Devolution and the governance of Northern Ireland

Manchester University Press

DEVOLUTION series
series editor Charlie Jeffery

Devolution has established new political institutions in Scotland, Wales, Northern Ireland, London and the other English regions since 1997. These devolution reforms have far-reaching implications for the politics, policy and society of the UK. Radical institutional change, combined with a fuller capacity to express the UK's distinctive territorial identities, is reshaping the way the UK is governed and opening up new directions of public policy. These are the biggest changes to UK politics for at least 150 years.

The Devolution series brings together the best research in the UK on devolution and its implications. It draws together the best analysis from the Economic and Social Research Council's research programme on Devolution and Constitutional Change. The series has three central themes, all of which are vital components in understanding the changes devolution has set in train.

1 **Delivering public policy after devolution: diverging from Westminster:** Does devolution result in the provision of different standards of public service in health or education, or in widening economic disparities from one part of the UK to another? If so, does it matter?

2 **The political institutions of devolution:** How well do the new devolved institutions work? How effectively are devolved and UK-level matters coordinated? How have political organisations which have traditionally operated UK-wide – political parties, interest groups – responded to multi-level politics?

3 **Public attitudes, devolution and national identity:** How do people in different parts of the UK assess the performance of the new devolved institutions? Do people identify themselves differently as a result of devolution? Does a common sense of Britishness still unite people from different parts of the UK?

already published

Devolution and constitutional change in Northern Ireland
Paul Carmichael, Colin Knox and Bob Osborne (eds)

Beyond devolution and decentralisation
Alistair Cole

Between two Unions
Europeanisation and Scottish devolution
Paolo Dardanelli

Territorial politics and health policy
UK health policy in comparative perspective
Scott L. Greer

The English Question
Robert Hazell

Using Europe: territorial strategies in a multi-level system
Eve Hepburn

Devolution and electoral politics
Dan Hough and Charlie Jeffery (eds)

The Northern Veto
Mark Sandford (ed.)

Towards a regional political class?
Professional politicians and regional institutions in Catalonia and Scotland
Klaus Stolz

Debating nationhood and government in Britain, 1885–1939
Perspectives from the 'four nations'
Duncan Tanner, Chris Williams, Wil Griffith and Andrew Edwards (eds)

Devolution and power in the United Kingdom
Alan Trench

Devolution and the governance of Northern Ireland

Colin Knox

Manchester University Press
Manchester and New York

distributed in the United States exclusively
by Palgrave Macmillan

Copyright © Colin Knox 2010

The right of Colin Knox to be identified as the author of this work has been asserted by him in accordance with the Copyright, Designs and Patents Act 1988.

Published by Manchester University Press
Oxford Road, Manchester M13 9NR, UK
and Room 400, 175 Fifth Avenue, New York, NY 10010, USA
www.manchesteruniversitypress.co.uk

Distributed in the United States exclusively by
Palgrave Macmillan, 175 Fifth Avenue, New York,
NY 10010, USA

Distributed in Canada exclusively by
UBC Press, University of British Columbia, 2029 West Mall,
Vancouver, BC, Canada V6T 1Z2

British Library Cataloguing-in-Publication Data
A catalogue record for this book is available from the British Library

Library of Congress Cataloging-in-Publication Data applied for

ISBN 978 0 7190 7436 3 *hardback*

First published 2010

The publisher has no responsibility for the persistence or accuracy of URLs for any external or third-party internet websites referred to in this book, and does not guarantee that any content on such websites is, or will remain, accurate or appropriate.

Typeset by Servis Filmsetting Ltd, Stockport, Cheshire
Printed in Great Britain
by CPI Antony Rowe, Chippenham, Wiltshire

To Veronica

Contents

List of illustrations viii
List of abbreviations xi
Acknowledgements xiii

Introduction 1

1 Devolution 7
2 The Northern Ireland Civil Service 47
3 Modernising government 79
4 Local government 110
5 Non-departmental public bodies 143
6 The third sector 172
7 Reconciled Northern Ireland? 202
8 Work-in-progress: community planning and central–local relations 234
9 Conclusions 267

References 282
Index 300

Illustrations

Figures

1.1	Devolved government in Northern Ireland, 1999	14
1.2	Northern Ireland Assembly, 2007: seats by political party	23
1.3	What has the Assembly achieved?	45
2.1	Northern Ireland public sector jobs, 2008	52
2.2	Departmental current expenditure, 2009–10	58
2.3	Northern Ireland Executive Programme for Government, 2008–11	59
3.1	Excellence and fairness: achieving world class public services Source: Cabinet Office (2008a).	83
3.2	Public administration in Northern Ireland: pre-Review of Public Administration, 2002	89
3.3	Two-tier model of public administration Source: OFMDFM (2005b: 22).	93
3.4	Framework for reform in Northern Ireland public services Source: Northern Ireland Civil Service (2004).	98
3.5	Public services modernisation in Northern Ireland Source: OFMDFM (2009).	102
4.1	Local councils by political party, 2009	111
4.2	Northern Ireland's 26 district councils, 2009	119
4.3	Councils' income, 2007/08	134
4.4	The 11 new councils from 2011 Source: OFMDFM (2005b).	136
4.5	Review of public administration implementation structures, 2009	138
7.1	Declining violence in Northern Ireland Source: PSNI Statistics to 31 May 2009.	209
7.2	Improvement in community relations among young people Source: Northern Ireland Young People Life and Times Surveys.	216

ILLUSTRATIONS ix

7.3	Improvement in community relations among adults	216
	Source: Northern Ireland Life and Times Surveys.	
7.4	Kind of society Northern Ireland has become, 2008	219
8.1	Omagh District Council, 2009	242
8.2	Community planning process, Omagh District Council, 2009	245
8.3	Baseline information, Omagh relative to Northern Ireland, 2008	251
8.4	Proposals for central--local relations	265
9.1	Has Northern Ireland got better?	274
	Source: Northern Ireland Life and Times Surveys.	

Boxes

1.1	Example of the legislative process	21
1.2	Chronology: power-sharing and devolution in Northern Ireland	32
2.1	Northern Ireland Civil Service: core values	54
3.1	'Northern Ireland Direct': a best practice case study	100
4.1	Belfast City Council best practice scheme	126
5.1	Guidance on accountability	153
5.2	Commissioner for Public Appointments: code of practice	157
5.3	The seven principles of conduct underpinning public life	159
6.1	Definition of voluntary/community organisations	174
6.2	Shared values: compact between government and voluntary and community sector	179
8.1	Omagh District Council . . . commitments: targets for action	248
8.2	Cardiff Council: local delivery agreement projects	260

Tables

1.1	Northern Ireland Executive and Assembly: devolved functions	16
1.2	Northern Ireland Assembly elections: seats by political party	23
1.3	Northern Ireland Assembly elections: votes by political party	24
1.4	Acts of the Northern Ireland Assembly	42
1.5	What has the Assembly achieved by political party affiliation?	45
1.6	Chi-square tests	45
2.1	Departmental structure of Northern Ireland Civil Service	50
2.2	Northern Ireland public sector jobs	51
2.3	Staff in 11 government departments by industrial status and gender	53

2.4	Public expenditure by department	58
2.5	Public service agreement: education example	61
2.6	Performance example: Department of Health, Social Services and Public Safety	63
2.7	Policy-making: pre- and post-devolution	71
3.1	Modernisation in the Programme for Government	105
3.2	Department of Finance & Personnel balanced scorecard	107
4.1	Northern Ireland local government elections since 1973: share of the poll	121
4.2	Northern Ireland local government elections since 1973: seats gained	122
4.3	Local government in Northern Ireland: current functions	130
4.4	Councils by population, spending and domestic rates	131
4.5	Council income sources, 2007/08	134
4.6	Councils merging	137
5.1	Types of public body and main features	145
5.2	Decisions on public bodies: review of public administration	147
5.3	Public bodies in Northern Ireland	149
5.4	Northern Ireland public bodies' expenditure	150
5.5	Public appointments	156
5.6	Public accountability	170
6.1	Primary purpose of organisations	175
6.2	Primary beneficiaries of organisations	176
6.3	Housing, urban regeneration and community development	200
7.1	Religion of pupils by school and management type	221
7.2	Religion by school management type	221
7.3	Number of integrated schools	223
8.1	The process of community planning	236
8.2	Omagh District Council, Community Plan	247
8.3	Baseline information: quality of life indicators	250
9.1	Monitoring delivery: Programme for Government	275
9.2	Monitoring delivery: PSA 20, improving public services	276

Abbreviations

C&AG	Comptroller and Auditor General
(C)CRU	(Central) Community Relations Unit
CRC	Community Relations Council
CSI	Cohesion, Sharing and Integration
CSR	Comprehensive spending review
DFP	Department of Finance and Personnel
DSD	Department for Social Development
DUP	Democratic Unionist Party
ESRC	Economic and Social Research Council
EU	European Union
IEF	Integrated Education Fund
IICD	Independent International Commission on Decommissioning
IRA	Irish Republic Army
LAA	local area agreements
LGSC	Local Government Staff Commission
MLA	Member of the (Northern Ireland) Legislative Assembly
NDPB	non-departmental public body
NGOs	non-governmental organisations
NIAO	Northern Ireland Audit Office
NICIE	Northern Ireland Council for Integrated Education
NICS	Northern Ireland Civil Service
NICVA	Northern Ireland Council for Voluntary Action
NIHC	Northern Ireland Housing Council
NIHE	Northern Ireland Housing Executive
NILGA	Northern Ireland Local Government Association
NIO	Northern Ireland Office
OCPA NI	Office of the Commissioner for Public Appointments for Northern Ireland
OFMDFM	Office of the First Minister and deputy First Minister
QUANGOS	quasi-autonomous non-governmental organisations

PAC	Public Accounts Committee
PfG	Programme for Government
PSA	public service agreement
PSNI	Police Service of Northern Ireland
PUP	Progressive Unionist Party
QoL	quality of life (indicators)
RPA	Review of Public Administration
SF	Sinn Féin
SLIG	Suffolk and Lenadoon Interface Group
SDLP	Social Democratic and Labour Party
STV	Single transferable vote
UDA	Ulster Defence Association
UUP	Ulster Unionist Party

Acknowledgements

This book evolved from an ESRC project within the Devolution and Constitutional Change Programme completed with my co-researcher Professor Paul Carmichael at the University of Ulster (ESRC Award number L219252108). I have worked with Paul on a number of research projects and owe much to his thinking and reflections on the ideas in this book. The on/off nature of devolution in Northern Ireland meant that I made various attempts to complete this work but only recently felt that the stability of the institutions provided a context for a narrative on devolution and the governance of Northern Ireland. Professor Bob Osborne, Director of the Social Policy Research Institute (University of Ulster), has been a constant source of support and intellectual stimulation on Northern Ireland. I would also like to acknowledge and thank Professor Charlie Jeffery, Edinburgh University, and former Director of the ESRC Devolution and Constitutional Change Programme for his academic leadership during the study and Tony Mason of Manchester University Press for his patience and help throughout.

The qualitative data contained in the book were gathered from a large number of civil servants, public officials, politicians and NGO leaders. They will recognise their views and ideas which have hopefully been reflected accurately in the text. I thank them for their generosity both in sharing their thoughts and taking time out of their busy schedules to speak with me. The peace building programmes delivered by a number of the case study organisations cited in this book were funded by Atlantic Philanthropies simply because government departments considered them 'too risky' to support. I am therefore grateful to Martin O'Brien, Dr Padraic Quirk and Gail Birkbeck from Atlantic Philanthropies for permission to use the case study materials.

Although the ideas in this book have been shaped by both formal research through data gathered from interviewees and informal conversations with academic colleagues, the author takes full responsibility for errors of fact or interpretation.

Colin Knox

Introduction

Northern Ireland has over the years, and for obvious reasons, earned the rather dubious title of 'a place apart' when considering the governance of the United Kingdom as a whole (Rose, 1971). What is different about Northern Ireland is that the abuse of power in the delivery of public services played a significant part in the demise of devolution (from 1921 to 1972) and paved the way for a distinctive system of public administration largely removed from the hands of elected representatives. Direct rule from Westminster became synonymous with a democratic deficit where local government had been stripped of key functional responsibilities. Major services such as health, social services, education and housing were vested in non-departmental public bodies and overseen by ministerial appointees. Although intended to be a short-term expedient until the wider political and constitutional problems were addressed, these governance arrangements became what one former Head of the Northern Ireland Civil Service described as a state of 'permanent impermanence' (Bloomfield, 1998: 144). One consequence of this is that governance scholars have largely ignored Northern Ireland as an aberrant region of the United Kingdom explained away by its uniqueness, and therefore less deserving of academic attention. Northern Ireland was, and is, of course fertile ground for a large political science literature on the various attempts to tackle the stubborn political impasse and eventually find a settlement where the two key protagonists in the conflict (the Democratic Unionist Party and Sinn Féin) now share power. It is hardly surprising therefore, in the face of more immediate political problems and associated violence, that the governance of Northern Ireland attracted limited academic scrutiny.

Yet the period of Direct Rule government from 1972 onwards has impacted adversely on the system of public administration which prevailed. Reflecting on the governance of Northern Ireland during that time, a member of the Public Accounts Committee in Westminster argued 'the quality of government services in Northern Ireland too often lets down people who are using them and who are paying for them through their taxes' (Lidington,

2004: 9). Senior civil servants had unfettered power and were largely unaccountable for public service delivery, an assertion they either reject or claim that such a responsibility was foisted upon them. Key political developments in the form of the Belfast/Good Friday Agreement 1998 ushered in a democratically elected Assembly in Northern Ireland 'inclusive in its membership, capable of exercising executive and legislative authority and subject to safeguards to protect the rights and interest of all sides of the community' (Belfast/Good Friday Agreement: 1998: 5). Devolution became a reality on 2 December 1999 when the Northern Ireland Assembly and its power-sharing Executive Committee of Ministers assumed powers of self-government under the Northern Ireland Act 1998. One of the major tasks facing the devolved Executive was public administration reform, in the words of the (then) First Minister 'this is the opportunity of a generation to put in place a modern, accountable, effective system of public administration that can deliver a high quality set of public services to our citizens' (Trimble: 2002: 5). However, faltering periods of devolution between 1999 and October 2002 when the Assembly was suspended for the fourth time witnessed a reversion to wider political problems and limited attention to improving governance. With the return to devolution on 8 May 2007, Northern Ireland is experiencing its first consistent period of administrative stability and it is therefore timely to take stock of the unfolding agenda of changes in governance.

This is the context for this book on *Devolution and the Governance of Northern Ireland*. Much like the tentative process to embed devolved government in Northern Ireland, this book has been written in staccato fashion. The on/off nature of devolution has proved challenging in attempts to capture, with accuracy, a reforming public administration agenda. Governance reform was an issue conceived by local politicians in the first mandate of the Northern Ireland Assembly, taken over by direct rule ministers when devolution collapsed, and re-examined and radically revised by returning Members of the Legislative Assembly who wanted to distance themselves from decisions taken by British Ministers on behalf of the people of Northern Ireland. It may even be premature at this point to reflect on governance arrangements under devolution as the picture is unfolding. For example, alongside the current radical restructuring of the public sector emerging from the Review of Public Administration discussed in some detail in this book, the Northern Ireland Assembly approved in January 2009 the following private members' business:

> That this Assembly recognises the importance of ensuring that the maximum amount of public spending is directed at front line services; and calls on the First Minister and deputy First Minister to bring forward proposals to reduce the number of Government Departments. (Hansard, Official Record, 19 January 2009)

There are therefore limitations in trying to 'hit a moving target'. Nonetheless, this book attempts to provide a cross-sectional view of the governance arrangements in Northern Ireland under devolution.

The narrative begins in chapter 1 by examining the rocky road to 'stable' devolution in Northern Ireland, if that is not tempting fate! It considers the four intermittent periods of devolved government and its restoration in May 2007. The architecture of devolution, the bodies established under the Belfast/Good Friday Agreement are unpacked: Strand 1 institutions – the structure, political composition of the Northern Ireland Assembly, the Executive, government departments responsible for the delivery of key public services and the civic forum; strand 2 institutions, North–South Ministerial Council and associated cross-border services bodies; and strand 3 institutions, British–Irish Council and British–Irish Intergovernmental Conference. The first chapter concludes by posing the question whether devolution in Northern Ireland is making a difference, albeit perhaps a little early to be definitive about such a question. In doing so, we consider examples of the topical and highly populist policy decisions which the Executive and Assembly have taken on: winter fuel payments, deferral of water charges and free prescriptions, and the very controversial and divisive debate on the abolition of academic selection. The chapter concludes by considering both the legislative record of the Assembly and public opinion on its achievements to date.

A key component of the book is an examination of core governance institutions: the civil service, local government, non-departmental public bodies, and the third sector in Northern Ireland. Chapter 2 therefore looks at the Northern Ireland Civil Service, the changes in its structure and functions from 6 to 11 departments under devolution to accommodate the needs of a power-sharing Executive. The challenge for devolved government in Northern Ireland is to re-skill its civil servants to serve a local elected Assembly and become policy advisors as opposed to simply 'reading across' public policies from Westminster – consistent with the period of direct rule. This demands professional skills training for officials. This chapter also considers how public services are funded, the *Programme for Government* which sets out the Executive's priorities and policies and how departments are held to account for performance against public service agreements (PSAs). Devolution has led to greater local scrutiny of the work of government departments. Examples are included of Northern Ireland Audit Office reports which have assisted the Public Accounts Committee of the Assembly to hold civil servants to account to a much greater extent than an infrequent appearance at the equivalent Westminster Committee under direct rule. Finally, this chapter compares policy-making pre and post devolution and the key influences on that process.

The public sector in Northern Ireland has lagged behind the rest of the United Kingdom in adopting a modernising agenda. Chapter 3 therefore examines the modernisation of public services in Great Britain by outlining the various initiatives from *Modernising Government* (Cabinet Office, 1999) through *Working Together: Public Service on Your Side* (Cabinet Office 2009b) and discusses, more generally, a conceptual framework (Pollitt and Bouckaert, 2004) which synthesises the process of reform in other countries. This provides the context to examine the more recent interest in public sector modernisation in Northern Ireland. Essentially this has taken a twin-track approach: structural reforms under the Review of Public Administration and a series of reform measures. The extensive nature of evidence gathering which informed the Review of Public Administration is outlined and the final decisions on reformed public sector structures listed. Alongside this, civil service reform projects and programmes are discussed to include: new working methods, technological improvements and enhancing the skills of civil servants.

The focus then shifts to consider local government in chapter 4. Local government in Northern Ireland has played an important, if sometimes controversial, role in the governance of Northern Ireland. To appreciate its significance we trace the history and evolution including the emasculated role of councils since 1973 and the politicisation of local government when councillors could find no other democratic platform to express wider views on constitutional developments. Despite their limited formal brief, councils began to demonstrate imaginative ways of expanding functional responsibilities in partnership working, economic development and in improving community relations. Local government is now grappling with a change agenda resulting from the Review of Public Administration. Not only will the number of councils be reduced from 26 to 11 in May 2011 but they will assume some increase in their functions and hope to have much greater influence through new statutory responsibilities in community planning and well-being. The nature of the changes at local council level begs the question whether, as a result, we will have 'stronger' local government in Northern Ireland.

Non-departmental public bodies have been a prominent feature of the governance landscape in Northern Ireland because of the lack of confidence in elected representatives to provide public services in a non-partisan way. Chapter 5 therefore begins by examining the history of quangos, including problems of accountability and ministerial patronage, and the non-departmental public bodies which were targeted for 'culling' under the Review of Public Administration. Specifically the issue of patronage and transparency in public appointments is considered further through the appointment of the Commissioner for Public Appointments in Northern Ireland and her public

INTRODUCTION

spat with senior officials in a bid to protect and assert her independence. The wider experience of culling quangos in Great Britain inform the discussions in the Northern Ireland context, including David Cameron's contribution (2009) to the debate on overhauling the existing system due to problems of accountability, cost and effectiveness. This chapter concludes by examining two Northern Ireland case studies, the *Local Government Staff Commission* and the *Northern Ireland Housing Council* as examples of an executive and advisory non-departmental public body respectively which were initially targeted for abolition but subsequently granted a reprieve. These examples are included to demonstrate the practical difficulties of matching the rhetoric of quango culling with the reality of cutting the number of non-departmental public bodies in Northern Ireland.

The voluntary and community (or third) sector has played a key role in the governance of Northern Ireland, particularly but not exclusively when 'normal business' was brought to a standstill through the turmoil of street violence and political stagnation. Chapter 6 therefore examines the history and evolution of the voluntary and community sector since the beginning of the conflict and its closer formal co-operation with government via the *Compact* and *Joint Forum*. A series of initiatives followed which marked the mutual dependence of the public and third sector through *Partners of Change*, *Investing Together* and *Positive Steps*. To illustrate the important role which the voluntary and community sector played, and continues to play, in peace building, the work of two case studies are considered in some detail: Suffolk and Lenadoon Interface Group and the role of ex-prisoners. Finally, this chapter considers recent moves by the third sector to codify the relationship with government through a White Paper which aims to advance the prospect of a participative democracy in Northern Ireland.

It would perhaps seem peculiar to an external observer of developments in Northern Ireland if, in a post-conflict scenario, we did not make some reference to whether the two main communities have reconciled their differences. Chapter 7 therefore charts the 'path to peace' by outlining the key political developments from the Anglo-Irish Agreement (1985) through the St Andrews Agreement (2006) to the current phase on devolution from May 2007. It takes stock of how major political progress has impacted on the nature of Northern Ireland day-to-day life, most notably a significant reduction in violence as the overt manifestation of political conflict, but it remains a highly polarised and divided society. The Direct Rule Government's attempts at tackling segregation are examined through the policy of *A Shared Future* and its subsequent rejection by the devolved administration. A long awaited replacement policy *Cohesion, Sharing and Integration* has yet to materialise. Two examples of using public services to promote reconciliation are examined in this chapter: integrated education and shared housing. The chapter concludes by addressing the question 'is Northern Ireland a reconciled society?'

Chapter 8, the final substantive chapter, offers a work-in-progress account of two important issues for the future governance of Northern Ireland: community planning and central–local relations. Both these matters are under active consideration at the time of writing (August 2009) and therefore the material presented is subject to change as they unfold. Community planning has been hailed as a significant development for local government in Northern Ireland because it will enshrine its legislative role in co-ordinating a number of government departments and agencies in the planning and delivery of public services within the new 11 councils from 2011. There are huge expectations in the local government fraternity as to what it can offer given their disappointment that significant powers were not returned to councils as a result of the Review of Public Administration. To inject a sense of realism, evaluation research on community planning in Scotland and Wales is outlined. In addition, through an examination of the first community planning pilot study in Northern Ireland (Omagh District Council), the process of community planning is described and the learning highlighted. The second theme of the chapter is central–local relations which are being redefined and will be secured in legislation. Here we draw on the experience of Wales which is helping to shape the debate and outline proposals which are under consideration to structure future relations between local government and the centre in Northern Ireland.

Northern Ireland is at an interesting point in devolution – the political battles have been fought, a power-sharing Executive is in place, and there has been stability in the institutions since May 2007. In simple terms the public has pocketed these gains and there is now a sense of urgency and growing frustration that we need to see the benefits of devolution in the daily lives of people in Northern Ireland. Populist policies have a limited shelf life and improvements in governance arrangements need to make an impact through better public services and quality of life improvements. This book commenced with the important question as to whether a devolved Assembly had made a difference (chapter 1). Although the public's perception of the success of devolution is significantly conditioned by their perspectives on the political settlement in Northern Ireland and associated power-sharing arrangements, from survey evidence 73.4 per cent of respondents believed that the Assembly has achieved 'a little' or 'nothing' (see chapter 1 for details). The message for our politicians is clear.

1
Devolution

This is indeed a momentous occasion, as Northern Ireland begins to put behind it the conflict, prejudice and division that has blighted the lives of everyone in both communities for a generation. For the first time, all shades of political opinion in Northern Ireland will have a stake in the future. After a quarter of a century, the curtain is finally coming down on direct rule. Of course, there will still be anger about the past, and real difficulties undoubtedly still lie ahead, but this generation is now turning the page to the future. In Stormont now, Ministers have been appointed and a Government formed. They are waiting only for their powers. Passing those powers to them is our job tonight. (Then) Secretary of State for Northern Ireland, Peter Mandelson introducing the draft Northern Ireland Act 1998 (Appointed Day) Order 1999 in Westminster to devolve powers to the Northern Ireland Executive and Assembly, (*Hansard*, Official Report, 30 Nov. 1999)

There is not one truly democratic country in the whole world which would, for one moment, accept the principle that armed gunmen, thugs and murderers, with their hands dripping with the blood of their fellow countrymen, their fellow co-religionists and their fellow citizens should, as of right, be given office in government. Where would we find another democracy passing a measure like this? . . . Now we are asked to pass a law to put criminals into office – and the Government think that the people of Northern Ireland should join in some happy ceremony on this occasion. They should go and tell that to the widows, the orphans and those with vacant seats in their houses, and they will get an answer. Rev. Ian Paisley's (DUP Leader) response to the Commons debate on the devolution of powers to the Northern Ireland Executive and Assembly (*Hansard*, Official Report, 30 Nov. 1999, Column 269)

The rocky road to 'stable' devolution

Power was devolved to the Northern Ireland Assembly and its Executive Committee of Ministers on Thursday 2 December 1999 following the signing of the Belfast/Good Friday Agreement on 10 April 1998. The Northern Ireland Act 1998 gave legal status to the implementation of the Agreement arising from multi-party talks and provide the legislative framework for devolution. Devolution simultaneously triggered the establishment of the North–South Ministerial Council, North–South Implementation bodies, the British–Irish Council and British–Irish Inter-Governmental Conference. The new Northern Ireland Assembly had first met in shadow form, without powers, in July 1998 in preparation for devolution. As the above quotations illustrate it was not without controversy. The (then) Secretary of State, Peter Mandelson judged that under the terms of section 3 of the Northern Ireland Act 1998, 'sufficient progress has been made in implementing the Agreement for me to set a commencement date for devolution to take effect in Northern Ireland' (Mandelson, 1999: 254). In contrast, the (then) leader of the Democratic Unionist Party, Dr Ian Paisley, argued that Westminster was being 'asked to approve a law that provides that those who have engaged in murder, the most heinous and atrocious of murders, must have a way opened for them to get into the government of Northern Ireland' (Paisley, 1999: 270). Commenting on the importance of the Belfast/Good Friday Agreement, Bogdanor noted:

> The Agreement has a double significance for the government of the United Kingdom since it proposes not only a solution to the Irish problem, but also recognition of the process of devolution to the non-English parts of the United Kingdom. (Bogdanor, 2001: 109)

This observation highlights the fact that devolution has been used by the British Government as a mechanism to advance the peace process – described by then Prime Minister Blair as a process of 'creative ambiguity' (Blair, 2003). The necessary concentration on the 'Irish problem' has had implications for the effective outworking of devolution in Northern Ireland (Knox and Carmichael, 2005b). Unlike Scotland and Wales, devolution in Northern Ireland has become inextricably linked to the divisive issues which precipitated its inception and characterise its operation in practice.

From the start, the Agreement was viewed differently by the two communities – described as 'asymmetry in attitudes' – republicans and nationalists more positive and loyalists and unionists more ambivalent (Wilford and Wilson, 2003a: 46). For some unionists it represented concessions (power-sharing) as well as the prospect of peace. Over time, unionist/loyalist support for the Agreement ebbed away, accelerated by the IRA's intransigence on decommissioning, whereas nationalists/republicans continued to support its full implementation. A key aim of the Agreement was to encourage republicans and loyalists into the democratic process and wean them away from violence. The only sanction available to the British Government when they defaulted however was to collapse the institutions upon which the Agreement is premised, hence 'expelling' them from the democratic process. This was self-defeating. Observers, however, caution against viewing devolution as a short-term fix: 'in Northern Ireland, more than any other part of the United Kingdom, devolution remains a process' (Bradbury and Mitchell, 2002: 311). Devolution in Northern Ireland has been intermittent in nature, fraught with political disputes and lacking, until its current period of operation, in stability. We consider the various phases of its development.

First period of devolution: 2 December 1999 to 11 February 2000

Devolution was welcomed by David Trimble the (then) leader of the Ulster Unionist Party who described direct rule as the 'debasement of democracy'. His party's agreement to share power with Sinn Féin was conditional upon their commitment to exclusively peaceful means and an acknowledgement that decommissioning was essential to the peace process. There had been no decommissioning of IRA weaponry in advance of devolution and Sinn Féin argued that it must take place in the context of the full implementation of the overall settlement. Unionists, however, were nervous that Sinn Féin in government might want to back its political demands with the tacit threat of a return to violence. By February 2000 devolution was in trouble as David Trimble had nothing to show for his policy of 'jumping first' into government with Sinn Féin in the expectation that the IRA would reciprocate with decommissioning. To further cement the link between devolution and the wider political agenda, the (then) Secretary of State announced to the House of Commons: 'if there is no decommissioning, there will be no implementation of the Good Friday Agreement, there will be no devolution in Northern Ireland. It is a matter of colossal regret, but it is a fact' (Mandelson, 2000). In short, the devolution agenda became mired in the search for a constitutional settlement and its effective implementation. With paramilitaries refusing to break the logjam on decommissioning, the Secretary of State argued that although progress had been made between the IRA and the Independent International Commission on Decommissioning (IICD), it was insufficient and he suspended the Assembly on 11th February 2000. Commitments to decommission, he demanded, had to be clear otherwise they could not command confidence in their intent.

Second period of devolution: 30 May 2000 to 10 August 2001

The stalemate on decommissioning continued until May 2000 at which point, according to the terms of the Agreement, it should have been completed. The mood changed with an IRA statement that they 'would initiate a process (within a defined context of British Government commitments) that would put their weapons completely and verifiably beyond use.' Unionists saw this as a statement on the modalities of decommissioning which failed to address *when* it would happen. Although an IRA arms inspection by independents in June 2000 heralded some movement by republicans, the IRA failed to decommission. Republicans claimed that London had not met their commitments on policing reforms and demilitarisation. First Minister Trimble resigned on 1 July 2001 but nominated his fellow UUP Minister (Reg Empey) as caretaker, triggering a six-week period in which to resolve the impasse over arms. Trimble's resignation as First Minister was an attempt to assuage hardliners in his own party and wrongfoot the anti-Agreement DUP. To avoid plunging Northern Ireland into an election, the Secretary of State (John Reid) decided to suspend devolved government from 11 August for one day to allow parties further time to consider the proposals of the two governments. This bought an additional six-week period for a deal to be brokered. Republicans accused the British Government of acceding (once again) to the unionist veto and the IRA responded by withdrawing their offer to the IICD.

Third and fourth periods of devolution: 12 August 2001 to 21 September 2001 and 23 September 2001 to 14 October 2002

Little improved in the intervening period. A second 24-hour (described as 'technical') suspension was announced by the Secretary of State on 21 September after failing to break the deadlock and reinstate the First Minister, permitting a further six-week breathing period. Ulster Unionists exerted further pressure by withdrawing their ministers from the power-sharing Executive. Within days the IICD witnessed a 'significant' quantity of IRA weaponry (arms, ammunition and explosives) put completely beyond use, described by Secretary of State Reid as taking the 'peace process on to a new political level – rarely has the whole community be so united' (Reid, 2001). The IRA claimed 'this unprecedented move is to save the peace process and to persuade others of our genuine intentions'. Despite much over-use of the words 'historic breakthrough', this move was considered just that because the IRA had previously looked upon disarmament as surrender. The Ulster Unionist leader, however, came under increasing pressure over time as unionist support for the Agreement ebbed and disillusionment with the peace process grew.

The fourth period of devolution lasted almost 13 months until it was indefinitely suspended by the Secretary of State in October 2002 for the fourth time since its inception in December 1999. The crisis was the result of (another) political impasse described at the time as 'a lack of trust and loss of confidence on both sides of the community' (Reid, 2002). This stemmed from concerns about Sinn Féin's commitment to exclusively democratic and non-violent means and accusations by each community of the other that they did not endorse the full operation and implementation of the Agreement. A climate of mistrust and uncertainty prevailed accentuated by events such as the trail of republicans in Colombia (allegedly involved in training the left-wing FARC group, Revolutionary Armed Forces of Colombia, but subsequently found not guilty), the break-in at Special Branch offices in Castlereagh Police Station (where personal details of Special Branch detectives were removed), and political espionage at Stormont implicating Sinn Féin. In the latter, unionists accused the IRA of exploiting Sinn Féin's membership of the Executive to gather information (names and addresses of prison officers) of use in future acts of violence. The power-sharing arrangements in the Assembly intended to build trust between parties appeared to have achieved the opposite.

The period following the fourth suspension was intended to restore confidence between the political parties, hold elections to the Northern Ireland Assembly and reinstate power-sharing as soon as possible. The Prime Minister called for radical 'acts of completion' by the IRA to rescue the political process, reassure unionists and provide the basis for restored devolution. A third act of IRA decommissioning (October 2003) aimed at kick-starting the political process foundered when the UUP leader pulled out of a (now hackneyed) 'historic' deal with Sinn Féin at the last minute which failed to meet unionist demands for a clear and transparent report – full disclosure on arms. Unionists needed very public reassurances that major acts of decommissioning had taken place to significantly impact on public opinion. Recriminations and counter-accusations of bad faith followed. The Assembly was formally dissolved in April 2003 in anticipation of elections in May of the same year. The political parties eventually went into the Assembly elections in November 2003 (postponed twice in the hope of political movement) against the background of a deadlocked process where there was the prospect of no Executive after an election – an Assembly but no government, described as an election to a ghost Assembly or restoration to a state of suspension. The election results saw Sinn Féin eclipse the SDLP to become the largest nationalist party in the Assembly. The Democratic

Unionist Party (DUP) topped the polls and displaced the UUP (tables 1.2 and 1.3 below).

Suspension and restoration of the Assembly

Following the 2003 elections the political parties began a review of the Belfast/Good Friday Agreement with the aim of restoration to devolved institutions. The Secretary of State created a non-legislative fixed-term Assembly, via the Northern Ireland Act 2006 from those MLAs elected in 2003 to provide a forum for the parties to begin preparations for devolved government. The Assembly members' key task was to elect people to hold the offices of First and Deputy First Minister and to ensure that the remaining ministerial portfolios were filled by 24 November 2006. In the event of failure to do this the Secretary of State could indefinitely postpone the Assembly elections scheduled for May 2007, dissolve the Northern Ireland Assembly elected in November 2003 and cease payments to members. The British Government took the view that a further election to a body which would not sit should not be held and direct rule would remain in place. The discussions between the parties informed the next round of talks called by the British and Irish Government, held at St Andrews in October 2006.

The two issues of central concern which formed the basis of talks to achieve full and effective operation of the political institutions were: the need to support policing and the rule of law across the whole community and eventually the devolution of policing and justice, and support for power-sharing and the political institutions. The British and Irish Government reached agreement on these issues as set out in the St Andrews Agreement of 13 October 2006, the details of which were given legislative effect in the Northern Ireland (St Andrews Agreement) Act 2006. The Act made provisions for a new transitional Assembly, set out a timetable to restore devolution, the date for the third election to the Northern Ireland Assembly, and made important amendments to the Northern Ireland Act 1998 which came into force with the restoration of devolved government. In the event, elections took place on 7 March 2007 and devolution was restored on 8 May 2007 (missing the 26 March 2007 deadline set down by the governments) following a high profile meeting and media event at which Ian Paisley (then DUP leader) and Gerry Adams (the leader of Sinn Féin) agreed to establish a power-sharing Executive comprising: 4 DUP, 3 Sinn Féin, 2 Ulster Unionists and 1 SDLP ministers with a DUP First Minister and Sinn Féin Deputy First Minister. The Northern Ireland Assembly and Executive have been in operation since then.

Devolution architecture

The architecture for devolved government in Northern Ireland (see figure 1.1) as set out in the Belfast/Good Friday Agreement can be summarised as follows:

1. democratic institutions in Northern Ireland: the Northern Ireland Assembly, Executive and Civic Forum (strand 1);
2. the North–South Ministerial Council: to bring together those with executive responsibilities in Northern Ireland and the Irish Government (strand 2); and,
3. the British–Irish Council: to promote the harmonious and mutually beneficial development of the totality of relationships among the people of the United Kingdom, Isle of Man and Channel Islands (Guernsey and Jersey); and, British–Irish Intergovernmental Conference: to bring together the British and Irish Governments to promote bi-lateral co-operation at all levels on all matters of mutual interest within the competence of both Governments (strand 3).

A key element in securing the agreement of nationalists and republicans to any internal (strand 1) settlement was a power-sharing government and the provision of safeguards to copperfasten inclusion and avoid regression to unionist hegemony characteristic of Stormont regime from 1921 to 1972. As one prominent Sinn Féin MP and MLA put it:

> The provisions in the Agreement regarding the new institutions were vital in securing the support of both communities for the establishment of the Assembly and other institutions. Nationalists, in particular, had deep concerns about the re-establishment of a Northern Assembly, given our historical experience under the old Stormont. Therefore, rigorous checks, balances, and guarantees had to be secured to ensure our participation in the Assembly. The concepts of power-sharing, ministerial positions, Chairs and Deputy Chairs, as of right under d'Hondt, and the requirement for cross-community support for key decisions all point to the fact that this is a new and inclusive political dispensation in which the rights of both communities, and others, are protected. All who signed up to the Agreement have a duty to protect and promote that inclusiveness. (Murphy, 2002: 22)

The institutional structures of devolution in Northern Ireland which have been established to ensure effective power-sharing arrangements are rooted in consociational theory (Lijphart, 1968; 1975), although this suggestion is contested (Dixon, 1997; 2005). Consociation is described as:

> The name of a political system used in some culturally divided societies to share and divide government power and authority. Political power is shared by the

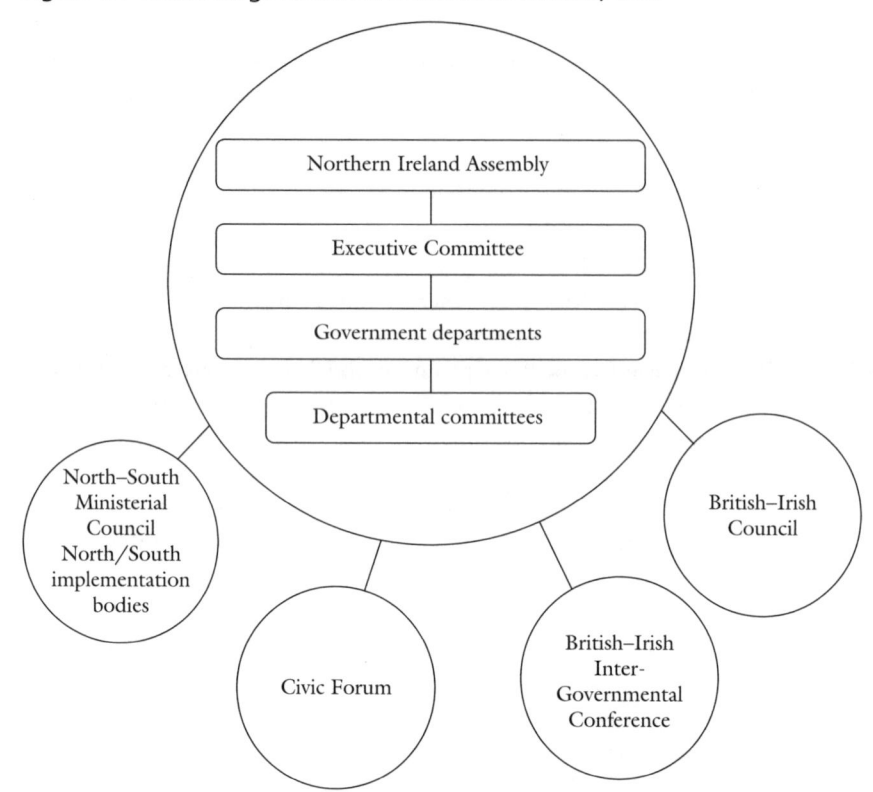

Figure 1.1 Devolved government in Northern Ireland, 1999

[Diagram showing: Northern Ireland Assembly → Executive Committee → Government departments → Departmental committees, with connected circles for North–South Ministerial Council / North/South implementation bodies, Civic Forum, British–Irish Inter-Governmental Conference, and British–Irish Council]

rival cultures on a proportional basis – in the executive, the legislature and public employment. Each cultural community enjoys rights of veto and autonomy. (McGarry and O'Leary, 1995b: 509)

Wilford (2001: 60–61) outlines how the 'consociational bargain' plays out in devolved government in Northern Ireland in the form of four key characteristics or safeguards which are integral to the design and operation of the Assembly and how wider society is organised:

- A partnership within and between the Executive and legislature: four-party coalition which makes up the Executive; the relationship between the Executive and the Assembly; and intra-Assembly arrangements among political parties within statutory committees.
- Proportionality in electoral systems, allocation of public expenditure and public employment.
- Autonomy over each community's sense of identity – the endorsement of social segregation.

- Mutual veto among political elites – unanimity among decision-makers in the form of 'key decisions' and 'cross-community' consent.

We consider the architecture of the devolved government which reflects the principles of, and safeguards to, power-sharing arrangements in Northern Ireland.

Strand 1 institutions

Assembly

The Northern Ireland Assembly has 108 elected members of the legislative assembly or MLAs from 8 political parties and meets in Parliament Buildings, Stormont, Belfast. The buildings, opened in 1932, were the former home of Northern Ireland Parliament until it was prorogued in 1972 and direct rule from Westminster introduced. The political symbolism of this is not lost on unionist politicians who remind nationalist and republican politicians of its origins. The Assembly has full legislative and executive authority for 'transferred matters' – the power to make laws and take decisions on all the functions of the 10 government departments and the Office of the First Minister and deputy First Minister (see table 1.1). 'Transferred' or devolved matters are functions where the Northern Ireland Assembly has been given power under devolution to make decisions and laws e.g. health, education, environment, agriculture etc. 'Excepted matters' are those functions which have not been transferred to the Northern Assembly and will remain the responsibility of the UK Parliament. They are usually matters of national importance e.g. foreign affairs, defence, nuclear energy, international relations and taxation. 'Reserved matters' are functions which will be transferred in the future, e.g. policing, security policy, prisons and criminal justice.

The Assembly carries out its work in plenary or full meetings of the Assembly and through its statutory or departmental, standing and ad hoc committees. Plenary meetings or 'sittings' are normally held twice weekly and in the Assembly Chamber in Parliament buildings. The Business Committee meets weekly and agrees the business for a plenary session and this is set out in an Order Paper for each day's sitting. Assembly decisions are made by way of motions with the 'question being put' to the Assembly for a decision on each motion. Most decisions are agreed by a simple majority of members. Certain 'key' decisions, however, require cross-community support. Issues subject to key decisions are either laid down in legislation or are listed in the standing orders of the Assembly (e.g. exclusion of a minister or members from holding office, a financial vote, a vote on making or amending standing

Table 1.1 Northern Ireland Executive and Assembly: devolved functions

Ministers	Departments	Functions
The Rt Hon Peter Robinson MP MLA, First Minister, and Martin McGuinness MP MLA, deputy First Minister. The two Junior Ministers, Robin Newton, MLA and Gerry Kelly MLA, assist them in carrying out the work of their department. They are jointly accountable to the First Minister and deputy First Minister	Office of the First Minister and deputy First Minister	Support for the Executive and liaison with the Assembly, the North–South Ministerial Council, British–Irish Council, Civic Forum and UK Departments; international relations; Programme for Government and the Executive's economic policies; promoting and monitoring implementation of equality of opportunity/good relations, tackling poverty and social exclusion, children and young people, victims and survivors, sustainable development; Maze/Long Kesh Regeneration; Review of Public Administration; Information Service; emergency planning; improving investment in infrastructure and the Statutory Publications Office.
Sammy Wilson MP MLA	Department of Finance and Personnel	Finance; Personnel; Civil Service accommodation; legal services; Northern Ireland Statistics and Research Agency; Land Registers; Land & Property Services Agency; Central Procurement; Civil Law Reform Division; General Register Office and building regulations.
Caitríona Ruane MLA	Department of Education	Schools funding and administration, pre-school, primary, post-primary and special education; the youth service; the promotion of community relations within and between schools; teacher education and salaries and school planning and provision.

Arlene Foster MLA	Department of Enterprise, Trade and Investment	Economic development policy including: business development, energy, telecoms, tourism; economic advice & research; research and statistics services; business regulation including: company law/registry, insolvency service, consumer affairs, trading standards; health and safety at work; social economy; mineral development; geological survey of NI; Invest NI; NI Tourist Board, Health and Safety Executive for NI and the Consumer Council for NI.
Michael McGimpsey MLA	Department of Health, Social Services and Public Safety	Public health; primary care services and community health and personal social services; family practitioner services; elderly and community care; child care and child protection; family policy; mental health; learning disability; physical and sensory disability; provision of hospital services and clinics; accident and emergency services; public safety – ambulance and fire and rescue services.
Margaret Ritchie MLA	Department for Social Development	Housing programmes; urban regeneration policy, strategy and programmes; Social Security Agency; Child Support Agency; support for the voluntary and community sector; social and charities policy and legislation; Rent Assessment Officer; Office of the Social Fund Commissioner; Northern Ireland Housing Executive; Charities Advisory Committee and the Disability Living Allowance Advisory Board for Northern Ireland.
Conor Murphy MP MLA	Department for Regional Development	Strategic planning; transportation strategy; ports and public transport; roads and water policy; providing and maintaining roads; water and sewerage services.

Table 1.1 (continued)

Ministers	Departments	Functions
Edwin Poots MLA	Department of the Environment	Planning control; environment and heritage; protection of the countryside; waste management; pollution control; wildlife protection; local government; local government reform; mineral resources (planning aspects); driver and vehicle testing and licensing; road safety and transport licensing and enforcement.
Michelle Gildernew MP MLA	Department of Agriculture and Rural Development	Food; farming and agri-environment policy; agri-food development; rural payments and inspection; veterinary matters; rural development; forestry; sea fisheries and rivers.
Nelson McCausland MLA	Department of Culture, Arts and Leisure	Arts and creativity; sport and leisure; inland fisheries; inland waterways; public libraries and museums; language diversity; Ordnance Survey of Northern Ireland; Public Records Office of Northern Ireland and advising on National Lottery distribution.
Sir Reg Empey MLA	Department for Employment and Learning	Higher education; further education; vocational training; employment services; employment law and labour relations; student support and postgraduate awards and careers advice and guidance.

orders). This is to protect against any one political group dominating the decision-making process or reversion to majoritarianism. This may be done in two ways:

- *Parallel consent* where over 50 per cent of Members voting, including over 50 per cent of nationalists and over 50 per cent of unionists voting, all agree to the motion; or
- A *weighted majority* which requires the support of 60 per cent of those voting, including 40 per cent unionist and 40 per cent nationalist support.

Cross-community voting demands ethnic self-designation. Members of the Legislative Assembly may therefore designate themselves as 'nationalist', 'unionist' or 'other' and can only change his/her community designation between elections if (s)he changes political party affiliation. Critics argue that designation reinforces sectarian divisions by accepting the pre-existing order of Northern Ireland society and the system is too rigid and acts as deterrent to non-aligned parties (Farry, 2009: 175). Another important safeguard for effective power-sharing arrangements is the 'petition of concern'. If, in accordance with the Northern Ireland Act 1998, 'thirty members petition the Assembly expressing their concern about a matter which is to be voted on by the Assembly, the vote on that matter shall require cross-community support'. Therefore, once the issue has become a key decision, it must then be subject to either of the two cross-community tests above.

Statutory committees are permanent committees of the Assembly which oversee the work of each of the 10 government departments (and in addition the Committee for the Office of the First Minister and deputy First Minister). Their powers are significant in that they exercise a scrutiny, policy development, advisory and consultation role in respect of their respective department and can initiate legislation. Specifically, they have powers to: consider and advise on departmental budgets and annual plans; consider secondary legislation and take the committee stage of primary legislation; initiate inquiries and write reports; and consider matters brought to their attention by ministers. In addition, there are six standing permanent committees of the Assembly which assist in its work on issues such as finance, procedures and the business of the Assembly as follows: the Public Accounts Committee; the Audit Committee; the Assembly and Executive Review Committee; the Committee on Standards and Privileges; the Committee on Procedures; and the Business Committee. Ad hoc committees are set up for a specific task and when their work is complete stand down. One current example is the Ad Hoc Committee – Private Security Industry (NI) Order 2009. This Committee has been established to consider the proposal for the Private Security Industry (NI) Order 2009, referred by the Secretary of State, and to submit a report to the Assembly by 30 June 2009. Most statutory and standing committees have 11 members including a chair and a deputy chair. Committee chairs and deputy chairs are appointed using a selection system (d'Hondt mechanism) that ensures each Assembly party is represented according to the votes it received in the election. Membership of the committees also reflects party strengths. The chairs and deputy chairs of statutory committees do not normally belong to the same political party as the relevant departmental minister (Northern Ireland Assembly, 2009c).

Specifically in terms of legislation, the Northern Ireland Assembly has the power to make primary legislation (or law) within those areas which have been devolved to it under the Northern Ireland Act 1998. Members of the Legislative Assembly make law through proposing, debating, amending and finally approving a Public Bill. There are three types of Public Bill: an Executive Bill which is introduced by a Minister; a Private Members Bill which is introduced by a Member; and a Committee Bill which is introduced by a Committee Chair. Ministers, committees and individual members can propose a Bill to the Speaker for consideration by the Assembly. If the Speaker is satisfied that it is within the competence of the Assembly, it is introduced and debated in the Chamber and scrutinised by the relevant statutory committee. The committee reports back to the Assembly for consideration by members who can propose amendments. It is then considered further by the Assembly and a final vote taken. Following approval by the Assembly and the Secretary of State, the Bill is given royal assent and becomes an Act of the Assembly (see box 1.1 as an example of the legislative process). Primary legislation or Acts provide the powers to make subordinate legislation in the form of statutory rules (regulations, rules, orders and by-laws) – primary legislation therefore sets the framework for more detailed statutory rules. Because primary legislation is a time consuming process for the Assembly, changes and amendments to the content of various legal measures can be hastened through subordinate legislation (Northern Ireland Assembly, 2008). In addition, under the accelerated passage procedure a Bill skips the committee stage and can pass all stages in as little as 10 days, but in no less time. According to standing orders of the Assembly this procedure is intended only for exceptional circumstances (Northern Ireland Assembly, 2009c: section 42). In such circumstances, reasons must be given for seeking accelerated passage, the consequences of it not being granted, and if appropriate, steps taken to minimise the future use of this procedure. The accelerated passage procedure requires cross-community support.

Box 1.1 Example of the legislative process

Public Authorities (Reform) Bill Northern Ireland Assembly Bill 19/07

The Public Authorities reform legislation originated in a decision by the former Secretary of State, Peter Hain to reduce, under the Review of Public Administration, the number of quasi-autonomous non-governmental organisations or quangos in Northern Ireland either through dissolution or transfer of their functions to other public bodies such as government departments, agencies or local authorities. The original provisions were set out in a draft Order in Council (a statutory instrument which equates to primary legislation used during direct rule) and open to consultation Jan–April 2007. The proposals were to abolish: the Fisheries Conservancy Board, Disability Living Allowance Board and the Northern Ireland Housing Council as well as a number of public appointments provisions. Following the consultation process and the restoration of devolved government the proposal to abolish the Housing Council and public appointments were withdrawn.

Primary legislation in the form of the Public Authorities (Reform) Bill was brought forward by the Northern Ireland Assembly to:

- Abolish the Fisheries Conservancy Board and transfer its functions (conservation and protection of salmon and inland fisheries) to the Department of Culture, Arts and Leisure.
- Abolish the Disability Advisory Board which provided independent advice to the Department of Social Development on two significant social security benefits (Disability Living Allowance and Attendance Allowance). The advice is to be given to the department by the equivalent Great Britain organisation.
- Separate subordinate legislation was used to dissolve: Enterprise Ulster, Pig Production Development Committee, and the Laganside Corporation

Stages and dates in the legislative process

- *First stage*: Public Authorities (Reform) Bill Northern Ireland Assembly Bill 19/07 introduced (17 June 2008).
- *Second stage*: general debate on the Bill with an opportunity for MLAs to vote on its general principles (30 June 2008).
- *Committee stage*: detailed investigation by the relevant committee (Committee for the Office of the First Minister and deputy First

Minister) which concluded with a publication for consideration by the Assembly (19 November 2008).
- *Consideration stage*: consideration by the Assembly of, and an opportunity for MLAs to vote on, the details of the Bill including amendments proposed to the Bill (9 December 2008).
- *Further consideration stage*: consideration by the Assembly of, and an opportunity for MLAs to vote on, further amendments to the Bill (12 January 2009).
- *Final stage*: passing or rejecting of Bill by the Assembly without further amendment (20 January 2009).
- *Royal Assent*: the Bill becomes law and the Act printed: *Public Authorities (Reform) Act (Northern Ireland) 2009* (16 February 2009).

Elections and political composition

There have been three elections to the Northern Ireland Assembly in 1998, 2003 and 2007. The single transferable vote (STV) proportional representation system is used for elections to the Assembly and in local and European elections in Northern Ireland. The Assembly is elected for a 4-year period but with the possibility of 'extraordinary elections' if two-thirds of its members resolve or a First and deputy First Minister cannot be elected. The elections are based on the 18 Westminster constituencies within which 6 seats are allocated (6 × 18 MLAs).

The composition of the Northern Ireland Assembly elected in 2007 is set out in figure 1.2 and shows the DUP as the largest party, followed by Sinn Féin, Ulster Unionist Party, SDLP and Alliance. The 2007 elections saw the Democratic Unionist Party increase its number of seats by 6 (to 36) over 2003 and obtain the highest share of first preference votes in the Assembly at 30.1 per cent (see tables 1.2 and 1.3). Sinn Féin also increased its number of seats by 4 over 2003 with a 2.7 per cent increase in first preference votes. The Ulster Unionist Party, on the other hand, lost 9 seats from 2003 and saw its share of first preference votes drop by a significant 7.8 per cent. The SDLP dropped 2 seats from 2003 and 1.8 per cent of first preference votes – it secured 2 seats less in the Assembly than the UUP despite a marginally better first preference voting performance (15.2 per cent and 14.9 per cent respectively). Alliance increased from 6 to 7 seats with an increase of 1.5 per cent in first preference votes. In terms of the smaller parties, the PUP retained its one seat although witnessed a drop of 0.6 per cent in first preferences, the UKUP lost its only seat and the Green Party secured its first seat in the Assembly.

DEVOLUTION

Figure 1.2 Northern Ireland Assembly, 2007: seats by political party

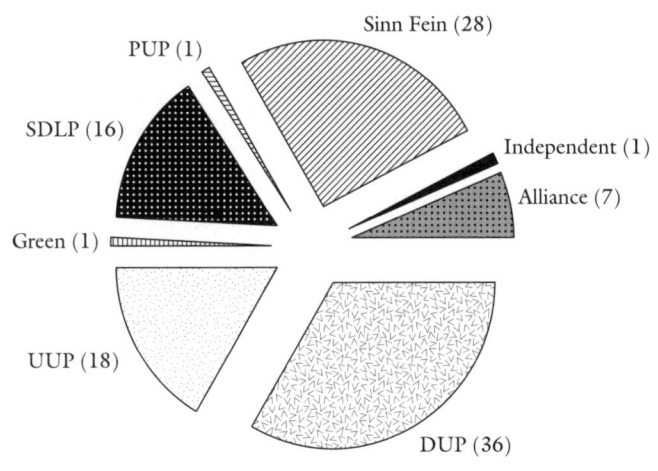

Pie chart showing: Sinn Fein (28), PUP (1), SDLP (16), Independent (1), Alliance (7), Green (1), UUP (18), DUP (36)

Table 1.2 Northern Ireland Assembly elections: number of seats by political party

	1998	2003	2007
Democratic Unionist Party	20	30	36
Sinn Féin	18	24	28
Ulster Unionist Party	28	27	18
Social Democratic and Labour Party	24	18	16
Alliance Party of Northern Ireland	6	6	7
Progressive Unionist Party	2	1	1
Green Party	–	–	1
Northern Ireland Women's Coalition	2	–	–
Independent/Others	3	1	1
UK Unionist Party	5	1	–
Totals	108	108	108

Turnout in the 2007 Assembly election was 62.3 per cent of the electorate and the 108 seats were contested by 257 candidates (although one candidate stood in all 6 constituencies). Some 79 per cent of transfers from unionist voters went to other unionist party candidates and 12 per cent went to nationalist party candidates. Some 64 per cent of transfers from nationalist voters went to other nationalist party candidates and 13 per cent went to unionist party candidates. Of the 108 MLAs, 29 did not hold office in the 2003–07 term and 18 were women, the same as in the 2003 election (Northern Ireland Assembly, 2007b: Research Paper 01/07; Tonge, 2008).

Table 1.3 Northern Ireland Assembly elections: share of first preference votes by party (%)

	1998	2003	2007
Democratic Unionist Party	18.1	25.7	30.1
Sinn Féin	17.6	23.5	26.2
Ulster Unionist Party	21.3	22.7	14.9
Social Democratic and Labour Party	22.0	17.0	15.2
Alliance Party of Northern Ireland	6.5	3.7	5.2
Progressive Unionist Party	2.5	1.2	0.6
Green Party	0.1	0.4	1.7
Northern Ireland Women's Coalition	1.6	0.8	–
Independent/Others	5.8	4.2	4.5
UK Unionist Party	4.5	0.8	1.5
Totals	100	100	100

Sources: The Electoral Office for Northern Ireland; Northern Ireland Assembly Research Paper 01/07; Gay and Pak (2007).

The Executive

The Executive Committee exercises executive authority on behalf of the Assembly and comprises each of the departmental ministers and the First and deputy First Ministers. Under the Belfast/Good Friday Agreement the First and deputy First Minister were jointly elected into office by the Assembly voting on a cross-community basis. Under the St Andrews Agreement 2006 and subsequent legislation, there is no election – the largest party nominates the First Minister and the largest party within the 'other designation' nominates the deputy First Minister. In other words, the election of the First and deputy First Minister is decoupled. For all meetings of the Executive Committee the First and Deputy First Minister act as co-chairs which involves dealing with and co-ordinating the work of the Executive Committee and the response of the Northern Ireland administration to external relationships (Northern Ireland Executive, 2007). Ministers in the Executive and Committee Chairs and Deputy Chairs are allocated to parties on the basis of the d'Hondt system in relation to the number of seats each party has in the Assembly. The First and deputy First Minister do not collectively choose the overall membership of the Executive (these are allocated to and nominated by parties) and have no 'control' over those ministers outside their own party. The Executive has been described as 'a mandatory coalition' (NI Assembly, 2002) but as Wilford (2009: 181) argues, parties are not compelled to take up the option of seats to which they are entitled based on their electoral performance in the Executive– it is a matter of choice. Wilford (2007: 167) described the four-party coalition (DUP, Sinn Féin, Ulster Unionist and SDLP) in the Executive as 'not an agreed arrangement among more or less willing partners, but a confected grand coalition that, for its outset, resembled a loveless marriage'. Because most MLAs represent the main four political parties, there is no official opposition in the Assembly.

The Northern Ireland (St Andrews Agreement) Act 2006 provides for a new ministerial code and places a duty on ministers and junior ministers to act in accordance with the provisions on ministerial accountability in the Code. It also allows the Assembly via a 'petition of concern' raised by 30 members to refer an important ministerial decision, or one which contravenes the ministerial code, to the Executive Committee – a mechanism to protect against the so-called 'solo-runs' by ministers. The role of the Executive Committee is set out in paragraphs 19 and 20 of the Belfast/Good Friday Agreement and reaffirmed in the Ministerial Code:

- To provide a forum for the discussion of, and agreement on, issues which cut across the responsibilities of two or more Ministers, for prioritising executive and legislative proposals and for recommending a common position where necessary.
- To agree each year, and review as necessary, a programme (*Programme for Government*) incorporating an agreed budget linked to policies and programmes, subject to approval by the Assembly, after scrutiny in Assembly Committees, on a cross-community basis.
- Discussion and agreement upon significant or controversial matters that are clearly outside the scope of the agreed programme or which the First Minister and deputy First Minister acting jointly have determined to be matters that should be considered by the Executive.

In essence, the Executive performs a role which is similar to a cabinet in other legislatures but is not made up from the majority political party only. The Executive brings forward proposals for new primary legislation in the form of Bills, for introduction in the Assembly, and for subordinate legislation in the form of statutory rules made under a 'parent' Act. It also provides direction for the Assembly through the *Programme for Government* and agreement on how this will be funded yearly.

Civic Forum

The Civic Forum was established under the terms of the Belfast/Good Friday Agreement as a 'consultative mechanism on social, economic and cultural issues' (Belfast/Good Friday Agreement, 1998: 9). Beyond this, the

Agreement is not specific, other than to say that it will receive administrative support from the Office of the First and Deputy First Minister. The Civic Forum adopted the mission statement to 'exercise effective community leadership and directly influence the building of a peaceful, prosperous, just, cohesive, healthy and plural society'. It described itself as representing a 'broad cut of civic society in Northern Ireland' (Knox, 2003: 30).

The Forum comprised representatives of the business, trade union and voluntary sectors and 'such other sectors as agreed' by the two ministers. It is widely acknowledged that the Forum was the brainchild of the Women's Coalition Party which pressed for a civil society contribution to any new political dispensation as part of the negotiations which led to the Agreement. Arrangements for the Forum were formalised in the Northern Ireland Act 1998 which required the First and Deputy First Minister, acting jointly, to make arrangements for obtaining from the Forum its views on social, economic and cultural matters. It was made up of 60 members drawn from a variety of sectors, all of whom were appointed, following a selection process, by the First and deputy First Minister.[1] The Forum held its inaugural meeting in October 2000. Its work programme fell into three broad categories: responding to major consultation exercises; research and analysis of key social, economic and cultural issues; and business improvement measures. Significantly, its views were sought on the Executive's *Programme for Government* and the budget in 2002/03. The Forum also made submissions on a number of ongoing policy debates – 'Investing for Health Strategy', the 'Review of Post Primary Education' and 'Priorities for Social Inclusion'. Its research and analysis team had mapped out a number of future projects including work on: life-long learning, entrepreneurship and creativity; combating poverty; inclusiveness and a plural society; and creating a sustainable Northern Ireland. In less than 2 years of full operation the Forum cost £750,000. A review of the Forum was first proposed by First Minister and Deputy First Minister some 12 months after its inception but was deferred until spring 2002 to allow it to become established. This did not happen due to the suspensions of the devolved institutions. The original intention of the review was to examine the structure and effectiveness of the civic forum and make recommendations. However, by 2006 it was clear that MLAs were divided on whether the Forum, as originally constituted, was in fact the most appropriate mechanism for obtaining the views of civic society. Following restoration on 8 May 2007, the First Minister and the Deputy First Minister decided to commission a fresh review to examine the structure, membership and role of the forum. The terms of reference of the earlier review were expanded to take into account the changes in civic society during the intervening years and the wider concerns raised by MLAs.

In February 2009 as the review was ongoing DUP members (under private members business in the Assembly) proposed a motion that the civic forum which had not met since 2002 should not be re-established because it had provided no value, lacked public concern about its absence, and other ways should be investigated to interact with the public in shaping policy. As one DUP contibutor to the debate put it:

> The civic forum was not necessary when it was created; it was not heeded when it spoke; it was not valued enough by its members for them to attend; it was not noticed when it fell; it is not missed in its absence. It encumbered the ground for long enough during its brief, pitiful life. It was put out of its misery in suspension, and it should never see the light of day again. (Moutray, 2009: 214).

In an even more scathing attack on the Forum another DUP, MLA argued that it failed mainly because it was not truly representative of Northern Ireland society; its make-up was 'anti-unionist, anti-orange and anti-evangelical' and designed to ensure that the majority of unionist opinion, which was opposed to the Belfast/Good Friday Agreement, was in the minority on the Forum (McCrea, 2009: 218). What is interesting about this motion on the civic forum is that a 'petition of concern' was presented and accepted by the Speaker of the Assembly which ensured that the vote on the motion was held on a cross-community basis. The SDLP saw the motion as part of a wider agenda by the DUP as follows:

> Those [DUP] statements (above) are part of a pattern of attitudes towards some of the people of Northern Ireland, and towards the institutions of the Good Friday Agreement, and, as such, people must wake up, catch on and draw conclusions. An attempt is being made to unpick one of the structures that brought about agreement politics in the North, and to dismantle the architecture of those agreement politics as expressed through the Civic Forum, 10 Departments and the North–South Ministerial Council. Let us not be naive about the DUP's ambitions and intentions. The motion is part of that pattern, and of a family of motions, designed to achieve that strategic outcome. (Attwood, 2009: 221)

The DUP motion was defeated on a cross-community vote. In May 2009 the DUP launched policy proposals *Driving Forward a Reform Agenda* in which it also flagged its intention not only to abolish the civic forum but also to streamline the Human Rights Commission, Equality Commission and the Office of the Commissioner for Children and Young People. In July 2009 the First Minister, Peter Robinson, launched what was described as a 'searing attack' on the Equality Commission when he said: 'It is outrageous that a mere 34 per cent of the staff of the Equality Commission is drawn from a Protestant community background. Furthermore, if we look at the commissioners themselves, I cannot identify a single person who would share the views of the tens of thousands of people who vote for the main unionist party in Northern Ireland' (Robinson, 2009b: 1). The future of the civic forum is still under consideration as parties have now divided along political lines in support or opposition.

Strand 2 institutions

The North–South Ministerial Council was established under the Belfast/Good Friday Agreement (strand 2) to develop consultation, co-operation and action within the island of Ireland. It brings together those with executive responsibilities in Northern Ireland and the Irish Government to work on matters of mutual interest and within the competence of the administrations both North and South. It is made up of ministers from the Northern Ireland Executive and the Irish Government, supported by a joint secretariat based in Armagh and staffed by civil servants from Northern Ireland and the Republic. All decisions of the council must be agreed by both sides. The Belfast/Good Friday Agreement provided that a work programme for the North–South Ministerial Council covering at least 12 subject areas should be agreed based on co-operation and implementation for mutual benefit. In practical terms this has translated into 6 areas where co-operation takes place through existing mechanisms within each of the jurisdictions separately (agriculture; education; environment; health; tourism; and transport), and 6 areas which are implemented through designated North–South bodies (food safety; Foyle, Carling and Irish Lights Commission Sector; Inland Waterways; Language (Irish and Ulster-Scots); special European Union programmes; and trade and business development). The establishment of any additional North–South bodies must be agreed by the Ministerial Council and be endorsed by the Northern Ireland Assembly and Oireachtas.

There are three formats for North–South Ministerial Council meetings: plenary, institutional and sectoral. In plenary format the Council takes an overview of co-operation on the island and of the North–South institutions – these sessions are led by the First Minister and deputy First Minister (NI) and the Taoiseach (Republic of Ireland). Some recent issues for debate and agreement at the plenary sessions have been: co-operation on the swine flu outbreak; a framework for the removal of waste illegally dumped in Northern Ireland from rogue operators in the Republic; and an all-island Animal Health and Welfare Strategy to facilitate free movement of animals. In institutional format, institutional and cross-sectoral issues are considered, including matters on the European Union. Recent discussions have included: the current economic downturn and the budgetary challenges facing the two jurisdictions; obstacles to cross-border mobility; cross-border banking charges; and transfer of pension rights on a cross-border basis. In sectoral format the aim is to oversee co-operation in the agreed 12 areas or sectors. Issues discussed reflect the range of activities involved but have included: *language* – co-operation between the two constituent language agencies, *Foras na Gaeilge* (The Irish Language Agency) and *Tha Boord o Ulstèr Scotch* (The Ulster Scots Agency); *education* – educational under-achievement and Traveller education; and *health* – suicide prevention measures, child protection and food safety (North–South Ministerial Council, 2009). Writing in advance of the restoration of devolution in 2007, Coakley (2007: 273) noted that the absence of political direction (for the North–South Ministerial Council) 'set clear limits to the extent to which the new implementation bodies may respond in a creative and innovative way to changing circumstances'. It therefore remains to be seen whether the restoration of devolution will improve the impact of the North–South Ministerial Council.

Strand 3 institutions

The British–Irish Council includes members from the two sovereign governments of the United Kingdom and Ireland, devolved institutions and Crown dependencies. The British–Irish Council is the only international forum where all eight members from this group participate. The role of the British–Irish Council is set out in the Belfast/Good Friday Agreement (1998: 14): 'to exchange information, discuss, consult and use best endeavours to reach agreement on co-operation on matters of mutual interest within the competence of the relevant administrations.' The British–Irish Council, much like the North–South Ministerial Council, meets in different formats – summit level and specific sectoral level, with participants represented by the appropriate minister. The Council has agreed a list of priority areas for work largely around: early years, misuse of drugs, the environment, social inclusion, transport, tourism, health, indigenous, minority and lesser used languages and demography (understanding migration and its impact; healthy independent ageing; investigating policy interventions, fertility, and student flows). Members of the British–Irish Council take a lead on specific areas. Recent discussions at the summit sessions have included the impact of the global economic downturn on members' respective economies and developing the role of the voluntary and community sectors during this time by helping to deliver services, develop communities, and support the vulnerable. A sectoral meeting on the environment, for example, considered topics on climate change, Sellafield and radioactive waste, and integrated coastal zone management (British–Irish Council, 2009). Walker (2001: 139) commented that the British Irish Council 'gripped the imaginations of many people in these islands, independently of its connections to the Belfast Agreement', and in the context of an expanding European Union it could offer 'a possible way forward politically, socially, culturally, and economically for the British Isles as a whole.' Coakley (2007: 271) is less sanguine in his assessment of its operation in practice when he commented: 'the work of the British Irish Council has not ignited the popular imagination, and it has singularly failed to attract the sustained involvement of the jurisdiction, Northern Ireland, that was responsible for its very creation'.

The British–Irish Intergovernmental Conference was set up under the Belfast/Good Friday Agreement to deal with 'the totality of relationships' and brings together the two governments 'to promote bilateral co-operation at all levels on all matters of mutual interest' within their competence (Belfast/Good Friday Agreement, 1998: 15). The Conference meets at summit level (Prime Minister and Taoiseach) but can be represented by appropriate ministers such as the Secretary of State for Northern Ireland and Minister for Foreign Affairs. A reported meeting took place in February 2007 when the Conference reviewed progress on the implementation of the St Andrews Agreement and restoration of the power-sharing institutions. The Conference also discussed security, policing and justice, human rights and equality issues. Reflecting on the achievements of strand 3 institutions, Coakley (2007: 274) noted 'the level of progress has been more consistent (than other strand 2/3 institutions) but also much more modest. This may well be due to the absence of any single interest driving the process in this domain, and may also reflect another reality: that the bitter relationship between the two islands that was so dominant in the past has now been overcome'.

Commenting on the overall consociational arrangements which are evidence in the architecture of devolved institutions in Northern Ireland, Alliance MLA, Dr Stephen Farry (2009: 166–167) notes:

> All of the main elements of consociational systems are present in the current governance arrangements for Northern Ireland. The mandatory coalition executive is a form of grand coalition. The system of designation and the related voting systems within the legislature and within the Executive reflect mutual vetoes. The twin-hatted nature of the offices of the First Minister and deputy First Minister also reflects this aspect. Proportional representation is used in elections to the Assembly and other elected bodies. In turn, proportionality is used to determine the composition of the Executive. It is further used in terms of some aspects of public appointments and recruitment to the police service. Moreover, there is substantial functional autonomy for what are treated as separate communities, with the state either implicitly providing duplication of goods, facilities and services.

Whilst accepting these features of consociationalism, Farry does not believe (with the exception of the PR electoral system) they will result in stability, an open civic society and a sustainable economy in Northern Ireland.

Farry's analysis is rejected by McGarry and O'Leary (2009: 51) who argue 'we think it is straightforwardly true that the Agreement, consociational in its prefiguration and in its content, and in its renewal, and with all its attendant difficulties, is clearly causally associated with a highly significant reduction in political violence'.

Devolution: making a difference?

On 26 March 2007 Ian Paisley the (then) leader of the Democratic Unionist Party issued a statement which heralded his party's intentions to share power with Sinn Féin – this included a specific reference to devolution:

> After a long and difficult time in the Province, I believe that enormous opportunities lie ahead for Northern Ireland. Devolution has never been an end in itself but is about making a positive difference to people's lives. I want to make it clear that I am committed to delivering, not only for those who voted for the DUP, but for all the people of Northern Ireland . . . With hard work and a commitment to succeed, I believe we can lay the foundation for a better, peaceful and prosperous future for all our people. (Paisley, 2007)

This announcement on power-sharing marked another 'historic moment' in Northern Ireland. It also demonstrated that the implementation of the Belfast/Good Friday and St Andrews Agreements have become synonymous with devolution which means that the fate of the former (political settlements) will dictate the destiny of the latter (devolution). Moreover, this blurring of boundaries between trying to achieve a political settlement and, at the same time, introduce constitutional change under devolution has served to merge these issues in the minds of the public – see box 1.2 on the chronology of events leading to power-sharing/devolved government and how these were reported in the local press.

Devolution has therefore appeared to be less about the role played by the Assembly and Executive in the day-to-day business of running Northern Ireland and more to do with issues of 'high' politics. The stance of the main political parties has compounded the merger and devolution is no longer seen as a circumscribed policy of constitutional change. Hence, devolution in Northern Ireland has suffered by association with the Agreement(s) which were aimed at resolving long-standing constitutional, security and human rights/equality issues. Each crisis in the implementation of the Agreement became a crisis for devolution. This despite the fact, as Lord Holme (2002: 1209) pointed out, 'devolution is *one* plank in a rather complicated edifice represented by the Agreement'. Yet the wider public do not differentiate between devolution and the political agreement which led to power-sharing.

Chronology: power-sharing and devolution in Northern Ireland

1994, 31 August: The IRA announce 'a complete cessation of military activities', followed 43 days later with a similar ceasefire announcement by the main loyalist paramilitaries.

1996, 9 February: The IRA ends its 17-month ceasefire with the bombing of London's Docklands and the killing of two innocent civilians. Government breaks off links with Sinn Féin.

1997, 20 July: IRA announces renewal of its ceasefire and the recently elected Blair government resumes contact with Sinn Féin.

1998, 10 April: The Belfast/Good Friday Agreement paves the way for the establishment of a power-sharing executive, new cross-border links and a British military scale down.

1999, 29 November: After much wrangling the Assembly finally meets and nominates Executive ministers – only to be suspended the following February by Northern Ireland Secretary Peter Mandelson because of the IRA's failure to decommission any of its weapons.

2000, 29 May: Unionists agree a return to Stormont and resumption of devolution on the basis of the arms issue being dealt with while the Assembly continues to function.

2002, 14 October: The Northern Ireland Assembly and power-sharing Executive is suspended after the arrest of Sinn Féin's head of administration, Denis Donaldson, and three others for allegations of an IRA spy ring gathering intelligence at the heart of government.

2002, 17 October: Prime Minister Tony Blair travels to Belfast and warns republicans they cannot continue the twin track of politics and power-sharing while holding onto weapons.

2003, 1 May: Tony Blair postpones Assembly elections to buy more time for David Trimble's Ulster Unionists and Sinn Féin to strike a power-sharing deal.

2003, 4 September: The Independent Monitoring Commission is set up to monitor the activities of paramilitary groups in the face of Sinn Féin opposition.

2003, 23 October: Peace process choreography involving the Ulster Unionists and Sinn Féin goes wrong when David Trimble claims there was not enough transparency around the IRA's third act disarmament for him to deliver his end of the deal.

DEVOLUTION

2003, 26 November: The Democratic Unionists emerge for the first time as the largest party in new Assembly Elections and Sinn Féin as the major voice of nationalism. Ian Paisley warns he will not sit in government with republicans until the IRA disarms and disbands.

2004, 5 January: Assembly members Jeffrey Donaldson, Arlene Foster and Norah Beare defect from the UUP to the DUP.

2004, 18 September: After three days of intense negotiations involving Tony Blair, Taoiseach Bertie Ahern and the Northern Ireland parties, the DUP and Sinn Féin resolve to keep talking.

2004, 4 October: Ian Paisley holds discussions with Bertie Ahern in Dublin.

2004, 8 December: After the DUP and Sinn Féin fail to strike a devolution deal, Tony Blair and Bertie Ahern travel to Belfast to publish their proposals for restoring power-sharing.

2004, 21 December: The IRA is accused of carrying out the £26.5m robbery of the Northern Bank in Belfast city centre, the biggest UK bank robbery ever.

2005, 30 January: The Provisional IRA come under huge pressure after they are accused of trying to cover up the murder of Robert McCartney outside a Belfast city centre bar.

2005, 6 April: Gerry Adams makes an appeal to the IRA to revitalise the political process by abandoning its armed campaign.

2005, 6 May: The DUP makes huge gains over David Trimble's Ulster Unionists in the general Election.

2005, 7 May: David Trimble quits as Ulster Unionist leader.

2005, 24 June: Sir Reg Empey becomes UUP leader.

2005, 28 July: The Provisional IRA announces a formal end to its armed campaign.

2005, 26 September: General de Chastelain and two clergymen acting as independent witnesses announce the IRA has completed its disarmament process.

2005, 8 December: The Stormont spy ring case collapses.

2005, 16 December: Gerry Adams stuns republicans by expelling Denis Donaldson for confessing to being a British spy.

2006, 4 April: Denis Donaldson is shot dead in Donegal. The IRA denies involvement.

2006, 6 April: Prime Minister Tony Blair and Taoiseach Bertie Ahern give the parties a deadline of 24 November to set up a power-sharing executive.

> *2006, 13 October:* After three days of talks in St Andrews, Ian Paisley agrees to a road map to devolution but he makes power-sharing with Sinn Féin dependent on them signing up to policing.
>
> *2007, 28 January:* Sinn Féin members back their leadership's proposal to get involved in policing in Northern Ireland if power-sharing returns.
>
> *2007, 6 March:* Following Sinn Féin's decision to endorse the police in Northern Ireland, the province goes to the polls and returns both the DUP and Sinn Féin with increased numbers of seats. Horse trading ahead of the 26 March devolution deadline gets into full swing and four days before the date, Chancellor Gordon Brown unveils a £5.1bn financial package to entice parties back into power. However, on 24 March, the DUP executive signals they will not nominate on 26 March and want power-sharing delayed until an agreed date in May.
>
> *2007, 9 March:* The DUP and Sinn Féin further strengthen their hold on the Assembly in a new Stormont election.
>
> *2007, 25 March:* Northern Ireland Secretary Peter Hain signs the order, convening the Assembly to nominate a new power-sharing government or come up with an agreed plan for achieving devolution within weeks. The minister warns that if the main parties cannot find an agreed path back to devolution, direct rule by English, Welsh and Scottish ministers would be prolonged.
>
> *2007, 26 March:* Ian Paisley and Gerry Adams announce on camera they have struck a deal to revive power-sharing on May 8.
>
> *2007, 27 March:* Jim Allister MEP quits the DUP over its power-sharing deal.
>
> *2007, 2 April:* At a meeting at Stormont, it is decided the DUP will take the finance, economy, environment and culture ministries. Sinn Féin opts for education, regional development and agriculture. The UUP chooses health and employment and learning, while the SDLP claims social development.
>
> Devolution is ongoing.
>
> Sources: 'Sinn Féin and DUP strike power-sharing deal', David Gordon, *Belfast Telegraph*, 26 March 2007: 1; 'Month by month: the tortuous road to devolution', *Belfast Telegraph*, 8 May, 2007: 1

Wilford and Wilson (2003: 116) argue 'it is not the idea of devolution *per se* that was the casualty of the shift in popular opinion. Rather, lack of trust in the republican movement subverted Protestant support'. They go on to highlight the lack of public affinity with devolution:

> Part of the difficulty was the only limited evidence, as in Scotland and Wales, that the citizens of Northern Ireland had developed an instrumental commitment to devolution. Particularly among Protestants, there was merely lukewarm affirmation of the devolved ministers' mantra-like claim to 'making a difference'. Indeed, substantively, the record from December 1999 – however rationalised by suspensions – was limited. (Wilford and Wilson, 2003: 84)

This observation captured the state of play at the beginning of the fourth period of suspension for the Assembly (14 October 2002–7 May 2007). Since then, the second mandate of the Northern Ireland Assembly has demonstrated a degree of political stability and it may now be timely to ask 'has devolution made a difference' in terms of public policy issues. We consider, selectively, some of the key 'successes' of devolution.

Winter fuel payments

The huge increases in the cost of energy became a key issue for the devolved Assembly in the winter of 2008, particularly amongst the elderly and most vulnerable in Northern Ireland. The Department of Social Development, as the lead agency, stressed its commitment to tackle the problem through: implementing the winter fuel payment (£250) towards the cost of heating for people aged 60+, and a means-tested Warm Homes Scheme to support energy efficiency measures (insulation, replacement heating systems) in the home. Such was the radical increase in electricity and gas prices, however, more people, particularly those on fixed incomes or state pensions, fell into the fuel poverty trap and looked to the devolved administration to alleviate hardship. The Minister, Margaret Ritchie, responded with urgent relief proposals to provide a £200 payment off the heating costs of the most vulnerable. The proposals however became entangled in the political stand-off between the DUP and Sinn Féin which had led to no meetings of the Northern Ireland Executive for a 5-month period from June 2008.

Meanwhile advocates for older people exerted very public pressure on their politicians including a high profile media march on Stormont. Age Sector Platform, Help the Aged and Age Concern Northern Ireland launched a campaign to establish a link between the state pension and average earnings around the rallying call 'Can't Heat or Eat' – highlighting the choice older people used to make between eating *or* heating their home did not now exist, some were struggling to do both. They supplemented their campaign with research which calculated that the winter fuel payment covered a third of average fuel prices when it was first introduced but now accounted for less than one-fifth and demanded that it be increased to at least £500 to help older people in Northern Ireland. Minister Ritchie, in turn, lobbied the

(UK) Secretary of State for Work and Pensions for an increase in the winter fuel payment. On 15 December 2008 the First Minister and deputy First Minister announced that the Executive would make a payment of £150 to over 100,000 householders on pension credit and income support, costing the devolved administration £15m.

A particularly interesting aspect of dealing with this issue was that the Executive and Assembly initiated legislation (through accelerated passage) which allowed them not only to direct funds towards the most vulnerable in society at a time of exceptional need in relation to fuel costs, but also to enable financial assistance to be provided to tackle poverty, social exclusion or patterns of deprivation when funding arrangements were unsatisfactory. The Financial Assistance Act (Northern Ireland) 2009 now provides the Executive with flexibility in the allocation and distribution of resources across all departments so that it may be able to respond quickly and effectively to *any* crisis situation or in tackling poverty and social exclusion. The speed with which the devolved administration acted, despite wider political disagreements was seen as a major success – the Bill was first introduced in the Assembly on 12 January 2009 and received Royal Assent on 4 February 2009, an example of the Assembly responding to local needs in a timely fashion.

Water charges

The Direct Rule administration presided over major reforms to the water and sewerage services in Northern Ireland in which the Water Service Agency, located in the Department for Regional Development, was restructured as a government owned company (GoCo) – a statutory trading body owned by central government but operating under company legislation, with substantial independence from government. The government also announced the introduction of domestic water and sewerage charges from April 2006, a hugely controversial decision since rate payers, branding it a 'tap tax', claimed to be paying for these services already through regional rates. Average household water bills were estimated at around £415 by 2008. These charges, the (then) Minister (John Spellar) claimed, were to pay for improvements to the water and sewerage system without diverting cash from other public services. An estimate of £3b was given to upgrade Northern Ireland's utilities over 20 years. He argued that the average rates bill in Northern Ireland was £500 by comparison with household bills for property taxes and water charges of around £1,200 in the rest of the United Kingdom.

In the budget projections for 2006/07, the financial year in which the water tax was due to start, the minister threatened that the Treasury would reduce the block grant to Northern Ireland by £50m if charges were not introduced. Minister Spellar claimed that the Stormont Executive during its first mandate had signed up to water charges as part of an agreement with the Treasury on a major reinvestment package for Northern Ireland. He also said he saw no prospect of extra money coming from the UK Exchequer for the package. The Treasury had agreed to a three-year phasing-in of charges and 25 per cent discount for the poorest households. In the minister's view the Treasury had gone further than in England, Wales and Scotland. Slippage occurred until April 2007 on the introduction of charges, due to be based on the rateable value of homes, because of revisions needed to the household valuation list and time needed to procure a billing and charging system. Local politicians revealed that the introduction of water charges also became part of the negotiations (in December 2004) with the Northern Ireland Office to reach a political accommodation and restore devolved government in which the introduction of water charges would be rolled out over a 5-year period instead of the intended three. The direct rule administration, despite significant opposition from consumer groups and local political parties, pushed ahead with legislation to introduce charges and the Water and Sewerage Services (NI) Order 2006 was approved in November 2006. Once again the prospect of introducing water charges (and other issues such as rural planning restrictions, Irish Language Act) were raised as the deadline for devolution or dissolution of the Assembly arrived (26 March 2007 at midnight) following the St Andrews Agreement. Local politicians were faced with the prospect of direct rule ministers implementing some unpopular policies. When the political deal came on power-sharing, water charges were deferred.

In May 2007 the Assembly deferred the introduction of domestic water charges pending the outcome of an independent review set up to examine the arrangements for the delivery of water and sewerage services in Northern Ireland – including funding. The review completed its work in January 2008 and the Executive has consulted on its recommendations. For 2009/10, the Executive decided to defer the introduction of household payments for water and sewerage services – meaning that charges will not now be introduced on 1 April 2009. In April 2009 Regional Development Minister Conor Murphy asked his Executive colleagues to back a further two-year deferment, until at least 2012, with the option of continuing the extension again at a later date. No decision has been reached on when water and sewerage charges will be introduced at the time of writing.

Free prescriptions

Gordon Brown's plans, announced at the Labour Party conference in September 2008, to scrap drug charges for all cancer patients in England

and, eventually, for long term chronic illnesses did not extend to Northern Ireland and could only be adopted if the Assembly decided to do so. Wales and Scotland already offer their cancer patients free medicines. Northern Ireland would then have been the only region in the United Kingdom where people with cancer, believed to be around 50,000 people according to Macmillan Cancer Support, still have to pay for their prescriptions. Health Minister Michael McGimpsey had initiated a cost–benefits review of prescription charges in Northern Ireland and was considering a range of options. He had made it clear that giving cancer patients the medication they require could mean long-term savings for the Health Service. If patients are able to manage their condition with the aid of drugs, then they will be able to live in the community and not require expensive hospital treatment. Public pressure to remove the charges was given added impetus when the (then) Finance Minister, Nigel Dodds said he could see 'no obstacles' to the scrapping of prescription charges for cancer sufferers in the province. At the end of September 2008 the Northern Ireland Health Minister announced that *all* prescription charges, which stood at £6.85 per item, would be completely abolished within 18 months (by April 2010), with an interim reduction to £3 per item in January 2009. He said the £13m gap, or 3.5 per cent of the overall drugs bill created in his annual budget by the decision could be accommodated without damaging other services within the Health Service. In announcing the decision he pointed out:

> It is simply unacceptable that those who are ill should have to worry about finding money for vital drugs which they cannot afford. This is totally against the ethos of a health service which promises free health and social care to all . . . This is a historic and happy day for the health and social care service in Northern Ireland. It brings to an end an inequitable system which caused only anxiety to thousands of people who were already suffering from serious illnesses. It is also a testament to what can be achieved by a local administration responding to local needs and wishes. The people of Northern Ireland deserve no less from their own Government. (McGimpsey, 2008)

The newly resumed Executive, after a hiatus where no meetings took place, approved the measure in November 2008.

The above policies provide a snapshot of the more high profile policies adopted by the Northern Ireland Assembly. The criticism made however is that the power-sharing administration has opted for populist public policies and neglected the more difficult policy choices on which there are fundamental differences between the DUP and Sinn Féin. These populist policies have been critiqued by independent sources. In a 2009 report from the Economic Research Institute of Northern Ireland (ERINI), aimed at spelling out the options available to the Executive and Assembly during the recession, they noted:

The Executive have already taken a range of actions to lower the cost of services to citizens. These include:

- Not imposing separate water charges for 2009/10.
- Freezing domestic rates. This is costing £40 million this year and will be increasingly expensive as time goes on.
- Lowering the cap on capital values for rating (legislation pending).
- Freezing non-domestic rates at an estimated cost of £15 million.
- Free prescription charges from 2010/11 at a cost of at least £13 million per year.
- Free travel for the elderly at an additional cost of £4 million per year.

These subsidies do keep down the cost of living in the short term but they carry very high levels of dead weight and are quite indiscriminate . . . Before straying further along the road of dispensing subsidies it would be highly desirable if the Executive actually took stock of the true cost of the wide range of existing subsidies before proceeding further. (Economic Research Institute of Northern Ireland, 2009: 16–17)

The DUP disagreed with the proposals as outlined, arguing that they would reverse the policies adopted by their party in government. If the above example could be described as populist policy successes, the following controversial issue is a stark reminder of difficulties which have faced the devolved administration.

Education reforms

In December 2007 Sinn Féin Education Minister Caitríona Ruane outlined proposals to reform what she described as an outdated 1947 education model, which had divided children into two school types, either grammar or non-grammar: crudely perceived to be high performing/selective and less academic/non-selective, respectively. Central to the Minister's reform agenda was the underlying principle of equality of access and opportunity which she asserted had been denied to children through an academic selection process at the age of 11 (the so-called 11+ exam). Her Sinn Féin colleague Martin McGuinness had announced the ending of the test in 2002 and her proposals were to apply to children entering post-primary schools in September 2010. As part of a wider programme of change, which included the phased introduction of a revised curriculum; the expansion of subjects available to study at secondary level; and the establishment of a new Education and Skills Authority, she promised a 'world class education system fit for the twenty-first century'(Ruane, December 2007). She proposed to move from a system of academic selection via the 11-plus transfer test to a 14-plus system of election where pupils transferring to post-primary schools would do so largely on the basis of their school preferences. Her plans allowed a 3-year transition period during which the grammar schools had the option to engage in a scaled-down selection process.

The Minister however 'locked horns' with the Education Committee in the Assembly over her plans, where there is still strong support for the grammar school system, and the Northern Ireland Executive refused to table a debate on the Minister's proposals for change. As a result, the Minister withdrew her plans, ended the 11+ selection process in 2009 and issued guidance to all those involved in post-primary transfer from 2010 onwards. The guidance enables post-primary schools to develop their own admissions criteria which they should communicate to parents. The Minister advised schools that they should *not* use academic admissions criteria. Grammar schools have refused, given the non-legislative basis of the minister's guidance, to adopt this course of action (although they must 'have regard to' the Department's guidance) and have developed their own entrance examinations as the basis of selection. An unregulated system of post-primary transfer has now emerged with the Minister refusing to back down on her plans to reform. In short, there is a shambles and the education policy landscape is dominated by the selection debate.

A difference?

Two-plus years into the second mandate of the devolved power-sharing administration (at the time of writing) offer the opportunity for some reflection. As a legislative and executive forum, achievements to date have been modest. It must of course be readily acknowledged that the very existence of a power-sharing devolved administration in the first place is a huge political accomplishment. One example of the political maturity which has developed is the collective response of the First and deputy First Minister to three murders in March 2009 when dissident republicans killed two soldiers and a police officer. Deputy First Minister Martin McGuinness joined First Minister Peter Robinson in pledging his 'whole-hearted support' to the PSNI in the face of escalating dissident republican violence and called on all members of the community to give any information they may have on 'these traitors to the island of Ireland' to the police. He made his address alongside Mr Robinson and then Chief Constable Sir Hugh Orde at Stormont Castle, an important and symbolic display of political unity. Their reaction to this chain of events was described as follows:

> Martin McGuinness's commendable unequivocal condemnation of the killers as 'traitors to the island of Ireland' would have been unimaginable a few years ago.

So would Ian Paisley's description in the House of Commons on Monday of the words of a Catholic priest who led his parishioners in praying for the souls of the dead soldiers as 'one of the greatest speeches I have ever heard from a man of the cloth'. As Dr Paisley put it, we are seeing 'something we never thought we would see' – not just in the appalling return to political murder, but also in the way reactions to that return have not been split along tribal or sectarian lines. (*Irish Times*, 2009)

In public policy terms or the capacity of the devolved government to 'make a difference' to the lives of people in Northern Ireland, there is much to be done. Squabbling over seemingly innocuous policy issues between the DUP and Sinn Féin does not instil confidence in the minds of the public and the populist polices adopted to date are short-term sweeteners. The 'wicked' public policy issues remain, hastened by the recession and a squeeze on public spending. The lack of an effective political opposition is raised as an impediment to decision-making and holding the two power brokers (DUP and Sinn Féin) to account. The SDLP and UUP claim that Executive decisions are arrived at through negotiations between the two largest parties and their political advisors in a secretive, behind-closed-doors manner. The law making record of the devolved administration has been equally unimpressive (see table 1.4) with 63 Acts from 1999, some of which are on relatively minor matters. Perhaps the final arbiter on whether the Assembly is make a difference should be the general public. We draw on the Northern Ireland Life and Times Survey data 2008 to make an assessment on this crucial question. The probability survey interviewed 1,216 respondents between 1 October 2008 and 28 February 2009, 18 months or more into the second mandate of the Northern Ireland Assembly.

The question posed to interviewees was as follows:

Overall, do you think that the Northern Ireland Assembly has achieved:
- ✓ A lot
- ✓ A little
- ✓ Nothing at all
- ✓ Too early to say

The results are set out in tables 1.5 and 1.6 and illustrated in figure 1.3.
The results indicate the following:

- Sinn Féin (13.7 per cent) followed by SDLP (8.7 per cent) respondents felt the Assembly had achieved *a lot*.
- UUP (26 per cent) followed by DUP (24.1 per cent) respondents saw the Assembly as having achieved *nothing*.

Table 1.4 Acts of the Northern Ireland Assembly

2000	2001	2002	2007	2008	2009
Allowances to Members of the Assembly Act (Northern Ireland) 2000	Adoption (Intercountry Aspects) Act (Northern Ireland) 2001	Budget Act (Northern Ireland) 2002	Budget Act (Northern Ireland) 2007	Budget Act (Northern Ireland) 2008	Budget Act (Northern Ireland) 2009
Appropriation Act (Northern Ireland) 2000	Budget Act (Northern Ireland) 2001	Budget (No. 2) Act (Northern Ireland) 2002	Children (Emergency Protection Orders) Act (Northern Ireland) 2007	Budget (No. 2) Act (Northern Ireland) 2008	Budget (No. 2) Act (Northern Ireland) 2009
Child Support, Pensions and Social Security Act (Northern Ireland) 2000	Budget (No. 2) Act (Northern Ireland) 2001	Carers and Direct Payments Act (Northern Ireland) 2002	Welfare Reform Act (Northern Ireland) 2007	Charities Act (Northern Ireland) 2008	Building Regulations (Amendment) Act (Northern Ireland) 2009
Financial Assistance for Political Parties Act (Northern Ireland) 2000	Defective Premises (Landlord's Liability) (Northern Ireland) 2001	Children (Leaving Care) Act (Northern Ireland) 2002		Child Maintenance Act (Northern Ireland) 2008	Financial Assistance Act (Northern Ireland) 2009
Weights and Measures (Amendment) Act (Northern Ireland) 2000	Department for Employment and Learning Act (Northern Ireland) 2001	Game Preservation (Amendment) Act (Northern Ireland) 2002		Commission for Victims and Survivors Act (Northern Ireland) 2008	Health and Social Care (Reform) Act (Northern Ireland) 2009

Dogs (Amendment) Act (Northern Ireland) 2001

Electronic Communications Act (Northern Ireland) 2001

Family Law Act (Northern Ireland) 2001

Fisheries (Amendment) Act (Northern Ireland) 2001

Government Resources and Accounts Act (Northern Ireland) 2001

Ground Rents Act (Northern Ireland) 2001

Health and Personal Social Services Act (Northern Ireland) 2002

Industrial Development Act (Northern Ireland) 2002

Limited Liability Partnerships Act (Northern Ireland) 2002

Local Government (Best Value) Act (Northern Ireland) 2002

Open-Ended Investment Companies Act (Northern Ireland) 2002

Personal Social Services (Preserved Rights) Act (Northern Ireland) 2002

Health (Miscellaneous Provisions) Act (Northern Ireland) 2008

Libraries Act (Northern Ireland) 2008

Local Government (Boundaries) Act (Northern Ireland) 2008

Mesothelioma, etc., Act (Northern Ireland) 2008

Pensions Act (Northern Ireland) 2008

Pensions (No. 2) Act (Northern Ireland) 2008

Presumption of Death Act (Northern Ireland) 2009

Public Authorities (Reform) Act (Northern Ireland) 2009

Table 1.4 (continued)

2000	2001	2002	2007	2008	2009
	Health and Personal Social Services Act (Northern Ireland) 2001	Railway Safety Act (Northern Ireland) 2002		Public Health (Amendment) Act (Northern Ireland) 2008	
	Planning (Compensation, etc.) Act (Northern Ireland) 2001	Social Security (Northern Ireland) Act 2002		Taxis Act (Northern Ireland) 2008	
	Product Liability (Amendment) Act (Northern Ireland) 2001	State Pension Credit Act (Northern Ireland) 2002			
	Social Security Fraud Act (Northern Ireland) 2001				
	Street Trading Act (Northern Ireland) 2001				
	Trustee Act (Northern Ireland) 2001				

DEVOLUTION

Table 1.5 What has the Assembly achieved by political party affiliation?

Political party affiliation	What has the Assembly achieved? % within Political Party (n)				Total
	A lot	A little	Nothing	Too early	
DUP	4.4% (11)	54.6% (136)	24.1% (60)	16.9% (42)	100% (249)
Sinn Féin	13.7% (20)	44.5% (65)	20.5% (30)	21.2% (31)	100% (146)
UUP	6.7% (14)	48.1% (100)	26.0% (54)	19.2% (40)	100% (208)
SDLP	8.7% (18)	50.2% (104)	19.8% (41)	21.3% (44)	100% (207)
Alliance	5.8% (5)	67.4% (58)	10.5% (9)	16.3% (14)	100% (86)
Total	7.6% (68)	51.7% (463)	21.7% (194)	19.1% (171)	100% (896)

Table 1.6 Chi-square tests

	Value	df	Asymp. Sig. (2-sided)
Pearson chi-square	27.691[a]	12	0.006
Likelihood ratio	27.695	12	0.006
Linear-by-linear association	0.478	1	0.490
No. of valid cases	896		

Note: [a] 0 cells (.0 per cent) have expected count less than 5. The minimum expected count is 6.53.

Figure 1.3 What has the Assembly achieved? Survey responses, 2008/09

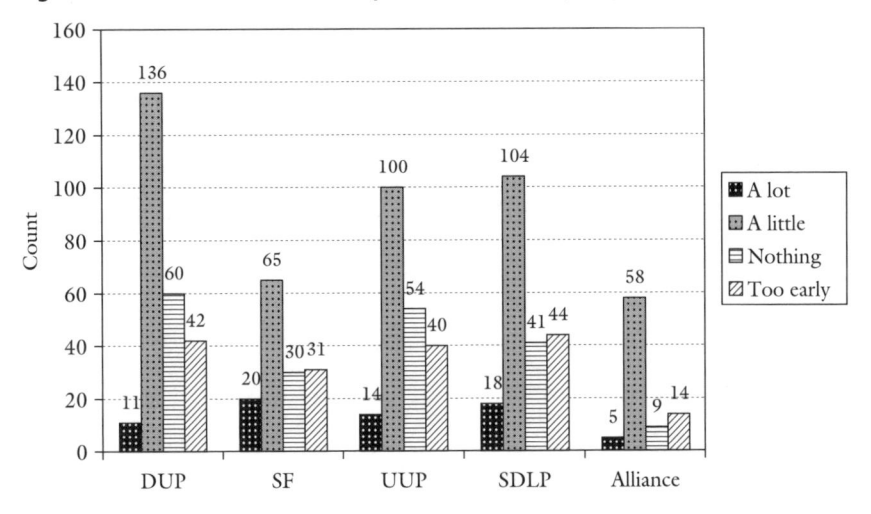

- Alliance (67.4 per cent) followed by DUP respondents (54.6 per cent) felt the Assembly had achieved *a little*.
- The SDLP (21.3 per cent) and Sinn Féin (21.2 per cent) respondents claimed it was *too early to tell*.

Overall, there *is an association* between the political party which people are closest to and their opinion of how well the Assembly is performing, χ^2 (12, N = 896) = 27.7, p < 0.05.

The public's perception of the success of devolution is still significantly conditioned by their perspectives on the political settlement and concomitant power-sharing arrangements, exemplified by the large percentage of DUP supporters (78.7 per cent) who felt the Assembly has achieved 'a little' or 'nothing' despite their party taking the lead role in government.

Note

1 The Forum comprised members from: business (7); agriculture & fisheries (3); trade unions (7); voluntary and community sector (18); churches (5); culture (4); arts and sport (4); victims (2); community relations (2); education (2); appointees of the First Minister and the Deputy First Minister (6); and an independent chair.

2
The Northern Ireland Civil Service

One must, however, consider the possibility that the six Northern Ireland departments will yet again pass under democratic control. In that event, it is to be hoped (although not confidently expected) that the efficient delivery of the public services will be considered of comparable weight to the purely political criteria. (Sir Kenneth Bloomfield, 1997: 145, former Head of the Northern Ireland Civil Service 1984–91)

Background

The Northern Ireland Civil Service is constitutionally separate from the Home Civil Service, a legacy of the creation of the Northern Ireland Parliament set up in 1921. It faces different issues in terms of geography, supporting a power-sharing government and a regional public sector reform agenda. As Birrell notes the Northern Ireland Civil Service is 'a unique example of a regional civil service within the United Kingdom completely separate from the UK civil service' although its structures and procedures tended to replicate the Great Britain model (Birrell, 1978: 305; Birrell, 2009). UK Civil Service departments employ staff in Northern Ireland in 'excepted' and 'reserved' matters such as: Immigration and Nationality Directorate; HM Revenue and Customs; Maritime and Coastguard Agency; Ministry of Defence; Northern Ireland Court Service; Northern Ireland Office; Identity and Passport Service. Together, this group makes up the Northern Ireland Home Civil Service Network.

The current structure of the Northern Ireland Civil Service dates back to December 1999 when 11 departments were set up as part of the Northern Ireland Executive by the Northern Ireland Act 1998 and the Departments (Northern Ireland) Order 1999. The former gave legal effect to the political outworkings of the Belfast or Good Friday Agreement (1998) and allowed provision to be made 'by the Act of the Assembly for establishing new Northern Ireland Departments or dissolving existing ones' (Section 21 (2), Northern

Ireland Act 1998). Devolution in Northern Ireland was part of wider constitutional reform agenda of the Labour Government which has seen powers devolved to the Scottish Parliament, Welsh Assembly and London Assembly. Devolved government in Northern Ireland witnessed the 6 pre-existing government departments responsible for public services under Direct Rule reconfigured and expanded to 10 departments with an additional department (Office of the First Minister and Deputy First Minister, OFMDFM) established to manage the *Programme for Government* and the agenda of the new Executive. The number of Civil Service departments had nothing to do with administrative criteria deemed necessary to discharge public services but, rather, was the product of political compromise to ensure the main political parties secured ministerial positions. As Wilson (2001: 74) describes it: 'the unspoken calculus was that Sinn Féin would not be satisfied with only one Executive seat, ten departments were required to ensure the party enjoyed two'.

The background to the current structures was also outlined during an Assembly debate on the organisation of government departments:

> There were six Departments during the Direct Rule years, but in December 1998, the pro-Agreement parties agreed to the establishment of the Office of the First Minister and Deputy First Minister and to the increase in the number of Departments to ten, as well as agreeing to the staff who came with them. The reason for almost doubling the number of departments was not to ensure efficient delivery for the people of Northern Ireland, but rather to ensure that all the pro-Agreement parties would be rewarded by gaining ministerial office and to ensure that from the outset of devolution, Sinn Féin had a position at the Executive table. Those political considerations also explain the reason for the inflated number of Assembly Members, which was to ensure that the small pro-Agreement parties, such as the Women's Coalition, the Progressive Unionist Party and the Alliance Party, would all be represented in the Chamber. (Ross, *Hansard*, Official Report, Northern Ireland Assembly 19 January 2009).

Politically derived administrative changes were not, however, a completely new experience for Northern Ireland. As one former Head of the Civil Sevice recounts, 'in 1973–74 when departmental structures were last re-examined in the context of impending devolution, a major influence was the imperative to find ministerial posts capable of accommodating a specific political balance in a coalition context' (Bloomfield, 1997: 146).

Functions

There are clear differences both in substance and context when considering the Northern Ireland Civil Service compared to other parts of the United Kingdom best described by Carmichael when he noted:

> Undoubtedly, the Northern Ireland Civil Service is closely modeled on its larger counterpart, the UK Home Civil Service, from which it takes many aspects of its structure and internal procedures, partly because a pervasive British Unionist ideology among the upper echelons of the service stressed its affinity with its 'mainland' cousin. However, the context within which public administration functions in the more normalised setting of Great Britain is distinctly different to that in Ulster . . . The Northern Ireland Civil Service is a key actor in the forefront of the Province's affairs and senior civil servants have 'enjoyed' a far higher public profile than their Whitehall counterparts. (Carmichael, 2002: 45)

The 'profile' of civil servants has undoubtedly changed under devolution and there is a much greater degree of accountability and scrutiny, something which officials found difficult get used to.

The Departments (Northern Ireland) Order 1999 established five new Northern Ireland departments and renamed certain existing departments (see table 2.1). Eleven government departments are now responsible for the bulk of 'transferred' public services and, under devolved government arrangements, are accountable to ministers who liaise with their respective statutory committees for each department. The committees are there 'to advise and assist each Northern Ireland Minister in the formulation of policy with respect to matters within his/her responsibilities as a Minister' (Northern Ireland Act, 1998: section 29). What is obvious even from the titles of civil service departments in Northern Ireland is that they have responsibility for key public services which would otherwise be delivered through local government in other parts of the United Kingdom. Hence, functions such as education, housing, social services and libraries fall within the remit of councils in Great Britain but have been retained in the highly centralised system of public administration that is Northern Ireland. The Northern Ireland Executive and Assembly seem reluctant to devolve any significant additional functions to local government. There are ongoing discussions between the political parties about the devolution of policing and justice powers to the Northern Ireland Assembly. The St Andrews Agreement (Northern Ireland, 2006: section 7) encouraged political parties 'to agree the necessary administrative arrangements to create a new policing and justice department' arguing that the implementation of the Agreement would build the necessary community confidence to allow a request by the devolved administration for transfer by May 2008. There have however been major political difficulties in resolving this issue between the DUP and Sinn Féin and a review committee at Stormont is now considering how best to proceed on the matter. In the interim, the murder of two young British soldiers and a police officer by dissident republicans (March 2009) has been met by a combined response from the DUP, Sinn Féin and the PSNI that such incidents will not disrupt the democratic process and stability of the

Table 2.1 Departmental structure of Northern Ireland Civil Service (pre- and post-devolution)

Pre-devolution (from 1982 onwards)	Post-devolution (1999 onwards)
Secretary of State: Northern Ireland Office Central Secretariat	Secretary of State: Northern Ireland Office
	Office of the First Minister and Deputy First Minister
Finance and Personnel	Finance and Personnel
Economic Development	Enterprise, Trade and Investment
	Regional Development
	Social Development
Agriculture	Agriculture and Rural Development
Health and Social Services	Health, Social Services and Public Safety
Environment	Environment
	Culture, Arts and Leisure
Education	Education
	Employment and Learning

Assembly. Difficulties remain however on whether there is adequate funding available for the new department of justice, police and judiciary and which political party will assume the ministerial portfolio.

The large number of existing departments has resulted in criticisms from the business and voluntary and community sectors about the lack of coherent government and the need to interface with several departments in the course of their day-to-day business. Dr Stephen Farry of the Alliance Party outlined the extent of the duplication involved as follows:

> The lines that divide our Departments are arbitrary. The Department for Employment and Learning (DEL), for instance, is responsible for the needs of the unemployed, but the Department for Social Development (DSD) looks after a large part of the benefit system. Likewise, both the Department of Education and the Department for Employment and Learning have responsibilities for functions within education. A number of Departments have roles relating to the economy. The Department of Enterprise, Trade and Investment (DETI) plays quite a small role in that area: it has responsibility for tourism, and, in that regard, interfaces with the Department of Culture, Arts and Leisure (DCAL). The most acute example of the failure to deliver joined-up government relates to planning. At the macro level, the Department for Regional Development (DRD) is responsible for strategic planning and the Department of the Environment (DOE) for the implementation of planning. DOE has the lead in the consideration of individual planning applications, and, alongside that Department, Roads Service and Northern Ireland Water, under the remit of DRD, play a consultative role. Those overlaps create obstacles. The Department for Social Development comes into the picture for matters relating to urban regeneration. Therefore, three Departments have a role to play in planning. That is baffling

for individuals in Northern Ireland – and even more so for businesses that are trying to deliver results. (*Hansard*, Official Report, Northern Ireland Assembly 19 January 2009)

In addition to the overlap in functional responsibilities outlined above, the transfer of some central government functions (urban regeneration, public realm aspects of roads functions etc.) to the reconfigured local authorities in 2011 will hollow out some of the civil service departments and make the scale of their activities as separate departments questionable (Knox and Carmichael, 2005a).

Form

Up-to-date and accurate statistics on the number of civil servants are difficult to access because of the outworking of the Review of Public Administration which has significantly changed the administrative architecture of Northern Ireland. During the Review process estimates of those working in the public sector were given (in 2005) as: Northern Ireland Civil Service (31,000); Health Service (68,000); Education (50,000); Local Government (10,000); Non-departmental public bodies (41,000) – a grand total of 200,00 public sector employees (*Review of Public Administration in Northern Ireland: Further Consultation* (2005: 103). More up-to-date figures, but in a different classification format, are available from the Department of Enterprise, Trade and Investment (Quarterly Employment Survey 2008) – see table 2.2 and figure 2.1.

The size of the public sector in Northern Ireland, as measured in terms of employment share (30.8 per cent), has often attracted negative commentary

Table 2.2 Northern Ireland public sector jobs[a] (at December 2008)

NI central government (including health trusts)	114,854
Bodies under aegis of NI central government	78,034
UK central government	5,816
Local government (district councils)	11,816
Public corporations	9,467
Total public sector jobs	**219,987**
% of employee jobs (excludes self-employed)	**30.8**

Note: [a]Public sector jobs comprise central government (including bodies under the aegis of central government), local government and public corporations. 'Public corporations' are companies or quasi-corporations controlled by either central government or local government. These companies receive more than half their income from the sales of goods or services into the market place.

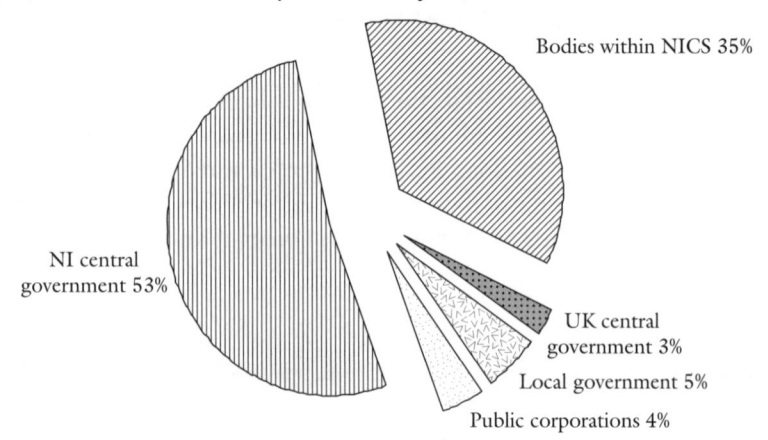

Figure 2.1 Northern Ireland public sector jobs, 2008

- Bodies within NICS 35%
- NI central government 53%
- UK central government 3%
- Local government 5%
- Public corporations 4%

by comparison to the rest of the United Kingdom which is significantly lower (at around 20 per cent). But when measured in terms of public employment as a proportion of the overall population it is similar to other parts of the UK (at around 12–13 per cent). As the Northern Ireland Executive (2008a: 21) points out 'this suggests that the greater concern should be the relative size of the private sector in the local economy'.

The Northern Ireland Civil Service is responsible for 'transferred' matters and comprises a wide range of jobs broadly categorized under the following headings:

1 *General Service*: Administrative Officer, Executive Officer 1, Deputy Principal.
2 *Secretarial*: Typist, Personal Secretary
3 *Scientific*: Scientific Officer, Fisheries Officer, Microbiologist
4 *Technology*: Graduate Trainee Quantity Surveyor, Electrical Engineer, Architect, Tracer
5 *Legal*: Legal Assistant, Law Clerk
6 *Computing*: Programmer, Systems Analyst
7 *Specialisms*: Graduate Trainee Valuer, Inspector of Schools, Veterinary Officer
8 *Centralised Services*: Messenger, Security Guard, Telephonist
9 *Industrial*: Road Workers, Porters, Industrial Technicians.

The Occupational Groups listed 1–8 above are collectively known by the term 'non-industrial' civil servants. Non-industrial grades are grouped into salary bands as follows: Senior Principal (Grade 6); Principal (Grade 7); Deputy

Table 2.3 Staff in 11 government departments by industrial status and gender[a]

	Female		Male		Total
	No.	%	No.	%	No.
Non-industrial	13,032	52.6	11,762	47.4	24,794
Industrial	44	2.0	2117	98.0	2,161
Total	13,076	48.6	13,879	51.6	26,955

Source: *Equal Opportunities in the Northern Ireland Civil Service*. Belfast: Department of Finance and Personnel (2008).

Note: [a] These data do not include: direct recruits of the Police Service of Northern Ireland; direct recruits of the Northern Ireland Assembly; home civil servants working in the Northern Ireland Office; or prison grades in the Northern Ireland Prison Service.

Principal (DP); Staff Officer (SO); Executive Officer 1 (EO1); Executive Officer 2 (EO2); Administrative Officer (AO); and Administrative Assistant (AA). The senior civil service comprises the following grades:

- Grade 5 (Assistant Secretary)
- Grade 3 (Deputy Secretary)
- Permanent Secretary
- Head of the Northern Ireland Civil Service.

The breakdown in staff across the 11 government departments according to industrial status and gender is shown in table 2.3.

All civil servants, regardless of their grade, must adhere to a code of ethics which outlines their commitments to the long-standing core values of public service: integrity, honesty, objectivity and impartiality (see box 2.1). As civil servants made the transition from Direct Rule to devolved government in Northern Ireland these core values have become much more apparent. Their direct accountability to local ministers, appearances before statutory departmental committees and responding to questions from the Assembly emphasizes the role which they must play in supporting elected representatives largely absent under Direct Rule arrangements.

Devolved government has also challenged the Northern Ireland Civil Service to develop skills and capacities in areas such as policy-making which have been lost in an operating environment where public policies were simply 'read across' from Westminster. One clear manifestation of their willingness to invest in developing civil servants is the Professional Skills for Government

> **Box 2.1 Northern Ireland Civil Service: core values**
>
> 1. The Civil Service is an integral and key part of the government of Northern Ireland. It supports the Government of the day in developing and implementing its policies, and in delivering public services. Civil servants are accountable to Ministers, who in turn are accountable to Parliament.
> 2. As a civil servant, you are appointed on merit on the basis of fair and open competition and are expected to carry out your role with dedication and a commitment to the Civil Service and its core values: integrity, honesty, objectivity and impartiality. In this Code:
>
>   - 'integrity' is putting the obligations of public service above your own personal interests;
>   - 'honesty' is being truthful and open;
>   - 'objectivity' is basing your advice and decisions on rigorous analysis of the evidence; and
>   - 'impartiality' is acting solely according to the merits of the case and serving equally well Governments of different political persuasions.
>
> 3. These core values support good government and ensure the achievement of the highest possible standards in all that the Civil Service does. This, in turn, helps the Civil Service to gain and retain the respect of Ministers, Parliament, the public and its customers.
> 4. This Code sets out the standards of behaviour expected of you and all other civil servants. These are based on the core values. Individual departments may also have their own separate mission and values statements based on the core values, including the standards of behaviour expected of you when you deal with your colleagues.
>
> *Source: Northern Ireland Civil Service Staff Handbook.*

(PSfG) initiative which has been implemented across the Northern Ireland Civil Service from April 2006. Aimed initially at the senior civil service, acquiring professional skills is now an integral part of how the performance of officials is assessed and incentivised. The initiative is part of a wider Whitehall policy designed to develop the skills and experience needed to deliver twenty-first-century public services.

Professional Skills for Government aims to:

- ensure that civil servants wherever they work have the right skills and expertise to enable their departments and agencies to deliver effective services; and
- provides clarity about the skills individuals need to develop and progress in the Civil Service.

Skills and expertise are defined in a series of frameworks for four core areas of development at each grade level and for each career grouping in the civil service. The four core areas are as follows:

- *Leadership*: Civil Service leadership qualities sit at the centre of the framework. These are to: provide direction for the organisation; deliver results; build capacity for the organisation to address current and future challenges; and act with integrity (as this lies at the very heart of leadership within the Civil Service).
- *Core skills*: Every civil servant needs certain core skills to work effectively. At Grade 7 the four core skills are: people management; financial management; analysis and use of evidence; and, programme and project management In addition to these skills, those in or aspiring to the senior civil service need to demonstrate skills in communications and marketing, and strategic thinking. Government Skills, in partnership with departments, has developed a common core skills framework for civil servants below Grade 7. This framework, launched in July 2008, will be embedded in departmental frameworks by 2012.
- *Professional expertise*: related to the job/career grouping. Job-specific professional skills are related to the work of individual civil servants. Everyone in the Civil Service requires some professional skills to do their job, whether they work in policy development, operational delivery, corporate services or provide expert advice (for example, scientists, economists and communicators). This area of the professional skills competency framework is supported by Heads of Profession, who set standards for all professions in the Civil Service.
- *Broader experience* of working in more than one career grouping. For senior officials and those aspiring to the senior civil service, both depth and breadth of experience are important. Deep professional knowledge is valuable, but with career progression breadth of experience becomes increasingly important. Heads of profession are leading work to define what broader experience looks like in each professional context. This experience could be gained within a profession, within another part

of the Civil Service or in other sectors (*Building Professional Skills for Government: A Strategy for Delivery*, 2008).

Northern Ireland has developed its own action plan for delivering the professional skills agenda for the civil service and makes recommendations aimed at improving the organisational capacity and quality of public services. The action plan is organised around three themes:

- Develop and drive up professional standards and use them to manage careers.
- Take common action on common skills.
- Develop a working relationship between government employers and the higher and further education sectors to strengthen the skills of the talent pool from which government recruits.

The action plan acknowledges that the 'devolved administration focuses on Northern Ireland solutions to Northern Ireland issues' (Skills Sector Council for Central Government, 2008).

Finance

Given the highly centralised system of public services in Northern Ireland it is important to examine how core activities are funded. Northern Ireland's public expenditure comes from four key sources as follows:

1   Share of UK Public Expenditure allocations calculated using the Barnett formula referred to as 'unhypothecated' funding which means the Northern Ireland Executive/Assembly can make their own decisions on how to spend the money, determining their own priorities and programmes.
2   Regional rates: income collected by a tax on business and domestic property in Northern Ireland and paid as a rates bill. The rates bill comprised two parts: regional rate which is to pay for the costs of centrally provided (government department) public services; and the district rate or funds collected to pay for services provided by local government. Regional rates income is also unhypothecated making it available for allocation on whatever priorities for public spending are decided by the Executive and Assembly.
3   Borrowing under the Reinvestment and Reform Initiative (RRI): money can be borrowed for capital investment each year under this initiative. The borrowing is subject to annual limits determined by the Treasury and is £200m per annum at present.

4   EU funding: money available from the European Union to assist Northern Ireland in various ways. For example, PEACE is a European Union structural funds programme aimed at reinforcing progress towards a peaceful and stable society and promoting reconciliation. The INTERREG Programme is a cross-border territorial co-operation programme for Northern Ireland, the Border Region and Western Scotland which aims to support strategic cross-border co-operation for a more prosperous and sustainable region.

These sources of funding represent: Treasury (91.6 per cent); rates (5.8 per cent); RRI (2.1 per cent) and EU funds (0.4 per cent) in 2007–08 (Northern Ireland Executive 2008a: 31–32).

With increasing pressure on the devolved budget in Northern Ireland there have been discussions about the potential to revise or scrap the allocation of funding using the Barnett formula. This, despite the fact that by comparison with other parts of the UK, Northern Ireland has the highest per capita spending at £9,789 compared to England at £7,535 (HM Treasury, 2008: 127). Such comparisons, however, can be misleading because the funding allocation does not reflect variations in the regional needs of the population. Instead, the formula relies in broad terms on: changes to the assigned budgets of the devolved administrations; relative population proportions; and a comparability element between UK departmental programme and services delivered by each devolved administration. Key criticisms of budget allocations to the devolved regions include the argument that per capita spending does not reflect the tax base that pays for public spending – in other words, English taxpayers subsidise Stormont (and other devolved administrations). Equally, there is no real electoral accountability between taxation and spending in the devolved regions – they spend what they get as they see fit from the Treasury but do not have to justify unpopular increased taxation to their electorates (Northern Ireland Assembly, 2009). Despite political agitation about the unfairness of Barnett in allocating resources to Northern Ireland one public expenditure scholar offers the following advice on the abolition of the Barnett formula:

> Proceed with caution, as you might find that what you wish is unpleasant. Whether or not the future of present arrangements is called the Barnett formula, the substance or present arrangements are beneficial to Northern Ireland in both resource and procedural terms. (Heald, 2009)

It is not surprising to note that when the £8.5 billion annual budget is allocated across departments that the key spending areas are in health and education at 47.4 per cent and 21.9 per cent respectively (see figure 2.2 and table 2.4).

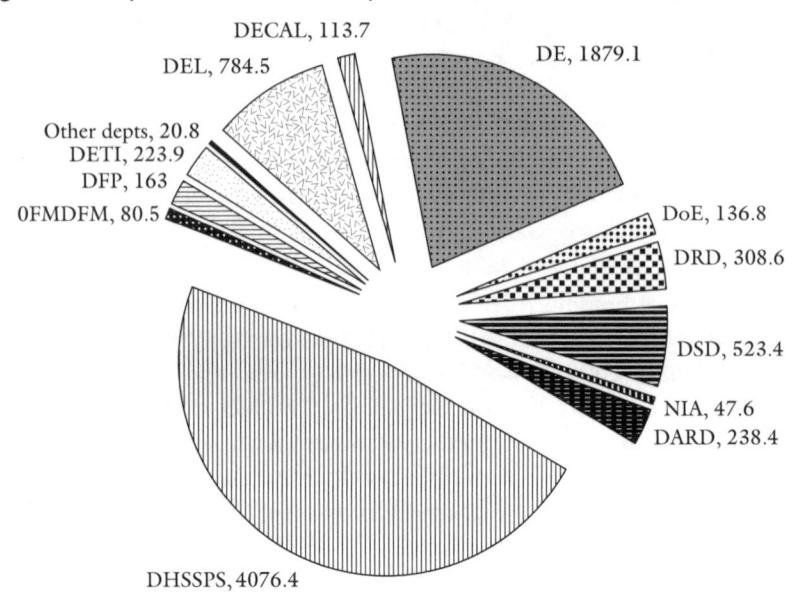

Figure 2.2 Departmental current expenditure, 2009–10

Table 2.4 Public expenditure by department

Department	2009–10 (£m)	%
Agriculture and Rural Development	238.4	2.8
Culture, Arts & Leisure	113.7	1.3
Education	1879.1	21.9
Employment & Learning	784.5	9.1
Enterprise, Trade & Investment	223.9	2.6
Finance & Personnel	163.0	1.9
Health, Social Services & Public Safety	4076.4	47.4
Environment	136.8	1.6
Regional Development	308.6	3.6
Social Development	523.4	6.0
Office of the First Minister & Deputy First Minister	80.5	0.9
Northern Ireland Assembly	47.6	0.6
Other Departments	20.8	0.2
Total current expenditure	**8596.7**	**100**

THE NORTHERN IRELAND CIVIL SERVICE 59

The Programme for Government

The Programme for Government is the Northern Ireland Executive's priorities and policies for government which includes an agreed budget linked to these policies and programmes. Each year the Executive reviews the budget for the following year and rolls the programme forward for the 3 years ahead. The Programme for Government highlights the key goals and actions the Executive will take to drive forward its priority areas. The Programme includes a detailed Public Service Agreement Framework which sets out the actions and targets departments will take in support of the Executive's priorities. 'Growing the Economy' is the Executive's top priority over the lifetime of this Programme for Government. A strong economy, it argues, is vital if we are to provide the wealth and resources required 'to build the peaceful, prosperous, fair and healthy society in Northern Ireland, supported by quality public services and infrastructure' (Northern Ireland Executive, 2008b: 6). The priority areas are interconnected and the Executive recognise that economic growth cannot be taken forward in isolation from efforts to transform a post-conflict divided society and enhance the environment. The components of the Programme for Government are shown in figure 2.3. Aside from these key priorities, the Executive has committed to two cross-cutting themes: a

Figure 2.3 Northern Ireland Executive Programme for Government, 2008–11

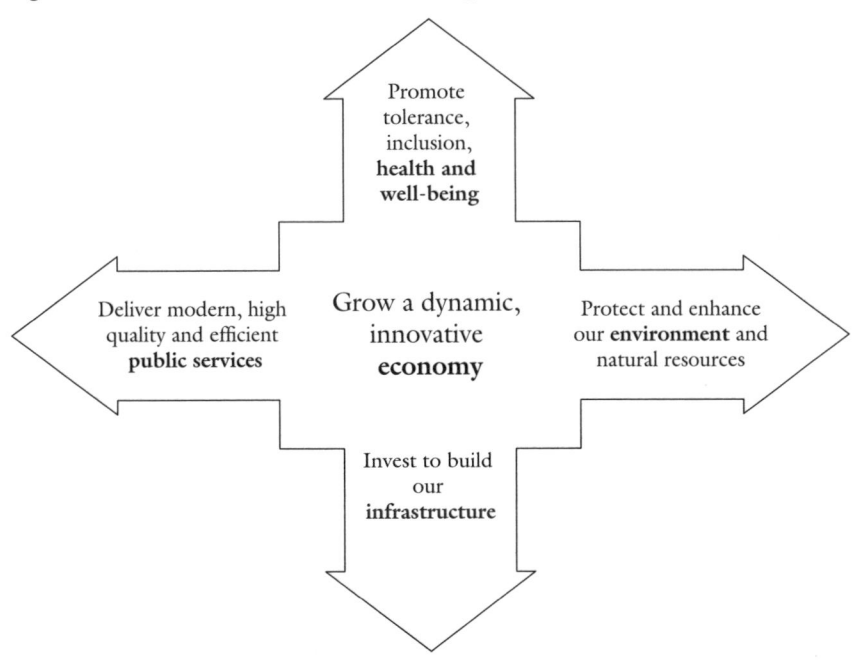

- Promote tolerance, inclusion, **health and well-being**
- Deliver modern, high quality and efficient **public services**
- Grow a dynamic, innovative **economy**
- Protect and enhance our **environment** and natural resources
- Invest to build our **infrastructure**

shared and better future for all to tackle issues of equality, fairness, inclusion and the promotion of good relations; and sustainability in their economic, social and environmental policies and programmes. There has been some disagreement amongst the political parties about the need to radically review the programme in light of the global economic downturn.

Public service agreements (PSAs) are the mechanism through which the priorities of the Northern Ireland Executive, as outlined in the Programme for Government, are operationalised within the 11 government departments. The purpose of PSAs is to provide accountable government by setting targets for public service delivery. Government departments are expected on an annual basis to report on progress against the attainment of their targets. A typical example of a public service agreement is outlined in table 2.5 which shows how the Executive intends to raise standards in schools. The PSA shows the overall aim and objectives to be achieved under this agreement, what actions need to be taken, targets to aim for, and the department(s) responsible for delivery. One criticism made of these agreements is that they are set by, and for, civil servants and hence targets tend not to be 'stretched'. For example the Child Support Agency in Northern Ireland has rising levels of debt (gross debt at March 2008 was around £82.6m) yet their debt collection target, according to the Northern Ireland Audit Office and the Public Accounts Committee, is not considered to be challenging enough.

More generally the Northern Ireland Audit Office (NIAO, 2009a) has been critical of how government departments were measuring performance against their PSA targets. These criticisms included two broad areas: the design of data systems, the operation of these systems and reporting on performance as follows.

Design of data systems

- The NIAO found that senior management tended to be primarily concerned with ensuring targets were in place and that progress against targets was monitored. There was less evidence that they took an active interest in underlying data systems or issues relating to quality control and data accuracy.
- PSA data systems need to be clearly and comprehensively documented and departments are required to publish technical notes. The NIAO found that departments tended to rely on existing data sources, such as administrative databases or established surveys, and there were a number of examples where these were not fully adequate for PSA purposes. The general quality of the technical notes was inadequate and, in some cases, baselines were not being set and key terms not being defined.

Table 2.5 Public service agreement: education example

PSA 19: Educate and develop our young people to the highest possible standards to deliver improved outcomes for all young people, including measurable reductions in the gap in educational outcomes between highest and lowest attainers.

Objectives	Actions	Targets	Department responsible
Improve the overall performance of schools	• Implementation of the Revised Curriculum • Implementation of School Improvement Policy • Complete a review of school leadership and management training	• By 2011, 68% of students gaining a Level 2 qualification by the time they leave school. • By 2011, 65% of students undertaking A level examinations gaining 3+ A levels A–C or equivalent in Year 14 • Raise the participation of 16/17 year olds in full-time education of vocational training to 95% by 2011	Department of Education
Improve the fundamental skills of literacy, numeracy and ICT, with particular focus on those schools currently with low levels of achievement or which draw their pupils from areas of high socio-economic deprivation	Implementation of the Revised Curriculum and the Literacy and Numeracy Strategy	• 55% of students gaining a Level 2 qualification, including GCSEs A*–C in English/Maths (or equivalent) by the time they leave school by 2011 • 30% of students with entitlement to Free School Meals gaining GCSE A*–C in English and Maths by the time they leave school in 2011 • 90% of students gaining GCSE A*–C in English and Maths (or equivalent) by the time they leave school by 2011	Department of Education
Ensure that mainstream pupils leave schools with formal qualifications	Implementation of School Improvement Policy, Special Educational Needs Policy and a revised policy for Alternative Education Provision	Reduce percentage of year 12 pupils with no qualification at GCSE level or equivalent to 1.5% by 2011	Department of Education

Operation of data systems and reporting of performance

- NIAO identified a number of PSA targets which suffered from methodological weaknesses such as the data system not measuring all aspects of the stated target and in some cases identified substantial time lags which have prevented timely reporting.
- PSA targets should be consistently stated and should not be subject to unnecessary change. NIAO found a number of cases where departments had made changes without any documented explanation of the need for, and nature of, the changes.
- The introduction of PSAs has formalised the process for reporting performance to the Assembly and the public, and OFMDFM co-ordinates and produces an annual progress report on achievement against PSA targets. NIAO found that the format of this report did not allow for the adequate reporting of target performance.

In his report, the Comptroller and Auditor General acknowledged assurances from departments that, since devolution in May 2007, steps have been taken to ensure that the monitoring and reporting of performance against PSA targets is robust. However, these new targets were introduced after the Comptroller and Auditor General's study commenced and were therefore not examined as part of the report.

A typical example (table 2.6) of reporting performance using the PSA framework in the Department of Health, Social Services and Public Safety (DHSSPS) illustrates how the NIAO arrived at their conclusions. The example shows a selection of PSA targets within the area of health prevention and access to primary care. In determining the extent to which the department has successfully measured performance the following criteria were used by auditors:

- was there a specified and appropriate baseline against which improved performance could be assessed?
- were terms in the PSA properly defined?
- was there a clear quantification of 'success'?
- was there an appropriate description of the data system?
- were there quality assurance arrangements in place to validate the data?
- was there an assessment of the data system's limitations and risks?

The example (table 2.6) shows significant weaknesses reporting performance against PSA targets.

Table 2.6 Performance example: Department of Health, Social Services and Public Safety (DHSSPS)

Targets	Specified and appropriate baseline	Comprehensive definition of terms	Clear quantification of success	Appropriate description of data system	Description of quality assurance arrangements	Assessment of data system limitations and risks
PSA 9: By encouraging people to take preventative measures and promoting access to health and social services, reduce the gap in life expectancy between those living in the fifth most deprived electoral wards and the NI average by 50% for both men and women between 2000 and 2012.	✓	✓	×	✓	×	×
PSA 10: By 2011, reduce the proportion of adult smokers to 22% or less, with a reduction in prevalence among manual groups to 27% or less.	✓	×	✓	×	×	×
PSA 11: By 2010 stop the increase in levels of obesity in children (joint target Department of Education and Department of Culture, Arts and Leisure)	×	×	×	×	×	×
PSA 12: By March 2008, all patients who request a clinical appointment through their general practice for other than emergencies, to be able to see an appropriate primary care professional within two working days	×	×	×	×	×	×

Source: Northern Ireland Audit Office (2009), *Public Service Agreements: Measuring Performance.*

External scrutiny

The performance of civil service departments in delivering public services under Direct Rule arrangements since 1972 attracted criticism. As one politician put it: 'the quality of government services in Northern Ireland too often lets down the people who are using them and who are paying for them through taxes. That is in part, although not entirely, a legacy of nearly four decades of violence' (Lidington, 2004). The Northern Ireland Housing Executive and its parent department (Department for Social Development) were severely criticised by the Public Accounts Committee (PAC) for their failure over a long period to get to grips with the homelessness problem (Public Accounts Committee, 2004a). The Roads Service and the Water Service, both in the Department for Regional Development (at the time) were attacked by the Public Accounts Committee for 'disgracefully high' levels of sickness absence costing over £2m per year in direct costs. The Accounting Officer could give no explanation for the widespread failure to apply procedures and had not considered the possibility of a wider systemic malaise in other areas of management (Public Accounts Committee, 2004b). Additional examples included the Social Security Agency and Child Support Agency where the Comptroller and Auditor General for Northern Ireland (C&AG) was unable to form an opinion on the financial statement of the Department for Social Development (parent department) for two consecutive years (2001–03). Identified errors included fraudulent benefits claims, overpayments and inaccurate assessments of child maintenance allowance (Northern Ireland Audit Office, 2004).

If the examples outlined above could be 'explained away' as a legacy of Direct Rule and, as a result, less oversight of public services by a local administration, then departmental performance was expected to improve under devolution. There are however more recent examples which highlight significant weaknesses in the delivery of core public sector functions. We consider two important examples to illustrate this point.

Example 1: unemployment

Unemployment is a significant public policy issue and is increasingly exercising politicians in the global economic downturn. During the period January–March 2009 unemployment in Northern Ireland was estimated at 6.1 per cent or 49,000 people (Department of Enterprise, Trade and Investment, 2009). One key element of government support for the unemployed was the *New Deal 25+ Programme*, introduced in November 1998. This was a mandatory programme which provided participants with assistance to overcome barriers to employment in the form of work experience and/or training. By the end of March 2007, 74,000 participants had taken part in New Deal 25+ at a cost to the Department for Employment and Learning (DEL) of around £69million. In September 2008, New Deal 25+ was subsumed within the Department's *Steps to Work Programme*. However, lessons learned from New Deal 25+ remain particularly relevant given the current challenging economic conditions. In an Audit Office study the DEL was criticised for a number of shortcomings:

- New Deal 25+ support resulted in 6,300 (18 per cent) of the 35,000 participants moving into sustained employment. However, the majority of leavers (54 per cent) returned to benefits. Older participants, particularly those aged 50 and over, were much less likely to get a job.
- By March 2007 around two-thirds of participants had been on the programme before, including a small number which had been on it more than five times. The audit report identified the need to improve outcomes for these repeaters – the likelihood of repeaters getting a job diminished with each New Deal episode.
- The report noted significant variances in outcomes across the different programme options. The main option, the *Preparation for Employment Programme* (i.e. work placements) which accounted for 60 per cent of all option starts between April 2002 and March 2007, was the least effective – only 7 per cent achieved sustained employment.
- A sample survey of participating employers indicated that just under one-quarter used New Deal 25+ as a source of low-cost labour (Northern Ireland Audit Office, 2009b).

Example 2: social housing

The second example relates to the area of social housing in Northern Ireland which comprises approximately 115,000 dwellings with a total rental income per year (based on figures in 2006/07) of £344m. The social housing landlords responsible for collecting rents are the Northern Ireland Housing Executive (NIHE) and Housing Associations. A report which considered the performance of landlords in securing rental income was critical in a number of areas:

- The Northern Ireland Housing Executive's only corporate target has been that year-end gross arrears should not exceed the previous year-end balance. Assessed against this target, NIHE performed well over recent years. However, the reduction in gross arrears over this period had been achieved largely through writing-off high levels of tenant debt – while gross tenant arrears fell by £3.3m from 2001/02 to 2006/07, total write-offs over the same period amounted to £10.6m. The report notes a number of underlying issues in relation to NIHE's rent income performance, including a reduction in the percentage of total rent collected and high levels of individual arrears.

- Annual performance statistics supplied to Department of Social Development by Housing Associations for the period 2001/02 to 2005/06 indicate significant increases in gross arrears for the sector overall. However, concerns with the completeness and accuracy of arrears data in recent years undermine its usefulness and relevance (Northern Ireland Audit Office, 2009c).

External scrutiny is therefore an important source of independent oversight of civil service performance. In addition, however, pressure is building on the Northern Ireland Executive to provide more and better-quality public services with limited opportunities to raise additional income (other than through the regional rate). Politicians are now looking to improve efficiencies in the public sector. The deferral of the introduction of water charges, freezing regional rates (equivalent to the council community charge) and the fall in sales of social housing has resulted in pressure on the public budget. More fundamentally, devolution requires a change in the culture of the Civil Service accused of running Northern Ireland with limited political oversight for more than thirty years.

The Social Democratic and Labour Party (SDLP) has targeted the Civil Service as part of a comprehensive package of reforms to reduce public expenditure. The SDLP highlight the major pay disparity between 'junior civil servants working at the coalface delivering services directly to the public and the senior civil service: mandarins primarily involved in policymaking and strategic management' and call for a review of the bonus system for Permanent Secretaries and a freeze on recruitment or promotion into the civil service at Grade 5 or above (SDLP, 2009: 27). The Democratic Unionist Party has made similar suggestions for changes in the civil service. The DUP Party Leader and First Minister launched proposals entitled *Driving Forward a Reform Agenda* (May 2009) in which he describes 'a truly radical reforming agenda'. He argued:

> At the present time Northern Ireland is hopelessly over-governed. We want to see a reduction in the number of Assembly Members and government departments ... We want to reduce the number of government departments from the present eleven to a more practical six. We want to erase the Belfast Agreement legacy of expensive and cumbersome government. We support reducing the number of

MLAs. It is our desire to save money and ensure that people get the best possible service for the lowest cost. (Robinson, 2009a: 1)

Specifically, the DUP has targeted the North–South implementation bodies (six bodies established by international agreement between the British and Irish Governments to implement all-island policies agreed by Ministers in the North–South Ministerial Council) as representing poor value for money coincident with their political stand-point on cross-border co-operation. The DUP argues that the Northern Ireland Civil Service has 'an excessive number particularly of senior civil servants even by Whitehall standards' (DUP, 2009: 8). The Party refers to 'an industry in equality and human rights in Northern Ireland'. One element in their proposals is to streamline/merge several of these bodies and abolish the Parades Commission, a long-standing source of aversion for the DUP. Their Finance Minister has argued that cutting the number of government departments in half could potentially save between £40–50m per year as a result of duplicated services. Sinn Féin is suspicious that such moves are an attempt, under the guise of efficiency savings, by the DUP, to dismantle the structures set up to safeguard equality and human rights issues. Other political parties have identified the need to reform the top-heavy structure of 11 civil service departments as a way of rationalising the civil service and providing more coherent public service delivery. In short, devolved politicians are becoming restless and impatient with the weight of bureaucracy. A debate in the Northern Ireland Assembly resolved the following:

> That this Assembly supports, in principle, the restructuring of the Northern Ireland Executive and the Assembly in order to improve the efficiency and effectiveness of government; and calls on the First Minister and Deputy First Minister to update the Assembly on the proposals for the creation of an Efficiency Review Panel, as announced on 9 April 2009, and to agree to implement a review and produce a report on the issue of the number of MLAs and government departments in the next Assembly, within the next six months. (*Hansard*, Official Report, 18 May 2009)

Restructuring now looks likely for the Executive, Assembly and civil service departments. Civil servants who 'escaped' the reaches of the Review of Public Administration will not now relish an upheaval in their own back yard.

Policy-making

Policy-making is 'the process by which governments translate their political vision into programmes and actions to deliver outcomes' – desired changes in the real world (*Modernising Government*, White Paper, Cm 4310,

1999: 15). Making public policy in the Northern Ireland Civil Service has changed significantly, largely because of the moves from Direct Rule to devolved government (Carmichael and Osborne, 2003). During the period of Direct Rule (1972–99), British Ministers were pre-occupied with constitutional and security issues leaving policy matters to civil servants whose job it was to maintain basic public services during the chaos of the 'troubles'. This resulted in a significant concentration of power vested in the hands of unelected officials with limited input from other parts of civil society. The deeply divided sectarian nature of Northern Ireland society and the enduring conflict dominated the policy debate and provided limited space for positive change agents.

Many public policies were simply 'read across' from Great Britain with no local political input and levels of accountability for public spending were 'light touch' – it was a rare (and daunting) occasion for a Northern Ireland Permanent Secretary to have to appear in front of the Public Accounts Committee in Westminster. An emasculated system of local government/ councils, with few public service functions, simply accentuated the limited opportunities to influence public policy in Northern Ireland. Key public services such as health, education and housing were located in non-departmental public bodies (health and education boards and the Northern Ireland Housing Executive respectively) and governed by hand picked quangocrats with ministerial endorsement. Policy-making was stripped of political input and public services subjected to the most limited form of accountability. When major change occurred, it came in the form of top-down legislation or as a result of international pressure normally to address systemic sectarianism (e.g. Fair Employment Act 1976 or when American companies threatened to disinvest in Northern Ireland unless a set of employment principles (McBride campaign) were implemented) – see Osborne, 1992 and Osborne and Shuttleworth, 2004.

Political gains, devolved government and a significant decline in the levels of violence have created new opportunities for local policy-making, although it has taken some time for regional government in Northern Ireland to bed down. The two main parties in the Executive (DUP and Sinn Féin) have clashed on major policy issues and the Executive did not meet for a 5-month period in 2008. Moreover, there has been an uncomfortable transition for senior civil servants who ran public service fiefdoms moving from a position of dominance to accountability through local elected Members of the Legislative Assembly (MLAs). Equally, the role of voluntary and community sector has changed as local politicians strut their elected credentials and seek to minimise NGO access to key decision-makers. As Keating observed in discussing policy-making under devolution in Scotland:

> Political devolution may have had the ironical effect of demobilizing the active civil society that previously served as the vehicle for expression of ideas and opposition in Scotland, so reducing the vitality of debate. This is not an argument against devolution, any more than the dying down of civil society in central and eastern Europe is an argument against democracy, but it does point to the need for devolved institutions to be matched by other voices, and for the institutions to be able to think creatively and contribute to policy development. (Keating, 2007: 240–241)

The staccato nature of devolved government from December 1999 until May 2007 has not allowed for the flow of legislative business that would have been expected or for statutory committees to initiate public policy and exercise the level of accountability over government departments. While the locus of power has therefore changed from a public policy arena dominated by senior civil servants, devolved government has not yet realised its full potential. The stop–start policy environment gives rise to mixed circumstances – some old guard civil servants continue to exert significant influence, particularly in the face of weak and/or relatively inexperienced ministers within an Assembly which is often distracted by issues that allow politicians to revert to type (sectarian politics). The power-sharing executive has disagreed on key public policies such as: the end of academic selection in schools; granting legal status to the Irish language; building a 'conflict transformation centre' at the site of the former Maze prison (now rejected by the DUP Culture, Arts and Leisure minister); how to address the issue of victims of the conflict (four victims commissioners and the controversial Eames–Bradley report); and, devolution of policing and justice powers to the Assembly.

Politicians and officials recognise that the 'cost' of arriving at consensus between the two main political parties has been at the expense of tackling 'hard' political issues. Hence, in a bid to shore up or consolidate the power-sharing institutions, politicians from Sinn Féin and the DUP have not been able to address contentious public policy issues. The replacement for *A Shared Future* (the long awaited *Cohesion, Sharing and Integration Strategy*) is an example. One politician described it as follows: 'what is good for power-sharing has not necessarily been good for public policy. Power-sharing in our case does not equal good governance'. Wilford describes the structure of the Executive Committee in this way:

> A testament to the maximal inclusiveness of its consociational design, this four-party voluntary coalition, unlike those struck in Edinburgh and initially Cardiff – was not an agreed arrangement among more or less willing partners, but a confected grand coalition that, from its outset, resembled a loveless marriage. It encompassed the staunch loyalism of the DUP, the unapologetic republicanism of Sinn Féin, together with the ostensibly more forgiving unionism of the UUP and the pragmatic nationalism of the SDLP. (Wilford, 2007: 167)

Using Weiss' framework (1999) which lists the key factors that shape public policy we examine how policy-making has changed pre- and post-devolution (a framework also used by Nutley *et al.*, 2007 to discuss what shapes the use of research to inform public services). Weiss identifies interests, ideology, information and institutions as key factors that shape public policy as follows:

- *Interests* are first and foremost the self-interests of those engaged in the policy process, whether these are political (advancing a particular cause) or personal (advancing one's career).
- *Ideology* means the systems of beliefs, moral and ethical values and political orientations that guide policy-makers' actions.
- *Information* represents the array of knowledge and ideas from multiple sources that crowd for attention in the policy field and that are used by policy-makers to make sense of current issues and problems.
- *Institutions* are the organisations within which policy-makers act, with their own histories, cultures and constraints, and that in turn will shape how policy-makers define their interests, ideologies and information, and the way in which decisions are made. (Weiss, 1999: 477–78 cited by Nutley *et al.*, 2007)

We adopt this framework and consider the changes which have taken place in the Northern Ireland policy-making context pre- and post-devolved government (see table 2.7). The unfortunate reality for Northern Ireland is such that public policy issues, however important, do not yet have electoral significance. Put in the form of a question: does public policy matter? We have not reached the stage of political maturity where people vote on a political party's performance in delivering a public policy agenda. Does this instil complacency amongst our politicians that we will continue to vote along traditional sectarian cleavages? Those seeking to influence policy-making need to be aware that the political process is not yet as electorally sensitive to their demands as might be expected. Even in extreme cases it is doubtful, for example, that Sinn Féin voters will desert the party over the highly contentious post-primary education transfer policies adopted by Minister Caitríona Ruane or DUP voters over Minister Sammy Wilson's unconventional remarks on the environment.

The policy-making landscape and the role played by civil servants in that process has changed since devolution in a number of ways which we now consider.

Accessibility

It is perhaps stating the obvious that local ministers are more easily accessible and the devolved Assembly more accountable. This accessibility

Table 2.7 Policy-making: pre- and post-devolution in Northern Ireland

Factors influencing change	Direct rule	Devolution
Interests: The self interests of those engaged in the policy process, whether these are political (advancing a particular cause) or personal (advancing one's career)	• The politics of opposition: 'power without responsibility' – local parties snipe at public policies imposed by Westminster • Hugely influential role of civil servants	• Individual interests of ministers in pursuing a successful political career and promoting their political parties • Risk-averse senior civil servants made more accountable through devolution, assembly committees and the Public Accounts Committee
Ideology: The systems of beliefs, moral and ethical values and political orientations that guide policy-makers' actions	• Northern political parties driven by key constitutional issues. • Inter- and intra-political rivalry to capture the unionist/loyalist or nationalist/republican vote. • Public policy issues irrelevant in elections	• Sinn Féin's pursuit of the ubiquitous equality agenda • DUP ideology under Peter Robinson – wants to see devolution succeed: 'The DUP is a devolutionist party, but first and foremost a Unionist Party' (Robinson, 2008)
Information: The array of knowledge and ideas from multiple sources that crowd for attention in the policy field and that are used by policy-makers to make sense of current issues and problems	• Public policy field dictated by 'read across' agenda from Great Britain. • A process of elite decision-making where senior civil servants controlled the flow of information. • Local political input into key public policies minimal.	• Policy field crowded with education debate, devolution of policing and justice, victims issues, Irish Language, Bill of Rights • Other policy issues can get squeezed (example: long awaited Cohesion, Integration and Sharing Strategy: OFMDFM) • Strict adherence to the Programme for Government framework and therefore reluctance by civil servants to think beyond its parameters

Table 2.7 (continued)

Factors influencing change	Direct rule	Devolution
Institutions: The organisations within which policy-makers act, with their own histories, cultures and constraints, and that in turn will shape how policy-makers define their interests, ideologies and information, and the ways in which decisions are made	• Creation of alternative structures of government and progressive legislation. • No local (durable) political forum to execute public policy-making. • A weak system of local government/ councils with limited functional responsibility. • Westminster business on Northern Ireland centres on political, constitutional and security issues	• Local (durable) political forum to execute public policy-making? • Mutual vetoes (DUP and Sinn Féin) for all major decisions can be used to frustrate business • Power-Sharing Executive: lack of collective responsibility

means that MLAs and local councillors, a number of whom 'double-job' (dual mandate) as Assembly members, can be influenced by local groups. The growth of all-party Assembly groups set up to facilitate a forum on an issue which attracts cross-party collaboration is emerging as a key policy driver (e.g. children and young people; ethnic minority communities). Lobby groups have elicited political support by carefully targeting elected representatives with a particular interest in a topic, who then become champions for the cause in the course of their work in the Assembly.

> Ministers want to make themselves as accessible as possible and to engage with groups. We sometimes have difficulty getting them to delay meeting with groups particularly if we are snowed under with work in the department . . . Ministers go out and about and talk to people in their public engagements. Door stepping a Minister can result in him/her turning to civil servants for advice on matters raised by chance encounters. MLAs in general are influenced by the correspondence they receive, their constituency case loads and what they hear in surgeries. Individually they will have contacts in the NGO sector that will also influence their thinking. (Interview with senior official)

Contentious policy issues

The nature of the power-sharing Executive, an involuntary coalition of four political parties, means that consensus is often difficult to achieve and seemingly innocuous issues can become politicised in Northern Ireland (e.g. post-primary education transfer and siting of a national sports stadium). Where these policies come within the remit of the Office for the First Minister and Deputy First Minister (OFMDFM), they enter a much more complex decision-making arena. The structure includes 2 ministers, 2 junior ministers, and 8 special advisors (4 Sinn Féin (SF) and 4 DUP). Decisions will not be taken quickly and it is crucial to secure the endorsement of special advisors whose role cannot be overstated. For issues which must go for Executive approval, support from the two main parties (DUP and SF), by dint of the decision-making arithmetic, becomes imperative.

> The policy-making agenda is not as open and pluralist as might be expected in an elected democratic Assembly with the two main parties retaining close ownership at the centre. When issues become sensitive the wagons are circled and DUP & Sinn Féin play their cards fairly close to their chest. There is not the same degree of NGO involvement and the role of special advisors becomes paramount in trying to broker a consensus between the political parties. A key organ is the 'ministerial representatives group' which meets weekly and many would say is as important as Executive meetings where public policy is decided. (Interview with senior politician)

Non-contentious policy issues

Where public policy issues are non-contentious, statutory committees of the Assembly can become a key source of influence. Each committee undertakes a scrutiny, policy development and consultation role in relation to their respective departments and plays a key part in the consideration and development of legislation. The potential of statutory committees has not yet been fully realised and some have become bogged down in departmental operational detail rather than strategic decision-making (Osborne, 1998, 2002). There are however examples where statutory committees in the course of taking evidence and holding public inquiries have been very influential in the policy-making process (e.g. inquiry into Child Poverty – Committee for the Office of the First Minister and deputy First Minister; and Charities Act (NI) 2008 – Committee for Social Development). The committees set their own agenda and hence there are opportunities for members to influence the nature of the work.

Three additional considerations are important here. First, issues which have a cross-border relevance will be particularly attractive to Sinn Féin

Ministers and MLAs. Second, officials point to the potential influence that other devolved regions (Scotland and Wales) can have on public policy in Northern Ireland (and vice-versa). The whole rationale for devolution makes political parties more reluctant, and in the case of Sinn Féin openly unwilling, to look towards Westminster/Whitehall as the source of public policy. Second, NGO groups could make better use of the potential for lobbying on the grounds of policy transfer where deemed successful from other regions of the UK. Third, a No-Day named motion (a term given to a motion for which no date has been fixed for debate in the Assembly) can be a useful mechanism through which individual MLAs can initiate a debate in the Assembly. An example was a no-day motion (March 2009) on childcare strategy promoted by Sinn Féin MLAs (Jennifer McCann, Sue Ramsey and Martina Anderson): 'that this Assembly expresses its concern at the lack of availability of affordable, quality childcare and calls on the Executive to implement a coherent and properly resourced childcare strategy'.

> It is easy for local politicians to get behind the demands of the age sector but much more difficult to get agreement around integrated education or the Bill of Rights because they are politically contentious. There are therefore 'wicked' public policy issues on which it is hugely challenging to advocate for social change because they go to the heart of what divides Northern Ireland along sectarian lines. I don't believe these hard issues will bring the structures down because they don't challenge any party's commitment to the institutions or non-violence but they do pose real questions about the effectiveness of governance in terms of delivering public policies for Northern Ireland. So far we have been given a pass because of the generous financial settlement from the Treasury and huge international good-will. But these will only paper over the cracks for so long and give people freedom not to tackle the hard issues. (Interview with NGO leader)

New opportunities

Beyond the simple dichotomy of contentious/non-contentious policies there are opportunities for lobby groups to inject new thinking into the public policy agenda. Devolution has, in reality, only functioned consistently since May 2007 (and even then with a period of no Executive meetings). Officials, politicians and the NGO sector are in agreement that the Executive and Assembly have under-performed on delivering public policies and failed to tackle the 'hard issues', in part to stabilise the power-sharing institutions but also through political immaturity or lack of experience. Thus far the Executive has become known for its populist policies or what one politician described as its 'lady bountiful role' – delay in introducing water charges, free public transport for older people, free prescription charges etc. The guiding policy framework, *Programme for Government 2008–2011*, is seen as the product of political compromise based on what the DUP and Sinn Féin could jointly agree. As one civil servant described it 'the *Programme for Government* is a nicely written document but it doesn't contain a lot – the fact that it makes no reference to post-primary education transfer is a measure of the compromise involved'. The further we move away from violence and consolidating the political structures however, the greater the need for new policy thinking and inputs from lobby groups and other stakeholders.

> We [officials] are having to learn. We didn't do much policy in Northern Ireland because we didn't have to. Policy was something that arrived from Westminster and the job, not to oversimplify it, was scoring out 'England and Wales' and inserting 'Northern Ireland' in a policy paper or a piece of legislation. When you are not exercising a skill over a long period of time, it tends to atrophy. We also lost whatever political astuteness that [*sic*] we had – we had become disconnected from the local body politic because for 30 years it wasn't necessary to listen to people. It was only necessary to look to Westminster. The NGO sector has a role to play in initiating and promoting policy change. (Interview with senior official)

The role of civil servants

By their own admission civil servants are much less influential under devolution than Direct Rule although they argue that their former role was much exaggerated. As one official put it: 'we were benign autocrats under Direct Rule who could sit above party politics and do things because we thought they were the right things to do for Northern Ireland'. Lobby groups should not ignore the importance, however, of including senior officials in their advocacy efforts under devolved government. Civil servants continue to have a significant influence on *how* policy happens although perhaps less on *what*. Officials want to be 'at the table' when wider stakeholders engage with politicians otherwise expectations can be raised and the practicalities of implementation are not fully considered. In short, senior civil servants do not like to be bounced into decisions after the event.

> People need to remember that civil servants are here to provide the evidence base and facilitate the process of decision-making and then to help implement policies. It is therefore helpful to the civil service for outside stakeholders to engage with them when lobbying ministers and MLAs. There is an advantage in everyone having a shared understanding of what the issues are. (Interview with senior official)

Partnerships or coalitions

The plethora of NGO groups and the disparate nature of their demands call into question their varying levels of effectiveness in promoting public policy change. Some groups are professional, know the devolved system, and have built up relationships with politicians and civil servants over a long period of time. Generous European funding over the years has resulted in a growing number of groups and increased competition for resources. Groups working in the same broad sector however, have not found common cause. Individual effort, however well-planned, is much less effective than a well-managed coalition pushing a single message. Importantly, NGO leaders have stressed the need to recognise that policy change can be a long-haul process, retelling the same message or a 'drip-drip-drip' approach. It must be recognised that the 'long haul' may be inconsistent with the short-term political cycle within which key political players can change.

> I was involved in the Children's Commissioner legislation and had dealings with NGOs in the children sector (Children's Law Centre, Early Years, NSPCC, Barnardo's and others). They were very professional, well run, effective and articulate in expressing their views. The NGOs had been developing evidence based policies for some years and arguing very cogently for this particular policy development and we as officials had to catch up. They were successful in influencing the policy agenda via a number of individual MLAs and particularly the SDLP which took that agenda on board and ran with it. Their success was that they build a coalition of NGOs large and small (about 14 groups) and realised that one NGO has little capacity to influence but acting together they were effective. They had to hammer their message home for a number of years but it was successful and for them has pointed the way ahead. (Interview with senior official)

Evidence

The importance of evidence in the policy-making process cannot be underestimated but it must be seen as part of a wider strategy – a necessary but insufficient pre-requisite for influencing the policy process. There are two important questions here. First, what constitutes 'evidence' and, second, how is it communicated? Politicians are particularly sensitive to public opinion, however that is expressed, hence 'evidence' for them can come in the shape of topics discussed on the Stephen Nolan radio/TV show, a populist overhyped discussion of current issues, through to organisations appearing before statutory committees of the Assembly with well-researched arguments. What is clear, however, is that evidence needs to be communicated to decision-makers (whether elected representatives or officials) in more imaginative ways to capture their attention. Long detailed research reports, however robust, are unlikely to impact on decision-makers who are already submerged in paperwork. Rigorous research must therefore provide the necessary underpinnings for a more succinct and stylised message to decision-makers. Evidence also needs to be timely. Responding to topical policy issues demands a fast turnaround which can pose problems for the rigour of research. Politicians welcome NGO and other independent research evidence as an alternative source of advice to that available via civil servants/government departments.

> The pressure point for effecting major social change is public opinion. Politicians are generally good at detecting public opinion and are sensitive to it – they would commit political suicide by ignoring it. They are also good at detecting the difference between messages espoused by a handful of activists as opposed to a groundswell of public opinion. Hence politicians sat up and took note of the campaign organised by age sector about winter fuel payments – older people are consistent voters and have political influence. Major policy change is effected by: gathering evidence of the need for change; communicating the evidence along with a strategy for policy change arrived at through a consensus among key stakeholders; and reaching a tipping-point where change becomes necessary. (Interview with senior politician)

Accountability and rights

Lobby groups have attempted, to a limited extent, to exploit existing and emerging accountability mechanisms and human rights treaties to which the UK Government is a signatory. The range of accountability mechanisms is wide and the scope for holding public bodies to account extensive. This can include such things as monitoring the delivery of government departments against public service agreement targets in the *Programme for Government*, through their statutory obligations under section 75 of the Northern Ireland Act 1998, to strategic litigation via judicial review of departmental/ministerial decisions. In other words NGOs can overlook ways of calling government (or duty-bearers) to account for their existing performance. There are legal, administrative and political accountability mechanisms which could better promote new policies or change existing public policies if vigorously pursued by lobby groups. Public bodies are sometimes complacent in their responsibilities – challenge can provide a very effective way of focusing the mind. If the Assembly is deemed to be under-performing in public policy delivery, then accountability becomes an important way to tackle this. Seeking to influence public policy in Northern Ireland was limited until recently because the policy agenda was dominated by two major issues: conflict resolution and high levels of unemployment. Post-conflict, other issues have begun to emerge.

> Advocating for social change is a long hard slog. There are no overnight success stories. Social change comes slowly and requires persistence by advocates who need to be wary of a government strategy as the official response to their demands. The plague in Northern Ireland has been launching strategies. Northern Ireland used to have a reputation for launching ships, now we launch strategies! Civil servants are good at developing policy options, announcing a consultation process

and developing a strategy on the back of this, all of which takes an inordinate amount of time. The challenge however is trying to ensure the strategy is implemented. Public bureaucracies have a great potential just simply to absorb things, tick boxes and make it seem like change is happening e.g. (PAFT [Policy Appraisal and Fair Treatment] and section 75). And even when senior civil servants are signed up to these strategies there are many gatekeepers at middle management level who can thwart implementation. (Interview with senior NGO leader)

This chapter has considered the functions, form and finance of the Northern Ireland Civil Service and the public services they are charged with delivering. It has outlined the Executive and Assembly's *Programme for Government* as the framework within which their priorities are expressed and from which public service agreements emanate for civil servants to deliver on those priorities. It has also provided examples of external or independent scrutiny of the work of government departments both during Direct Rule government and since. Finally, we examined how public policy is made in Northern Ireland, ways in which this has changed as a result of devolution and, how key stakeholders can more directly influence the policy process.

3
Modernising government

To get the best out of public services, it is essential that they are joined up locally around the citizen, are responsive to local circumstances and, crucially, harness the capacities of communities to identify and solve their own problems. In this way we will make public policy more sensitive to 'place' – not only to recognise that places are different and need different solutions, but also to unlock the energy and creativity of people on the front line. To do this we need greater devolution and decentralisation not just to local councils, but crucially to individuals, families, community groups, and professionals working in local public services. And at the same time, it is important that national agencies continue to respond flexibly to local priorities. (Cabinet Office, 2009b: 57)

Modernisation: Great Britain

The public sector in Northern Ireland, with its separate civil service, limited local government, and plethora of non-departmental public bodies has not, until recently, engaged with the wider British agenda of modernisation. Key policy initiatives in the rest of the United Kingdom such as *Modernising Government* (Cabinet Office, 1999), *Reforming our Public Services: Principles into Practice* (2002) and the policy debate contained in *The Future of Local Government: Developing a 10 year Vision* (Office of the Deputy First Minster, 2004) have all but bypassed Northern Ireland. Indeed there appears to have been little discussion amongst Northern Ireland politicians and officials of the emerging new public management agenda (Hood, 1991; 1998), so preoccupied were they with creating constitutional and security stability. Hence, Northern Ireland did not overtly engage in the wider debates around moving award from traditional approaches of public administration – reducing the role of the state, facilitating entrepreneurial skills, learning from the private sector or the modernisation agenda which grew out of the new public management narrative in other parts of the United Kingdom (Massey, 1993).

We outline some of the more recent reform initiatives from Whitehall by way of illustration and to demonstrate how uninvolved the Northern Ireland Civil Service was in these developments. Massey and Pyper (2005) trace the link between the emergence of new public management, re-engineering or re-inventing government, and the modernisation process in Great Britain. Referring to the *Modernising Government* White Paper they argue:

> The White Paper's contents epitomised the government's approach and emphasized the significance and centrality of the new public management in the New Labour project. The pace of reform was incessant, however, and only two years after its launch the Modernising Government initiative effectively evolved into a component of the new 'focus on delivery' and 'reforming public services' agenda. (Massey and Pyper, 2005: 58)

An interesting example which illustrates just how peripheral and insular the Northern Ireland Civil Service was to the wider modernising agenda is found in the discussion paper *The UK Government's Approach to Public Service Reform* (2006). The 100-page document was prepared by the Prime Minister's Strategy Unit in support of a conference '21st Century Public Services: Putting People First' hosted by the National School of Government in June 2006. It set out the Government's approach to public service reform as having four main elements:

- Top-down performance management (pressure from government).
- The introduction of greater competition and contestability in the provision of public services.
- The introduction of greater pressure from citizens including through choice and voice.
- Measures to strengthen the capability and capacity of civil and public servants and of central and local government to deliver improved public services. (Cabinet Office, 2006: 7)

Despite the fact that the document was entitled **UK *Government's Approach to Public Service Reform*** (author's emphasis), there is no reference to the Northern Ireland Civil Service or the different circumstances which prevail.

In a follow-up paper aimed at continuing the advances made in public services reform (*Building on Progress: Public Services*, 2007) the contention was that although a great deal had been achieved in key areas of health, education and law and order, public expectations of services provision had also increased. The overall vision contained in *Building on Progress: Public Services* was:

> To create self-improving institutions of public service, independent of centralised state control, drawing on the best of public, private and third sector provision. These institutions must be free to develop in the way they need to, responsive to the needs and preferences of citizens, and with a flexible workforce that is able to

MODERNISING GOVERNMENT

innovate and change. Out of this vision will come a new concept of modern public services: one built around the user of the service. (Cabinet Office, 2007: 7)

In order to improve public services over the next 10 years, the government argued, there was a need to do more in the following areas:

(1) Take further steps to empower citizens to shape services around them. Specifically, this means providing the tools, the information and the mechanisms necessary for citizens to exercise effective influence over services so that they change to meet their needs.
(2) Open up the supply side, where appropriate, so that the greatest possible diversity of provision is encouraged. In particular, the Government should develop a stronger focus on the commissioning of services and should use contestability and incentives to drive innovation and improvement in all appropriate areas of public services and to move in the direction of a level playing field between sectors.
(3) Foster workforce innovation and development, and engage with public service workers. This means breaking down the old demarcations between professions, which limit what many can do, and creating new roles where they are needed. It also means having better ways for staff to feed in to policy development.
(4) Help the hardest to reach. As fewer people now live in poverty and more people are helped by a range of policies – from tax credits to the minimum wage – the Government must develop new and specific approaches to those sectors of the population who have, so far, still proved hard to reach, raising their aspirations so that they too demand better services.
(5) Balance rights and responsibilities. In today's world, on issues from climate change to public health and fostering respect in local communities, the Government cannot and should not try to do it all alone. Government pressures and policies can set the goals, but the success of these depends on individuals contributing to their own well-being, that of their families and that of the communities in which they live. (Cabinet Office, 2007: 6–7)

Northern Ireland, once again, did not feature in the debate and the assumption was this approach to public services reform applies across the regions of the United Kingdom. A former Head of the Northern Ireland Civil Service, Sir Kenneth Bloomfield, explained how Northern Ireland as a region of the United Kingdom found itself at the margins of public sector reform as follows:

Under Direct Rule, while Secretaries of State have a fair degree of discretion, it tends to be the case that the broad ideological thrust of government in Britain in terms of public service structure and organisation will become evident in Northern Ireland, sometimes after a time delay. Thus the process of agentisation, contracting out and privatisation have been operated in Northern Ireland as in Great Britain, sometimes in the teeth of real reluctance by local interests. (Bloomfield, 1997: 147)

To illustrate Northern Ireland Civil Service detachment from the wider reform agenda Knox and McHugh (1990) examined the process of creating government agencies in Northern Ireland. To some extent a type of agency already existed by dint of political circumstances. The Northern Ireland Housing Executive, for example, had been set up in 1971 as a response to discrimination in public sector housing delivered through local authorities and operated at arm's length within the Department of the Environment since then. Knox and McHugh noted:

> The commitment of Northern Ireland departments to the agentisation initiative was lukewarm at the outset compared with the enthusiasm expressed in Whitehall. This stemmed from the fact that the research for the Efficiency Unit report did not include any contact with Northern Ireland civil servants. Inevitably the reaction within the Northern Ireland Civil Service was that *Next Steps* represented a Whitehall-specific initiative and had little relevance to Northern Ireland (Knox and McHugh, 1990: 266).

Devolved government in Northern Ireland, particularly since it stabilised (from May 2007), may well serve to compound the detachment from the Home Civil Service and the wider reform/modernisation agenda.

The more recent policy document *Excellence and Fairness: Achieving World Class Public Services* (Cabinet Office, 2008a: 6) posits a further phase of reform which would entail: developing new approaches to empowering citizens who use public services; fostering a new professionalism across the whole public service workforce; and providing strong strategic leadership from central government captured in figure 3.1. The paper points out that the suggested approach to achieving world class standards over the next few years does *not* include aspects of public service policy that are devolved in Scotland, Wales and Northern Ireland.

Excellence and fairness, it is argued, will be driven by empowering service users and unlocking the potential of the public service workforce with a more strategic role for government (Cabinet Office, 2009a). The drivers of excellence and fairness are therefore:

(1) Increased *citizen/user empowerment* with evolving relationships between service users/citizens and public service professionals:
 - Choice wherever possible
 - Users empowered to become genuine partners to services
 - Much greater transparency
 - Greater opportunities for citizens to hold their local public services to account.
(2) *New or enhanced professionalism* with a commitment to achieving world class performance within a decade:
 - A skilled, flexible, innovative workforce that can deliver a personalized service.

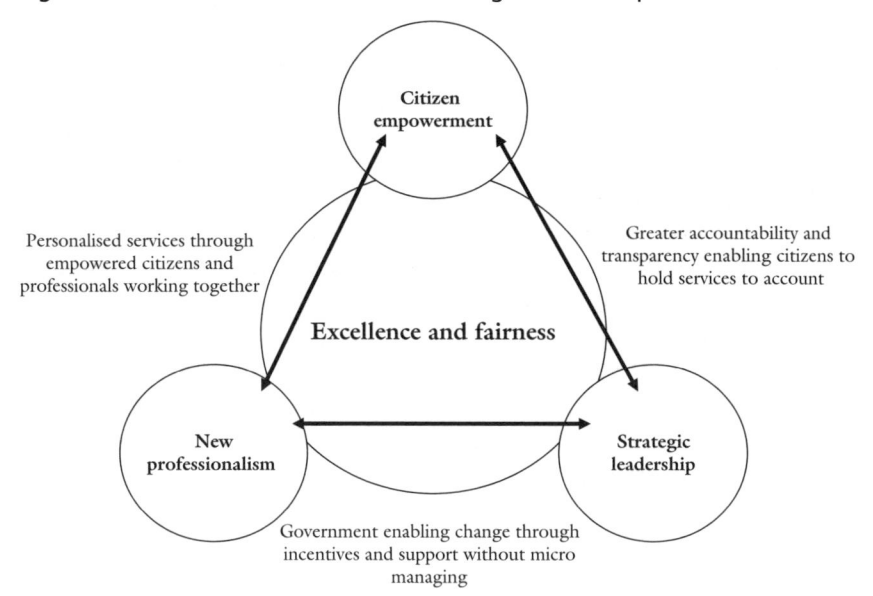

Figure 3.1 Excellence and fairness: achieving world class public services

Citizen empowerment

Personalised services through empowered citizens and professionals working together

Greater accountability and transparency enabling citizens to hold services to account

Excellence and fairness

New professionalism

Strategic leadership

Government enabling change through incentives and support without micro managing

- Consistent and reliable high-quality processes
- Increased empowerment for the front line
- Change of emphasis from 'top down' to 360 degrees accountability.

(3a) A *strategic role for central government* to provide a long term platform for improvement:
- Raising aspiration
- Establishing a direction of change, setting boundaries and standards
- Strategic investment
- Promoting innovation
- Building skills and capacity
- Stakeholder management.

(3b) *More devolution to local government* to give immediate political leadership where appropriate (Cabinet Office, 2009a: 6).

The contrast here with Northern Ireland could not be starker where local government has secured limited additional powers under the Review of Public Administration initiated in 2002 but still at the implementation phase. A recent publication entitled *Working Together: Public Service on Your Side* (Cabinet Office 2009b) acknowledges the existence of devolved government and the requirement to tailor regional policies and thus deliver public services to meet the specific needs of their areas. 'We will work closely with the devolved administrations to continue our common aim of further strengthening public services, whilst recognizing the particular and varying responsibilities across the different parts of the United Kingdom' (Cabinet

Office, 2009b: foreword). The UK Government describes the reform of public services as a 'quiet revolution' in two phases. In the first stage of work, clear national standards and targets were used to improve performance along with investment in public services. Part of that process also involved, according to the Government, more freedom, flexibility and incentives at the front line to push progress. The second phase, outlined in *Working Together: Public Service on Your Side* entails: fewer, sharper targets and standards, new freedoms for front-line staff and institutions, coupled with greater choice and diversity for citizens, including from private and third sector providers. As the quality of public services improves, the Government is determined to drive out low standards and ensure that all public services will be both excellent and fair for all (Cabinet Office, 2009b: 8). These reform initiatives from Whitehall set the context for a more detailed examination of the belated interest of the Northern Ireland Civil Service in public sector improvement. Before that we draw on the wider literature on public sector reform.

Public sector reform

The whole process of administrative and structural reforms of government has been debated in the literature. Wright (1994: 108), for example, argued that since the early 1980s Western Europe appears to be 'caught in a frenzy of administrative reform activity' as a result of convergent pressures to reshape the state. These included: reducing the size, resources and scope of the public sector; budgetary, planning and evaluation reforms; the need to improve public management; dismantling the traditions of the civil service (permanence, tenure); democratising the public sector (greater public consultation); more user-friendly public services; reorganising administrative structures; and transforming the culture of the public sector. He observed that significant differences remained in the nature, intensity, timing and pace of reforms which could be explained 'in terms of the opportunities afforded by the politico-institutional and cultural environment in which they are pursued' (Wright, 1994: 101). Wright categorised the various types of reform programmes as those introduced: as part of an ongoing process of internally induced modernisation; a reaction to specific political pressures; piecemeal, pragmatic and instrumental in nature; necessitated by the management of the above reform programmes; or, as part of a wider programme of political change. Since the origins of the Review of Public Administration in Northern Ireland were rooted in the *Programme for Government* in which the Executive pledged from the outset 'to lead the most accountable form of government in Northern Ireland' (OFMDFM, 2002: 7), this would suggest a reform programme linked directly to the outworkings of the Belfast Agreement and devolved government. In short, the Belfast Agreement resulted in a devolved power-sharing Executive and regional Assembly which, in turn, prompted the need for a radical overhaul of governance arrangements.

Rhodes (1997: 44) stressed that 'administrative reform is always political' and described how the Conservatives from 1979 onwards acted to cut back government spending and control the administrative machine. He noted six broad elements in their reform programme – introducing the minimalist state, reasserting political authority, extending regulation and audit, reforming the structure, reforming public management, and transforming the culture. The reform agenda has continued with Labour under the flag of 'modernisation'. As Massey and Pyper (2005: 59) report, the Labour Government 'has attempted to differentiate its approach from that of the previous Conservative governments, and effectively give its managerialism a softer, friendlier and more accommodating image'. Hence, they argue, there is a greater emphasis on constitutional and political reforms rather than mere market reforms.

Toonen suggests that the empirical study of administrative reform as a process is best conceived of as somewhere on a continuum between 'planned change' on the one hand and 'emerging strategy' on the other. In many cases, he claims, reform is 'often presented as the outcome of planned effort, politicised to some degree, and in intent and presentation certainly not incremental in nature' (Toonen, 2003: 472). In reality, however, Toonen concludes that reform is often long term, less rationally designed, piecemeal and a cyclical process. The process is 'full of inconsistencies, self-induced consequences and unexpected serendipities, which in the long run, may actually generate some decent results, next to the misses inherent to any experimental and learning process' (Toonen, 2003: 473). What constitutes 'decent results' or even 'misses' however, add to the idiosyncratic nature of administrative reform outcomes.

In considering *why* the actuality of administrative reforms is so distinctive across states, Pollitt and Summa (1997) offer four possible factors. First, the economy is always likely to be a background factor of some importance – the need to restrain the rate of growth of public spending. Second, the nature of the political system offers a powerful explanation for differences in reforms. Centralised states with strong single-party governments could force through changes in administrative reforms. Third, the nature of the administrative system which often reflects the political system in which it is located is an important determinant of reform. A strong core executive can impose reform throughout the whole of the public administration system. Finally, party political doctrine is offered as having some influence, although a less neat explanation of the nature of administrative reforms. Pollitt and Summa conclude that the most convincing explanations of reform trajectories in their empirical observations of four countries (Finland, New Zealand, Sweden and the UK) were not economic performance or party doctrines but, rather, the characteristics of the political and administrative systems already in place. 'It was these system characteristics which most significantly influence what was possible in terms of scope, process and speed of reform' (Pollitt and Summa, 1997: 15).

Pollitt and Bouckaert (2004: 25) refine this explanatory approach further by devising a conceptual map 'depicting the broad forces which have been at work in both driving and restraining change' – it synthesises the process of reform in many countries. Therein they suggest that interactions between background socio-economic influences, political pressures and characteristics of the existing political and administrative systems are shaping influences in the reform process. At the centre of their model is the process of elite decision-making where change is conceived and executed 'top-down' by executive politicians and/or senior civil servants. Whilst sympathetic to Pollitt and Bouckaert's institutional approach, Bevir *et al.* criticise the model on two grounds: 'it does not unpack the idea of path dependency by describing how and why the system got to where it is today' and does not fully explore 'the role of individual agency as a cause of change – there is little of the beliefs and actions of elite actors' (Bevir *et al.*, 2003: 3). They argue for an 'interpretive approach' as a way of understanding public-sector reform. This requires historical narratives of elite constructions of reforms or the reconstruction of 'the beliefs of elites to unpack the ideas that inform the changing actions and practices of governance' (Bevir *et al.*, 2003: 15). Using this approach, Bevir *et al.*, (2003) analyse public sector reform and draw out a number of implications, two of which (at least) speak directly to administrative changes in Northern Ireland. First, 'there is no toolkit applicable within or across countries. Governance is constructed differently and continuously reconstructed so that there can be no one set of tools' (Bevir *et al.*, 2003: 203). This is already evident in the Northern Ireland context where attempts to modernise local government, in line with reforms in Great Britain, have met with problems. Second, 'reform is a continuous, political process in which the meaning of change is contested' (Bevir *et al.*, 2003: 204). Hence, politicians in Northern Ireland are already fixated with which reformed council areas they are likely to politically control and how a (marginally) stronger local government tier will relate to a devolved Assembly, as opposed to whether these offer the 'best' mechanisms for delivering high quality public services.

Modernisation in Northern Ireland

How has the modernisation agenda played out in the context of Northern Ireland? Not surprisingly attention to improving public services assumed a much lower priority than tackling constitutional and security issues in Northern Ireland. So isolated was it from mainstream British influence that it earned the rather dubious title of 'a place apart' (Rose, 1971). Ironically, however, it was the abuse of power in the execution of public services which played a significant part in the demise of devolution from 1921 to 1972 and paved the way for intervention by the British Government through Direct Rule. The Belfast (Good Friday) Agreement in 1998 and the associated devolution of power to an elected Assembly in Stormont prompted a radical rethink about both the size and shape of the public sector in Northern Ireland and ways to improve public service provision. As Bell observed when commenting on the potential for administrative reforms under the Direct Rule period:

> So long as successive United Kingdom governments remain committed to the reintroduction of some form of devolution as a practical objective and not simply as a long-term aspiration, proposals for improving the efficiency of the government apparatus must be compatible with devolution. They must seek neither to erect significant administrative obstacles to a return to devolved government, nor to raise public doubt about the government's intentions regarding the constitutional future of Northern Ireland. (Bell, 1987: 217)

Devolution therefore impelled an examination of the overall architecture of government. The creation of the Northern Ireland Assembly and a regional tier of government added to an already congested political landscape which now features: 3 MEPs, 18 MPs, 108 Members of the Legislative Assembly (MLAs) and 582 local councillors for a population of 1.7 million people. In addition, a complex mosaic of government departments, agencies, local authorities, non-departmental public bodies, boards, trusts and quangos, prompted the criticism that Northern Ireland was both 'over-governed' and 'over-administered' (Knox and Carmichael, 2006; Carmichael and Knox, 2005).

In essence a twin-track approach was adopted to modernisation in Northern Ireland: structural reforms in the shape of the Review of Public Administration; and a series of measures aimed at improving public services. This agenda for change featured prominently in the early stages of devolution. The (then) First Minister noted in an Assembly debate:

> The Review of Public Administration is one of the major tasks facing the Executive and will be central to the way in which we deliver, structure and organise our public services in the future. This is an opportunity of a generation

to put in place a modern, accountable, effective system of public administration that can deliver a high quality set of public services to our citizens. (Trimble, 2002: 371)

The system of public administration in Northern Ireland was a piecemeal response to political circumstances and had over time become unwieldy, anachronistic and complex for a small population. Aside from repackaging six civil service departments into eleven to accommodate devolution in 1999, public administration structures remained largely unchanged since 1973. At that time the civil rights movement demanded major reforms in local government to address unionist hegemony consolidated through gerrymandered electoral wards, restricted franchise and discriminatory housing practices (O'Dowd et al., 1980). Reforms came in the shape of the Macrory Report (Review Body, 1970) which divided services into regional (requiring large administrative units) and district (suitable for small areas) services. The Stormont Parliament was to take responsibility for regional services and district councils would administer district services.

Macrory recommended the establishment of 26 borough or district councils and the setting up of appointed boards to decentralise the administration of centrally provided health and education services. The recommendations were subsequently passed into law under the Local Government Act (Northern Ireland) 1972. Macrory's proposals were however overtaken by the abolition of Stormont in 1972 and the imposition of Direct Rule from Westminster in the absence of a regional tier. What has emerged since then is an emasculated form of local government with limited functional responsibilities, a plethora of boards, trusts and non-departmental public bodies superimposed with civil service departments which have responsibility for public services ordinarily delivered by councils in the rest of the United Kingdom (see figure 3.2). Public administration in Northern Ireland was described by the Comptroller and Auditor General as 'disastrously fragmented'. Almost every body in Great Britain that carries out any function of government, he argued, 'is duplicated on a tiny scale within Northern Ireland and that is an impediment to clarity and an enormous inefficiency' (Dowdall, 2004).

The structure of public administration and efforts to reform its institutions were inextricably linked to the various political and constitutional initiatives which emerged in Northern Ireland including, since 1999, the on/off attempts to stabilise devolved government (Knox and Carmichael, 2005a). To ensure public services remained outside the political (and the possibility of sectarian) sphere, more key functional responsibilities were vested in non-departmental public bodies (quangos) resulting in a patchwork of

Figure 3.2 Public administration in Northern Ireland: pre-Review of Public Administration, 2002

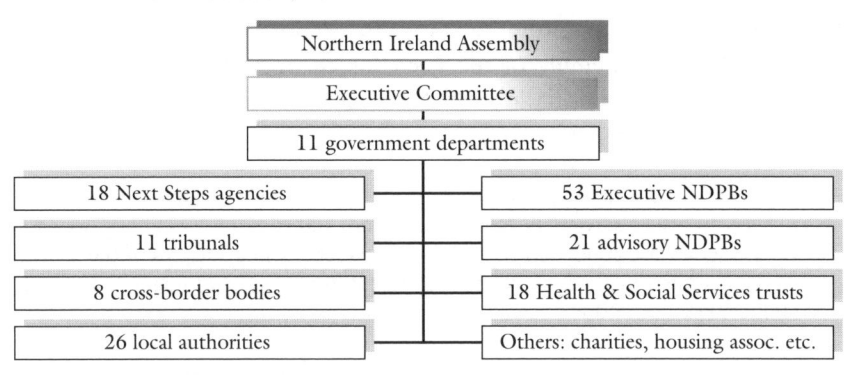

```
                    Northern Ireland Assembly
                    Executive Committee
                    11 government departments
  18 Next Steps agencies              53 Executive NDPBs
  11 tribunals                        21 advisory NDPBs
  8 cross-border bodies               18 Health & Social Services trusts
  26 local authorities                Others: charities, housing assoc. etc.
```

unaccountable organisations with a large proportion of the public budget. A line of Direct Rule ministers buttressed and expanded these structures piecemeal. Ministers could dispense largesse by placing benign appointees least likely to cause controversy ('yes [wo]men') on quangos. Add to this an active and engaged voluntary and community sector which had service delivery capacity and confidence as a key stakeholder, and we have the administrative landscape that existed in Northern Ireland. Not only was the system overtly complex, but it also suffered from a significant lack of public accountability. Health trusts, education and library boards, and quangos, for example, consumed some 45 per cent of the public budget. There was no political representation on health trusts; education and library boards comprised to 40 per cent local councillors; and quango appointees were in the gift of ministers. The most democratic forum, local government, had responsibility for a meagre 4 per cent of the public budget. With devolution came the opportunity for wholesale reform of a public administration system which, over time, had become ineffective and unaccountable. As Lord Glentoran (2004: 65) argued in a debate in the House of Lords: 'I believe that the Government is now guilty to a considerable extent of maladministration in terms of waste of public money in many different areas. Northern Ireland is grossly over-administered.' In sum, the administrative arrangements for a small population were complex, hugely bureaucratic and confusing to the public. One observer described the infrastructure of the Northern Ireland state apparatus as 'bloated, unwieldly and not fit for purpose'. He argued 'it is more collectivist than Stalinist Russia, more corporatist than Mussolini's Italy and more quangoised than the Britain of two Harolds' (Smith, 2004: 67). An eloquent, if over-the-top, description containing, nonetheless, a modicum of truth (Knox and Carmichael, 2005b).

Modernisation: the Review of Public Administration

Criticisms of 'over-administration' and an acknowledgement within the Northern Ireland Assembly of the need for change set the scene for the Review of Public Adminstration which was launched in 2002 with the following terms of reference:

> To review the existing arrangements for accountability, administration and delivery of public services in Northern Ireland, and to bring forward options for reform which are consistent with the arrangements and principles of the Belfast Agreement, within an appropriate framework of political and financial accountability. (Hansard, 2002)

The review, whilst attracting widespread political support, was criticised on two fundamental issues. In the first instance the 11 civil service departments were excluded from the remit of the review on the grounds that this could be used to renegotiate the Belfast/Good Friday Agreement 'by the back door' since the power-sharing executive was predicated on the four main political parties holding ministerial portfolios (Wilson, 2001). Any proposals by opponents of the Agreement to dismantle government departments under the Review of Public Administration could therefore have wider political consequences for a power-sharing executive. The second criticism was on the review mechanisms. The fact that civil servants from the Office of the First Minister and Deputy First Minister led the review did not satisfy the need for independence and compounded the idea that reforms would largely focus on all bodies outside of the central government – a kind of 'not in my back yard' mentality.

The review covered over 140 organisations within the public sector: 18 government agencies; 26 district councils; and 99 public bodies on which 2,065 public appointees sat (OFMDFM, 2004). The focus of the work was 'on the major public services which have most impact on citizens, and the organisations which deliver them' (OFMDFM, 2003: 8). This seemed at odds with the exclusion of 11 core civil service departments which had responsibility for some 40 per cent of public spending. In seeking to 'establish the optimum arrangements for public administration in Northern Ireland' the terms of reference of the review required any proposals to satisfy the following characteristics: democratic accountability; community responsiveness and partnership working; cross-community concerns; equality and human rights; subsidiary; quality of service; co-ordination and integration of services; scope of the public sector; efficiency and effectiveness; and innovation and business organisation (OFMDFM, 2003: 13).

Despite the fact that the Review of Public Administration was billed at its launch as 'one of the major tasks facing the Executive' (Trimble, 2002: 371) it fell to Direct Rule ministers to carry it forward. The on/off nature of devolution which was suspended for four times during the period December 1999 and October 2002 resulted in a review process overseen by British ministers. That process involved a comprehensive evidence gathering exercise as follows:

- *Attitudinal surveys*: Six separate Northern Ireland-wide attitudinal probability surveys were conducted between September 2002 and July 2005 with around 1,200 respondents in each survey. The aim of the surveys was to gather the views of the general public on their experiences of public services.
- *Listening to people's views*: The Review of Public Administration team and panel of independent experts listened (as part of a pre-consultation exercise) to the views of over 70 organisations including all 26 district councils, the 5 education and library boards, and all the health and personal social services organizations. In addition, they commissioned several research consultations.
- *Study visits*: The Review of Public Administration team undertook a series of study visits to other jurisdictions (Australia, Finland, Germany, Ireland, USA, Netherlands, New Zealand, Canada, Spain and Sweden) to consider how public services were organised elsewhere.
- *Mapping the public sector*: The complex structure of the pre-existing Northern Ireland public sector was mapped in two ways. First, maps were drawn showing the organizational structure of the system of public administration to include staffing levels, budgets and detailed functional responsibilities. The maps also depicted financial and accountability arrangements between parent departments, agencies, boards, trusts and non-departmental public bodies. Second, 'service to citizen' maps were drawn which grouped services in a way that indicated how citizens accessed them and their location within the Northern Ireland Executive's priorities in *Programme for Government*.
- *Briefing papers and research reports*: The review commissioned a number of academics to provide briefings on issues such as: public sector reform, multi-level governance, civic leadership etc. Several specific research reports dealt with a range of topics which evolved as the review progressed. These included work on: a Northern Ireland - Scotland comparison which examined the relative size, structure and funding arrangements of the public sector in Northern Ireland compared to Scotland. Research was also conducted on the distribution of the property wealth base across Northern Ireland aimed at assessing how a reconfiguration of local

government areas would affect income from district and regional rates (Northern Ireland has a property based rates system based on capital value).
- *Major public consultations*: Two Northern Ireland-wide public consultation exercises were held. The first took place between October 2003 and February 2004 and sought public reaction to how/by whom public services might be provided within a range of five models outlined in the consultation document (status quo; centralized services; regional and sub-regional public bodies; enhanced local government; and strong local government). The second consultation ran from March to September 2005 and sought views on the future shape of local government, the administration of health and social services, the administrative support for education, the future of non-departmental public bodies, and the development of leadership and capacity within the public sector.

Central to the consultation proposals was a two-tier model of public administration. The first tier would be a regional tier encompassing the Assembly, government departments and regional authorities, the focus of which would be policy development, setting standards and delivering regional services. The second tier, a sub-regional tier, would encompass organisations that ideally operate within common boundaries to include councils, health bodies, sub-regional bodies and delivery units of regional bodies. The model assumed delivery at the sub-regional tier unless economies of scale (or other factors) dictated delivery on a regional basis (see figure 3.3). Northern Ireland Office Minister (at the time), Ian Pearson, offered his views on the final reform model:

> I envisage the Assembly with departments sitting at regional level with responsibility for policy, strategic planning, setting standards and monitoring performance. At local level, larger more powerful councils could have responsibilities for an increased range of functions . . . I will also be examining the scope for significant reductions in the number of public bodies, in particular, the administrative structures around health and education. (Pearson, 2004: 1)

The 'final' decisions of the Review of Public Administration announced by the (then) Northern Ireland Secretary of State (Peter Hain) were contained in the document, *Better Government for Northern Ireland* (2006). Hain pointed out that 'ideally local politicians in a local Assembly should be taking decisions on all the key issues affecting the people of Northern Ireland'. In the absence of devolved government (at that time) the outcomes of the review were to ensure that 'taxpayers will get better value for money through the savings made in reducing bureaucracy being redirected

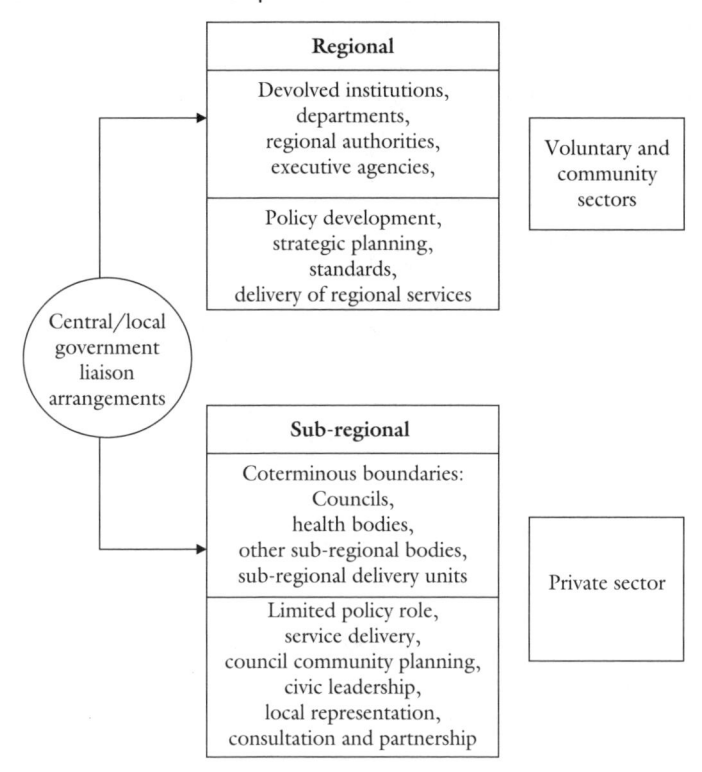

Figure 3.3 Two-tier model of public administration

```
                    ┌─────────────────────────────┐
                    │         Regional            │
                    ├─────────────────────────────┤
                    │  Devolved institutions,     │
           ┌───────▶│  departments,               │     ┌──────────────┐
           │        │  regional authorities,      │     │ Voluntary and│
           │        │  executive agencies,        │     │  community   │
           │        ├─────────────────────────────┤     │   sectors    │
           │        │  Policy development,        │     └──────────────┘
           │        │  strategic planning,        │
    ╭──────┴──╮     │  standards,                 │
    │Central/local│ │  delivery of regional services │
    │ government  │ └─────────────────────────────┘
    │  liaison    │
    │arrangements │ ┌─────────────────────────────┐
    ╰──────┬──╯     │       Sub-regional          │
           │        ├─────────────────────────────┤
           │        │  Coterminous boundaries:    │
           │        │  Councils,                  │
           │        │  health bodies,             │
           └───────▶│  other sub-regional bodies, │     ┌──────────────┐
                    │  sub-regional delivery units│     │Private sector│
                    ├─────────────────────────────┤     │              │
                    │  Limited policy role,       │     └──────────────┘
                    │  service delivery,          │
                    │  council community planning,│
                    │  civic leadership,          │
                    │  local representation,      │
                    │  consultation and partnership│
                    └─────────────────────────────┘
```

to front-line services': *Better Government for Northern Ireland* (2006: 3). The savings from the review (based on certain assumptions around its implementation) were estimated at £200m per year (Deloitte, 2006). The reforms included the reduction in local councils from 26 to 7 by spring 2009 and a new Education and Skills Authority to be established (April 2008), and Health and Social Services Authority replacing 4 existing health and social services boards.

The restoration of devolution and the establishment of a power-sharing Executive on 8 May 2007 witnessed local political parties revisit the outcomes of the Review, in particular the proposals for local government. This is hardly surprising given that, during consultation, 4 of the 5 main political parties were in favour of 15 councils and expressed concerns about the loss of local identity and the potential for 'balkanisation' of Northern Ireland with a significant east-west split in religious segregation. Since then, there have been several key developments.

Health Minister, Michael McGimpsey announced (6 July 2007) that he needed more time to consider the establishment of the proposed Health and Social Services Authority which was intended to replace Northern Ireland's existing four health and social services boards. The Minister claimed in a memo to his staff that 'the Review of Public Administration is not my plan, as I was not involved in the decisions taken under Direct Rule' (McGimpsey, 2007: 1). A delay in this key structural reform in health was announced despite the fact that many of the senior management appointments had already been made to the new Authority.

Education Minister, Caitríona Ruane stated (19 July 2007) that 'the Review of Public Administration project in education is too big and complex' to try to implement by April 2008 (Ruane, 2007b: 2). She therefore agreed, with the endorsement of the Northern Ireland Executive, to postpone the setting up of the new Education and Skills Authority by up to one year. The Minister pointed out in drawing up her plans for change in the education sector that 'there is adequate time for scrutiny of legislation by the Education Committee and the Assembly'.

Finally, Environment Minister, Arlene Foster, announced (6 July 2007) a new review of local government which considered 3 elements:

- developing a shared vision for local government;
- the number of councils; and
- the functions to transfer to local government.

In short, a range of structural and functional reforms for local government were re-examined – a 'review of the review', if you will (Knox, 2008a).

The move away from the seven-council model as a result of the Department of Environment review impacted on the fundamentals of the original reform package in a number of ways. The reforms were predicated on the four principles of: subsidiary, equality and good relations, common boundaries, and strong local government. Co-terminosity will now be much more difficult to achieve and almost certainly not on a 1:1 basis between local government and other public services such as health, planning and roads. The two-tier regional/sub-regional model of public administration which informed the original thinking of the review is now in some doubt. The model envisaged the role of the regional tier (Assembly, Executive and central government departments) to develop and shape policy and legislation, and set strategic objectives for services. The sub-regional tier should have, at its core, strong local government based on council areas sharing common boundaries with other service providers. The sub-regional tier should also be responsible for service delivery co-ordinated by councils through new statutory powers in community planning. With an agreement now reached to establish 11 councils, the balance will shift towards more centralised service provision, undermining the original two-tier model.

The *final* decisions from the Review of Public Administration reached by the devolved administration are as follows:

Local government

- The number of councils will reduce from 26 to 11 by May 2011. The Local Government Boundaries Commissioner submitted his recommendations to the Department of the Environment on the new boundaries in June 2009.
- The councils will have a statutory duty to lead a community planning process, and all other agencies must work with the councils. Councils will also be given the power of well-being.
- A range of functions will transfer to local government including: aspects of planning, rural development, the public realm aspects of local roads functions, urban regeneration and community development, a range of housing related functions, local economic development and tourism.

Health

- The 18 health trusts were reduced to 5 and have been fully operational since April 2007 (the Ambulance Service remains as a separate trust).
- Four new organisations were established in April 2009:
  - A single *Health and Social Care Board* replaced the existing four Health and Social Services Boards. It focuses on commissioning, resource management and performance management and improvement.
  - A *Public Health Agency* incorporating and building on the work of the Health Promotion Agency but with a much wider responsibility for health protection, health improvement and development to address existing health inequalities and public health issues for all the people of Northern Ireland.
  - A *Business Services Organisation* providing a range of support functions for the whole of health and social care system. The Central Services Agency was dissolved and the majority of its services was undertaken by the new organisation.
  - A single *Patient and Client Council* replaced the Health and Social Services Councils with five local offices operating in the same geographical areas as the existing trusts, to provide a strong voice for patients, clients and carers.

Education

- An Education and Skills Authority will replace the current five Education and Library Boards by January 2010. The new Education and Skills Authority (ESA) will take over the functions currently carried out by the: five Education and Library Boards; Council for the Curriculum Examinations and Assessment; and the Regional Training Unit. It will also be responsible for the front-line support currently undertaken by: Council for Catholic Maintained Schools; Northern Ireland Council for Integrated Education; and Comhairle na Gaelscolaiochta (Irish Schools).
- The new ESA will absorb the role of the Education Staff Commission, which dealt with recruitment, training and terms and conditions of employment of officers of the education and library boards. It will also undertake some of the functions currently performed by the Department of Education.
- The Youth Council will come under the ESA, as will youth services administration.
- A new statutory Advisory Forum will be established as a major source of advice between education sectors and the Department of Education

Libraries

- A Library Authority was established in April 2009 assuming the relevant responsibilities from the Education and Library Boards.

It is clear from the above outcomes that the review majored on structural reforms, the reorganisation of the machinery of governance. It also faced significant political developments. Devolved government ministers did not want to simply accept the decisions of a process presided over by 'direct rulers'. In an overview of the outcomes of the Review of Public Administration, Birrell argues that:

> The reforms represent a reduction in the number of existing organisations and some reconfiguration of functions, as well as demonstrating an institutionalist and somewhat traditional approach focused on existing traditional sectors and institutions . . . In practice, the final outcome consists of a package of disparate changes, representing a number of influences, streamlining of structures, cost cutting, and enhancing the functions for local government, but also of increased centralisation of other functions. (Birrell, 2008: 791)

An emphasis on structural reform is, more generally, highlighted by Frost (2002) who comments on the attraction of the one-off 'big-fix' solution to public service shortcomings:

> Changing organisational structures can, at some considerable human and financial cost, address structural problems. If the problems are more directly related to managerial practices and support systems, or to weak or uncertain ethical frameworks, structural solutions are an expensive method for answering the wrong question. (Frost, 2002: 90)

Yet the (Direct Rule) Minister with responsibility for the review noted at the time 'improving services to the public lies at the heart of any new model of public administration' (Pearson, 2004). Structural reconfiguration, in itself, was not going to achieve this. As Bell noted: 'The history of government in Northern Ireland tends to confirm the American experience . . . where it is suggested, the principal lesson is that reorganisation does not of itself promote economy or efficiency' (Bell, 1987: 192). In the absence of a modernisation agenda 'read across' from Great Britain, Northern Ireland somewhat belatedly started to consider ways in which it could improve public services set alongside the emerging reorganisation of the structures of its public bodies. It is to this process of modernisation that we now turn.

Modernisation: public services reform

One of the first signs of movement on the wider modernisation agenda for public services in Northern Ireland came in the form of a report entitled *Review of the Northern Ireland Civil Service: Response to Devolution* (2002). The report was commissioned by the (then) Head of the Northern Ireland Civil Service 'to examine the effectiveness of Northern Ireland departments in responding to the requirements of devolution, and to identify ways and means of improving that effectiveness' (Northern Ireland Civil Service, 2002: 3). The report acknowledged that devolution could be seen as part of a wider agenda of constitutional reform and made reference to the *Modernising White Paper* (1999) and its specific objectives for devolution, one of which was:

> Modernising the approach – devolution is regarded as a stimulus to fresh thinking, for example reducing bureaucracy, allowing people choice, better service delivery and 'joined up thinking' to provide a much greater customer focus. (Northern Ireland Civil Service, 2002: 13)

There is an acceptance in the report that 'the modernising issues are peripheral to the question of how we have responded to devolution' by comparison with other parts of the United Kingdom. External stakeholders who were consulted to inform the findings of the report referred to the public service as 'bureaucratic and risk averse, lacking customer focus and making insufficient use of information technology' (Northern Ireland Civil Service, 2002:

27). Recommendations emerging from the *Response to Devolution* report were:

- To develop the Civil Service culture to embrace the key themes of modernising government within the Civil Service reform agenda:
  - the Permanent Secretaries modernisation sub-group should draw up a modernisation strategy to address the cultural issues identified by the review
  - Departmental Boards should each consider how they could align their departments' policies and operations around the themes of modernisation and draw up a strategy to implement a modernisation programme (Northern Ireland Civil Service, 2002: 86).

As a follow-on to these recommendations a report entitled *Fit for Purpose: The Reform Agenda in the Northern Ireland Civil Service* (Northern Ireland Civil Service, 2004) set out a framework for providing high-quality public services. Whilst acknowledging that the Northern Ireland Civil Service shared many of the drivers for change with counterparts in the rest of the United Kingdom and Ireland, the argument was that it faced some unique challenges. These included the fact that there were tougher equality laws and, as an employer, the civil service had to promote equality of opportunity and demonstrate best practice in these areas. Officials also had to help develop and implement policies within new and unique political structures. For these reasons and because of the challenges the report argued:

> The Northern Ireland Civil Service will pursue a reform agenda appropriate to the Northern Ireland context, with the aim of creating and sustaining public services that citizens need and expect; affirming the essential principle of equality and integrity; and characterised by responsiveness, flexibility and efficiency. (Northern Ireland Civil Service, 2004: 8)

The framework proposed for reforming public services is illustrated in figure 3.4.

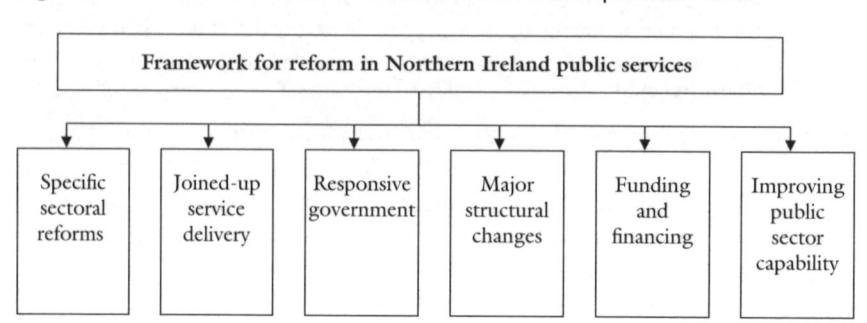

Figure 3.4 Framework for reform in Northern Ireland public services

```
┌─────────────────────────────────────────────────────────────┐
│     Framework for reform in Northern Ireland public services │
└─────────────────────────────────────────────────────────────┘
       │         │          │          │         │         │
       ▼         ▼          ▼          ▼         ▼         ▼
  ┌────────┐ ┌────────┐ ┌──────────┐ ┌────────┐ ┌────────┐ ┌──────────┐
  │Specific│ │Joined-up│ │Responsive│ │ Major  │ │Funding │ │Improving │
  │sectoral│ │ service │ │government│ │structural│ │  and  │ │  public  │
  │reforms │ │delivery │ │          │ │ changes │ │financing│ │  sector  │
  │        │ │         │ │          │ │         │ │         │ │capability│
  └────────┘ └────────┘ └──────────┘ └────────┘ └────────┘ └──────────┘
```

The various components of this reform package were described as follows:

- Specific sectoral reforms are those which directly make step changes in outcome for citizens such as: action on acute hospitals, waiting lists, post-primary education and public transport.
- Joined-up service delivery is co-operation between different government departments and agencies in areas such as: welfare reform, road safety, neighbourhood renewal, and investing in health.
- Responsive government is about making significant changes to the involvement of citizens in the processes of government. Compliance with Freedom of Information is an important element of responsive government.
- Major structural changes are aimed at improved citizens outcomes and enhancing accountability of which the Review of Public Administration is a key driver.
- Funding and financing of public services is about reforms which make a significant impact on quantum, timing or efficiency of resources for public services such as water and rating reform.
- Improving public-sector capability for the Northern Ireland Civil Service means the key activities which will enable the service to deliver and support the other reforms and raise the general standards of public services in Northern Ireland.

The civil service therefore committed to taking forward a new reform programme containing three key elements:

(1) Putting the priority front-line services first so that resources are focused on meeting the needs and aspirations of the community. Achieving this means, amongst other things, a smaller and more efficient Civil Service, with rationalised support services, less absenteeism, and better management of pay and workforce issues.
(2) Building capability, for example, by enhancing leadership and professionalism, developing talent, better performance management, and employee relations.
(3) Embracing diversity by more external recruitment and interchange, more outreach to groups who may be under-represented, and enhanced equal opportunities/diversity monitoring. (Northern Ireland Civil Service, 2004: 3)

One initiative established in 2004 with the aim of providing real examples of quality improvements in the delivery of services to citizens was the *Northern Ireland Best Practice Scheme*. Through the scheme, staff from the wider Northern Ireland public sector and the voluntary and community sectors are given the opportunity to visit host organisations, assess working practices, and benchmark their own performance against key aspects of service improvement. Participants can then use the experiences of others to develop their own knowledge and skills in order to improve their service delivery. The dissemination of good practice is also captured in case study format by the *Public Service Improvement Unit* which is responsible for the scheme. As an example we include a summary of NI Direct (discussed below) – a reform aimed at simplifying citizen access to public services in Northern Ireland through multiple electronic channels, but initially concentrating on telephony (see box 3.1).'

Box 3.1 'Northern Ireland Direct': a best practice case study

NI Direct, in the Department of Finance and Personnel, provides a virtual contact centre for the Northern Ireland Civil Service (NICS).

A review of telephonist services between 2004 and 2005 concluded that: customer experience was very poor; there was a high volume of abandoned calls and handling times were too long.

An improvement strategy was developed which resulted in the setting up of a Service Improvement Team. Greater stakeholder involvement was encouraged which included consultation with staff and their representatives. Relevant training programmes for staff and supervisors were also put in place.

The overall improvement strategy has resulted in considerable improvements in service and satisfaction levels. For example the organisation handles in the region of 400,000 calls per month. The average percentage of calls abandoned has dropped considerably and recent survey information has revealed that over 96 per cent of calls are now answered within 12 seconds.

Another one of the main outcomes was that the organisation began to provide 'one and done' services for a number of key agencies/departments. Today, these include Planning Service, Land & Property Division, General Register Office and the Department of Agriculture and Rural Development. NI Direct provides a wide range of services which includes form distribution, surveys, avian flu advice and help in relation to the recording of births, deaths and marriages.

An example of a successful collaborative partnership is with the Planning Service. NI Direct worked in partnership with the organisation as part of a pilot project in defining processes, collaborating on training and addressing areas of concern. The benefits include: more efficient use of staff resources; prior knowledge of cases before customer contact is made;

response targets now in place and general enquiries are resolved at the first point of contact. Following the success of the pilot the 'information line' went live in July 2007.

Over the last few years the organisation has undergone radical change and will continue to evolve as the Northern Ireland Civil Service modernises and transforms. Their experience will be of considerable benefit for staff involved in project management and customer service improvement.

Source: Reform Delivery Unit, Delivery and Innovation Division (2008).

Reform programmes and projects

A much greater emphasis and focus on public sector reform resulted from devolved government. A number of factors, in particular, forced the pace of change started under *Fit for Purpose*: citizens' expectations increased, demanding much more local accountability and higher quality public services. The Northern Ireland Executive's Programme for Government outlined what the devolved administration had committed to delivering within the constraints of the budget available to them. This, in turn, demanded efficiencies in order to release resources for frontline services. Recent operational plans for delivering civil service reforms are seen as a transformational change process leading to major improvements in quality, efficiency and effectiveness across all 11 departments in the Northern Ireland Civil Service. It is about modifying the way in which public services are delivered. The key approach taken to transformational change is to:

- make government departments much more accessible to the public;
- create a new working environment for civil servants;
- develop newly skilled officials who have access to up-to-date technology, and
- employ new working methods.

All of this is being done through a series of projects and programmes. These include: Records NI; HR Connect; Account NI; Workplace 2010; Centre for Applied Learning; ICT Shared Service Centre; NI Direct; and Network NI (see figure 3.5 for the modernisation model). These projects provide for a service-wide consolidation and redesign of business processes into stand-alone centres or 'shared services' projects. The value of these projects is estimated to be in the region of £2.9b. In short, the Northern Ireland Civil Service modernisation agenda is to deliver better public services through

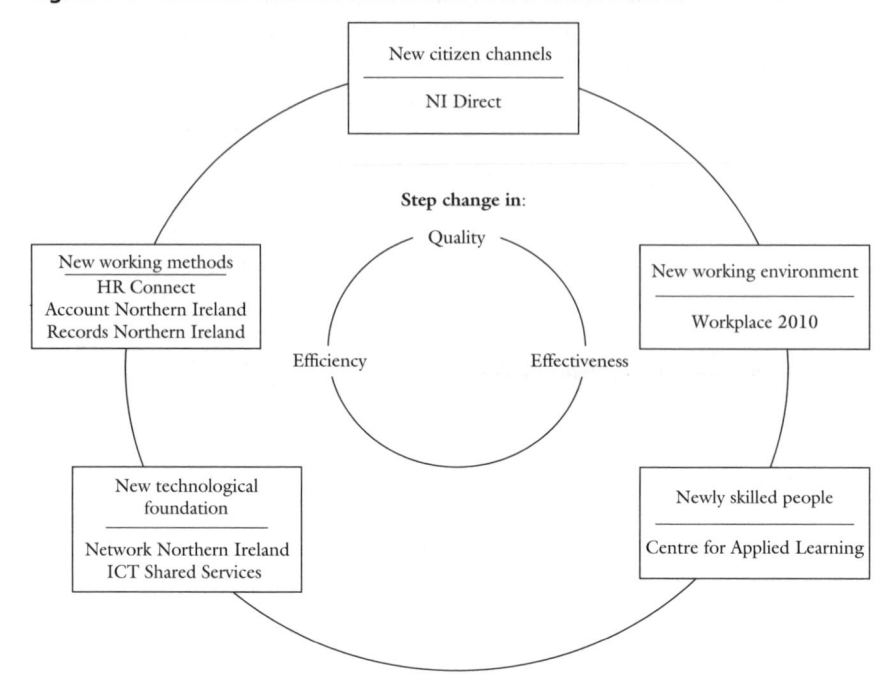

Figure 3.5 Public services modernisation in Northern Ireland

```
                    New citizen channels
                    ─────────────────────
                         NI Direct

                      Step change in:
                         Quality

New working methods                         New working environment
  HR Connect                                ─────────────────────────
Account Northern Ireland                         Workplace 2010
Records Northern Ireland
              Efficiency    Effectiveness


  New technological                              Newly skilled people
     foundation                                ─────────────────────────
  ─────────────────────                         Centre for Applied Learning
  Network Northern Ireland
    ICT Shared Services
```

improving capacity and providing civil servants with the necessary technology and facilities. They are doing this in four broad areas: reform (business transformation and best public service improvement/best practice); innovation (a range of IT-enabled reforms); new technologies, and delivery of services. We outline some of the detail of the projects and programmes integral to the modernisation approach.

New citizen channels: NI Direct

This project is aimed at simplifying and improving access to public services through a single telephone point of contact for Northern Ireland public service enquiries. It will also provide an improved range of contact channels for citizen access to public services – single website presence for government departments and agencies to include a range of transactional services. The aim is to reduce barriers to citizens accessing online public services through the delivery of a digital inclusion programme. See, for example, the NI Direct website at www.nidirect.gov.uk/ billed as the official government website for Northern Ireland citizens. There is also a Citizens' Online Programme which will develop the OnlineNI portal. It comprises a number of projects involving increasing the uptake of, and simplifying connection to, the government gateway for smaller service organisations, the trialling of public service kiosks in public space and identity management.

New working methods

These include: HR Connect, Account NI, and Records NI.

- *HR Connect* is an outsourced shared human resource service centre aimed at providing modern, cost effective support to the Northern Ireland Civil Service and offering consistency in the interpretation of policies across departments.
- *Account NI* is a major transformation programme to provide a common accounting system across the civil service aimed at improving the efficiency and effectiveness of the delivery of financial services. It offers a new integrated resource accounting and budgeting system for the Northern Ireland Civil Service. Account NI is a shared service financial centre which processes all invoices and purchase orders across the government departments (on a rolling implementation basis).
- *Records NI* is a single corporate service for managing records and documents electronically which aims to improve access, reduce the costs of physical file storage and administration and provide better information for such things as auditing and freedom of information requests. Records NI will also open up the sharing of information and knowledge throughout the civil service by introducing electronic records management.

New technological foundation

- *Network NI* provides network services for the Northern Ireland Civil Service that meets their business needs. Joined up network services should ensure better value for money and a level of usefulness and flexibility that would not be attainable by individual departments working in isolation. The network services provided through this project will facilitate additional applications, such as Voice over IP (VoIP) and video conferencing.
- *ICT Shared Services* is a single shared service centre for ICT office systems across the Northern Ireland Civil Service which provides a common infrastructure and consistent desktop services to officials in the office, at home or when mobile working.

Newly skilled people

- *Centre for Applied Learning* is a single shared service which provides generic training and development for the Northern Ireland Civil Service aimed at delivering the necessary skills and capacity needed and in support of the reforms implementation. It is designed to be the 'one-stop shop' for generic training within NICS.

New working environment

- *Workplace 2010* was a 5- to 7-year programme of work to transform the Northern Ireland Civil Service office estate, improving the office environment for many staff and facilitating new ways of working that demonstrates value for money for the taxpayer. Workplace 2010 intended to introduce new accommodation standards, including open plan working to enable the civil service to rationalise its existing estate and dispose of surplus, poor-quality accommodation. It promised to deliver: modern, flexible and efficient workspace for staff; accommodation that meets business needs; a smaller, more efficient estate; value for money for the taxpayer; and an environment that will support and enable significant and lasting change. The initiative however came to a premature end with the global economic decline. The Department of Finance and Personnel terminated the procurement of Workplace 2010 (in February 2009) due to 'exceptional market conditions which made it difficult to obtain debt finance for this type of property-related contract and because of the fall in the value of commercial property' (Department of Finance and Personnel, 2009).

The whole package of modernisation reforms feature in the Executive's *Programme for Government 2008–11* as Public Service Agreements (PSA 20 and 21) see table 3.1. They also feature in the balanced scorecard of the Department of Finance and Personnel (see table 3.2). The Head of the Northern Ireland Civil Service (Bruce Robinson) sees these reforms as part of a wider process of modernisation which includes:

- *Building a stronger performance culture* with a focus on outcomes for the citizen. Part of this has involved £250m value-for-money gains over a 3-year period (to March 2008) from public procurement, but also a reduction of 2,300 in the number of full-time equivalent posts in the Northern Ireland Civil Service over the same time.
- *Developing a much sharper customer focus* and more effective joined-up

MODERNISING GOVERNMENT

Table 3.1 Modernisation in the Programme for Government

	PSA 20 improving public services	
Objective 1	Actions	Target
Deliver a programme of civil service reform	Take forward NICS reform programme to deliver modern, high quality and efficient public services by improving NICS capacity and providing NICS staff with the necessary tools and technology	Deliver shared NICS corporate services and commence the benefits realisation process through the implementation of the following reform programmes: • Financial and accounting services through Account NI – full implementation by April 2009 • Human resource services through HR Connect – full implementation by November 2008 • ICT services through the ICT Shared Service Centre – full implementation by April 2009 • Network services through Network NI by September 2009 • Office estate services through Workplace 2010 – commence implementation by June 2009 • Complete the implementation of Records NI to move to full electronic records across NICS by October 2008
	PSA 21 enabling efficient government	
Objective 2	Actions	Target
Build the capacity of the Civil Service to deliver the Government's priorities by improving leadership, skills, professionalism, diversity and equality	Deliver high quality cost-effective training services through the Centre for Applied Learning to meet the needs of NICS Departments Encourage applications from under-represented groups and address barriers, real and perceived, to employment in the NICS	To deliver the Centre for Applied Learning Business Plan as agreed with the Centre for Applied Learning Strategy Board To identify priorities for the commissioning of training from the Centre of Applied Learning, in line with NICS business needs The NICS is more reflective of the diversity of Northern Ireland's society by 2011 Align the NICS competency framework and internal processes with the Professional Skills for Government framework by March

Table 3.1 (continued)

	PSA 21 enabling efficient government	
Objective 2	Actions	Target
	The Professional Skills for Government framework fully embedded in all NICS human resources practices and processes Develop a new Senior Civil Service Leadership Development Programme	2009 and embed Professional Skills for Government fully within the NICS by April 2010 By June 2008 to revise and publish a new Learning and Development Strategy for the Senior Civil Service which aligns with Professional Skills for Government

delivery. The NI Direct project will create opportunities to effect improvements, through a single telephone number access point, and in citizen satisfaction with the delivery of public services. Cross-sectoral and cross-departmental partnerships have been developed to tackle the lack of coherence for users of public services.

- *Growing officials*: the Northern Ireland Civil Service has now in place a new people strategy to ensure officials are well placed to respond to the changed labour market, rising citizen expectations and to ensure the reforms are implemented (Northern Ireland Civil Service People Strategy 2009–13. Belfast: Department of Finance and Personnel).

Bruce Robinson concluded:

> I believe that the pressures and challenges provide the imperative for transformation in order to achieve a step change in the quality, efficiency and effectiveness of public service delivery. It is a long term strategy but we will continue building on the sound progress that we have been making. Everyone – citizens, businesses, service users, and service providers, has a stake in the success of public services. It is our responsibility in the civil service to focus on implementing the Executive's *Programme for Government*, transform the delivery of government services, and to ensure the Northern Ireland Civil Service makes its contribution to building a successful, dynamic local economy that benefits people throughout Northern Ireland. (Robinson, 2008: 7–8)

Despite the optimism of Northern Ireland's most senior official, the Northern Ireland Audit Office sounded alarm bells in a report published in 2008 entitled *Shared Services for Efficiency: A Progress Report* (Northern Ireland

Table 3.2 Department of Finance & Personnel balanced scorecard: 'Leading reform, delivering value and promoting sustainability'

Results	Customers
• To implement and deliver Northern Ireland Civil Service reform • To secure, plan, manage and monitor public expenditure • To improve financial management across the Northern Ireland public sector • To ensure that corporate NICS human resource policies and services are in place • To contribute to sustainable development • To deliver DFP Executive Agency targets	• To provide high quality services which meet the needs and expectations of our customers • To promote and improve access to public services and information in Northern Ireland • To ensure the provision of efficient, effective and high quality shared services to the NICS and wider public sector
Internal processes	**Organisation and people**
• To rationalise our processes to enable us to live within our budgets • To communicate in an effective, timely and appropriate manner • To develop enhanced processes for human resource and workforce planning	• To lead modernisation and change through positive, visible leadership and management at all levels in DFP • To ensure staff are equipped with the necessary skills and competencies to deliver DFP objectives and the implementation of reform • To embed a culture of engagement, innovation and continuous improvement within DFP • To review, agree and embed DFP organisational values • To ensure compliance with data protection legislation

Source: Department of Finance & Personnel Operational Plan, 2009–10.

Audit Office, 2008). The Audit Office highlighted the importance of the modernisation projects which constituted the reform agenda (as set out in figure 3.5 above) and acknowledged that in some cases change was already underway but also identified projects which had produced challenges for the Department of Finance and Personnel.

The Comptroller and Auditor General (C&AG) included in his findings:

- Some projects have gone through significant changes during the procurement process. For example, in HR Connect a shift in the procurement

approach and extension to the contract period resulted in the cost increasing from an original estimate of £328m to £465m. In contrast, the cost of Network NI reduced significantly from an original estimate of £48m to £29m; this was mainly from a change in scope and the successful bid being significantly lower than expected.
- Generally projects have taken longer to procure and implement compared with original estimates. Contract signature has been reached 9 to 18 months later than initially planned, with Workplace 2010 experiencing a longer delay. The reasons include initial timetables based on optimistic assumptions, changes at preferred bidder stage, unforeseen complexity and, in the case of Workplace 2010, a legal challenge by one of the unsuccessful bidders.
- The Audit Office found the HR Connect and Records NI contracts reflected good practice.

The Comptroller and Auditor General noted in his conclusions that 'it is still too early to reach a firm conclusion as to whether these new services are delivering the efficiencies and benefits envisaged' (Northern Ireland Audit Office, 2008: 3- 5).

As a follow-on to the C&AG's report, the Public Accounts Committee of the Northern Ireland Assembly found that the Department of Finance could have difficulties completing the implementation of £3 billion reform agenda. The PAC Chair noted:

> There is an enormous challenge ahead for the Department of Finance and Personnel (DFP) to complete the implementation phases of the various Reform Agenda projects and to move to successful operation. In the Committee's view, the Department's capacity to do this is still unproven. In addition, whether value for money has been achieved is still to be demonstrated. (Maskey, 2009b: 1)

To cast doubt on the value for money of this set of reforms is to raise fundamental questions. The model on which this modernisation process is predicated has at its heart, to secure a step change in quality, efficiency and effectiveness (see 3. 5 above). The PAC highlighted the absence of measurable data to enable departments to identify baseline costs. This will make it much more difficult for the Department of Finance and Personnel to demonstrate, and for the Public Accounts Committee to validate, whether value for money has been maximised. The PAC concluded that 'without any clear specification of the benefits at the outset, we may still end up with systems that are not fit for purpose'. This is a major indictment of the reform agenda so far.

This chapter began by outlining the ongoing public sector modernisation agenda in Great Britain and highlighted the fact that the Northern Ireland Civil Service had lagged well behind efforts elsewhere to tackle reform of its public services. In part this can be explained by the wider constitutional and security issues which pre-occupied Direct Rule politicians but there was also a detachment from the reform agenda on the part of senior officials in Northern Ireland justified by 'unique' circumstances. When reforms came, a two-part approach was adopted – a series of structural reforms initiated through the Review of Public Administration and a range of programmes and projects centred around improved technology, providing better access to services, a more efficient approach to service delivery, and building the capacity of civil servants. The Review of Public Administration, launched in 2002 is still being implemented. Its entire focus on structural reform which excluded one of the most important elements in service delivery, government departments, would suggest an incomplete job. The fact that political parties are now calling for a review of civil service departments substantiates this claim. These structural reforms at local or central government level have political overtones which appear to have little to do with whether the new structures are fit for purpose but rather the political control of the new councils and unravelling of the Belfast/Good Friday arrangements, respectively. The second element of the reform agenda has had mixed reviews thus far and both the Northern Ireland Audit Office and the Public Accounts Committee remain to be convinced of the cumulative impact of the projects and programmes which comprise the modernisation agenda. More generally, politicians and officials are acutely aware that there is no correlation between quality public services and electoral accountability in Northern Ireland. Voting patterns remain firmly sectarian and hence the modernisation agenda, whilst important, will ultimately present no real electoral threat to politicians through lack of substantial progress or, at worse, failure to deliver on its promises.

4
Local government

Debate too often focuses on which services local government is responsible for, as if this is the true measure of the importance and worth of local representative government. A new conception of the role for local government needs to go further, to reflect the well-being and place-shaping agenda. Whatever the legal and constitutional arrangements for the provision of a service or function, if it has impacts on local people, then the local authority should have a role on representing the community interest and influencing that service. That requires not just the joining-up of resources and activities, but also a leadership and influencing role to ensure that the efforts of all agencies are focused on the outcomes of greatest importance to local people. Local government is well-placed to play this convening role. (Lyons Report, 2007: 3)

Local government in Northern Ireland

History

Local government in Northern Ireland currently comprises 26 district councils, with 582 councillors elected through the single transferable vote system of proportional representation for a 4-year term. Elections were held in 2005 and the current term extended due to the reorganisation of local government effective from May 2011 (see figure 4.1). Net council expenditure for the year 2007/08 was £458m for a population of 1.72 million people in Northern Ireland – this represents less than 5 per cent of the total public expenditure devolved budget. Although politically symbolic, as a locally electoral forum, in functional terms these statistics illustrate the relatively minor role played by councils in public service delivery.

Local government in Northern Ireland has had a turbulent past but also played a key role in leading the way to the political accommodation which now exists in the power-sharing Executive today. It is the product of the

LOCAL GOVERNMENT

Figure 4.1 Local councils by political party, 2009

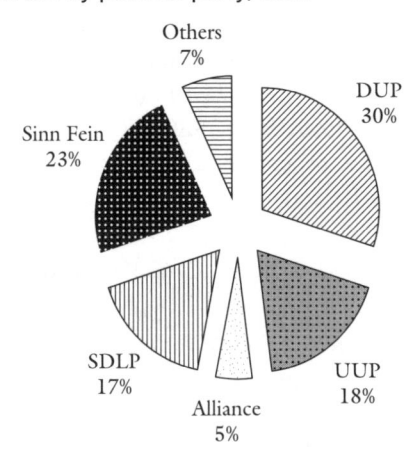

- Others 7%
- DUP 30%
- Sinn Fein 23%
- SDLP 17%
- Alliance 5%
- UUP 18%

Local Government (Ireland) Act 1898 which, in turn, derived from the 1888 and 1894 legislation for England and Wales. Alexander (1979) summarised the provisions of the 1898 Local Government (Ireland) Act as follows: first, the Act established a two-tier system of local government in which county boroughs (the six largest towns: Dublin, Cork, Limerick, Waterford, Belfast, Londonderry) and county councils formed the upper tier; and urban and rural districts formed the lower tier. Second, the public health functions of the poor law guardians in rural areas were transferred to the rural district councils. Third, the Act rationalised local government boundaries and eliminated overlapping jurisdictional areas. Fourth, a simplified rating system based on a single assessment for all local government purposes was introduced. Finally, the Act extended the local government franchise to include all adult male ratepayers, a provision which made the new county councils a focus of growing nationalist agitation for the separation of Ireland from the United Kingdom. The Act of 1898 established the structure of local government that obtained in Ireland at the time of the establishment of the Irish Free State and the devolved government in Northern Ireland.

When the 'free state' was created in 1920, the devolved government of Northern Ireland consisted of 6 Irish counties which formed the administrative state of Northern Ireland. Within the 6 counties the local government framework comprised: 2 county boroughs, 6 county councils, 10 boroughs, 24 urban districts and 31 rural districts – a total of 73 local authorities, serving a population (by 1966) of about 1.4 million people, ranging from Tandragee Urban District with 1,300 people to the city of Belfast with 407,000 (Birrell and Murie, 1980: 155, 159). Elections were held every three years and all councils except rural district had rating functions. They fulfilled the same role as their British counterparts with the exception of protective services such as police and civil defence. In the post-1920 period a number of controversial changes took place, described by Tomlinson as 'the invincibility of the Unionist local government system was carefully constructed and maintained from 1920 onwards' (O'Dowd *et al.* 1980: 98).

The first step in this process of change began with the 1922 Local Government (Northern Ireland) Act which:

1 Replaced proportional representation with the simple majority method of election. Proportional representation had been introduced into Ireland in 1918 by the Westminster Government to ensure representation by Unionist minorities throughout Ireland as a whole and to minimise the Sinn Féin vote in the South. The first-past-the-post system now corresponded with British local elections.
2 Presented the opportunity for redrawing electoral divisions and ward boundaries once proportional representation had been removed. The electoral areas within county boroughs and urban districts (wards), counties and rural districts (district electoral divisions) had been established in the 1840s prior to the proportional representation system.
3 Altered the franchise by incorporating property ownership as a qualification for the vote. Prior to the 1922 Local Government (Northern Ireland) Act anyone occupying land or premises, whether rated or not, could be registered for a local government vote. The 1922 Act restricted the franchise by limiting the vote to those holding land which had a valuation of £5 or more.

Later in the 1920s the franchise changed again following the introduction of a company or business vote, which allowed all limited companies to nominate up to six electors, one for every £10 valuation of their premises. Britain had abandoned the property vote and reverted to universal suffrage in 1945, and the Republic of Ireland introduced adult suffrage for local elections in 1935. Unionist politicians considered that to be a dangerous strategy since some local authorities would be lost to them. As Tomlinson (1980) explained:

> While Britain and the Irish Republic had been democratising local government, the Unionist Government was consolidating its grip on local politics by fixing ward boundaries, by distributing votes to the propertied and by disenfranchising the propertyless . . . The abolition of proportional representation and the reconstruction of wards and the franchise meant that, for the rural and county councils, elections were hardly necessary. The only question for the Unionists to resolve was who was to be chosen to serve on the local council. (Tomlinson, 1980: 100–101)

LOCAL GOVERNMENT

A growing recognition of the inadequacy of local government machinery to provide local services efficiently existed from 1940 onwards. Loughran (1965: 35) noted that 'local government has not made any considerable contribution to the development of Northern Ireland since the war'. This is evidenced by the growth of *ad hoc* statutory bodies and the removal of centralisation of local government functions. The Northern Ireland Hospital Authority was established to administer hospitals, specialist and ancillary services. Statutory boards became responsible for fire services and electricity. The Northern Ireland Housing Trust, set up in 1945, had the task of building houses for the whole province. This was seen as a measure to bolster housing provision by local authorities unable to cope with demand from within their own resources.

Pressure to reform local government came from two quite distinct but complementary sources. First, the Northern Ireland Government at Stormont began to modernise local government (beginning in March 1966) and remedy its defects and second, ongoing dissatisfaction with its performance contributed to the disturbances of 1968. Tomlinson (1980) noted the inherent resistance to pressure for change in an entrenched local government system from 1920 to the mid-1960s:

> Protestant bourgeois patronage, operating through the local government system on the basis of carefully concocted electoral districts and a restricted franchise, was well fortified against the political and economic forces for change which emerged in the 1950s and the 1960s. (Tomlinson, 1980: 101)

The main defect was the large number of small local authorities which existed and created an obstacle to the proper functioning of local government. Alongside the 73 directly elected local authorities, there were 24 statutory committees exercising special powers with a further 30 joint authorities or specialised bodies. Twenty-seven of the 73 councils had a population of fewer than 10,000 and 46 local authorities had a rateable valuation in which one penny in the pound produced less than £500. With a small rate base and associated financial resources, many could not employ the necessary professional and technical staff, nor could they justify the comprehensive provision of services. Local authorities also increasingly depended on central government as a source of income. By 1970 approximately 75 per cent of expenditure was borne by Exchequer grants resulting in a financially weak local structure dependent on central government which exerted considerable day-to-day control over its affairs (Birrell and Hayes, 1999). A wide disparity existed in the size and resources of various authorities, particularly in the south and west of the Province, yet all had similar statutory functions. This resulted in the proliferation of joint and *ad hoc* authorities, mentioned above, and the attendant problems of co-ordination and accountability. Many councils were therefore neither administratively nor financially viable. One local government official, Maurice Hayes (then Town Clerk of Downpatrick Council), summarised the problem thus:

> Our present local government structure was erected to meet a set of problems in Victorian times on a foundation of previously determined area boundaries and financial procedures . . . the stability of the foundations has been threatened by the running sands of population movement and social change; the whole edifice is now lop-sided and unable to support the more sophisticated organisation needed to cope with the problems of a complex modern society. (Hayes, 1967: 82)

The Northern Ireland Government responded by initiating a series of consultations between the government and Local Authorities Association culminating in a White Paper published in December 1967. The paper accepted that the present local government system stemmed from the nineteenth century and 'it is now, by common consent, in need of overhaul' (*The Reshaping of Local Government*, Cmnd 517, 1967). The White Paper recommended structural reorganisation based on a simplified, two tiers, local government system with 12–18 new administrative areas and the existing county councils. For reform purposes the three tests of local government had to be satisfied: 'efficiency, economy and the effective representation of local aspirations, all in harmony with public policy as a whole' (*The Reshaping of Local Government*, Cmnd 517, 1967).

Further proposals were set out in a follow-up White Paper published in July 1969 *The Reshaping of Local Government: Further Proposals* (1969) Cmnd 530 advocating 17 area councils and the abolition of county councils. Areas councils would comprise clusters of urban authorities with their surrounding rural areas. An independent commission would be set up to draw the boundaries of electoral districts within the new council areas and functions limited to environmental services, including housing, urban redevelopment and water supply. Planning and development, according to the proposals, would be central government responsibilities, with councils preparing sub-area plans for approval by the Ministry of Development in the context of overall strategic planning.

Sectarianism and local government

The proposals had a disappointing reception. The public showed little interest in the prospect of reform and in the preceding consultations and discussions. The reactions of political groups were generally predictable. Debate centred almost entirely on the likely political complexion of the proposed area councils. Anti-partition groups, on the whole, were satified with the

LOCAL GOVERNMENT 115

recommendations since they expected to gain control over four of the proposed areas in the south and west of the Province. An element of extreme unionist opinion condemned the reform proposals, especially in the west. Very little was heard about the merits of the reforms on the grounds of economy, efficiency or democracy. In short, both White Papers were opposed by local interests, even though the proposals had not addressed the political problems of local government. Predictably the political issue was to prove crucial for local government reform.

The politics of local governnent were dominated by sectarian considerations. Unionist continued to control an unbalanced share of local authorities with disproportionately large majorities – few councils changed hands at local elections. There were 12 local government areas which had a Catholic majority in the population with a Protestant/Unionist majority on the council. The situation resulted in allegations of council discrimination against Catholics. Buckland offered the following summary:

> Local government remained an outstanding grievance, with unionist majorities still bolstered up by discriminatory housing policies, carefully-drawn electoral areas and the persistent refusal to adopt the British practice of one man (*sic*) one vote . . . Protestants continued to receive preferential treatment in the allocation of local housing and a disproportionate share of local government jobs. (Buckland, 1981: 116)

Housing proved the most controversial council function. Catholics alleged that houses were strategically located to enhance unionist electoral prospects and their allocation remained in the hands of an elite core of Protestant councillors determined, in the vernacular, to 'look after their own'. Such a view is tenable in the absence of any clear housing allocation policy which at best operated in an *ad hoc* manner and, at worse, provided an opportunity for patronage and sectarianism. Hayes described councils approach to housing provision at the time in this way:

> There is little consistency among local authorities in their measurement of (housing) 'need'. Some operate points schemes, weighted in various ways, most do not. In some councils the allocation of houses is a council responsibility, in others it is the business of the housing committee. In some rural districts the allocation of houses within an electoral division is the prerogative of the local councillor. The methods adopted by local authorities in determining their house building programmes are often even more mysterious. There is little evidence of demographic or social investigation as a preliminary to policy-making. (Hayes, 1967: 93)

Hewitt, on the other hand, claimed that the pre-1968 system of local government could *not* be regarded as 'particularly inequitable' (Hewitt, 1981: 370). Unionists argued in response to charges of discrimination that they were greatly exaggerated. Nationalist councils, they claimed, were equally guilty of discrimination and such unfairness as took place was justified by the perceived disloyalty of the Catholic population to the British State. John Darby's comprehensive research on the period concluded that some discrimination charges were unsubstantiated and others exaggerated, but proven cases were sufficiently numerous to constitute 'a consistent and irrefutable pattern of deliberate discrimination against Catholics' (Darby, 1976: 43). This conclusion is also supported by Whyte (1983) who studied the period in detail.

Grievances concerning religious discrimination by some local authorities in employment and housing, and the manipulation of council boundaries for political purposes culminated in the civil rights protests of 1968 and the subsequent outbreak of civil disturbances. Budge and O'Leary (1973) in a study of Belfast Council made the general comment that:

> It is in fact the Unionist hegemony in local government which has been a major focus for the disturbances which began in 1968 and which persist. Given the circumstances from which it emerged and the religious hostilities which have supported it, Unionist predominance in local government could hardly fail to be criticised. (Budge and O'Leary, 1973: 173)

Protests came via the principal pressure group, the Northern Ireland Civil Rights Association (NICRA), which had six basic demands, four of them directly concerned with local government. These were:

- One man (*sic*), one vote.
- Removal of gerrymandered boundaries.
- Laws against discrimination by local authorities and the provision of machinery to deal with other complaints.
- Allocation of public housing on a points system.

The first civil rights march took place on 5 October 1968 and received worldwide publicity due to the violence which ensued. Their protest strategy proved successful in provoking a series of reforms initiated by the Stormont Government (in November 1968) and backed by British Prime Minister Harold Wilson and James Callaghan, Home Secretary. As Tomlinson (1980) remarked:

> It is at this moment that the seemingly separate trajectories of the politics of administrative reform and the growing extra-parliamentary anti-Unionist civil rights movement intersected. The transcendence of the Unionist state and the reform of local government merged as a single political issue. (Tomlinson, 1980: 109)

The government reform package indicated that it intended to complete a comprehensive review and modernisation of the local government structure by the end of 1971, to reform the franchise, including the abolition of the company vote, to encourage a points system for housing, and to appoint a Parliamentary Commissioner for Administration for regional government activity. Farrell (1976: 248) described the package as 'too little, too late; it was enough to outrage the loyalists without satisfying the civil rights movement'. In fact the package represented a substantial compromise by Northern Ireland's Prime Minister Terence O'Neill, but during 1968 law and order broke down and the situation became more polarised until eventually in August 1969 the British Government and its troops became directly involved.

To date there had been two White Papers, guidance on housing allocation and a firm government commitment to reform local government, including the franchise, yet violence continued and mounted. James Callaghan (British Home Secretary at the time) visited Northern Ireland and announced the creation of two joint working parties to investigate the allocation of houses by public authorities, the employment policies of public agencies and the possibility of setting up a Northern Ireland community relations programme. By October 1969 local government had been stripped of its responsibility for housing and a decision taken to create a centralised housing agency. This new body, the Northern Ireland Housing Executive, assumed control of all public housing in the Province. The most controversial function of local authorities was therefore removed, clearly as a result of political considerations.

Emasculated local government

The removal of housing from councils marked a radical departure from the existing system and introduced an entirely new factor in reshaping local government. For one thing, housing up to that point had been recognised by the Stormont Government as one of the more important functions entrusted to local authorities. Its removal undermined many of the assumptions upon which the proposals in the White Papers had been based. Housing was the local government function in which many councillors took great interest. A concerted housing programme by the new central housing authority required the provision of supporting services such as water, sewerage, roads and the prompt release of land. Thus, the decision to transfer housing responsibilities from local authorities called for a complete reappraisal of existing proposals for reshaping local government. John Oliver, then Permanent Secretary in the Ministry of Development, described what happened:

> A crucial decision was taken by ministers in October 1969, in consultation with James Callaghan, the British Home Secretary. This was to lift the whole subject of housing in all its forms out of the hands of local councils and the Housing Trust

and give it to a new statutory board. Everyone saw that whatever the merits of this decision it would tear the heart out of local government as we knew it and render it impossible to create a new system with anything approaching a full range of functions in the British or Irish tradition. (Oliver, 1978: 90)

Just prior to the 'crucial decision', referred to above, the Cameron Commission, set up to investigate the reasons for the outbreak of violence after the civil rights march, reported in September 1969. It found in the County Borough of Londonderry and in some district councils:

1. Inadequacy of housing provision by certain local authorities.
2. Unfair methods of allocation of houses built and let by some local authorities, in particular, refusals and omissions to adopt a points system in determining priorities and making allocations.
3. Misuse in certain cases of discretionary powers of allocation of houses in order to perpetuate unionist control of the local authority. (Disturbances in Northern Ireland, Cameron Report, 1969: paragraph 260)

In December 1969, Brian Faulkner, Minister of Development with overall responsibility for local government, appointed a high-powered review body under the independent chair of Patrick Macrory, a prominent businessman, to:

- Review existing published government proposals for reshaping local government in Northern Ireland.
- Examine any further proposals which may be made to the review body.
- Examine the consequences of the decision upon housing control and its implications for other services currently provided by local government.
- Advise upon the most efficient distribution of the relevant functions, on the role of public opinion and the number of local government areas. (Review Body on Local Government, 1970)

The Review Body was not, however, empowered to recommend precise boundaries for local authority areas. Tomlinson suggested that:

Macrory's task had already been 'depoliticised' to some extent by the decision on housing and by commitments to the abolition on plural voting and the introduction of universal adult suffrage. (Tomlinson, 1980: 113)

Indeed proposals had also been made to reorganise the health service and personal social services in a Stormont Green Paper in 1969 through a system of area boards. This represented a further constraint on Macrory whose final recommendations divided services into two categories: regional services requiring large administrative units, and district services suitable for small areas. The Stormont parliament, government and ministers would take responsibility for regional services and district councils would administer local services. The report listed 17 functions, in addition to housing which were

Figure 4.2 Northern Ireland's 26 district councils, 2009

currently provided wholly or partly by local authorities that would pass to regional control. These included services such as education, personal health, welfare and child care, planning, roads and water. This allocation left local authorities with matters of a purely local nature to administer.

Macrory recommended the establishment of 26 borough or district councils (see figure 4.2), the abolition of county councils and boroughs, and the setting up of appointed area boards to decentralise the administration of health and education services. The recommendations were subsequently passed into law under the Local Government (Northern Ireland) Act 1972. The review body accepted the abolition of the statutory divide between town and country in local government and thus supported the earlier proposals for unitary local authorities. Not more than 26 councils were recommended on the principle that local authorities should be small enough to provide for close local contact and to encourage democratic participation. The increase in the number of units from 17, in the 1969 White Paper proposal, to 26 may be seen as a reaction to increased control of those services such as housing, water-supply and sewerage, which required large authorities for their effective finance and organisation and to the suggestions of the Cameron Commission for greater democracy. Birrell and Murie (1980: 171) noted: 'Macrory's recommendations were very different from those contained in the 1967 and 1969 White Papers. The 1967 White Paper expressly rejected centralised forms of administration as depriving services of valuable elements of local interests and initiative'.

Mackintosh (1971) saw the main recommendations as predictable and influenced by the Wheatley Commission on Scottish local government with its broad classification of regional and district services. Having decided on 26 district councils based on the main centres of population, the controversial question of ward and council boundaries passed to a Boundary Commission established with that objective. The new boundaries were established, adult suffrage introduced and the voting system changed by the British Government to proportional representation and used for the first district council elections in May 1973. The new councils became executive on 1 October 1973 and the functions of former authorities which were regional in character were transferred to departments (as the Northern Ireland ministries became known) after the passing of the Northern Ireland Constitution Act 1973. The Act provided for a Northern Ireland Assembly and an Executive instead of a parliament and government.

District councils were given four key functions: ceremonial, executive, representative and consultative.

1. Ceremonial functions refer to the dignities and ceremonial traditionally associated with local government, such as allowing district councils to become boroughs, with the chairman retitled mayor.
2. Executive functions which councils provide: (a) regulatory services such as licensing cinemas, dance-halls, street trading, building regulations and environmental health inspection and (b) provision of certain services. These include: cleaning, refuse collection and disposal, burial grounds and crematoria, recreation facilities and tourist amenities.
3. Representative functions. Macrory recommended that local councillors should be represented on relevant bodies to express views on the provision and operation of major public services not under their charge. Thus education and library services were administered through five education and library boards with 40 per cent of the board members being local councillors appointed by the Department of Education (Northern Ireland) following nomination by their respective councils. A similar system existed for the health and personal social services, except that there were four area boards and 30 per cent councillor membership.
4. Consultative functions. District councils had to be consulted on matters

of general national interest and central government functions which affected their area such as planning applications, housing and roads.

Alexander in reviewing the reform period argued:

> Just as the reform proposals of the government of Northern Ireland in the 1960s were overtaken by events, so were the recommendations of Macrory overtaken by the abolition in 1972 of the devolved government of Northern Ireland and the introduction of direct rule from Westminster. (Alexander, 1982: 61)

The regional tier at Stormont anticipated by Macrory did not happen (referred to as the 'Macrory gap') and responsibility for regional services rested with the British Government working administratively through the Northern Ireland Office. In spite of the councils significantly reduced powers, local government elections since 1973 have been the focus of revitalised electoral competition based on proportional representation and universal adult suffrage. In 1973 there were 1,222 candidates for 526 seats compared with the previous local government elections in 1967 where the majority of seats were uncontested. The political composition of councils also reflected the proportional representation electoral system in that there were relatively few councils where one party had an overall majority and there is greater representation of minority parties (see tables 4.1 and 4.2 for local government election results from 1973 onwards). As Tomlinson (1980: 187) described it: 'the reforms have given rise to a great expression of political tendencies than was possible in the past'. Equally, however, stripping local government of key responsibilities (and the

Table 4.1 Northern Ireland local government elections since 1973: share of poll by political party (%)

Year	UUP	DUP	Ind. U	PUP/UDP	Alliance	SDLP	Sinn Féin	Con	Others
1973	17.0	4.3	23.2		13.7	13.4			28.4
1977	29.6	12.7	8.5		14.4	20.6			13.2
1981	26.5	26.6	4.2		8.9	17.5			15.3
1985	29.5	24.3	3.1		7.1	13.4	11.8		5.8
1989	31.4	17.7	3.9		6.8	21.2	11.2	1.1	7.0
1993	29.3	17.2	2.7		7.7	21.9	12.5	1.5	7.2
1997	27.8	15.6	2.5	2.2/1	6.6	20.7	16.9	1.0	5.7
2001	22.9	21.4	1.5	1.6	5.1	19.4	20.7		7.4
2005	18.0	29.6	0.1	0.7	5.0	17.4	23.2		6.0

Note: Key to political parties: UUP: Ulster Unionist Party; DUP: Democratic Unionist Party; Ind. U: Independent Unionists (assorted individuals); PUP/UDP: Progressive Unionist Party/Ulster Democratic Party (fringe loyalists); Alliance: Alliance Party; SDLP: Social Democratic and Labour Party; Sinn Féin; Con: Conservative Party; Others: assorted individuals.

Table 4.2 Northern Ireland local government elections since 1973: seats gained by political party

Year	UUP	DUP	Alliance	SDLP	Sinn Féin	Others	Total
1973	194	21	63	82		166	526
1977	175	71	70	114		96	526
1981	151	142	38	103		92	526
1985	190	142	34	101	59	40	566
1989	191	110	38	121	43	63	566
1993	197	103	44	127	51	60	582
1997	185	91	41	120	74	71	582
2001	154	131	28	117	108	44	582
2005	115	182	30	101	126	28	582

imposition of direct rule from Westminster) was the portent for a very long period where Northern Ireland experienced a democratic deficit. As Jenkins described it:

> Apart from what are little more than parish councils, Northern Ireland's all embracing public sector is ruled either personally by British Ministers or boards appointed by them. For 20 years (at the time of writing) no ruler of Northern Ireland has been elected by its people. In no reputable sense of the term is Northern Ireland a democracy. It is a colony. Its people react as colonial people normally react, by turning to the political extremes. (Jenkins, 1993: 16)

This may be an over-simplification of the role ascribed to the new councils but it nonetheless puts the reforms in context.

The politicisation of local government

Following the reorganisation of local government in 1973 some councils struggled to provide basic public services in the prevailing context of violence, bombings and shootings. Local government had been stripped of major functional responsibilities and was initially resistant to, and resentful of, its downgrading. Belfast Corporation had a staffing level of 15,000 prior to reorganisation which was reduced to 3,000 and seen by officials as an attack on the democratic process. One senior local government officer commented 'I think it is a pity for Northern Ireland that democracy is getting knocked, taking responsibility from people who need more not less' (Smith, 1973: 105). Hadden (1975: 10) also pointed to the 'widespread and growing disenchantment with the new local government structure'. He criticised the allocation of key services such as education, health and social welfare to regional boards because of their uncertain status between the Ministries and local councils. Hadden argued for a gradual return to general-purpose local government in the 26 new district councils with specific central controls to prevent a retreat to the sectarian discrimination which featured in some of the former local authorities. All but a few observers criticised reorganised local government and some acquiesced in the absence of anything better. Fitzgerald (1978), for example, obtained the views of senior politicians and management on the day-to-day operation of local government. Reflecting on their opinions she stated: 'this is an unrepresentative system. But the detached observer tends to conclude that it works and its introduction may have contributed towards the more peaceful state of affairs now evident in Northern Ireland' (Fitzgerald, 1978: 1079).

An assessment of the reorganised system of local government is offered by Birrell and Murie (1980: 155–190) who highlighted three features of councils' operation: the politicisation of local government; the councils' performance in providing services; and their consultative role, and concluded:

- It is difficult to assess whether reorganisation has produced a more efficient system of administration.
- The injection of the expertise and specialisation which was a key feature of the new system was achieved at the expense of public accountability and participation.
- The work of the Commissioner for Complaints and the reorganisation of local government would seem to ensure more impartial administration and provide safeguards against discrimination.

Connolly (1983: 12) was not impressed and argued that the absence of significant executive functions amongst councils contributed to the 'politics of irresponsibility'. This was endorsed by Kilmurray (1981: 13) who suggested that consigning councillors to the role of consultees on major public services could lead to influence without responsibility and the 'supremacy of the big mouth'. Councillors had no incentive to make temperate demands from the various statutory bodies with jurisdiction in their areas. Indeed they had a considerable incentive to decry the efforts of quangos and central government departments as being undemocratic and unresponsive to local needs. Connolly concluded:

> In short, the reduced powers of local government, together with the absence of a devolved parliament, have introduced a new conflictual dimension into Northern Ireland policy viz, the alienation of unionists from governmental structures . . . Members of the SDLP believe that many unionist dominated councils still do not act impartially. Unionists believe that the old system was equitable. (Connolly, 1983: 12)

In an overview Connolly argued that the reduction of powers within local government had *not* abated the community divisions and in some ways had increased them. What it *had* done was to reduce the range of possible conflicts in local government.

This view is also articulated by McConaghy who described what he termed the demise of local government in Northern Ireland. He pointed out that the Northern Ireland example had serious implications for all centralising states. Although the final collapse began with the Local Government Act 1972, the real turning point was the centralisation of housing under the Housing Executive Act 1971. As a result, there was a marked decline in financial and political accountability within Northern Ireland. Traditional local government was now almost extinct according to McConaghy. He quoted an official who said: 'the choice for Ulster has been limited democracy with stability or unlimited democracy without stability' (McConaghy, 1978: 138). Centralisation he claimed promoted new extremism and this was evident amongst councillors who pressed for political demands without executive power and responsibility: 'what can lead to irresponsible attitudes sometimes, is a tendency to support all constituents regardless, since central agencies bear the odium for adverse decisions . . . and the bill!' (McConaghy, 1978: 130).

Frustrations also grew among councillors, voiced through the unionist dominated Association of Local Authorities. The Vice President of the Association conveyed the feeling of limited progress since 1973:

> Northern Ireland in the past nine years has had a quasi or sham local government with truncated executive powers, and councillors endeavouring to mediate to their ratepayers and electors administrative decisions and policies from faceless bureaucrats about important and key functions that affect the daily lives of ordinary people. (Semple, 1982: 2)

Frustration and calls by unionists for increased powers in the early 1980s turned to anger and vitriolic attacks on central government over two highly significant factors which dominated local government from 1985 onwards. The first of these events was the election of 59 Sinn Féin councillors representing the political wing of the Provisional Irish Republican Army. Unionists perceived Sinn Féin's electoral strategy, the infamous 'ballot box and armalite' mantra, as a threatening new dimension in local government and they disrupted its operation to mark their displeasure. Some councils adjourned business and all 18 unionist controlled councils refused to carry our normal duties. Varying degrees of conflict ensued with occasional fist fights breaking out in council chambers over the presence of Sinn Féin.

The period witnessed an increasing intervention by the courts as a key strategy in resisting unionist tactics (Connolly and Knox, 1988). Both the Official Unionists and the Democratic Unionists accused central government of double standards by refusing to deal directly with Sinn Féin while at the same time expecting collaboration between parties in councils. The burgeoning local government protest against Sinn Féin was superseded by a hard-line campaign against the Anglo-Irish Agreement (November 1985). All unionist councils adjourned in protest and refused to strike district rates. The courts ordered several indicted councils to resume normal business and set a rate. The local government forum, by this stage, had become embroiled in a constitutional protest of defiance against the Agreement well beyond its remit. It remained at the forefront of politics through a series of clashes with central government and the courts.

New emergency legislation (Local Government Temporary Provisions Northern Ireland Order 1986) empowered the government to appoint commissioners when day-to-day services were at the point of breaking down. This was followed by high court fines against recalcitrant councils (Belfast £25,000 and Castlereagh £10,000) and legal censure of others (Lisburn, Antrim and Coleraine). In the face of such setbacks a gulf emerged between the two unionist parties accentuated by the defeat of a mass councillor resignation strategy proposed by the Democratic Unionist Party. Support for the protest dwindled and from early 1988 the strategy was moribund. By way of an olive branch to dispirited unionists, the government announced proposals aimed at councillors who espoused violence, in which those standing for election to local council would be required to declare that they will 'neither support nor assist' the activities of any banned organisation. Although primarily aimed at Sinn Féin it included anyone who openly supported a proscribed paramilitary organisation. The proposals aimed to address complaints from unionists that it was offensive to ask them to work in council chambers with Sinn Féin members who sought to justify the IRA's terrorist campaign. Local government came under pressure of various sorts related to the wider political context in Northern Ireland, an example of which was dissension over the Anglo-Irish Agreement. The reason for this is that councils were the only mechanism available to express the voice of local elected representatives and their constituents. Hence, at times of intense political conflict local government became the conduit for macro politics. Despite the limited range of functional responsibilities within the remit of councils, local government was for some time the only elected operational forum in Northern Ireland.

The local government elections of 1989 marked a turning point in council chambers, with a degree of moderation not unrelated to the decline in representation from the political extremes (see tables 4.1 and 4.2 above). From this stable political context an experiment in 'responsibility sharing' developed – this term evolved in deference to unionist sensitivities over the words 'power-sharing'. Dungannon District Council is credited with leading the way in rotating the council chair between two main political parties, the SDLP and UUP, although some councils (Down, Omagh, Newry & Mourne, for example) claim to have been doing this for years in a less high-profile manner. In addition, the Enniskillen bombing of November 1987 appears to have had a profound impact on local politicians. One observer noted that councillors 'felt the need to bring an end to sterile adversarial politics . . . and found in their opposition to political violence more in common than they had previously recognised' (Beirne, 1993: 7). In the wake of the 1989 local government elections, 11 local authorities appointed mayors/chairs and deputies from both political traditions. The power-sharing trend continued after the 1993 elections and there were encouraging signs of a climate of accommodation, conspicuously absent at the macro level (Knox, 1996). Even the more tempestuous councils (such as Belfast and Craigavon at that stage) boasted power-sharing arrangements. The 1997 local government elections produced Belfast's first nationalist Lord Mayor in its 150-year history and 12 councils, mainly nationalist controlled or hung, operated power-sharing arrangements.

Innovative local government

Despite the paucity of functional responsibilities, local government began to emerge as a serious player in a largely fragmented system of public administration in Northern Ireland. Two examples serve to highlight the innovative role which councils have played building a more inclusive society in Northern Ireland. An example of best practice in Belfast City Council is also included (see box 4.1).

Box 4.1 Belfast City Council best practice scheme

Belfast City Council (BCC) is the largest Council in Northern Ireland, employing more than 2,600 people and serving a population of 269,000. The Council's commitment to continuous improvement and excellence has been recognised through a number of awards and accreditations, including Investors in People, Charter Mark, ISO and the Mark of Excellence. The Council promoted several aspects of best practice working to include:

- *Operation Clean-up*: a highly successful Community Safety initiative which reduces and prevents criminal and anti-social behaviour by removing 'runaround' cars from public roads. Some 6,500 vehicles have been seized over a 3-year period, removing the enabler for

---

car-related crime and leading to a substantial reduction in the number of abandoned vehicles reported.
- *Women into Non-traditional Sectors*: Belfast City Council is leading the Women into Non-traditional Sectors (WINS) project to attract more women into jobs such as street cleansing, grounds maintenance, construction and driving. The project was able to access support from the European Social Fund and the Department for Employment and Learning under the EQUAL Community Initiative Programme for Northern Ireland. Belfast City Council is working in partnership with a number of organisations including Translink, the Northern Ireland Housing Executive, the Construction Industry Training Board, the Department for Employment and Learning, and Queen's University.
- *Step up to Learn*: It was recognised that some Belfast City Council staff had problems with reading and writing and had not benefited from access to formal qualifications. This has implications for service delivery, employee participation and inclusion. To help rectify this, Belfast City Council worked closely with the trade unions to introduce an essential skills programme.
- *Waste Collection*: Belfast City Council has recently introduced a new alternate week kerbside recycling collection. This has been extremely successful and a key contributory factor was the innovative communication strategy that the council deployed. A recent independent survey revealed that 84 per cent of customers were satisfied with their bin collection (78 per cent in 2004) while 74 per cent were satisfied with the doorstep recycling service. Only 1 per cent of responders were unaware of the changes to the recycling service. The data management and communication of the alternate week collection was lauded by the chair of the EU Eurocities conference in 2006 as a model for EU emerging states.

Source: Northern Ireland Best Practice Scheme, Department of Finance and Personnel, Reform Delivery Unit: Delivery and Innovation Unit (*Information Bulletin* 4: September 2008).

Partnerships

Local authorities became pivotal brokers in partnership arrangements designed to deliver European funded programmes (Greer *et al.* 1999). In 1995, the European Union launched the Special Support Programme for Peace and Reconciliation, a 300 mecu (£215m) package designed to reinforce progress towards a peaceful and stable society following the cease-fires. The ways in which the European initiative suggested this could be achieved were by supporting projects in economic development and employment, promoting urban and rural regeneration, developing cross border co-operation and extending social inclusion (European Commission, 1995). The European Commission expressed a preference that funded initiatives should be embedded in local participative structures through the creation of new partnerships. District partnerships, representing each of the 26 district council areas, were set up in 1996 comprising nominees from the community/voluntary sectors, public bodies, trade unions and business to advance the objectives of the programme.

After some initial problems associated in particular with fears around usurping the role of elected bodies and representatives, local authorities demonstrated a readiness to both enter into partnerships and make them succeed. The ideological baggage which participants brought to the process was left outside meetings. In part too, however, the willingness to entertain 'responsibility sharing' had extended to involving as many people/sectors as possible in the decision-making processes of district partnerships – the emergence of participative democracy in Northern Ireland. The creation of district partnerships therefore provided a mechanism which mobilised elected representatives, community and voluntary sector nominees, with participants from business and public bodies. Local government played a key role in the success of this groundswell of collaborative community energy not unconnected to the compromise which was needed to shift political hardliners at the macro level. The (then) direct rule Minister for the Environment, Lord Dubs, offered a useful summary of the contribution made by district partnerships:

> The District Partnership Sub-Programme is to my mind one of the most encouraging and worthwhile initiatives in recent years. I have no doubt that the lessons learnt from the implementation of the sub-programme will be invaluable to other regions throughout Europe wishing to devise a bottom up participative response to tackling difficult issues such as community divisions and social exclusion. The district partnerships work for the reconciliation of the people of Northern Ireland. They are bridging the gap between unionist and nationalist and between advantaged and disadvantaged. They seek to unify rather than separate, begin dialogue that will bridge differences, replace misconceptions with trust and consensus, and seek solutions to problems that appear insurmountable. (Dubs, 1997: 2)

District partnerships, in which councils played a key role, were able to forge agreement, consent and, above all, cross-community engagement. In that sense the level of spending, marginal in the context of the public sector budget for Northern Ireland, was almost incidental. What proved important was the process of changing attitudes, creating social inclusion and capacity building. Local government was at last emerging from the bear pit of sectarianism (Knox, 1998).

Community relations

Local councils had been actively involved in community development work for some time but in 1989 a number of local authorities responded to an initiative promoted by central government to become involved in improving community relations in their areas. The Central Community Relations Unit (CCRU) in central government invited councils to participate in a programme aimed at developing cross-community contact and co-operation, promoting greater mutual understanding and increasing respect for different cultural traditions. The CCRU offered 75 per cent grant-aid for the employment of community relations staff by councils, the provision of financial support for appropriate cross-community activities, and assistance with the development of local heritage and cultural activities.

Councils responded to the CCRU invitation with varying degrees of enthusiasm. The first council (Dungannon) joined the scheme in February 1990 but it was not until 1993 that all 26 local authorities were involved in the initiative which, at the outset, received funding for three years. Despite the staggered starting pattern of councils, the inexperience of newly appointed community relations officers and the scope of the task, funding sources were renewed and the programme extended following a favourable evaluation. Given the conditions associated with joining the initiative, for example agreement on a cross-political party basis to participate, vesting responsibility for community relations in local councils was, from a government perspective, a way of promoting consensus at the political level and in turn, by example, in the community. The community relations remit put consensus firmly on the policy agenda of councils which was symbolically important in making progress on the wider political front. Moreover, an active involvement in this area, given the chequered history of discrimination and sectarianism in local government, added to the emerging climate of cross-party co-operation and stability within which councils demonstrated a more responsible approach to an incremental increase in devolved powers. The community relations programme was subsequently replaced with a *Good Relations Challenge Programme* to reflect legislative changes in the form of the Race Relations Order (Northern Ireland) 1997, and the Northern Ireland Act 1998 which places a legislative duty upon councils to: 'have due regard to the desirability of promoting good relations between persons of different religious belief, political opinion or racial group'. Local government has been at the vanguard in promoting community or good relations work – an unlikely proponent of this function given its history of divisiveness.

Table 4.3 Local government in Northern Ireland: current functions

Direct services:	Representative role:[a]	Consultative role:
• Advice and information • Arts and entertainment • Building regulations • Burial grounds and crematoria • Civic ceremonials • Community services • Dog control • Economic development • Harbours • Health inspection • Leisure and community centres • Licensing • Markets and fairs • Museums and art galleries • Parks and open spaces • Pollution control • Public conveniences • Recreation grounds and services • Refuse collection and disposal • Street naming and cleansing • Tourism development • Consumer safety • Community relations • Food standards • War memorials	• Education • Health and social care • District policing partnerships • EU partnerships • Community safety partnerships	• Water • Infrastructure/ utilities • Roads • Planning

Note: [a] The representative role of local government is changing in some functional areas (e.g. health and education) as the Review of Public Administration is implemented.

All change

Functions

Local government in Northern Ireland is currently responsible for a limited range of public services and therefore a relatively small amount of public expenditure. Councils are also, by standards in Great Britain, relatively small units of populations (see tables 4.3 and 4.4 respectively). The functional responsibilities of councils will change from May 2011 following reorganisation, but to a limited extent. The Northern Ireland Local Government Association (NILGA) estimates that the new functions will require about a 25 per cent increase in council budgets and 12 per cent increase in council

Table 4.4 Councils by population, spending and domestic rates 2007/08

District	Population	Net expenditure (£)	Domestic rate (£)
Antrim	50,530	15,852,995	0.2875
Ards	75,279	16,111,706	0.2409
Armagh	55,755	14,505,284	0.3174
Ballymena	60,738	15,306,702	0.2874
Ballymoney	28,730	6,032,134	0.2768
Banbridge	44,778	10,358,975	0.3003
Belfast	267,999	107,879,703	0.2423
Carrickfergus	39,175	9,364,157	0.2986
Castlereagh	65,665	12,835,602	0.1871
Coleraine	56,565	14,458,260	0.2506
Cookstown	34,102	7,804,487	0.2444
Craigavon	84,679	23,116,579	0.3395
Derry	107,296	30,754,000	0.3365
Down	67,436	16,054,247	0.2873
Dungannon	50,747	11,779,024	0.2284
Fermanagh	59,712	11,024,867	0.2032
Larne	31,067	8,717,488	0.3236
Limavady	34,147	7,750,773	0.3335
Lisburn	111,521	23,728,543	0.2275
Magherafelt	41,819	7,425,777	0.2214
Moyle	16,515	4,635,785	0.3245
Newry & Mourne	91,572	21,358,841	0.2672
Newtownabbey	80,834	21,773,983	0.2832
North Down	78,272	18,522,282	0.2235
Omagh	50,730	12,182,525	0.3243
Strabane	38,745	8,639,468	0.2937
Total	1,724,408	457,974,187	0.2677

Source: Department of the Environment (Northern Ireland) – District Rate Statistics 2007/08

staffing. This suggests a (new) annual net expenditure for councils of around £520m out of a total devolved budget of £8b – almost 7 per cent of the public purse. Despite claims contained in the Review of Public Administration to be strengthening local government, in functional terms council responsibilities are still very limited.

Councils are involved in the development and implementation of community safety strategies (with the Northern Ireland Office) and work with the police on issues such as drug, alcohol abuse and the provision of youth clubs and other social amenities to reduce the potential for crime. Local councils also have a central role in the District Policing Partnerships and, more recently, emergency planning. Councils play a key role in dispensing EU funds normally within cluster groups. There is an increasing emphasis on improving local environmental performance, particularly in waste management in the context of diminishing landfill capacity and restrictions on construction of new incineration plants. Some councils have initiated programmes to reduce overall energy consumption and to meet a growing proportion of their energy requirements from renewable sources of energy such as wind and solar power.

Finance

Northern Ireland up until 2007 operated a rating system or a property based tax designed to raise revenue for local services. The valuation of all rateable property was fixed on the basis of rental value. The net annual value (NAV) was the yearly rent for which the property could be let, assuming that it was vacant and that the tenant agreed to pay the rates, kept the property in repair and was responsible for its insurance. The rateable value is generally the NAV but may be varied by statute in the case of property deemed exempt either partially or in full.

Raising revenue for 'local services' is complicated in Northern Ireland due to the fact that councils do not have responsibility for such basic functions as: education, housing, personal social services, roads and water. Because of this, the rates levy in Northern Ireland comprises two key elements:

- *Regional rate*: this finances those local services that are not administered by councils and is struck by the Department of Finance and Personnel at a uniform rate for all councils. While non-domestic ratepayers pay the full rate poundage, domestic ratepayers enjoy a reduction known as the domestic rate aid grant.
- *District rate*: varies from one council area to another and finances those local services that are directly administered by local authorities. On average around 65 per cent of a district council's income is met from the district rate. As a result of revaluation of domestic properties in 1996 district councils were required to strike a separate rate for domestic and non-domestic sectors.
- The regional and district rates are both collected by the Land & Property Services Agency and the product of the district rates is paid over to each council (Sources: CIPFA, Northern Ireland Local Government Association, Local Government Staff Commission, and National Association of Councillors).

Local councils have long objected to the fact that because these two rates are collected in a single rates demand to their constituents, local government assumes responsibility or blame for the regional element of the rates (as well as the district rate) yet has no control over increases in the former. Hence councils may feel they have been prudent in service provision and public spending as reflected in the district rate element but cannot hold central government to account for increases in the regional rate. Moreover, there has been much debate and controversy over which centrally provided services the regional rate pays for and how expenditure is calculated and passed on to councils in the form of the district rate.

Following a rating review, the system changed in 2007 from rental valuations, as outlined above, to an individual assessment of the capital value of every residential property in Northern Ireland using sales evidence from the housing market. A discrete capital value system is used, involving the application of a single tax rate to an individual assessment of each property. The capital value of each domestic property was assessed by the Valuation and Lands Agency through a combination of information already held on each property, outdoor visual inspections and sales evidence. This system contrasts with the English system of banding, where households are allocated to one of a number of different bands according to their capital value. The band determines the amount of council tax to be paid, with all households within the same band paying the same amount. Legislation requires, among other things, the maintenance and updating of the valuation list. That list is based on each of the 26 district council areas, sub-divided into wards with properties arranged street by street in alphabetical order and shows the net annual value of all properties. Ratepayers have the right to inspect the list and extract information.

Revenue expenditure needed by district councils in Northern Ireland to support day-to-day running costs of services and to service loan charges is currently funded from a number of sources: district rates revenue, general exchequer grant or equalisation grant, specific grants, and fees and charges.

- *District rate revenue from domestic and non-domestic properties*: by far the most significant source of revenue is the district rate met by the collection of rates from the authority's ratepayers. The proportion of the rates bill that is used to pay for the local council's services is known as the 'district rate'.
- *General exchequer grant*: central government (through the Department of the Environment) makes a general contribution towards the overall net revenue costs of council services. The amount of general grant received varies significantly between individual councils and comprises two parts: the derating element which compensates councils for loss of income from derated properties; and the resources element which is paid to councils

whose rateable value per head of population falls below a standard determined each year by the Department of the Environment.
- *Specific revenue based government grants:* sometimes government departments make a contribution to the running costs of services. An example of such assistance would be the community relations grant towards the cost of employing a Community Relations Officer and providing a programme of cross-community events.
- *Fees and charges:* these represent monies raised by the authority itself charging for some of its services. Examples would include admission charges to leisure centres, building inspection fees, trade waste collection charges, and catering franchises.

See an example of income sources for councils' expenditure in 2007/08 (table 4.5 and figure 4.3)

In order to strike the district rate, each council draws up detailed estimates of revenue expenditure and income for each incoming financial year,

Table 4.5 Council income sources, 2007/08

	£ (m)	%
Income: specific grants, fees and charges	126.2	21.2
General grant	44.4	7.4
District rate revenue	401.6	67.2
Transfers, reserves	25.3	4.2
Net operating expenditure	597.5	100

Source: Department of the Environment (Northern Ireland), District Rate Statistics 2007/08.

Figure 4.3 Councils' income, 2007/08

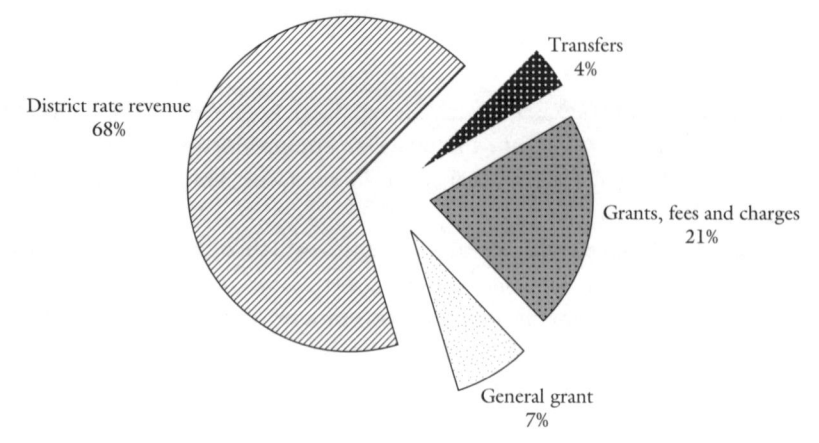

- District rate revenue 68%
- Transfers 4%
- Grants, fees and charges 21%
- General grant 7%

which runs from 1 April to 31 March. These documents are referred to as the 'annual estimates' and council officials spend a great deal of time in preparing the detail of these financial data. The annual estimates serve two purposes: they enable the council to calculate the district rate income which it will need; and they serve as detailed budgets of revenue income and expenditure. Each council must fix its district rate not later than 15 February each year. Councils may also carry forward a reserve surplus on the annual accounts to cater for unanticipated demand. In addition, the council may make contributions to, or allocations from, a repairs and renewals fund. The use of such reserve funding can assist councils in their financial planning. Councils also have the power to borrow but long-term borrowing must fulfil specific criteria and requires Department of the Environment approval.

Following the restoration of devolution (2007) in Northern Ireland the (then) Finance Minister Peter Robinson, froze the regional rate increase for domestic properties in Northern Ireland at their current level for a three-year period (the regional rate has therefore been fixed at no increase until 2011/2012) and deferred the introduction of highly unpopular water charges. He also pegged the increase in the non-domestic regional rate to the rate of inflation to ensure no increase in real terms for two years. With increasing pressure from the Treasury for UK-wide efficiency savings it remains unclear just how long the Northern Ireland Executive can continue with this pledge to the electorate and businesses faced with the impact of the global economic downturn.

Reorganisation

The Review of Public Administration launched in June 2002, and described in some detail in chapter 3, includes major changes to local government. The 'final' decisions of the review announced by the (then) Secretary of State, Peter Hain, in the *Better Government for Northern Ireland* (2006) were revisited by the incoming devolved government Minister, Arlene Foster who embarked on 'a review of the review'. She announced her vision for local government to the Northern Ireland Assembly in March 2008 as follows:

> Our vision is of a strong, dynamic local government that creates vibrant, healthy, prosperous, safe and sustainable communities that has the needs of all citizens at its core. Central to that vision is the provision of high-quality, efficient services that respond to people's needs and continuously improve over time. That vision resonates with the Executive's *Programme for Government* and its strategic priorities. It also reflects the strong desire that central and local government should work in partnership to deliver the *Programme for Government* and the vision for local government. (Foster, 2008)

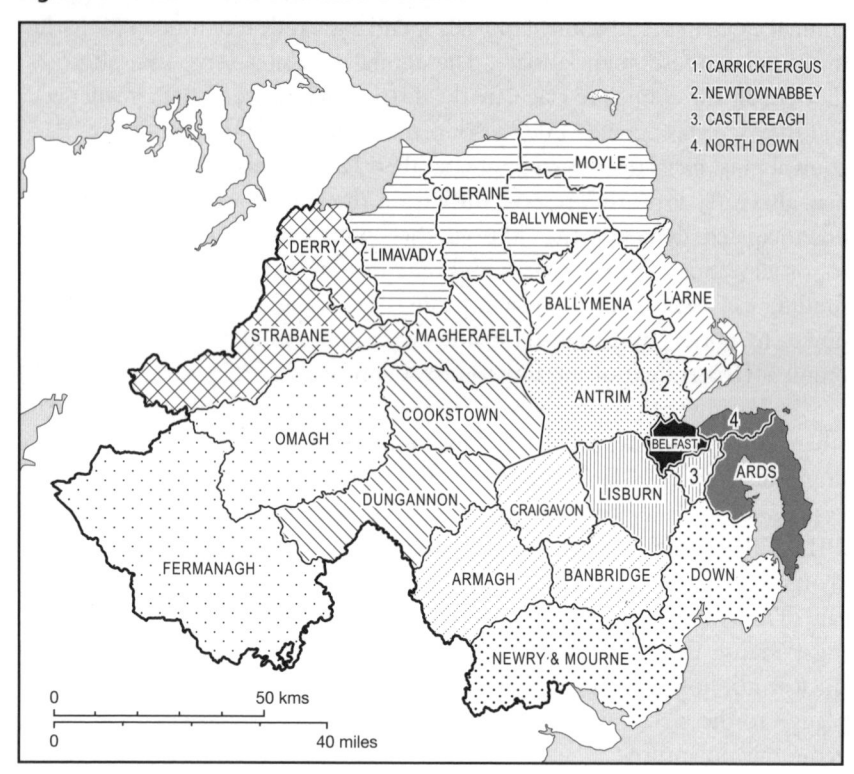

Figure 4.4 The 11 new councils from 2011

The main changes contained in her announcements were as follows:

- The rationalisation in the number of local authorities in Northern Ireland from 26 to 11, effective from May 2011 (see figure 4.4 and table 4.6). The new council areas which combine several existing councils incorporating changes recommended by the Boundaries Commission.
- The transfer of functions from central to local government will include: local development plan functions, development control and enforcement; local public realm aspects of roads functions including streetscaping; town and city centre environmental improvements; street lighting; off-street parking; urban regeneration and community development delivery functions including those associated with physical development, area based regeneration (such as Neighbourhood Renewal) along with some community development programmes and support for the voluntary and community sectors; housing related functions; and a number of

Table 4.6 Councils merging

Existing council clusters	Proposed new councils	Ward changes
Belfast City Council	Belfast City Council	60
North Down and Ards Borough Councils	North Down and Ards District Council	40
Down District Council and Newry and Mourne District Council	Newry City, Mourne and Down District Council	41
Craigavon Borough Council, Armagh City and District Council, and Banbridge District Council	Armagh City, Banbridge and Craigavon District Council	41
Lisburn City Council and Castlereagh Borough Council	Lisburn City and Castlereagh District Council	40
Antrim Borough Council and Newtownabbey Borough Council	Antrim and Newtownabbey District Council	40
Ballymena Borough Council, Larne Borough Council, and Carrickfergus Borough Council	Mid and East Antrim District Council	40
Moyle District Council, Ballymoney Borough Council, Coleraine Borough Council and Limavady Borough Council	Causeway Coast and Glens District Council	40
Magherafelt District Council, Cookstown District Council, and Dungannon and South Tyrone Borough Council	Mid Ulster District Council	40
Omagh District Council and Fermanagh District Council	Fermanagh and Omagh District Council	40
Derry City Council and Strabane District Council	Derry City and Strabane Regional Council	40
26 existing district councils	11 new councils	Overall reduction in wards and councillors from 582 to 462

functions associated with driving forward local economic development, local tourism and local arts, sports and leisure (current functions of local government are set out in table 4.3).
- The creation of new community planning and well-being powers for local government.
- Statutory governance arrangements.
- A further review will be carried out 12 months after the new councils become operational.

The timeline for the new changes is as follows:

- *Spring 2009*: Local Government Miscellaneous Provisions Bill
- *July 2009*: Outcomes of Boundaries Commissioner report accepted by Minister for the Environment
- *July 2009 – July 2010*: District Electoral Area Commissioner report
- *Spring 2011*: Local Government Restructuring Bill
- *May 2011*: Elections to the new 11 councils and new councils appointed
- *2009–2011*: Running alongside these activities will be a series of modernisation activities.

Implementation structures

Structures to support the implementation process have been agreed – a Strategic Leadership Board, 3 Policy Development Panels, 11 Transition Committees, a Communications Forum, a Joint Secretariat and officer advisory support structures (see figure 4.5).

The Strategic Leadership Board is a cross-party group of politicians supported by three chief executives of councils in an advisory role. The Strategic Leadership Board was established to give political leadership to the Review of Public Administration in local government. The Board is chaired by the

Figure 4.5 Review of public administration implementation structures, 2009

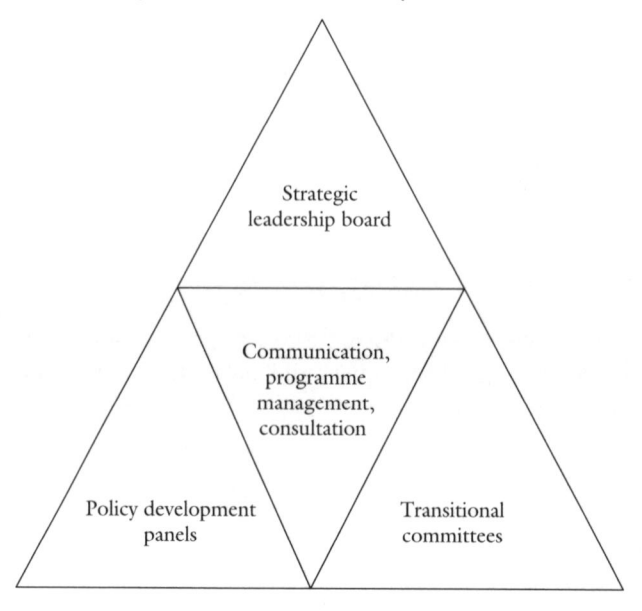

Minister of the Environment and the President of the Northern Ireland Local Government Association.

There are three policy development panels headed by cross-party local councillors and supported by local government and civil service advisors:

1. *Governance panel*: considers central/local relations and community planning. This panel has set up a capacity building work group of officials to develop a comprehensive training programme for local government and transferring function employees, and elected members. It has also developed an ethical standards framework for local government and the roll-out details of community planning.
2. *Service delivery panel*: with responsibility for developing strategies in: customer services; information systems; shared services; procurement; and a service delivery and performance improvement framework.
3. *Structural reform panel*: examines human resources; capacity building; finance; estates; regional and sub-regional design. This panel has established a human resources group of officials to take forward negotiation and consultation on all human resource related issues.

In addition, transitional committees have been established between cluster councils which will amalgamate to facilitate the re-organisation process. This will include the transfer of some 1,100 staff and £116m of expenditure from central to local government, according to the Minister of the Environment. They will ensure that the new councils are in a position to take full executive responsibility for services in May 2011 (immediately following the local government elections in that month). The elections to the 11 new local authorities will coincide with the next Assembly elections. New governance arrangements with appropriate checks and balances will be developed and a severance package made available to long serving councillors.

Stronger local government?

Local government in Northern Ireland emerged from a period of bitter sectarian entrenchment to become a model of voluntary power-sharing arrangements long before the present mandatory coalition in the devolved Assembly at Stormont. It might be argued that councils provided the local pilot for power-sharing at the macro-level where a significant number of councillors 'double job' as Members of the Legislative Assembly. Given the relatively minor functions which local authorities provide, power-sharing or 'responsibility sharing' was, and remains, easier at council level. Yet local government offered a non-threatening forum in which politicians across the political divide could forge relationships on issues of common concern to their electorate. Councillors were often the first port of call for constituents on matters over which local government had no direct control. There were also times in the tumultuous political history of Northern Ireland when local government remained the only democratic forum in place. As an elected forum, councils therefore played a vital role in fostering political relationships at grassroots level and an access point for the public in seeking advice, information and redress on public services provided by central government departments.

Is the implementation of the findings from the Review of Public administration likely to lead to stronger local government in Northern Ireland? Four of the original guiding principles outlined in the review were: strong local government, subsidiarity, equality and good relations, and common boundaries. It is difficult to find evidence that any of these inform the outworking of the review. Local government has been given relatively few additional functions; devolution has resulted in centripetal tendencies with power concentrated in Stormont rather that local government; the amalgam of some councils could exacerbate community relations; and the idea of common boundaries once hailed as a huge advantage for coherence in service delivery is now unworkable in an 11-council model.

Although the Lyons Inquiry in England warned against focusing only on the range of services for which councils are responsible as a true measure of its importance, the paltry range of functions even under a reformed system of local government in Northern Ireland is difficult to ignore. If, as Lyons suggests, the new conception of the role of local government needs to go beyond merely considering functions, to reflect the well-being and place-shaping agenda, it might be argued that giving councils in Northern Ireland statutory responsibility for community planning and well-being will provide such an opportunity. Yet, in reality councils need to have a certain critical mass of services if they are to fulfil their proposed leadership role in the community planning process. How is this facilitated by merely tinkering at the margins with the functions of local government under the Review of Public Administration? Given local government's emasculated starting point, those transferred functions under the Review of Pubic Administration do little to bolster support for the sector which will remain the poor relation at the community planning table.

One of the key constraints identified by Lyons in creating a modern local government is the high degree of central control over local government. The impact of the Review of Public Administration for local government is centralisation writ large. Even more controversially it demonstrates regulatory capture of the reform agenda by civil servants unhappy to concede, from the outset, the loss of functional responsibilities from their departments. Naturally devolved government Ministers also want to exercise power and influence in their new roles and there is a reluctance to strengthen local government at the expense of their departments. Their electoral popularity is not enhanced by shifting functions to local government. Ministerial careers are not built on stripping their departments of functions.

All of the above would suggest that rather than supporting the principle of subsidiarity, the consequences of the Review of Public Administration for local government is contrary to its underpinning rationale which was a two-tier model, based on a regional and sub-regional tier of public administration. The former was 'to develop and shape policy and legislation, and set strategic objectives for services' (the Assembly, Executive and central departments). The latter would provide service delivery (strong local government, health bodies and other sub-regional bodies). It now seems that central departments are unwilling to delegate powers to local government for service delivery. Initial hopes for a strong local government in Northern Ireland have crumbled. This is the most unfortunate outcome of a process which commenced in June 2002 with the expressed hope that it was 'an opportunity of a generation to put in place a modern, accountable, effective system of public administration that can deliver a high quality set of public services to our citizens' (Trimble, 2002). The reform agenda has been seized by senior civil servants who are now driving the process, keen to protect the functions in their departments. New Ministers in turn, who want to gain public approval for their performance in office, are reluctant to lose functions from their portfolios. In short, for local government the Review of Public Administration has been a prolonged, fudged public sector reform agenda shaped to a large extent by the vested interests of civil servants rather than a citizen focused outward facing reform process.

Local government has emerged from the review as a small stakeholder in the overall governance of Northern Ireland but clinging to the hope that it can exert influence well above its functional weight through community planning, the power of well-being and a regulated relationship with central government. Whether this will happen in the shape of 11 councils with a marginal increase in powers remains to be seen post-local government reorganisation from May 2011 onwards. Political parties have expressed a desire to see the removal of the dual mandate which is likely to impact negatively on local government. Double jobbers will want to opt for the much better paid and more high profile positions in the Assembly (and Westminster). This will leave a political capacity gap in local government. It is difficult to see how professionals could be encouraged to stand for political office in the new councils given the portfolio of services proposed. Councils in Northern

Ireland attracted the disparaging comment of having responsibility for 'baths, bins, births and burials'. This was to grossly understate the role which councils played in Northern Ireland. The Review of Public Administration has however done little to dispel the myth that local government remains the poor relation of a dominant civil service which has captured and driven the change agenda in its favour.

5
Non-departmental public bodies

The current arrangements were developed over the past 35 years to deliver services and deal with problems as they arose. The approach was that, when a service was needed, a new body was created. This was done because it was felt that, in certain circumstances, there was much to be gained by having arrangements operating at arms length from government, or that expertise was needed that could not be accessed within government. The result was the current plethora of organisations, most of which have a very narrow remit. While this has enabled organisations to focus on specific problems and services, it had resulted in fragmentation of service delivery and been expensive in terms of overheads. As we all know, narrow administrative silos are not a good way of responding effectively to people's needs. A more joined-up approach is required and that will be helped by reducing the number of public bodies involved in delivery public services. (Former Secretary of State for Northern Ireland, Peter Hain, 21 March 2006b)

Definition and Scope

Before looking at the detail of non-departmental public bodies it is important at the outset to understand how they are defined. The term 'non-departmental public body' (NDPB) has been in existence since 1980 when it was coined by Sir Leo Pliatsky in his *Report on Non Departmental Public Bodies*. A non-departmental public body is defined as:

> A body which has a role in the processes of national Government, but is not a government department or part of one, and which accordingly operates to a greater or lesser extent at arm's length from Ministers. (Cabinet Office, 2008b: 3)

This definition comes with the following rider: non-departmental public bodies have also been referred to as 'quangos' – quasi-autonomous non government organisations. There is no commonly agreed definition of what the term 'quango' means and it is often used to include local bodies such as universities, research bodies or housing associations to which the government gives grants. In addition, the term is misleading as NDPBs, for example, are governmental rather than non-governmental organisations (Department of Finance and Personnel, 2007: 2.2). The equivalent definition used in the Northern Ireland context is given as follows:

> A public body is not part of a government department, but carries out its function to a greater or lesser extent at arm's length from central government, although Ministers are ultimately responsible for the activities of the public bodies sponsored by their departments. (Office of the First Minister and deputy First Minister, undated: 5)

There are five types of NDPBs:

- *Executive NDPBs*, typically established in statute and carrying out executive, administrative, regulatory and/or commercial functions. Examples include the Northern Ireland Housing Executive, Northern Ireland Tourist Board, and Sports Council for Northern Ireland (see table 5.1).
- *Advisory NDPBs*, provide independent, expert advice to Ministers on a wider range of issues. Examples include Drainage Council, Council for Nature Conservation and the Countryside, and Historic Buildings Council (see table 5.1).
- *Tribunal NDPBs* have jurisdiction in a specialised field of law. Examples include the Fair Employment Tribunal, Northern Ireland Industrial Court and Planning Appeals Commission.
- *Independent monitoring boards* of prisons, immigration removal centres and immigration holding rooms, formerly known as 'boards of visitors', these are independent 'watchdogs' of the prison system.
- In addition, in Northern Ireland there are *various uncategorised bodies* such as the Community Relations Council and the Senate of the Queen's University, Belfast.

There are several reasons given for the establishment of non-departmental public bodies operating at arm's length from ministers. First, NDPBs have a degree of independence which allows them to offer impartial advice and provide expertise on technical and scientific matters that may have ethical and/or funding repercussions (e.g. Commission for Victims and Survivors of the conflict or Mental Health Commission for Northern Ireland). Second, tribunals and other quasi-judicial bodies are established to facilitate separation between the decision-making body and appeals against those decisions. Third, quangos can be more flexible and responsive to particular needs

Table 5.1 Types of public body and main features

Executive non-departmental public bodies:

- are set up by Ministers to carry out administrative, commercial, executive or regulatory functions on behalf of the government;
- are legally incorporated and have their own legal identity. This means that they are established by legislation, by Royal Charter, under the Royal Prerogative, or incorporated under Companies (Northern Ireland) Order 1986;
- employ their own staff;
- are allocated their own budgets;
- are not Crown bodies and do not have Crown status (apart from the few exceptions where the NDPB is specifically afforded Crown status e.g. Health and Safety Executive for Northern Ireland);
- appointments to the boards of the bodies are made by Ministers or by departments. Some may be made by the bodies themselves;
- ministers are ultimately answerable for the performance of the bodies and for their continued existence, e.g. ministers/departments have the power (subject to Assembly approval if necessary) to wind the bodies up.

Advisory non-departmental public bodies:

- are established by ministers, or departments, to provide independent expert advice or to provide input into the policy-making process;
- do not usually have staff but are supported by staff from their sponsoring department;
- do not usually have their own budget, as costs incurred come within the department's expenditure;
- are formal bodies with defined membership and clear terms of reference;
- meet on a regular basis (at least once a year);
- are standing bodies (i.e. in existence for more than twelve months);
- are not part of a department or agency, or part of some other organisation;
- appointments to the bodies are made by ministers or by officials on behalf of ministers; some may be made by the bodies themselves;
- those appointed to the body are independent of government and drawn from outside the public sector (a body made up of more than two-thirds public servants is unlikely to be classified as a NDPB); and
- ministers are ultimately answerable for the performance of the bodies and for their continued existence.

Source: Department of Finance and Personnel (2007) *Public Bodies: A Guide for Northern Ireland Departments.*

and circumstances than government departments or agencies because they operate as separate legal entities. This legal status entitles executive NDPBs to: make decisions in an autonomous way; enter into contracts; own assets and dispose of them; employ staff; make payments from their own bank accounts; and draw up accounts (Department of Finance and Personnel, 2008).

Government policy on NDPBs is provided in guidance notes to Northern Ireland departments. The main principles are that:

- The function of the NDPB is in line with Departmental/Government objectives.
- A new NDPB should only be set up where it can be demonstrated that this is the most appropriate and cost-effective means of carrying out the given function.
- NDPBs should be accountable to the Northern Ireland Assembly and to the public for the way in which they carry out their functions, i.e. through their Annual Report and Accounts.
- The relationship between each NDPB and its sponsor department must be clearly defined in a way which supports the appropriate degree of delegation and independence of the NDPB, while assuring the accountable minister and department that financial management arrangements ensure propriety, regularity and value for money, and that risks will be managed.
- All NDPBs should be reviewed regularly to ensure that the functions of the body are still required; and if so, if they are still best undertaken by the NDPB.
- Bodies which have completed their tasks or are no longer needed should be wound up. (Department of Finance and Personnel, 2007, 2.3)

In setting up a public body, departments are advised to ensure that they strike the right balance between (1) enabling the minister to fulfil his or her responsibilities to the Assembly and (2) giving the public body the desired degree of independence. The balance will depend largely on the nature of each public body's functions and on the reasons for distancing these from government. Conferring functions on a public body involves recognition that a degree of independence from departments (in carrying out those functions) is appropriate. Nevertheless, ministers may be answerable to the Assembly for the failure to take controls that are necessary or advisable, especially in the case of a public body which is to receive public funds. Ministers may also be answerable if, having taken responsibility by establishing such controls, the department fails to use the controls properly (Department of Finance and Personnel, 2007, 3.10)

The above statement by the (then) Secretary of State for Northern Ireland, Peter Hain, captures the approach taken by the Direct Rule government to reduce the number of non-departmental public bodies. His announcement was part of the wider Review of Public Administration which concentrated on major reforms in local government, health and education aimed at saving in excess of £200m per year through cutting waste and strengthening front-line services in Northern Ireland. Overall, the Review of Public Administration, including areas of local government, health and education aimed to reduce public bodies from 154 to 75, a cut of over half. This was a bold claim to cull the number of public bodies, the details of which are set out in table 5.2.

Table 5.2 Decisions on public bodies: review of public administration

Executive public bodies	
Northern Ireland Housing Executive	A range of non-core functions will transfer to local government
Invest NI	Local economic development functions transferring to local government
NI Tourist Board	To incorporate the NI Events Company and local tourism functions transferring to local government
Fisheries Conservancy Board	Functions transferring to Department of Culture, Arts and Leisure
NI Museums Council	Functions transferring to local and central government
Arts Council of NI	Some funding to transfer to local government
Sports Council for NI	Some funding to become responsibility of local government
Enterprise Ulster	Abolish
Construction Industry Training Board	Amalgamate with Construction Skills Sector Skills Council
Livestock & Meat Commission	Incorporate the functions of the Pig Production Development Committee
Agricultural Research Institute of NI	Functions transferring to new Agri-food Biosciences Institute
Pig Production Development Committee	Functions transferring to Livestock & Meat Commission
NI Fishery Harbour Authority	Functions transferring to local government
Rural Development Council	Functions transferring to local government and policy role to central government
Agricultural Wages Board	Abolish
Local Government Staff Commission	Functions transferring to local government when new councils are established
Central Services Agency	Functions transferring to HSS structures
NI Practice and Education Council for Nursing and Midwifery	Functions transferring to Health and Social Services Authority
NI Medical and Dental Training Agency	Functions transferring to Health and Social Services Authority
Mental Health Commission for NI	Functions transferring to the Regulation and Quality Improvement Authority
Fire Authority for NI	Transfer to local government as a shared operational service
NI Events Company	Functions transferring to NI Tourist Board

Table 5.2 (continued)

Advisory public bodies	
Disability Living Allowance Advisory Board	Functions will transfer to the equivalent Board in Great Britain, whose remit will be extended
Drainage Council	Functions transferring to new Environment Agency – subject to the outcome of the review of environmental governance
Council for Nature, Conservation and the Countryside	Functions transferring to new Environment Agency – subject to the outcome of the review of environmental governance
Historic Buildings Council	Functions transferring to new Environment Agency – subject to the outcome of the review of environmental governance
Historic Monuments Council	Functions transferring to new Environment Agency – subject to the outcome of the review of environmental governance
NI Housing Council	Abolition will precede the creation of the new councils

Tribunals	
Tribunals	Combined Tribunal Administration Service under NI Court Service

Source: Better Government for Northern Ireland: Final Decisions of the Review of Public Administration (2006).

Specifically, the intention was to cut the number of public bodies from 81 to 53, in addition to reorganisation and consolidation in the functional areas above. The existing 81 public bodies to which the Secretary of State referred were: 15 executive agencies; 39 executive and 16 advisory public bodies or quangos; and 11 tribunals. These excluded a number of non-departmental public bodies which come within the remit of the Northern Ireland Court Service and the Northern Ireland Office (such as the Parades Commission for Northern Ireland, Probation Board for Northern Ireland, Criminal Justice Inspection, and Northern Ireland Policing Board etc.).

The recommendations of the Review of Public Administration were however revisited by the Assembly following the restoration of devolution in May 2007 and several important changes were made to the restructuring process. Some MLAs however claim that there has been back-tracking on the initial intention to radically reduce non-departmental public bodies. As one member put it:

> All parties had the opportunity in the Review of Public Administration and the reform of local government to cut back on bureaucracy in the interests of

Table 5.3 Public bodies in Northern Ireland at 31 March 2008

Executive NDPB	Advisory NDPB	Tribunal NDPB	Health and personal social services bodies	Public corporations	Other	Total
39	13	7	14	2	3	78

efficiency and effectiveness – underpinned by equality and community balance – but they failed to do so. There remains in the RPA the clear need and ability to review and downsize the number of quangos. In every debate on this matter in recent years, Members regularly referred to the number of quangos or unaccountable bodies as some might call them. Yet we have never managed the type of cull that is required for a number of those agencies and groups. That is work that we need to undertake, and it is within the remit of the Review of Public Administration . . . I have heard plenty of demands but no commitments. (Maskey, 2009a)

The Department of Finance and Personnel (NI) reported on the number of public bodies, their expenditure and staff employed at 31 March 2008 (see tables 5.3 and 5.4). Although not comparing like-with-like according to the Secretary of State's target, the prediction to reduce the number of public bodies from 81 to 53 appears to have made limited progress.

History of quangos in Northern Ireland

Northern Ireland has a long history associated with the growth of quangos not unrelated to the wider political problems of discrimination in public services provision. It should be noted that prior to 1972, for reasons of inefficiency and small-scale local government, there had been a fragmentation of provision and a tendency to hive-off services from councils. Hence, boards became a key element in the structural configuration of public services, particularly in health and housing, as early as 1946 when the Northern Ireland Hospitals Authority was created and charged with administering hospital, specialist and ancillary services and a Health Services Board provided general medical and pharmaceutical services (Birrell and Murie, 1980). The creation of the Northern Ireland Housing Trust in 1945 also heralded a role for unelected bodies outside the remit of local authorities. But it was the imposition of direct rule government and the transfer of executive and legislative authority to Westminster in 1972 which witnessed the centralisation of powers and a significant growth in non-departmental public bodies in Northern Ireland. Key public services were relocated within structures which could

Table 5.4 Northern Ireland public bodies' expenditure by department and numbers employed 2007–08

Department	Government funding (£)	Total gross expenditure (£)	Staffing at 31 March 2008
Department for Employment and Learning	7,245	19,948	337
Department for Regional Development	254,394	290,600	1768
Department for Social Development	485,242	799,511	3288
Department of Agriculture and Rural Development	37,683	49,614	874
Department of Culture, Arts and Leisure	43,699	47,270	532
Department of Education	1,458,519	1,506,670	31435
Department of Enterprise, Trade and Investment	149,397	145,412	863
Department of Finance and Personnel	15	N/A	2
Department of Health, Social Services and Public Safety	6,061,241	6,590,074	62698
Department of the Environment	140	2,697	55
Office of the First Minister and Deputy First Minister	16,544	16,118	117
Totals on public bodies (2007–08)	8,514,119	9,467,914	101,969

Source: Data calculated from *Northern Ireland Public Bodies 2008*.

Notes: *Government Funding*: This generally represents grant or grant-in-aid from Government, but in the case of Advisory NDPBs represents the secretariat costs borne by the parent department, where identifiable. *Total Gross Expenditure*: Shows the public body's total gross expenditure for the financial year (the 'bottom' line expenditure figure in their income and expenditure account). This will reflect, where appropriate, income from sources other than Government funding eg fees, levies etc., and is not applicable for Advisory NDPBs.

not be influenced by sectarian politics synonymous with the operation of local government at the time. Area boards were therefore given responsibility for education, health and personal social services, and a centralised housing authority (the Northern Ireland Housing Executive) took control of housing policy and implementation, all for reasons of improved efficiency but, more importantly, to ensure public services remained outside the political (and the possibility of sectarian) sphere.

A large democratic deficit opened up as additional key functional responsibilities were vested in non-departmental public bodies, resulting in a patchwork of unaccountable organisations with responsibility for a large proportion of the public budget. A series of direct rule ministers buttressed and expanded these structures piecemeal. Ministers could dispense largesse by placing benign appointees least likely to cause controversy ('yes [wo men') on quangos. A new breed of appointee emerged, disparagingly referred to as the quangocrat. Meehan commented on the evolution of quangos in Northern Ireland as follows:

> On the face of it, the extensiveness of boards in Northern Ireland makes it like nineteenth-century Britain. But boards exist here [in NI] not as precursors of modern institutions, but in response to democratic defects in the institutions that did develop. However, even though boards might be used for benign reasons, they are still open to the perennial criticisms. (Meehan, 1997: 176)

The perennial criticisms to which Meehan refers included an overtly complex system for delivering public services and therefore less user-friendly, but it also suffered from a significant lack of public accountability. Morison (1996) argued that while quangos served to depoliticise government by removing many functions normally carried out by elected bodies in other parts of the United Kingdom, appointees to NDPBs reflected the political and religious composition of society to a greater extent than normal 'democratic' means. The quango he claimed 'remains a potentially more democratic mechanism than a straightforward election in an unevenly divided and polarised society' (Morison, 1996: 17). Health trusts, education and library boards, and quangos, prior to the changes stemming from the Review of Public Administration, consumed some 45 per cent of the public budget in Northern Ireland. There was no political representation on health trusts; education and library boards had up to 40 per cent of their membership as local councillors; and quango appointees were in the gift of ministers. The most democratic forum was local government which was responsible for a meagre 5 per cent of the public budget – in fact, the budget of the Northern Ireland Housing Executive was greater than the combined expenditure of all 26 councils (Knox and Carmichael, 2006).

The proper and effective operation of quangos was all the more important because of the absence, under Direct Rule, of a tier of regional government in Northern Ireland. As Wilford (1999: 138) described it: 'bereft of regional government, the Province under direct rule experienced a yawning democratic deficit that left much of the day-to-day administration of key services largely unaccountable to both politicians and people'. Some of the larger executive quangos delivered functions performed by local authorities in Great Britain. Yet evidence on the performance of quangos was far from impressive. The Northern Ireland Housing Executive (the largest quango outside of health and education boards and trusts) and its parent department (Department for Social Development) were severely criticised by the Public

Accounts Committee (PAC) for their failure to get to grips over a long period with the homelessness problem. The PAC report noted that planning for the provision of homelessness was inadequate and the Housing Executive took 14 years to develop its first formal homelessness strategy. This, the PAC concluded, 'shows a disturbing degree of complacency about meeting its statutory duty towards some of the most vulnerable members of society' (PAC, 2004a: 1). Two of the largest education quangos, the Belfast and South Eastern Education and Library Boards, were the subject of a statutory inquiry set up by (then) Northern Ireland Office Minister Barry Gardiner as a result of a substantial overspend in 2003–04 (£11.4m and £21.4m respectively). The report uncovered serious failings in the execution of responsibilities within both boards. Their chief executives were found to be in 'very serious breach' of their responsibilities and, as a result, their accounting officer status was put on a probationary basis until June 2006 (Department of Education: Jack Report, 2005). One political party's education spokesperson said of the report: 'it is so damning that the public will rightly question why more money should be made available to quangos (a reference to education boards' calls for increased resources) when they can't manage the money they already have' (Wilson, 2005: 1).

The other key criticism of quangos operating in Northern Ireland was the absence of accountability under a number of guises (O'Neill, 2001). In terms of political accountability, quangos were held accountable through direct rule ministers who, in turn, were answerable to the Westminster Parliament. Such was the constitutional and security crises which confronted ministers, however, that little time was available to oversee the functional responsibilities of quangos. The Northern Ireland Affairs Select Committee which was set up in 1994 as a way of improving political accountability had been judged as weak at exposing quangos to proper inspection. Wilford and Elliott (1999: 39) described it thus: 'at the outset, members regarded the Northern Ireland Affairs Select Committee as an instrument capable of bringing the regime of direct rule to account. However, at the tail end of the Parliament there was broad agreement that it had fallen well short of this objective'. The Northern Ireland Affairs Committee subsequently conducted a number of inquiries into the performance of quangos but these tended to be relatively small-scale studies involving bodies such as the Sports Council, Northern Ireland Tourist Board and Arts Council focusing on their administrative practices rather than public accountability issues. In addition, select committees at Westminster, despite having responsibility for the scrutiny of Northern Ireland departments offered limited oversight on Province-specific matters (Carmichael *et al.*, 1996). Quangos were established within the parameters set down by their parent department and could therefore be held accountable but departmental guidelines tended to give them considerable operational discretion (Connolly and Loughlin, 1990). This is confirmed by Livingstone and Morison (1995) who pointed out that, notwithstanding the departments' powers to give formal direction to quangos, these have rarely been invoked in practice. More recent guidance is offered to departments on the thorny issue of accountability (see box 5.1).

Box 5.1 Guidance on accountability: NDPBs

Whilst NDPBs are distanced from government, the responsible minister is accountable to the Assembly for the degree of independence which a NDPB enjoys; for its usefulness as an instrument of government policy; and so ultimately for the overall effectiveness and efficiency with which it carries out its functions. Ministers also remain accountable to the Assembly for public money spent by a NDPB, even though bodies operate at arm's length with their own designated accounting officers. NDPBs are also accountable to the public for the services which they provide.

Departments will need to identify whether, in the circumstances of a particular NDPB, ministers will need to retain control over and so be accountable to the Assembly for certain aspects of the NDPB's activities. For example:

- whether questions of policy can be left to the NDPB acting in accordance with the functions and responsibilities conferred by the instrument establishing it, or whether ministers will need to be able to direct or modify policy;
- whether decisions in individual cases can be left to the NDPB subject only to appeal to the courts or a tribunal, or whether appeal to ministers is needed on some matters;
- whether income will derive substantially from levies, fees or charges, whether their level needs to be specifically approved by ministers or the Assembly, or whether this can be left to the NDPB (subject to the restrictions set out in the NDPB's management statement or financial memorandum).

It is unlikely that all of the risks related to delivering a service will be transferred to the NDPB. The minister's accountability means that some kind of assurance that risks are being well managed within the NDPB will be necessary.

> *Financial accountability*: As accountable units of management within the public sector, all public bodies are required to demonstrate that they are conducting their operations as economically, efficiently and effectively as possible. Annual reports and accounts are the main vehicles for discharging this 'stewardship' function and enabling the Assembly, the taxpayer and customers to judge whether the body is securing value-for-money in its operations. The board of a public body has a collective responsibility for the proper conduct of the body's affairs and for ensuring that staff maintain the strictest standards of financial propriety.
>
> *Source:* Department of Finance and Personnel (2007) *Public Bodies: A Guide for Northern Ireland Departments.* Belfast: DFP.

Writers on quangos expressed the view that non-departmental public bodies had a more extensive presence in Northern Ireland than elsewhere in the United Kingdom (Livingstone and Morison, 1995; Connolly, 1996; Greer, 1999). Northern Ireland therefore presented as the *locus extremis* in which quangos continued to evolve on the back of an administrative system dogged by problems of electoral accountability. Research carried out by the Northern Ireland Council for Voluntary Action (NICVA) on quangos which worked with community and voluntary groups, revealed a stark absence of mechanisms for access or accountability. NICVA concluded that in Northern Ireland, where traditional accountability for service provision was largely absent 'this context could be seen by quangocrats as a challenge to devise new processes' . . . instead it 'has offered an excuse, at best, for avoiding the issue of accountability' (Bradley, 1994: 26). Charges of a quangocrats' clique characterised by a 'don't rock the boat' mentality were levelled at many of these bodies created under Direct Rule to fill the gap left by the absence of an elected regional assembly (the so-called Macrory gap). With devolved government their *raison d'être* was questioned and the Northern Ireland Assembly saw an opportunity to achieve administrative efficiencies through rationalisation or abolition.

Public appointments

The issue of patronage, given the role of ministers in the public appointments process to non-departmental public bodies, was examined as a UK-wide matter by the Nolan Committee on Standards in Public Life in 1995. The fear was that because of the degree of ministerial discretion, that appointments to public bodies were, or could be perceived to be, influenced by political factors with limited parliamentary oversight of the process. Concerns were also raised that the membership of quangos did not represent the composition of society as a whole, a particular problem for Northern Ireland given its history of unionist hegemony. The Nolan Committee therefore made a number of recommendations to the Conservative (John Major) Government to ensure greater openness and independent external scrutiny in the form of a Commissioner for Public Appointments to regulate, monitor and report on the operation of the public appointments process in Great Britain. An equivalent post was created for Northern Ireland in 1995 although both posts were initially held by the same person (Widdis and Moore, 2002). Greenwood *et al.* (2002: 162) pointed out that 'the greater transparency now accompanying appointments to quangos means that some of the earlier excesses of partisan behaviour are unlikely to be repeated on the same scale'.

The Commissioner for Public Appointments in Northern Ireland (OCPA NI), currently Mrs Felicity Huston, regulates and monitors Ministerial appointments to a number of public bodies. She is independent of Government and the civil service, or at least that is the theory. In a blunt assessment of the relationship between her office and the Office of the First Minister and deputy First Minister, the Commissioner reported the following:

> My office is still sponsored and funded directly by the Office of the First Minister and deputy First Minister. Even our computer files are held on an OFMDFM system. The problems regarding such arrangements have been recognised by politicians and stakeholders alike . . . There is a clear conflict in my regulating the work of a department that in turn funds and sponsors my office. In a nutshell the Office of the Commissioner for Public Appointments is not independent of the department it is charged with regulating. Although this conflict of interest is a clear as the nose on one's face to everyone else, the Northern Ireland Civil Service struggles to recognise it, let alone resolve the problem. I have been pushing the issue for more independent status and independent location and I will continue the struggle. (Huston, 2008: 16–17).

The overall number of public appointments in Northern Ireland held at 31 March 2008 was 1,672. This represented a reduction of 352 appointments when compared with 2,024 held at 31 March 2007. The number of public appointments held at 31 March 2008 broken down by gender and between chairs and members is shown in table 5.5.

The Commissioner's office provides guidance to NI government departments on procedures for making public appointments; audits and reports on appointments procedures annually; and investigates complaints about appointment processes within the remit of the Commissioner's office. The independent scrutiny role provided by the Commissioner is exercised through a pool of assessors who are recruited and trained by her office to ensure that

Table 5.5 Public appointments held at 31 March 2008

	Total	Male	Female	% male	% female
Chairs	85	66	19	78	22
Members	1,587	1,073	514	68	32
	1,672	1,139	533	68	32

Source: Office of the First Minister and Deputy First Minister, Central Appointments Unit, Public Appointments Annual Report, 2007/08.

public appointments comply with a Code of Practice. The Office of the Commissioner for Public Appointments for Northern Ireland allocates an assessor to sit as a full member of the selection panel to advise on correct procedures and to act as the 'eyes and ears' of the Commissioner, reporting to her if necessary (OCPA NI website). The guidance requires departments to monitor information about appointments within the Commissioner's remit. The data gathered are disaggregated by: gender, age, community background, remuneration, disability, political activity and ethnic background. These data are then published annually.

The Code of Practice sets out the regulatory framework for the public appointments process and is based upon the seven principles, as recommended by the *Committee on Standards in Public Life* (Nolan, 1995). It aims to provide departments with a clear and concise guide to the steps they must follow in order to ensure a fair, open and transparent appointments process that produces a quality outcome and can command public confidence. The seven principles that underpin the Code of Practice are set out in box 5.2. They are the foundations of the public appointments process and are designed to ensure appointment on merit and a quality outcome (Office of the Commissioner for Public Appointments for Northern Ireland, 2007: 8–9). The current *Code of Practice for Ministerial Appointments in Northern Ireland* is a hybrid based on the Code of Practice in Great Britain. The Commissioner is in the process of producing a new code which will be more reflective of the changed political climate in Northern Ireland (Office of the Commissioner for Public Appointments for Northern Ireland, 2008: 5).

The Office of the Commissioner for Public Appointments (NI) introduced a 'kitemark scheme' in September 2001 to give recognition and highlight the fact that many public appointments are made in accordance with OCPA NI procedures. It is used to indicate a properly regulated and audited appointment process where potential applicants will be treated equally and fairly. This kitemark covers appointments to all bodies which fall within the Commissioner's remit. It must be included in public advertisements for all such appointments. The OCPA NI must be sent copies of both the advertisement

NON-DEPARTMENTAL PUBLIC BODIES

> **Box 5.2 Commissioner for Public Appointments for Northern Ireland: code of practice**
>
> - *Ministerial responsibility*: The ultimate responsibility for appointments lies with ministers.
> - *Merit*: All public appointments should be governed by the overriding principle of selection based on merit, by the well-informed choice of individuals who, through their abilities, experience and qualities, match the needs of the public body in question.
> - *Independent scrutiny*: No appointment will take place without first being scrutinised by an independent panel, or by a group which includes membership independent of the department filling the post.
> - *Equal opportunities*: Departments should sustain programmes to promote and deliver equal opportunities principles.
> - *Probity*: Board members of Executive non-departmental public bodies and health and personal social services bodies must be committed to the principles and values of public service and perform their duties with integrity.
> - *Openness and transparency*: The principles of open government must be applied to the appointments process, its workings must be transparent and information must be provided about the appointments made.
> - *Proportionality*: The appointments procedures need to be subject to the principle of proportionality, that is, they should be appropriate for the nature of the post and the size and weight of its responsibilities.
>
> *Source:* The Commissioner for Public Appointments for Northern Ireland, *Code of Practice for Ministerial Appointments to Public Bodies* (2007: 8).

and the press release. In addition, an OCPA NI 'monitored kitemark' was introduced in October 2002 and can be applied to appointments to bodies falling outside the Commissioner's remit, though its use is purely voluntary. Many departments use the Code of Practice to make appointments to such bodies and by using the monitored kitemark, they are publicly demonstrating their commitment to the Code (OFMDFM, *Make Your Mark*, undated).

The relationship between the current Commissioner for Public Appointments for Northern Ireland and the civil service, as the quotation above illustrates, has been an uneasy one at times. A very public spat arose between her and the (then) Head of the Northern Ireland Civil Service, Sir Nigel Hamilton, following evidence which she gave to the Public Accounts

Committee in Stormont. The Commissioner expressed her frustration to MLAs about the attitude of civil servants towards public appointments:

> There is a code of practice. However, I think I could best sum up the attitude that I see on a daily basis by mentioning a phone call that one of my officials took recently from a civil servant who said: 'well we know who we want to appoint, now how do we get round this code of practice'. That is what I deal with on an almost daily basis. (Huston, reported by D. Gordon, 14 November 2008)

These remarks produced a frosty response from the (then) Head of the Northern Ireland Civil Service who sought clarification and evidence to substantiate the assertions made by the Commissioner that there were 'widespread failures' by departments in complying with the code of practice. Controversy also arose over public appointments to the Commissioner(s) for Victims and Survivors, a very high-profile and politically controversial affair, when information was leaked to the press about the candidates throughout the process. The Commissioner expressed her views thus:

> Northern Ireland is a small place and rumours of 'who's getting what' abound. However, I understand that in this competition some candidates heard the outcome of their application directly from the press before the department had been in contact with them! I was approached in venues as diverse as my local supermarket and an airport lounge with the names of successful candidates, well before such names had been announced. (Huston, 2008: 10)

The relationship between the Commissioner and senior civil servants remains a work-in-progress!

Those who are appointed to public bodies are expected to exhibit a standard of behaviour beyond reproach – the so-called seven Nolan principles of conduct, which are set out in box 5.3.

Culling quangos

Quangos, of course, are not a Northern Ireland-specific issue and their increase, UK-wide, was the subject of a comprehensive review (Democratic Audit: *Extra Governmental Organisations and their Accountability, 1994*) which exposed the extent of their growth and criticised their lack of accountability. Concerns tended to focus on the overall number of quangos, the scope for improvements in their efficiency and financial management and whether their functions were necessary, or could be performed differently. But there were also concerns about the procedures by which members were appointed to quango boards. In November 1997 the Labour Government issued a Consultation Paper *Opening Up Quangos* as a UK-wide document

> **Box 5.3 The seven principles of conduct underpinning public life**
>
> - *Selflessness*: Holders of public office should take decisions solely in terms of the public interest. They should not do so in order to gain financial or other material benefits for themselves, their family or other friends.
> - *Integrity*: Holders of public office should not place themselves under any financial or other obligation to outside individuals or organisations that might influence them in the performance of their official duties.
> - *Objectivity*: In carrying out public business, including making public appointments, awarding contracts, or recommending individuals for rewards and benefits, holders of public office should make choices on merit.
> - *Accountability*: Holders of public office are accountable for their decisions and actions to the public and must submit themselves to whatever scrutiny is appropriate to their office.
> - *Openness*: Holders of public office should be as open as possible about all the decisions and actions that they take. They should give reasons for their decisions and restrict information only when the wider public interest clearly demands.
> - *Honesty*: Holders of public office have a duty to declare any private interests relating to their public duties and to take steps to resolve any conflicts arising in a way that protects the public interest.
> - *Leadership*: Holders of public office should promote and support these principles by leadership and example.
>
> Source: The Commissioner for Public Appointments for Northern Ireland, *Code of Practice for Ministerial Appointments to Public Bodies* (2007: 45).

for public discussion, but its salience in Northern Ireland was paramount, given the problems of accountability and loss of democratic control associated with Direct Rule. Suggestions for improvement arising from the consultation (*Quangos: Opening the Doors*, June 1998) included encouraging non-departmental public bodies to offer greater access to information by publishing annual reports, publicising reports of meetings and, where possible, making meetings more accessible to the public.

Birrell (2008) describes the attempts made by the devolved administrations to rationalize quangos as a major objective of each of the new administrations in Scotland (Denton and Flinders, 2006), Wales (Cooke and Clifton, 2005) and Northern Ireland. He classifies the various approaches taken to achieve this rationalization process under devolution as: abolition, declassification, amalgamation, transfer to devolved government, transfer to local government, and division of functions. Birrell concludes on the efforts of the devolved regions to cut the number of quangos:

> The implementation of rationalisation in all three countries, while seeing a streamlining of the numbers of devolved quangos, has largely seen the functions and services remain within the quango sector of government without a more radical or comprehensive reconfiguration between departments, executive agencies, local councils and quangos. One reason for the limited implementation may be the influence of the lack of any rationalisation policies on quangos from the UK government relating to quangos under their control. (Birrell, 2008a: 42).

Quangos in England also continue to attract the attention of politicians. David Cameron, Conservative Party Leader, pledged (6 July 2009) to cut the number of unelected quangos in order to save money and increase accountability, by abolishing bodies such as the schools' Qualifications and Curriculum Development Agency (QCDA), which develops the national curriculum, and to strip the media regulator (Ofcom) of its policy-making functions. Cameron estimated that there were around 1,000 unelected organisations paid by the taxpayer to deliver aspects of government policy at a cost of £34 billion of public spending annually. He questioned the increasing number of quangos on the grounds of accountability, cost and effectiveness, recommended an overhaul of the system, and set out key elements of a reform agenda. These would include:

- Assigning quangos strictly administrative functions and removing them as actors in democratic politics and public debate.
- No quango will have the power to stray outside the scope of its responsibilities, unless instructed to do so by ministers.
- Quangos must operate wholly within the financial resources allocated to them by ministers.

For each quango the following key questions would be asked:

- Does this organisation need to exist?
- If its functions are necessary, which of them should be carried out in a directly accountable way within the department?
- And which, if any, should be carried out independently, at arm's length from political influence?
- If there really is a need for an independent quango, how can we make sure it is as small as possible, operating with maximum efficiency, frugality and respect for taxpayers' money?

Cameron concluded:

> The problem today is that too much of what government does is actually done by people that no-one can vote out, by organisations that feel no pressure to answer for what happens and in a way that is relatively unaccountable . . . The values underlying our [Conservative Party] approach are clear. We understand how frustrated people feel when they see big, bureaucratic, unaccountable government getting it wrong and offering no come-back. And we want to change that. (Cameron, 2009)

Despite the clamour around quangos by political parties whether in Great Britain or Northern Ireland, Hood (1981) argued that NDPBs are too useful to be abolished by politicians for the following reasons:

- Government will always need bodies from which it can distance itself in sensitive areas.
- There is value in having temporary organisations outside the permanent government service that can be scrapped when chances permit.
- The use of such bodies as an administrative means of bypassing other public organisations, along with the patronage dimension, contunues to attract politicians.
- They are useful as political 'window dressing' (cited in Greenwood *et al.*, 2002: 163).

The political issues dealt with by some quangos in Northern Ireland have made them the subject of criticism by specific political parties. Hence, bodies such as the Parades Commission, Human Rights Commission, Equality Commission, and the Community Relations Council, for example, have been accused of being self-serving. This criticism is best captured by DUP Finance Minister, Sammy Wilson MLA, who has been openly disparaging of what he described as 'the anti-racist industry'. Wilson argued the 'industry' exaggerates the level of racism in Northern Ireland for its own financial gain: 'Don't forget that Northern Ireland Council for Ethnic Minorities has a vested interest in this – they need to keep up the impression that there's rampant racism in Northern Ireland because they apply for grants on the basis that their services are required' (Wilson, 2009a: 2).

NDPBs: unravelling the Review of Public Administration

The bold claims made to reduce the number of non-departmental public bodies in the Review of Public Administration (table 5.2) have begun to unravel. In part this is due to the fact that the devolved government wanted to distance itself from decisions taken by direct rule ministers and stamp its own authority on the reform proposals. Local MLAs and Executive ministers are also subject to direct lobbying by NDPB stakeholders in ways which British ministers were immune. It is also true that the usefulness of the roles and functions performed by some of the quangos earmarked for abolition in the broad sweep of reforms becomes much more apparent with the prospect of closure. Two examples of bodies faced with abolition or wholesale transfer of their functions were: the Local Government Staff Commission, an executive non-departmental public body whose functions were to be transferred to the new councils when established in 2011, and the Northern Ireland Housing Council, an advisory quango. We consider these two quangos as case study examples of an executive and advisory quango respectively to demonstrate the unravelling of the sweeping proposals announced in the Review of Public Administration.

Local Government Staff Commission

The Local Government Staff Commission is an executive non-departmental public body established under the Local Government Act (NI) 1972. Its powers were later extended under the Housing Orders 1976 and 1981, and the Local Government (Miscellaneous Provisions) (NI) Order 1992. The Commission's strap line is 'Achieving Excellence through People'. The terms of reference for the Commission are:

> To exercise general oversight of matters connected with the recruitment, training and terms and conditions of employment of officers of councils and the Northern Ireland Housing Executive and of making recommendations to councils and the Northern Ireland Housing Executive on such matters. (Local Government Act (Northern Ireland) 1972 as amended by the Housing Orders (NI) 1976 and 1981)

The main activities of the Commission are: recommending and monitoring employment and promotion procedures; convening advisory appointments panels; human resource planning activities; promoting co-operation in the public service; training and development; ensuring effective negotiating machinery; and, advisory and support services. Through the delivery of these activities the Staff Commission sees its work as important to councils and the Northern Ireland Housing Executive in the implementation of local government reform, the modernisation agenda, and managing the transition to, and development of, reformed councils.

The Local Government Staff Commission's income in 2007/08 was £698k of which £585k came from district councils and the Northern Ireland Housing Executive. In other words, almost 85 per cent of the Commission's income derives from the organisations it is tasked to support (Local Government Staff Commission, 2008). Thematically the Local Government Staff Commission focuses its work on six core areas of business:

- Local government reform: the Commission is preparing a human resources framework in the transition to the reforms in local government structures and functions. It provides advice to the Strategic Leadership Board as associated committees in the lead up to the formation of 11 councils in 2011.
- Recruitment and selection: the Commission is working with individual councils and transition committees to provide advice and assistance on implementing a vacancy control system with the aim of safeguarding the employment of existing council staff as a result of decisions arising from the Review of Public Administration. It is also working on a staff transfer scheme and mechanism for filling new posts in the new council structures.
- Equality and diversity: the Commission is leading a *Women in Local Councils* initiative to ensure that each council and political parties are challenged and supported to make measurable progress towards addressing any gender under-representation, thereby creating a local government sector which more accurately reflects the community it serves. The Commission also launched an initiative *Disability in Local Councils* to work with individual councils to encourage the participation of people with disabilities at all levels.
- Learning and development: the Commission is working to build the capacity needs of officers, elected members and organisations in the implementation of changes brought about by the Review of Public Administration and subsequent ministerial announcements on local government.
- Employee relations: the Commission provides advice and support to the regional collective negotiating mechanism set up to deal with human resource issues relating to local government reform. It also provides advice and assistance to the Northern Ireland Joint Council for Local Government Services (NIJC) which is the negotiating body of employers and unions for all staff in councils in Northern Ireland (except chief executives). The national joint body negotiates collective agreements on pay and conditions for all employees of local authorities in England, Wales and Northern Ireland.
- Organisation design and development: the Commission works with local government stakeholders to strengthen and enhance the capacity of human resource practitioners, change management officers and senior

local government staff to respond to change and meet organisational needs in an environment of continuous improvement. It also works in partnership with councils to implement stress management standards, workplace health issues, promotion and prevention of sickness absence management and support systems, and the Health and Safety Executive NI to promote a protected working environment for council employees (Local Government Staff Commission, 2009: 4–5).

The Local Government Staff Commission was somewhat bewildered that the 'final' announcement in the Review of Public Administration was to transfer its functions to local government. The second consultation document of the RPA, for example, noted that that 'the functions undertaken by the Commission will be of crucial importance during the transition period when local government structures are introduced' and the Commission 'could also have a role in capacity building and training staff for new positions' (Office of the First Minister and Deputy First Minister, Review of Public Administration, 2005b: 176). In its submission to the RPA consultation the Local Government Staff Commission endorsed these ideas suggesting 'that the expertise of the Commission should be used to assist in the change process' (Local Government Staff Commission, 2005: 23). Beyond the implementation of local government reforms (and in advance of the changes announced by the Secretary of State on the future of quangos), the Commission suggested its future role as follows:

> Whilst the manner in which local government is delivered may change, there is a continuing need for a body to ensure consistency in employment matters and to provide independent support in ensuring equality of opportunity and fairness in the local government system. The future of the Local Government Staff Commission should be considered in line with the need for appropriate statutory safeguards and standards in relation to staff in local government organizations. (Local Government Staff Commission, 2005: 23)

While this is perhaps a predictable reaction from an organization faced with the transfer of functions, its continued role was firmly supported by the Society of Local Authority Chief Executives (SOLACE NI), the Association of Public Service Excellence (APSE), and the Public Sector People Managers' Association (PPMA). The devolved government's response to the proposals to transfer the functions of the Local Government Staff Commission came in an announcement by the (then) Minister for the Environment to the Assembly in March 2008 when, as part of her decision to adopt an 11-council model of local government reform, she stated:

> The Local Government Staff Commission will be a key part of the change process. I will shortly be initiating a review of the commission to ensure that it is resourced

appropriately to provide much-needed support during the implementation of the decisions on the future shape of local government. (Foster, Hansard, 31 March 2008)

The review (conducted by a retired Permanent Secretary, John Hunter) considered the functions of the Staff Commission and 'the extent to which they were appropriate to provide the level of support required to give effect to the implementation of the decisions by the Executive about the future shape of local government in Northern Ireland'. The report recommended that:

- The Policy Development Panel in the local government reform process should draw on the experience of the Local Government Staff Commission and consider the creation of an organisation to provide regional support services to the new Councils.
- The Local Government Training Group (a sub-group within the Local Government Staff Commission which has a statutory responsibility for promoting or assisting the development of, or providing, facilities for the training of officers) should make early arrangements for the delivery in 2009–11 of comprehensive training and development programmes to build capacity in both officers and elected members.
- Statutory Transition Committees will be established to implement the local government reform programme. In bringing forward regulations in relation to the composition, governance and functions of the statutory transition committees, the role of the Staff Commission should be formally extended to provide support to these committees on staffing matters. This extension should also cover the full range of functions and duties of the Staff Commission and its role in relation to the appointment and qualifications of officers of new/reformed councils.
- The Staff Commission should service new negotiating machinery established specifically to negotiate the implementation of the local government reorganisation. In addition, the Staff Commission should: complete its work on updating its Code of Practice on Recruitment and Selection; support the 11 Transition Committees in the appointment of new Clerks and senior staff; provide early guidance on vacancy control procedures; develop model staff transfer schemes; generally assist with the implementation of the Public Service Commission's ten Guiding Principles as they apply to local government; and generally support the work of the Strategic Leadership Board, the Regional Transitional Co-ordinating Group, the Policy Development Panels and the 11 Transition Committees.

The Review of the Local Government Staff Commission concluded with the following:

> I am pleased to record the general view across local government that over the years the Staff Commission has served a very useful purpose ... Nonetheless, there are some within local government who believe that the new and larger Councils from 2011 will be capable of managing their own affairs, in accordance with employment and equality legislation, without the need for a Staff Commission. While this may be true of the larger Councils, I believe that the regional model for human resource support services has merit, not least in promoting consistency and fairness across Councils, against a backcloth of continuing pressure to reduce costs ... I have concluded that the LGSC has a vitally important continuing role to play in the run up to the creation of the 11 new Councils in May 2011. (Hunter, 2009: 4, 10).

The (then) Environment Minister (Sammy Wilson, now Finance Minister) accepted the recommendations of the review and decided that the Staff Commission would continue to exist until 2012 at which point it would be further reviewed along with the new 11 councils (some 12 months after their operation). He pointed out: 'the Staff Commission plays an important role in working with others to give effect to the Executive's decisions on the future shape of local government and this will continue throughout the transition period' (Wilson, 2009b: 4). This decision represented a *volte-face* on the fate of an executive non-departmental public body. We now consider the case of the Northern Ireland Housing Council, an advisory non-departmental public body scheduled to be abolished under the Review of Public Administration.

Northern Ireland Housing Council

The Housing Council was established by the Housing Executive Act (Northern Ireland) 1971. The Council is consulted by the Housing Executive and the Department for Social Development (DSD) on all matters that affect housing policy in Northern Ireland. The Northern Ireland Housing Executive meets once a month with the Housing Council, explaining operations and strategy. The Housing Council is made up of one representative from each of the 26 district councils in Northern Ireland. There were until 2006 three Housing Council members on the Board of the Housing Executive who are appointed for a one-year period. Since then, on the recommendation of former Minister David Hanson, to allow wider (cross-party) political participation and in an acknowledgement of the value of Housing Council representation on the Board, the number of representatives was increased to four.

Under the 'final' decisions arising from the Review of Public Administration (*Better Government for Northern Ireland*, March 2006) two significant announcements were made: first, a range of non-core functions of the Northern Ireland Housing Executive were to transfer to local government; and second, the Northern Ireland Housing Council was to be abolished in advance of the creation of the new councils (originally scheduled for Spring 2009). With the return of devolution, the local Department of Environment Minister launched a 'review of the review' and produced an 'Emerging Findings Paper' in August 2007 which re-examined both the number of councils and functions of local government agreed in the Review of Public Administration.

The Emerging Findings Paper suggested retaining the Housing Council, noting:

> The Minister for Social Development wants to retain the Housing Council, along with the statutory nominating rights to the body, and set it a more challenging remit. (Emerging Findings Paper, 2007: 36, paragraph 36)

Social Development Minister, Margaret Ritchie, met with a Housing Council delegation in September 2007 and confirmed 'that she was not minded to abolish the Housing Council at this time' (note of meeting, 4 September 2007, Housing Council). She saw a clear role for the Housing Council where it could be consulted and influence the development of housing policy. The Minister then referred to the potential for an enhanced and more challenging role for the Housing Council and asked for ways in which this might evolve.

The formal roles of the Northern Ireland Housing Council are rooted in legislation. The Housing (Northern Ireland) Order 1981 (chapter 1, article 4) notes:

(i) The Northern Ireland Housing Council shall consider any matter affecting housing which:
   - Is referred to the Housing Council by the Department (for Social Development) or the Northern Ireland Housing Executive.
   - Appears to the Housing Council to be a matter to which consideration ought to be given.
(ii) Where it appears to the Housing Council to be desirable to do so, the Council may make recommendations to the Department (for Social Development) or the Northern Ireland Housing Executive with respect to any matter which it has considered; and the Department (for Social Development) or the Northern Ireland Housing Executive shall consider any such recommendations.

In short, the Housing Council has exercised three key roles to date:

- It can offer advice to the Northern Ireland Housing Executive (through membership of its Board) and the Department for Social Development, and is consulted on strategic developments in housing policy.
- It has a monitoring role in that it can examine the outworkings of housing policies – the Chief Executive of the Northern Ireland Housing Executive

and senior DSD officials attend the Housing Council's monthly meeting to report on housing issues.
- It has a representational role in that it reflects the collective views of all 26 councils in Northern Ireland on public housing matters informed by elected representatives' interaction with constituents/tenants. In fact, until the revival of the Northern Ireland Local Government Association, the Housing Council acted as the only cross-party (non-partisan) forum for local councillors over a period of many years.

In practical terms the work of the Housing Council is best captured in the 2007/08 Annual Report where it states:

> The Housing Council continues to provide an important challenge function in Northern Ireland and contributes regularly to policy development and implementation on a province-wide basis. It provides a valuable learning forum for Councillors, both new and experienced, while offering a sounding board for policy-makers and challenge conduit for local councillors.

In summary, the Housing Council can claim to have been successful in several ways. It has acted as an independent elected advisory and consultative forum for both strategic housing policy (top-down) and a wide range of operational issues (bottom-up). The fact that the Housing Council has for over thirty-five years acted as a corporate non-partisan forum, despite its diverse political constituency and the turbulence of that period, is testament to its sense of purpose. It has been valued by the Northern Ireland Housing Executive as a conduit for public opinion judged by the regular attendance of the NIHE Chief Executive and senior officials at Housing Council meetings. It is the source from which elected representatives are appointed to the Board of the Northern Ireland Housing Executive. It provides a valuable cross-departmental monitoring and accountability function which reflects the fact that social housing as a function has important links with other public services, in particular education, health and community care. Its legislative remit means that it has been taken seriously by other public sector stakeholders.

The Housing Council argued in a report to the Minister for Social Development that its role and functions as an advisory, consultative, monitoring and representational body have been effectively discharged to date and made the case to the Minister for an enhanced role in the future which should include:

(1) Monitoring: An increased monitoring role over:
- The work of housing associations, particularly in delivering the social housing development programme. The Northern Ireland Housing Council would like to work more closely with the Northern Ireland

Housing Executive and the Department for Social Development in their oversight and regulation of housing associations, respectively.
- The private rented sector. Accepting that the private rented sector is largely unregulated, the Northern Ireland Housing Council believes there are opportunities to monitor aspects of the private rented sector such as houses in multiple occupation.

(2) Housing finance/budgeting: A more strategic and influencing role between the Northern Ireland Housing Council and the Department of Social Development in relation to the yearly funding allocations for housing in advance of final budget agreement with both the Northern Ireland Housing Executive and Housing Associations.

(3) Key stakeholder meetings: The Housing Council wanted a more structured relationship with the Chairs of: the Northern Ireland Housing Executive, the Northern Ireland Federation of Housing Associations, Chartered Institute of Housing, and the Minister or her representative in the form of quarterly meetings. The Housing Council suggested submission of summary updates of its work to the Social Development Assembly Committee for information and comment.

(4) A forum for engagement: In addition to closer links between Chairs (above) and the Minister, the Housing Council offered to provide a forum for stakeholder meetings, acting as a sounding board for topical issues. In other words, it could afford opportunities for a dialogue between the main housing stakeholders where ideas could be floated and a two-way engagement encouraged. Housing Council members should also be invited to sit on relevant Department for Social Development working/steering groups or task forces.

(5) Corporate visioning and business planning: The Northern Ireland Housing Council could play a very useful role in tracking the progress of the Department of Social Development, Northern Ireland Housing Executive and larger housing associations against their corporate and business plans – how they are performing on targets set and ideas for inclusion in yearly business plans. This would necessitate a more formalised reporting role for the Department for Social Development to the Housing Council. None of the above should be seen as a mechanism to inhibit direct lobbying of the DSD Minister on housing issues.

(6) Research: The Housing Council sought a research capacity, where it could commission work independent of the Northern Ireland Housing Executive and the Department for Social Development. (Knox, 2008: 10–12)

The Northern Ireland Housing Council stressed the importance of its current role in holding the Northern Ireland Housing Executive to account, directly through meetings of the Housing Council and indirectly through the Board of the Housing Executive. Compare for example the accountability role exercised by the proposed new 11 councils and the Northern Ireland Housing Executive (see table 5.6). The table shows how a 10-person appointed NIHE board (comprising 4 elected representatives and 6 public appointees) holds the NIHE to account for £783m per annum (Housing Executive's budget

Table 5.6 Public accountability

Organisations	Yearly net expenditure	Accountability mechanism
Northern Ireland Housing Executive	£783m	10-person Board of Housing Executive selected through the public appointments process by the Department for Social Development following Ministerial approval NIHE accountable through its parent department (DSD) to the Minister for Social Development and scrutinised by statutory DSD Assembly Committee
Proposed 11 councils	£575m	460 elected councillors

2008/09) compared to 460 elected representatives (in the new councils) with accountability for £575m.

Given the wide ranging scope of the Department for Social Development and the functions of its statutory oversight Assembly committee, the Northern Ireland Housing Council sees its enhanced role as having a local government housing accountability brief. With the transfer of housing related functions to local government and associated statutory powers of community planning and well-being, the Housing Council sees itself in a pivotal position to represent the local government sector on the function of housing and to offer advice to, and be consulted by, the strategic housing authority in the form of the Northern Ireland Housing Executive and the Northern Ireland Federation of Housing Associations. In short, the Housing Council wants to act, through an enhanced monitoring role, as local government's voice on housing matters.

The Minister for Social Development has not (at the time of writing) responded to the Housing Council's proposals but has made positive noises including bi-monthly meetings with the Council as a form of regular engagement:

> Two years ago I was also presented with the recommendation (or decision already taken) to abolish the Housing Council, – one of the original Review of Public Administration recommendations. I chose not to do so as I felt that the Housing Council had worked well over the years in giving important legitimacy and accountability to housing when there was a lack of democratic accountability. Although we now have devolution, I believe the Housing Council still has an important role into the future – particularly in the context of retaining the core functions of our existing strategic housing authority. (Ritchie, 2009)

Here again the rallying call to cull quangos has been muted when politicians are faced with the realities of the useful advice and functions performed by these bodies.

Northern Ireland has a love–hate relationship with quangos. On the one hand previous sectarian practices in public bodies necessitated the removal of key public services and their location in non-departmental public bodies. This contributed to the democratic deficit synonymous with direct rule in Northern Ireland. On the other hand, quangos provide (as Hood argues above) both independence and distance from government, an important factor in Northern Ireland where seemingly innocuous functions can become politically sensitive. Issues around accountability have been addressed to a large extent and there are clearer mechanisms for holding quangos to account, not least a closer oversight role played by devolved government through the Assembly's statutory committees. A recent example of this is a review by the Committee of Culture, Arts and Leisure of the governance arrangements of eight 'arm's length bodies' in Northern Ireland to include quangos such as Sports NI, the Arts Council and the Museums Council. Concerns about ministerial patronage have also been tackled by the Commissioner for Public Appointments Office, although relationships have been fraught with some senior civil servants who find the transition to independent external intervention difficult, a legacy of their power under direct rule arrangements. What is clear however is that the intended cull of quangos, as other devolved regions have experienced, is much more difficult to achieve in practice and is an ongoing process which will continue to exercise local politicians perhaps more as a rhetorical gesture than axing bodies initially perceived as nugatory.

6
The third sector

> *The voluntary and community sector makes a significant contribution to life in Northern Ireland and is a key social partner working with the Government to deliver social, economic, cultural and environmental change. Voluntary and community organisations have a track record of tackling social need and deprivation and are well placed to develop and deliver improved frontline services, particularly to the most disadvantaged people in society . . . Many voluntary and community organisations have played a key role in recent developments in human rights, equality and good relations.* (Department for Social Development, 2005: 3)

Definition and scope of the sector

The first consideration in examining the third or voluntary and community sector in Northern Ireland is that of definition (source: VolResource). The sector is diverse, amorphous and complex. One definition of the sector used by the Home Office is:

> Registered charities, as well as non-charitable, non-profit organisations, associations and self-help groups and community groups. Must involve some aspect of voluntary activity, though many are also professional organisations with paid staff, some of which are of considerable size. Community organisations tend to be focused on particular localities or groups within the community; many are dependent entirely or almost entirely on voluntary activity.

Definitions of the sector are sometimes broken down into its component parts as follows:

> *Community sector:* Those organisations active on a local or community level, usually small, modestly funded and largely dependent on voluntary, rather than paid, effort. Can be seen as distinct from the larger, professionally staffed agencies which are most visible in voluntary sector profiles. Hence the phrase 'voluntary and community sector' to encompass the full range.

Voluntary sector: There are many definitions and refinements of this term, with often a wide and a core version. One approach is by reference to what the other sectors cover e.g. private/commercial, state/public and informal (family, friends) – what is left is voluntary! That gives the derivation of the term 'third sector'. The third sector includes voluntary and community organisations as well as social enterprises. These organisations sit between the private and public sector. Another issue in defining the sector is that although many perceive voluntary organisations are distinctly different from private and public ones, the boundaries are actually unclear. It is more of a continuum than a set of discrete boxes.

The Scottish Council for Voluntary Organisations (SCVO) defines a voluntary organisation as: non-profit driven, non-statutory, autonomous and run by individuals who do not get paid for running the organisation (SCVO website) – see box 6.1.

Civil society: Increasingly being used in international discussions in place of NGO, distinguishing society interests from political or business perspectives.

In the Northern Ireland context, rather than trying to define the sector, the Northern Ireland Council for Voluntary Action (NICVA) simply acknowledges the difficulty in arriving at a definition and instead sets out criteria which characterize organizations that make up the sector as follows:

Formality: people and their activities have an organisational form to exhibit this attribute. The organisation may have a recognisable structure with a constitution or a formal set of rules. However, any definition using this attribute only will exclude large numbers of informal, community-based activities and temporary forms of activity.

Independence: organisations that are constitutionally and institutionally separate from the statutory and private sectors. This criterion excludes non-departmental public bodies and educational establishments, e.g. universities and voluntary aided schools. While these bodies can register as charities with the Inland Revenue, they are generally not perceived to be part of the voluntary and community sector.

Non-profit distribution: organisations that do not distribute profits to shareholders or owners. This criterion does not preclude undertaking activities such as trading to generate profit or surplus. However, proceeds should not be for the personal benefit of any individuals connected with the organization and should be directed towards achieving the organisation's charitable objectives.

Self-governance: organisations that are truly independent in determining their own course. This would exclude, for example, organisations that are charities within the National Health Service on the basis that they are ultimately controlled by a statutory body.

Voluntarism: organisations where there is a meaningful degree of voluntarism in terms of money or time. The donation of time includes that given by management committee members.

Private benefit versus public benefit: organisations that exist solely for the benefit of their own members (such as friendly societies or independent schools) are excluded. Organisations that benefit the wider public are included. This may include certain organisations that mainly benefit a specific group of people or even just their members. This would be the case when the objectives of the

Box 6.1 Definition of voluntary/community organisations

Voluntary/community organisations are extremely diverse, and therefore it is not easy to provide a brief definition. The Johns Hopkins Comparative Non-Profit-Making Sector Project uses the following definition:

A voluntary/community organisation is:

- *Formal*: It has a formally constituted character (excludes informal groups, households, families and friends) and may be a company limited by guarantee, a housing association, an unincorporated association, a friendly society, etc.
- *Private*: It is not a part of government, established by statute or royal charter, or under a substantial degree of executive control by government (excludes universities and non-department public bodies); it may include consortia composed of local authorities and others (e.g. local regeneration and development bodies), if the consortium is formally constituted and, at the very least, given a name.
- *Self-governing*: It has its own decision-making system and usually a formal constitution with procedures for accountability to independent trustees or its own members or constituents (e.g., excludes any so-called 'self-help groups' which are in fact directly run by clinicians).
- *Non-profit-making and distributing*: It does not distribute any surpluses to owners or members but spends them on serving its basic purpose (excludes commercial concerns but includes organisations which charge users or the public for services, undertake contracts for statutory bodies or operate commercial subsidiaries which trade and transfer profits to parent organisations).
- *Non-political*: It is not engaged in supporting candidates for political office (excludes political parties but includes campaigning and pressure groups, even though they are not eligible for charitable status e.g. Greenpeace, Child Poverty Action Group).
- *Voluntary*: It has an element of involvement of volunteers (some voluntary and community organisations appear to be entirely reliant on paid staff; however, their trustees or committee members are, in fact, their only volunteers).

While this definition applies to formal organisations (those with constitutions or rules and which probably are registered with the Charity Commission, local authority or intermediary bodies, etc.), it should not exclude less-formal groups based in neighbourhoods or local communities.

Source: Home Office (2004).

organisation provide a function that would otherwise need to be provided by the public sector, as is the case with disability organisations or community transport. Because of these criteria sacramental religious bodies and political parties are excluded. However, activities that are undertaken by associated but separate entities of religious organisations, such as mother and toddler groups, are included. (Source: Northern Ireland Council for Voluntary Action, 2009a: 12–13)

NICVA points out that it is very difficult to obtain exact statistics on the size of the voluntary and community sector in Northern Ireland because of the absence of a centralised register and ways to record when organisations close. Their best estimate of the size and scope of the sector in Northern Ireland is as follows:

- There are around 4,700 active organisations and 500 local or branch offices and projects that are linked to voluntary and community organisations.
- The sector has an income of approximately £570.1m and expenditure of £544.5m.
- The sector employs 26,737 people and has 87,723 volunteers. (Northern Ireland Council for Voluntary Action, 2009a: 16)

NICVA also disaggregates these data on the 'primary purpose' of voluntary and community organisations working in Northern Ireland, accepting that some organisations are involved in several kinds of activities (see table 6.1). The data show that community development (20.0 per cent) is the most common pursuit of organisations in the sector followed by advice/advocacy/

Table 6.1 Primary purpose of organisations (%)

Community development	20.0	Cultural	1.5
Advice/advocacy/information	10.6	Religious activities	1.4
Disability	9.1	Overseas aid/famine relief	1.1
Education/training	8.4	Volunteering development	1.1
Playgroups/after schools	6.3	Rural development	1.0
Medical/health/sickness	6.0	Relief of poverty	0.7
Youth work/development	5.0	Economic development	0.7
Arts	4.7	Community transport	0.6
Counselling/support	4.4	Community enterprise	0.6
General charitable purposes	3.1	Gender	0.5
Environment/conservation	3.0	Criminal justice	0.5
Sport/recreation	2.5	Animal welfare	0.4
Cross-border/cross community	2.4	Human rights/equality	0.4
		Welfare/benevolent	0.3
Accommodation/housing	1.9	Search and rescue	0.1
Heritage/historical	1.6	Research/evaluation	0.1

Source: NICVA, 2009a: 20.

Note: Base: 3,030.

Table 6.2 Primary beneficiaries of organisations (%)

General public/local communities	31.4	Homelessness	1.2
Preschool (0–5 year olds)	7.4	Sensory disabilities	1.1
Youth (14–25 year olds)	6.8	Carers	1.1
Children (5–13 year olds)	6.2	Community safety	1.1
Older people	5.5	Specific areas of deprivation	1.0
Women	5.4	Unemployed/low income	1.0
Voluntary and community sector	4.3	Ex-offenders and prisoners	0.9
People with disabilities	3.7	Ethnic minorities	0.9
Adult training	3.2	Interface communities	0.7
Mental health	2.8	Language community	0.5
Learning disabilities	2.7	Sexual orientation	0.5
Parents	2.0	Men	0.4
Addictions (drug/alcohol abuse)	1.8	Asylum seekers/refugees	0.3
Physical disabilities	1.6	Tenants	0.2
Victim support	1.5	Travellers	0.1
Volunteers	1.4	HIV/Aids	0.1
Overseas/developing countries	1.2		

Source: NICVA, 2009a: 21.

Note: Base: 2,995.

information (10.6 per cent) and disability (9.1 per cent). Community development is defined in the *Compact* between the government and voluntary and community sector in Northern Ireland as 'a collective process whereby members of a community come together to effect change and to address the needs within the community based on principles of self help and inclusion' (Northern Ireland Office, 1998: 17). The most common 'primary beneficiary' of voluntary and community organisations according to NICVA data is the general public or local communities (31.4 per cent), followed by pre-school (7.4 per cent) and young people (6.8 per cent) – see table 6.2.

Role played by the voluntary and community sector

The voluntary and community sector in Northern Ireland has a long history which, unsurprisingly, is linked to the political, constitutional and security problems faced by its people. The prorogation of Stormont and the introduction of direct rule from Westminster in 1972 was certainly an important milestone in the evolution of the voluntary and community sector. Direct rule witnessed the demise of local government and the absence of political accountability for public services. British ministers had no local electoral base in Northern Ireland and were preoccupied with high politics – this vested significant powers in the hands of civil servants who paid scant regard to local councillors. The resulting democratic deficit stirred the first signs of self-help in the community. A number of community action groups emerged in response to the trauma of political violence but without government support. As Nolan described it:

> All over Northern Ireland there were people trying to help the families that had been burnt out, or establishing food co-operatives, or taking kids from the frontline areas off on holiday, or setting up peoples' assemblies, or trying to get dialogue going between Catholics and Protestants. There was prodigious energy, and an optimism that this ragbag of people could create a sort of counter-culture that would not only challenge the rising sectarianism, but would give expression to a new radical politics. (Nolan, 2000: 29)

Increasingly Northern Ireland Office ministers and senior civil servants recognised the contribution which community and voluntary groups could make to a wide spectrum of government programmes in: health and social services, urban renewal, economic development, poverty initiatives, and, most importantly, community relations. This, in turn, led to a more professionalised voluntary and community sector that worked with, and accepted more resources from, government in the 1980s and was well placed to support efforts to build a peace process in the 1990s. Self-help and community activism, however, were more evident in nationalist areas whose history depicted the state as unionist oppressor. Fearon (2000: 26) observed that 'groups were more likely to be found in areas of high economic deprivation and nationalist in hue. Unionist groups still saw community development as a rebellious activity, something that sought to subvert and undermine the state'. By 1993, the Government published a *Strategy for the Support of the Voluntary Sector and for Community Development in Northern Ireland* which stressed the importance of partnership arrangements with the sector and acknowledged, in particular, the role of community groups in helping to formulate and deliver social policies. The pre-existing working relationship between the sector and senior officials had been instrumental in the production of the 1993 strategy in which government recognised 'the intrinsic value of the voluntary sector and its capacity to generate and harness good will and motivation and to translate these into action in response to a wide range of needs.' The Government also acknowledged the important role played by the voluntary and community sector in social and economic life where 'in the context of Northern Ireland's special circumstances, it provides a forum for reflecting the views and concerns of individuals and communities to Government' (Department for Social Development, 1993: 5). The evolution and development of civil society from its origins of grassroots community activism and volunteerism was described by one practitioner in the late 1990s thus:

> In comparison with the 1970's, the funding and policy environment for the voluntary and community sector is unrecognisable. The sector has demonstrated maturity and effectiveness in helping to tackle social and economic needs and in fostering peace and reconciliation. This element of civil society in Northern Ireland has been pivotal in keeping hope alive in very difficult circumstances. (Sweeney, 1997: 61)

The growing goodwill between the direct rule government and the sector helped lay the foundations for developing a 'compact' or a framework to guide relationships between them. Compacts evolved from the recommendations of the Deakin Commission (*The Commission on the Future of the Voluntary Sector*, 1996) and the policy document, *Building the Future Together* (1997) published by the Labour Party. The Deakin Commission proposed a 'concordat' of principles to inform the relationship between government and the sector. The Labour Government adapted these proposals in the form of compacts. Hence, Northern Ireland (as in England, Scotland and Wales) formally launched its compact *Building Real Partnership* (1998). The aims of this compact were to clarify respective roles in the relationship between government and the voluntary and community sector, establish shared values and principles that underpin the partnership, and identify commitments to ensure these values and principles govern future relationships (Northern Ireland Office, 1998: 8) – see box 6.2 outlining shared values contained in the *Compact*.

In reviewing the substance of compacts throughout the United Kingdom, Morison (2000: 113) whilst acknowledging that they represented an important statement about a new relationship, argued that 'they appear as genuinely baffling documents and seem to be made up of mainly warm words, platitudes and generalities'. The Northern Ireland Office however, was not at all confounded. It viewed the compact as a partnership with the voluntary and community sector based on shared values and mutual respect working with government 'to identify and tackle social needs, strengthen communities, and build a more tolerant, participative, inclusive and peaceful society' (Northern Ireland Office, 1998: 4). A Joint Government/Voluntary and Community Sector Forum was set up following the publication of the compact to discuss issues of mutual interest and to monitor its operation in practice. Its remit was:

- To promote dialogue between the voluntary and community sector and Northern Ireland Government departments.
- To provide a formal mechanism by which the voluntary and sector can raise matters of common concern with Northern Ireland Government departments and *vice versa*.
- To promote general strategic discussions about issues affecting the voluntary and community sector and volunteering.

> **Box 6.2 Shared values: compact between government and the voluntary and community sector in Northern Ireland**
>
> Common ground, mutual understanding, shared perceptions, and joint aspirations are essential elements of strong relationships. In working together towards the achievement of a participative, peaceful, equitable and inclusive society in Northern Ireland, both Government and the voluntary and community sector value the following:
>
> - *Accountability*: Being answerable to all relevant stakeholders in relation to the propriety of policies, actions and use of resources.
> - *Active Citizenship*: Participation of people in society through volunteering, community involvement, and self-help initiatives.
> - *Community*: People working together in localities or interest groupings to strengthen and improve their lives by harnessing their experience, skills, creativity and potential and identifying issues, needs and imaginative solutions.
> - *Democracy*: A society that enables all its citizens to participate, to share rights and responsibilities, and which incorporates an independent voluntary and community sector.
> - *Equality*: Equality of opportunity in relation to employment and services, and equality of access to resources and decision-making processes for all the people of Northern Ireland.
> - *Partnership*: Creative relationships between the public, private and voluntary community sectors that broaden experience and understanding and promote the development of holistic approaches.
> - *Pluralism*: Upholding the rich diversity of cultures, identities and interests within Northern Ireland.
> - *Social Justice*: Cherishing all citizens equally, through the pursuit of fairness, tolerance, and social cohesion, opposing all forms of discrimination and ensuring the participation of those who are most marginalised.
>
> Source: *Compact between Government and the Voluntary and Community Sector in Northern Ireland* (1998), Northern Ireland Office.

- To encourage the discussion of issues on a co-operative basis and the development of a shared approach to issues and concerns so far as it is possible. (Cited in Business Development Service, 2005: 6)

The joint forum comprises officials from each government department and representatives from a wide cross-section of the voluntary and community sector. However, the compact's timing (December 1998) was such that it remained in abeyance until devolution happened one year later.

In summary, the first period of devolution in Northern Ireland (1921–72) witnessed the demise of Stormont, local government discredited as a political entity and its emergence as a denuded forum with limited executive powers. The ensuing political vacuum and sectarian violence during the direct rule period mobilised community activists in a new phase, largely characterised by self-help. Increasingly the voluntary and community sector became valued by the direct rule government and civil servants as potential partners in the formulation and delivery of social policies. As various attempts to break the constitutional impasse foundered, the voluntary and community sector became a stronger stakeholder. This was their status as they entered the next phase, devolved government from 1999 onwards (for a timeline on key developments see: Northern Ireland Assembly, 2007b; 2008a).

Engaging with the devolved administration

In general terms, some politicians are envious of the privileged access which the voluntary and community sector had to senior civil servants during the period of direct rule – as one Ulster Unionist MLA put it 'it is time for the sector to stand aside' (Cobain, quoted in McCall and Williamson, 2001). Yet there is also an acknowledgement of the valuable contribution which the sector can make to post conflict Northern Ireland (Williamson *et al.*, 2000; Cochrane, 2001; Hodgett and Johnston, 2001; Acheson and Williamson, 2007). Consociational arrangements brokered through the Belfast/Good Friday Agreement cannot, in themselves, deliver stability on the ground and require active engagement with civil society as key stakeholders in the community (Byrne, 2001). This approach has been described by Taylor as social transformation which 'challenges ethno-national group politics in favour of a democratic, non-sectarian future' (Taylor, 2009b: 327) although is rejected by McGarry and O'Leary (2009: 67) who argue that the political preferences of Northern Ireland's civil society 'do not differ significantly from those of political parties'. Where that engagement can take place at the level of a departmental strategy for collaboration it offers the potential for a constructive working relationship. When it enters the arena of 'high politics' and the mechanism for engagement is part of the architecture of the Belfast/Good Friday Agreement (e.g. the Civic Forum), then support is partial.

The Northern Ireland's Executive's *Programme for Government* (in 2001) made clear the new devolved administration not only embraced the spirit of the *Compact* but also sought to operationalise it.

Regeneration of our society – in the fullest sense means that we have to tackle issues of equality and human rights, poverty and social disadvantage, renewal of the most disadvantaged neighbourhoods, sustaining and enhancing local communities and improving community relations . . . In tackling these issues we have the advantage of a vibrant and extensive community and voluntary sector which already makes significant and critical contributions to many areas of life. A key challenge will be to build on this community capacity and to involve it in policies and programmes aimed at strengthening our community well-being. (Northern Ireland Executive Programme for Government, 2001: 2.1.1)

In recognition, the Department for Social Development's Voluntary and Community Unit launched its strategy document *Partners for Change* (2001–04) for the voluntary and community sector in Northern Ireland. The three-year strategy set out specific priorities and actions for government departments which would enable the voluntary and community sector 'to contribute more fully to their areas of business and subsequently the social, environmental and cultural life of Northern Ireland' (Department for Social Development, 2001: 9). There were also responsibilities on the voluntary and community sector to take actions to support the implementation of the strategy. Each government department described its current relationship with the sector in the strategy and then set out priorities and actions under three broad headings: capacity building, working together and resourcing the sector. Considering just one of these headings – 'Working Together' – illustrates the extent of engagement envisaged between Government and the sector:

Working together will entail three dimensions:

- Working together to ensure that the voluntary and community sector are actively involved, and afforded the opportunity to contribute to the development, implementation and monitoring of policy developments in order that their expertise might inform policy-making processes.
- Working together to share good practice, to build on the experience of Government and the sector, in addressing need and effecting change and to develop and maintain mechanisms enabling greater communication between Government and the sector.
- Working together to deliver services. (Department for Social Development, 2001: 15)

Although this is was billed as a government strategy it had been developed collaboratively with the Joint Government/Voluntary and Community Sector Forum. Each department committed to the preparation of an annual progress report on the *Partners for Change* strategy which the Minister had to endorse prior to its submission for consideration by the Joint Forum.

Partners for Change undoubtedly gave a very firm commitment to collaborative working between the devolved administration and the voluntary and community sector. This compares with local compact partnerships in England where researchers found 'a gap between language and action... The voluntary sector may be spoken of as "essential" but is then not mentioned in corporate plans, and is not involved in strategic planning' (Gaster and Deakin, 1998: 191). The language used by the Department for Social Development to herald the Northern Ireland strategy was bold by any standards – 'with over 5,000 voluntary and community groups in Northern Ireland, creation of this strategy is an ambitious and innovative exercise that is without precedent in the United Kingdom' (Department for Social Development, 2001: 10). The Voluntary and Community Unit (within the Department for Social Development) described how the voluntary and community sector had become a key social partner in the processes of government. That involvement, it argued, 'reflects a more developed and mature relationship and role within Government than anywhere else in the United Kingdom, Ireland or indeed Europe' (Voluntary and Community Unit, 2002: 1). Even after stripping away the departmental rhetoric, the strategy suggested a significant role for the voluntary and community sector in the decision-making process of every government department. Its strict monitoring arrangements, overseen by the Joint Forum which scrutinised annual progress reports that had to be signed-off by ministers, implied departments could not afford to pay lip-service to partnering the sector. The sector's co-chair of the Joint Forum commented at the time:

> Five years ago it was almost inconceivable that representatives from government departments would be meeting regularly with representatives of community groups and voluntary organisations to discuss issues of concern in a Joint Forum. The most significant area that has engaged the Joint Forum over the past two years has been the development of the Government's strategy to support the community and voluntary sector – *Partners for Change*. This is a unique document. It is the first time that a devolved administration in the United Kingdom has published a document that brings together departmental strategies for the support of the community and voluntary sector. It is unique in the way in which it has brought together representatives from the community and voluntary sector and departmental officials in jointly working to develop the strategy. It is unique in the way in which the ongoing monitoring arrangements for the strategy will include the community and voluntary sector. (Graham, 2002: 20)

A review of the Joint Forum commissioned by the Department for Social Development reported in 2005 that it 'has been effective in meeting its current remit' and recommended it should continue (Business Development Service, 2005: 25).

Perhaps because of the extent of the voluntary and community sector's involvement at central government level and the paucity of local authorities' powers in Northern Ireland, there has not been the development of local compact arrangements as in other parts of the United Kingdom (Craig *et al.*, 1999; Ross and Osborne, 1999). But there were important general lessons to be learned from that experience. Osborne and McLaughlin (2002), for example, chart the relationships between local government and the voluntary sector in England during the period 1979 to 2000 and examined the implementation of compacts at both national and local levels. They concluded that the voluntary sector compact 'has the potential to give substance to the rhetoric of community governance, by providing explicit processes for the community to impact upon policy formulation and service management at the local level' (Osborne and McLaughlin, 2002: 61). They highlight, however, some of the attendant threats – potential participative challenges to the tradition of representative democracy, and the loss of voluntary sector independence as an advocate for the marginalised and socially excluded through its incorporation into the machinery of the state. These threats were all the more real given the size of Northern Ireland, the scale of the voluntary and community sector and its close working relationship with senior officials.

As devolved government wobbled and was eventually suspended for the fourth time in October 2002, direct rule Minister, Des Brown, established a taskforce (February 2003) to develop a strategy to help ensure that the voluntary and community sector 'can continue to make a substantial contribution to the achievement of government objectives and the well-being of the Northern Ireland community' (Department for Social Development, 2003: 1). The Task Force reported (*Investing Together*) in October 2004 and found that the voluntary and community sector operated in a volatile funding environment without a medium to long-term resource commitment. Chasing short-term funding and lack of commitment by statutory agencies distracted organisations from their core tasks and created instability in the sector. Although there were potential benefits of engaging in the delivery of public services, many voluntary and community organisations had experienced barriers in becoming involved. These obstacles were similarly identified by a review which had been completed by HM Treasury that considered how Government could work more effectively with the sector to deliver high-quality services: lack of recognition by funders of full delivery costs, lack of investment in relevant skills and knowledge, and the need for a more secure funding base to facilitate bidding for public sector contracts (HM Treasury, 2002). Many voluntary and community organisations also felt under-resourced to engage in meaningful policy development work which was particularly important under devolution in Northern Ireland.

The recommendations contained in the Task Force's *Investing Together* report were wide-ranging and focused on strengthening the relationship between Government and the voluntary and community sector. In particular, they were designed to ensure the sector was better placed to cope with social and economic changes. Specifically, the report recommended: the need for Government to invest in the voluntary and community sector and provide more stable and longer-term funding; establishment of a community investment fund; streamlining the delivery and accountability of public funding to the sector, improved governance; and, a modernisation fund to enhance the capacity of voluntary and community organisations to deliver public services (Department for Social Development, 2004: 50–53).

The Government's response to *Investing Together* came in a report entitled *Positive Steps* (2005) which welcomed the recommendations above and agreed that these generally aligned with the government priorities, departmental objectives and a strategy to support the voluntary and community sector. *Positive Steps* set out a course of action by government on a range of issues: funding, community development, service delivery and internal governance of the sector and became the benchmark for change. Collective future actions included, *inter alia*:

- A commitment by Government to invest an extra £23m over a 3 year period and a longer term (7–10 years) outcome focused approach to programmes involving the voluntary and community sector. A community investment fund would be established to provide more strategic funding for the support of generic community development activity.
- In order to promote modernisation and change within the sector and strengthen the service delivery role, Government agreed to establish a modernisation fund of £3m over a 3 year period and a further £15m to support capital projects across Northern Ireland.
- The voluntary and community sector was given approval to include full overhead costs related to delivering contracted public services and the Government, in turn, intended to put in place mechanisms to check governance and accountability systems to ensure proper disbursement of public money.
- The Government recognised the need to strengthen the regulation of charity law in Northern Ireland and proposed setting up a register of charities and a Northern Ireland Charities Commission. There was also a commitment to the *Compact* as a mechanism for agreement and consensus between Government and the sector and a reaffirmation of its relevance. (Department for Social Development, 2005)

With no sign of a return to devolved government and the *Partners for Change 2001–04* strategy now obsolete, the Department for Social Development launched a new strategy *Partners for Change 2006–08* billed as an action plan which identified the work of government departments with the voluntary and community sector. The new strategy was described by the Department for Social Development as 'the practical outworking of commitments given in the *Compact* to help build stronger, more inclusive and cohesive communities across Northern Ireland and to enhance the delivery of public services' (Department for Social Development, 2006: 4). All government departments contributed to the strategy and committed to actions under the following broad headings:

- *Building communities/promoting active citizenship*: encourage voluntary activity and the involvement of communities (both 'geographic' and 'of interest') in the planning and decision-making process about matters which affect them.
- *Shaping policy development/working together*: ensure that the knowledge and expertise of the sector informs policy development and that policies are sensitive to the needs of those who experience disadvantage.
- *Investment in the sector/capacity building*: build the capacity of the sector and ensure sustainable resources necessary to enable the sector to make an effective, continued contribution to society in Northern Ireland.

This was a comprehensive document in which each government department outlined its relationship with the voluntary and community sector, and listed commitments (under each of the three themes listed above) to action points which would further the relationship between the department and the sector. Where appropriate, the action points were referenced to commitments already made by each department in *Positive Steps*. The symbiotic relationship between Government and the voluntary and community sector is accurately captured by a statement in the strategy document as follows:

> This plan (*Partners for Change 2006–2008*) recognises both the independence of the Voluntary and Community Sector and the interdependence of Government and the Sector in creating a more prosperous, equitable, peaceful and stable society. It endorses the need for investment in the Sector both by Government and the Sector itself to enhance its capacity in targeting disadvantage and social exclusion, in influencing policy, in contributing to improved public services, in helping build better relations within and between communities and in advocacy and challenging policy where unfairness exists. It recognises that the Sector must develop and change to meet the demands of a changing Northern Ireland. (Department for Social Development, 2006: 4)

To take forward *Positive Steps*, an implementation group comprising senior officials in each of the government departments, responsible for relations with the voluntary and community sector was put in place, charged with oversight of commitments therein. In addition, NICVA was tasked with monitoring progress made in *Positive Steps* on a six-monthly basis. In October 2008 NICVA issued its final monitoring report on the outworking of *Positive Steps*. The report was based on the views of their members elicited via a survey and a longitudinal panel study of 72 organisations which examined awareness and impact of *Positive Steps* on the sector. The results were a mixed bag. Participants in the monitoring process found funding arrangements clearer, and more had witnessed the inclusion of full cost recovery in projects they were delivering. Generally there was optimism that the nature of funding 'was moving in the right direction.' However, the monitoring exercise concluded with:

> The big message to come out of the evaluations is the disconnection between what government claims is happening behind the scenes and the sector's own experience of what *Positive Steps* has achieved. This has created an atmosphere in the sector which is characterised by a general sense of disappointment, disillusionment and apathy towards the document and the subsequent implementation process. Progress has been made but there remains the sense it has been a missed opportunity to radically overhaul the funding environment and how the government and the sector interact. (NICVA, 2008a: 43)

This is hardly a ringing endorsement of original claims by the (then) Minister (John Spellar) in *Positive Steps* that he was 'confident this agenda for change will be delivered together by the Government and the sector and will make a major contribution to the sustainability of the voluntary and community sector and the services it delivers' (Department for Social Development, 2005: 2).

The Government has a somewhat different view outlined in two progress reports on *Positive Steps* arising from its implementation group now chaired by Social Development Minister, Margaret Ritchie (Department for Social Development, 2007; 2008). In the most recent assessment the Minister is much more positive than the sectoral assessment and comments as follows:

> There has been progress against the majority of *Positive Steps* commitments, resulting in significant change and greater consistency of practice. A small number of relatively complex commitments have not yet been fully implemented. However, Government has plans in place to examine the complexities of these outstanding commitments and to identify options for ensuring full implementation as soon as possible. (Department for Social Development, 2008: i)

The Minister concedes that there is what she describes as an 'expectation gap' over the issue of long-term funding for the sector in which Government made a commitment 'to promote a longer-term (7–10 years) outcome focused approach to programmes that significantly involve the voluntary and community sector', but argued that the 3-year budgetary cycle made it difficult to commit much beyond this time period. Minister Ritchie highlighted the progress made to date as follows:

- In Northern Ireland three-year funding commitments from Government Departments are the norm – this is not the case in Great Britain where one-year funding is the norm.
- Significant progress has been made on changing the regulation of charities in Northern Ireland. A Charities Bill will be enacted in summer 2008 with the Charity Commission for Northern Ireland being established by the end of 2008.

- Departmental leads have been identified and taken forward strategic developments in key cross-cutting policy areas (Disability, Youth, Women and Rural Services).
- Information on funding to the sector from central government is now available via the Government funding database, and funding from local government and non-departmental public bodies will be included over time.
- The £5m Community Investment Fund in the Department for Social Development, for the three-year period 2006 to 2009 is providing more strategic support for community development activity.
- Rollout of the £18m Modernisation Fund to help support and facilitate change is ongoing.
- A *Best Practice Manual on Finance and Governance* and a *Code of Good Governance* have been published by Department for Social Development and disseminated widely.

One example of progress since this departmental report on *Positive Steps* has been the establishment of the Charity Commission for Northern Ireland as a non-departmental public body funded by grant-in-aid from the Department for Social Development. It was established under the Charities Act (NI) 2008 and became operational on 27 March 2009. Its mission is to introduce a regulatory framework for the charitable sector in Northern Ireland, in line with developments in the rest of the UK and Ireland. This will provide a structure and process through which charities can demonstrate their contribution to society, and assure the public how charities are spending any donations. The Government, in turn, can assist in the better governance of the charity sector.

One of the significant differences in the work done by the voluntary and community sector from its counterpart in Great Britain is the key role it has played in rebuilding communities torn apart by sectarian divisions as a result of the conflict. We consider two case studies of the work undertaken – a peace building project at an interface area and the role of ex-prisoner community groups. By their nature case studies cannot capture the breadth of work which community groups at grassroots level are involved in, but will perhaps provide an insight into the very difficult circumstances faced by people determined to reinvest in rebuilding or renewing their communities.

Community sector: a case study in peace building

The Lenadoon Estate is a public sector housing scheme with over 9,000 residents situated on the outskirts of West Belfast, on the boundary between

Belfast and Lisburn City Councils. The estate was built during the mid-1960s just before the outbreak of 'the troubles' in Northern Ireland. Housing tenure was originally mixed religion but as civil unrest spread, the nature and development of the estate suffered significantly from population shift. A largely Protestant population living in the lower part of the estate (Lenadoon Avenue and Horn Drive) moved out during the early 1970s and their homes were filled with Catholics fleeing sectarian strife from other parts of Belfast. These population shifts created a fragmented community with a common adversary – sectarian violence. A Lenadoon community worker described the evolving situation thus:

> As a result of the conflict many local people were killed and scores more injured in incidents in the area. Hundreds of local people were imprisoned and this placed a heavy burden on the community . . . Despite this adversity, people showed a strong attachment to the area and a determination to work collectively to improve the estate and challenge the neglect of successive governments and statutory bodies. (Lenadoon Community Forum, 2003: 5)

As Lenadoon became the refuge of Catholics from other parts of Belfast, Protestant families living on the estate were forced to either move out because of sectarianism and intimidation or shift to the Suffolk estate (at the lower end of Lenadoon and the south side of the Stewartstown Road) which became an enclave for Protestants living in West Belfast. As Catholic families grew on the Lenadoon estate, Suffolk became the repository for Protestants who had chosen to remain – in effect a small commune of public houses with around 1,000 people surrounded on all sides by their Catholic neighbours. The result was a small Protestant community which felt under siege and insecure within an ascendant and what might be described as an increasingly territorial nationalist/ republican area. Suffolk residents living through this period argued that the British Government actively facilitated the evacuation of Protestants in collaboration with the Republican movement. One resident recalled how she recently encountered a senior British Army Officer who 'had waited nearly 30 years to apologise' to Protestant people in the area:

> He proceeded to tell me that while he was the local commander he had actually been negotiating with the Republican movement to kind of stage-manage the evacuation of the Protestant families. He said that there were hundreds of displaced Catholic families looking for houses and if they had descended on Lenadoon at the same time there could be wholesale slaughter. So they were being put into houses vacated by Protestants in small groups. (cited in Hall, 2007: 7–8)

Republicans in the area rationalised this as a pragmatic response by the Army to hugely difficult circumstances during 'the war in the North of Ireland'. There were accusations that the British Government actually paid the Republican movement to help resettle Catholic families in houses which Protestants were forced to evacuate. Catholics, in turn, were being burned out of their homes in other parts of Belfast and had to be relocated. With a group of isolated Protestant people living in Lenadoon, it was easier to force them into Suffolk and move Catholics into two increasingly segregated communities which were easier to police. This managed 'security solution' in the early 1970s created an interface area between Lenadoon and Suffolk estates (the boundary of which is Stewartstown Road) which endues to the present day – euphemistically known as 'the peace line'. One Lenadoon resident at the time described it thus:

> By 1976–7, most Protestant residents in Lenadoon had moved across the Stewartstown Road into Suffolk, while their houses had been resettled by Catholic families burnt or intimidated out of other parts of Belfast. And that's when the Stewartstown Road became the permanent interface, the peace line. And for most Catholics this road had become somewhere you didn't cross, if you could avoid it. (Hall, 2007: 12)

Apart from this territorial divide, both Suffolk and Lenadoon estates suffer from significant economic disadvantage. Suffolk and Lenadoon estates are part of the Outer West Belfast Neighbourhood Renewal area, defined as the top 10 per cent of deprived neighbourhoods in Northern Ireland.

Community development groups evolved in both areas to tackle social disadvantage and became affiliated to their respective umbrella groups. Lenadoon Community Forum was established in 1992 to co-ordinate the community development needs of some twenty member groups on the estate. Suffolk Community Forum was set up in 1994 'to work towards creating a stable, secure and confident community in Suffolk' (Insight Consulting, 2006: 3). Both forums subsequently moved to co-operate. The spirit of the early joint meetings in 1995/96 was 'to discuss things we think we have in common, the difficulties between us and how we can be better neighbours' (O'Halloran and McIntyre, 1999: 5). From these early informal meetings, as trust developed, a formally constituted Suffolk and Lenadoon Interface Group (SLIG) was established in 1999. An important aspect of building trust was recognition by SLIG that both communities faced common problems. The British Government reduced and eventually closed community employment schemes (ACE projects) on both sides of the interface; poverty presented itself as a real issue for the two estates; and protocols were established to deal with issues (parades, interface violence) during periods of heightened tensions.

The journey towards greater co-operation between Suffolk and Lenadoon encountered a number of setbacks. Wider political problems (contentious parades and sectarian killings) played out in the form of community interface violence within Suffolk and Lenadoon. There were ongoing problems over disputed land and territory. Catholics in Lenadoon point to an increasing need for social housing and vacant publicly owned land available in Suffolk. Residents in Suffolk however perceive this as 'their land' which should only be used to enhance housing or community facilities for Protestants. Community activists involved in SLIG also risked a backlash from within their own communities for moving at a pace of shared working inconsistent with the wishes of the majority of people living in both areas. In an attempt to summarise the evolution of SLIG, researchers involved in interface work in Belfast noted two key points. First, although violence subsided in areas such as West Belfast (and Northern Ireland more generally) this was not tantamount to 'peace': rather it emphasised the significant amount of work to be done within communities coming out of years of conflict. Second, joint development that results in real and meaningful inter-community work can be a 'very slow and frustrating process' (O'Halloran and McIntyre, 1999: 27).

The International Fund for Ireland funded an initial project in 2001 under the auspices of SLIG for youth and community work in both areas for a 3-year period. The project, specifically aimed at conflict management, was conceived as a diversionary programme on a single identity/community basis which sought to draw young people away from the interface and direct their energies into activities. The work was crucially important in terms of reducing interface tension and violence. The International Fund for Ireland reinvested for an additional 3-year period which enabled SLIG to employ staff and implement cross-community activities. At the same time, a regeneration project on the peace line (Stewartstown Road) was initiated by the Suffolk Community Group which identified a semi-derelict building owned by the Northern Ireland Housing Executive as the basis for a joint project. SLIG jointly applied for funding to create a shared space on the site and developed a mixed use building of 1,000m^2 with retail, office and community space. Such was the success of this venue that a second phase has just been completed including a modern childcare facility attracting parents and toddlers from Suffolk and Lenadoon estates. The residents attribute little of this to support from the public sector in Northern Ireland. As one Lenadoon resident put it:

> The civil service gave us no amount of hassle [*sic*], putting us through endless hoops and obstacles. They openly called our initiative a 'white elephant', questioned what was in it for Lenadoon, or Suffolk, and passed the opinion that it wouldn't be used, it would just stand idle . . . I remember after we had applied for further funding to develop the project into its second phase, a representative from the Belfast Regeneration Office said at a meeting: 'you've cured the interface, so why would you need more funding?' As if it was some sort of disease to be 'cured'! The stability of an interface depends upon hard work of the two communities to keep it that way; an interface remains, even at the best of times, potentially volatile. (cited in Hall, 2007: 28)

In January 2007, as a direct result of ongoing collaborative work, SLIG attracted a major investment of £2m over 3 years from Atlantic Philanthropies[1] for the implementation of a (joint) SLIG peace building plan to support community based reconciliation through the promotion of shared services, facilities and public spaces. Specifically the joint plan has involved delivery of cross-community activities across four key strands:

1. Peace building activities: these include shared pre-school provision, transformation of the controlled (Protestant) Suffolk Primary School into an shared space youth facility, a health and women's development project, cultural initiative, youth activities and sports development schemes.
2. Joint advocacy: lobbying government agencies on a joint community basis to address the social and economic needs of Suffolk and Lenadoon and the legacy of the conflict.
3. Building capacity for peace through community leadership and widening and deepening the basis of community self-help beyond the established activists who constitute the respective community forums.
4. Developing shared space by targeting derelict land and premises which could be reclaimed or refurbished as joint community facilities owned and managed by local people from the two communities.

The project has achieved significant success. These achievements have been recognised by the Community Relations Council through awards to founding members of the SLIG interface group. The case study exemplifies self-help exercised through community groups at its best.

Ex-prisoner groups: a case study in reintegration

It is estimated that 24,000 to 30,000 people have spent time in prison due to the conflict in, or about, Northern Ireland. The vast majority were young men when convicted. The Belfast/Good Friday Agreement acknowledged the role of prisoners in the peace process and their influence in wider peace building initiatives.

> The Governments (London and Dublin) continue to recognise the importance of measures to facilitate the reintegration of prisoners into the community by providing support both prior to and after release, including assistance directed towards availing of employment opportunities, retraining and/or re-skilling, and further education. (The Good Friday/Belfast Agreement, April 1998: 25)

Under the provisions of the Agreement, 450 prisoners (196 loyalist, 242 republican and 12 non-aligned) were released back into the community. Since then, 22 people have had their licences suspended who were believed to have breached the terms of their release. Of these, 18 were life sentence prisoners and 4 were determinate sentence prisoners. Ten of the 22 (4 determinates and 6 lifers) were for alleged involvement in terrorist offending behaviour and 12 for alleged involvement in non-terrorist offending behaviour (Northern Ireland Prison Service).

There is a gulf between the two main parties, DUP and Sinn Féin, in the power-sharing administration on this issue historically. The DUP was firmly against the early release of prisoners under the Belfast/Good Friday Agreement stating at the time 'all decent people recoil with moral contempt at the prospect of the mass release of those who have murdered and maimed the innocent' (DUP, 1998: cited in Shirlow *et al.*, 2005). Neither the DUP nor Sinn Féin made reference to the issue of ex-prisoners in their 2007 Assembly Elections Manifestos: *Getting it Right* and *Delivering for Ireland's Future* (*Saoirse, Ceart agus Síocháin*) respectively.

The early release of prisoners has therefore been politically charged, as has funding to support their efforts to reintegrate. Initiatives taken by direct ministers have not always found favour under devolution. For example, a conflict transformation initiative received (direct rule) government funding but subsequently attracted adverse media attention and caused political discord in the power-sharing Executive. Loyalist conflict transformation initiatives were established by community organisations in working-class Protestant areas following the cease-fires and staffed by people from the Ulster Volunteer Force and Red Hand Commando constituency. The broad aim of their work was to move from old conflicts to more self-confident communities that could engage with government in policy development and service provision that effect their communities.

Direct Rule ministers had agreed funding of €1.2m to support a UDA-linked conflict transformation initiative to encourage loyalist organisations to abandon violence and criminality. A research report highlighted some of the political benefits of such transformation initiatives in loyalist areas: they both represent and challenge existing thinking and practice within loyalism; they help diffuse tense and violent situations which assist stabilising the wider peace process; they actively engage with statutory bodies and government, seeking to influence policy on conflict management; they constructively engage with former adversaries; they act as conduits between statutory bodies and the loyalist community, many of whom are alienated from what is perceived as mainstream society; and, they seek to develop a transferable model of peace building (Gribbin *et al.*, 2005).

However, Social Development Minister (Margaret Ritchie) blocked the funding to the initiative (November 2007) on the grounds that the UDA failed to decommission and end its illegal activities. Ms Ritchie's decision sparked a clash in the Assembly between her and one of her power-sharing cabinet colleagues, (then) Finance Minister Peter Robinson, who accused her of failing to follow proper legal and ministerial advice before acting. The Minister's decision was the subject of a judical review which found that she had not acted in accordance with the provisions of the Ministerial code. The DUP Minister accused Ms Ritchie of acting in what amounted to 'little more than a party political frolic' which she rejected saying that 'the judge, in effect, ruled that the problem was an error in procedure' (McAdam, 2009: 24)

Notwithstanding the political sensitivities which surround former prisoners, Kilmurray (2007) has stressed the positive contributions they are making to wider goals of demilitarisation and community peace building. These include the following:

1. The ability of ex-prisoner groups to influence thinking on the ground, particularly in 'hard to reach' communities, with the aim of supporting the rule of law and discouraging violent responses to issues.
2. Working with local communities to reduce and, where possible, help prevent, anti-social behaviour, recreational rioting and criminality.
3. Helping ex-prisoners, ex-combatants and single identity local communities make the transition from 'conflict' to 'normality' by adopting a leadership role.
4. Work at interface areas, particularly with young people and during periods of heightened community tensions.
5. Providing opportunities for meaningful cross-community engagement, facilitation and addressing common problems.

Philanthropic funding supported ex-prisoner community groups because of the above contributions under two broad headings: re-integration and developing capacity.

Re-integration

These groups attracted independent funding because of the positive contributions which ex-prisoners were making to the political process at the macro-level, particularly on demilitarisation and community peace building efforts. The funds supported core costs of ex-prisoner centres serving a range of paramilitary groups typically engaged in the following type of activities:

- Advice and welfare support for individual ex-prisoners and their families, particularly in trying to secure employment and connect to the wider ex-prisoner community.

- Peace-building and conflict transformation, where ex-prisoner centres, located in the heartland republican and loyalist areas, serve as a focal point to address inter-community tensions. They have become centres for local dispute resolution and play an important role, through the actions of ex-prisoners, in for example the removal of paramilitary murals and symbols.
- Political development – ex-prisoner groups have played a significant, if understated role, in copper-fastening the political momentum by making their members aware of, and securing support for, risk-taking initiatives, not least in relation to the demilitarisation process.
- Acknowledging the legacy of the past – working with the victims and survivors of the conflict to address issues surrounding their loss and to assist them in trying to come to terms with their personal tragedies.

An important aspect of this work was to set up a cross-community Policy Development Group which brought together various ex-prisoner factions in a forum for exchanging views and channelling their collective pasts into creating a positive force for the future. It should of course be recognised that the constituent loyalist and republican groups were sworn enemies before the cease-fires so bringing them together in such a forum, in itself, represented a significant achievement. During periods of on-off political developments, the policy development group also acted as an important cross-community bridge which offered a sense of stability at the grassroots activist level.

Developing capacity

Additional philanthropic funding was invested to sustain the work of the ex-prisoners' centres and to support an ongoing advocacy campaign to ensure that government delivered on its commitment to mainstream funding. The lack of support from the government has been criticised. As Shirlow (2008: 27) has argued:

> With regard to former prisoner groups their future work must be related to exact statutory recognition. There is no overall approach towards former prisoners by the statutory sector and, as a result of this, statutory representatives have a tendency to only meet/respond to former prisoner representatives during periods of crisis . . . It is also noted that the Northern Ireland Office has taken no responsibility in this area.

Research and evaluation evidence indicates the significant role which ex-prisoners have played and continue to play in conflict transformation An external evaluation of the philanthropic funding to ex-prisoners found significant achievements as follows:

(i) Former prisoner groups possess the skills and a model of conflict transformation required to develop a meaningful inter-community relations approach within deprived communities and, in particular, those communities that were affected most by violence.
(ii) The model of conflict transformation promoted by former prisoners is well established and the removal of this model would create a distinct peacebuilding and community void.
(iii) The nature of the inter-group partnership being advanced by the former prisoner community is identifiable, robust and coherent. This partnership has had a major impact upon reducing violence and the reproduction of violence.
(iv) Former prisoners constitute an enabling agent that has encouraged and continues to promote approaches to post-conflict transformation that embeds peaceful methods (Shirlow, 2008: 1).

Despite this evidence, there is no mention of a strategic commitment to the work of ex-prisoners in the *Programme for Government 2008–11* – the priorities for the devolved administration over the four-year period. In fact, ex-prisoners do not feature in the document or the accompanying *Northern Ireland Executive Budget 2008–11*. Yet it is clear that former prisoners' community groups have been at the vanguard in progressing some of the most difficult issues in the peace process including: work at interface areas which can become a flashpoint for violence, negotiations on contentious parades, decommissioning of paramilitary weapons, engagement with the victims of political violence and promoting and encouraging the emerging debate on truth recovery. These contributions are summed up in research on the ex-prisoners groups as follows:

> The contribution of former prisoners and the groupings to which they belong has been highly significant to date. Despite significant obstacles . . . and an arguably lacklustre government follow-through upon the commitments in the Agreement, former prisoners have well used the resources afforded them. Through the reintegration framework, they have become key agents of embedding the process of conflict transformation in Northern Ireland in communities most affected by violence and from which violence would emerge first if the process were to fail. (Shirlow and McEvoy, 2008: 151)

These findings provoked a strong reaction from the DUP. Strangford Assembly Member, Simon Hamilton, argued that the research was insensitive and hurtful – the prisoner-release programme was a 'perversion of justice' and was sufficient grounds for many to oppose the Belfast Agreement itself. 'Just because the flinging open of the doors of the Maze and the freeing of terrorists from all sides happened almost a decade ago, the hurt and pain felt by victims and survivors is no less intense today,' he claimed.

> The authors of this book can sit in the ivory towers of academia and theorise over the supposed value of the early-release scheme all they want. But their conclusions

are deeply insensitive to many victims and survivors, and could in some cases cause victims to experience more harm. (Hamilton, quoted in Keenan 2008: 10)

Mr Hamilton argued that calling the early-release scheme a success 'completely ignores the very many people in Northern Ireland who consider it an appalling abomination'. Despite the political controversy which surrounds this highly sensitive topic, it is clear that the role of ex-prisoners' community groups has been central to peace building and consolidating political gains. Former prisoners were well placed to help 'keep the lid' on capricious community problems which had the potential to derail the political process: contentious parades, flashpoint violence, demilitarisation and interface areas. Government bodies, on the other hand, were unwilling to fund ex-prisoner groups because of the political sensitivities and the furore which accompanied their early release, not least from victims of paramilitary violence. It is clear from this example that ex-prisoner groups with external/philanthropic funding have been able to play a significant role within communities.

Participative democracy?

What can be concluded from the role played by the third sector and its relationship with the devolved government? Have we moved towards a model of participation and deliberation in Northern Ireland? NICVA has argued that Northern Ireland has an under-developed relationship between government and the voluntary and community sector by comparison with arrangements in Ireland, England and Wales. In a report making the case for a White Paper, NICVA claims that something stronger than the current Compact mechanism is needed to establish an enduring relationship with the Northern Ireland devolved administration – a participative democracy. Developing such a paper, according to NICVA, would demand that government address fundamental questions about the voluntary and community sector, viz.:

- What does government want and expect from the sector?
- What is the sector's role in service provision?
- What other roles in communities and in democratic processes does the sector play?
- How does government intend to support the sector in these various roles?
- What structures would need to be in place to do this?

This call for a White Paper points to fact that current relations between government and the voluntary and community sector are perceived by the latter as unsatisfactory. It could also been seen as a way of legally codifying the relationship and, to that extent, securing a firmer commitment from government. In a fairly blunt assessment from the sector's perspective NICVA argues:

> We do already have the *Compact* and it is now ten years since it was signed. All parties to it recognise that it is a largely aspirational document, which sets out very important principles and commitments for both sector and government. However, it is generally ignored in everyday practice and this makes it relatively meaningless to most organisations.
>
> *Positive Steps* was to be the policy that clarified some of the aspects of the relationship between government and voluntary and community organisations in Northern Ireland, but opinions differ between government and the sector as to whether the substantial issues dealt with in it have been implemented in a way that has made any impact. In addition . . . many of the issues with which a *White Paper* could deal move far beyond the issue of funding to exploring and expressing the role of civil society, and within that, the voluntary and community sector in a modern healthy democracy. (NICVA, 2008b: 1 and 2)

The call for a White Paper was endorsed by all political parties in a debate in the Northern Ireland Assembly (November 2008) although MLAs widened the appeal from the sector to include better cross-departmental funding to support the delivery of Programme for Government targets using the third sector's capacity. One DUP MLA noted in the debate 'In many ways, the strong community and voluntary sector reflects our history over the past number of decades, as it has done lots of work that the Government were unable to do, or did not want to do, and it was absolutely necessary for the work to be done on the ground. Slowly but surely, in recent times, political parties, and, most importantly, the Government, are starting to recognise that contribution' (Hamilton, 2008: 292). Whilst the Minister for Social Development welcomed the Assembly motion in support of the White Paper and also acknowledged the vital role which the sector played in delivering local services and tackling social needs, she expressed some reservations:

> Although I want the relationship between Government and the voluntary and community sector to be, dare I say it, intimate, I do not want it to be overly paternalistic. I do not consider Government or the Department for Social Development as the voluntary and community sector's employers because that could become a stranglehold . . . I am aware of NICVA's call for a White Paper to be prepared. Although I remain to be convinced that that is necessary to deliver the change that is required, I am, nonetheless, content to explore that option with my officials. (Ritchie, 2008b: 296–97)

Aside from trying to put the relationship and role of the voluntary sector on a firmer legislative footing with government, NICVA has identified several key issues in the changing political, economic and social environment which will impact on the work of the sector over the next three-plus years. These include, *inter alia*:

- The introduction of community planning will bring major challenges and opportunities to see voluntary and community organisations playing a key role in shaping policies for their local area.
- The current political dispensation is not well disposed to tackling issues of sectarianism and segregation. The issue of division and sectarianism is still the biggest underlying problem in Northern Ireland which affects and influences the political stances that parties in government take. Northern Ireland is still prone to the notion of being a 'zero-sum game'.
- The Civic Forum has not been reinstated – the voluntary and community sector is structurally absent from the devolved institutions. There may be the possibility to secure a new and better structure based on social partnership, as in the Republic of Ireland, and discussions continue on a North–South Consultative Forum.
- Relationships with the EU will no longer be about funding and will be about developing closer links, policy participation and working more within mainstream EU partnerships and structures, e.g. networks of cities, regions.
- The Northern Ireland Executive has placed a firm emphasis on the economy but has shown an unwillingness to raise the necessary resources. Freezing of rates benefits the better-off most and shows little appetite for equality. There is no recognition of the limits to growth dictated by sustainability or of the policies necessary to redistribute.
- Households will still be hit hard by new rates and water charges, increasing costs of energy and food. Political commitments, taken from the UK, to halve child poverty by 2010 and end it by 2020, are unlikely to be met and there is no evident will within government for a robust anti-poverty strategy with a coherent central action plan and budget. In the current climate this suggests worsening poverty and the return to problems of unemployment.
- Devolution of policing and justice in Northern Ireland will present challenges and opportunities. The sector, as a service provider in the criminal justice system, has a role to play. There will also be the obvious political ramifications. However, beyond this is the potential for a broad debate around citizenship, the state and justice in a devolved context (NICVA, 2009b).

Does the Assembly's endorsement of a White Paper augur well for the sector? Even though *Positive Steps* was conceived during the suspension of the

Assembly, its implementation has (since May 2007) rested with the devolved administration. The sector has been less than impressed on follow-through. On the one hand, the *Partners for Change* strategy provided the voluntary and community sector with, according to civil servants, 'unprecedented' access and influence over departmental policy-making and accountability arrangements back to the Joint Forum. On the other hand, the formal institutional arrangements for consulting social partners, the Civic Forum (on which the voluntary and community sector had 30 per cent membership) is castigated by some political parties (in particular the DUP) and has not been rejuvenated during the second mandate of the Assembly. The Civic Forum is a construct of the Belfast/Good Friday Agreement which is strenuously opposed by the DUP. In the wider unionist 'family', however, there are long-held suspicions of the voluntary and community sector. The hegemonic unionist state (1921–72) produced a self-help culture amongst nationalist and republicans and a corresponding reliance by unionists and loyalists on a benevolent public sector. Things have changed significantly since the 1970s. A highly mobilised voluntary and community sector in republican areas led to accusations that Catholics secure a disproportionate amount of grant-aid (particularly from European funding) compared to Protestant areas lacking in social capital. Even where community 'leaders' emerge in Protestant areas, there is an absence of mutual trust at the grassroots level and a perceived inability in their capacity to represent the disparate factions within unionism/loyalism (Purdue, 2001). Sinn Féin's community politics have been influential in the sector's development within their residential areas and hence unionists are wary of what they would see as an assertive republican element with political aspirations well beyond their nominal brief.

The Northern Ireland Executive's *Programme for Government 2008–2011* is minimalist in its commitment to the voluntary and community sector. There are a couple of platitudes where the First and deputy First Minister mention the Assembly 'working together with the public, private and voluntary and community sectors to build a shared and better future for all' and needing all 'to address the challenges we face – Government cannot do it alone but can provide a lead' (*Programme for Government 2008–2011:* 3, 23). However, in terms of public service agreements (PSAs) or the key actions that departments will take in support of government priorities, there is a rather general and somewhat feeble commitment to the sector (see table 6.3).

The voluntary and community sector has undoubtedly made a significant contribution to social, economic, cultural, reconciliation and environmental changes in Northern Ireland. Attempts to forge a more permanent relationship with the devolved administration seem like an obvious way to gain a foothold in government as a long-term social partner. Unionist parties appear to have mellowed towards the voluntary and community sector if their reactions

Table 6.3 Housing, urban regeneration and community development (PSA 12)

Objective	Actions	Target	Lead department
Promote a strong vibrant and sustainable voluntary and community sector to enable better delivery of services	• Deliver a sustainable network of advice centres meeting the needs of people. • Establish a robust system of regulation for charities in Northern Ireland • Improve partnership and recognition across government of the role of the voluntary and community sector in government objectives support	• Implement the Advice Services Strategy by 2009 • Establish a Charities Commission for Northern Ireland by the end of 2008, subject to legislation • Monitor and report on *Positive Steps* implementation by December 2008	Department for Social Development

Source: Northern Ireland Executive: *Programme for Government 2008–2011*: 41.

to White Paper proposals are indicative. The sector's dependence over a long period on European funding is coming to an end and voluntary and community groups must look for alternative sources of funding. While public service delivery and partnership arrangements with government departments offer an obvious source of funding, the very independence of the sector could be compromised as they become incorporated into the structures and processes of the public sector. What this chapter has attempted to illustrate is that some community groups, in particular, have taken huge risks in the peace building process, often supported by external/philanthropic funding to do things which the Government did not, or perhaps could not, support. The sector, naturally, is pushing for mainstream funding for these activities and to secure a long-term commitment by the devolved government to a participative democracy in Northern Ireland.

Note

1 Atlantic Philanthropies is a philanthropic organization funded by American Charles Feeney which aims to bring about lasting changes in the lives of disadvantaged and vulnerable people. They work on four main issues – ageing, disadvantaged children and youth, population health, and reconciliation and human rights within seven countries: Australia, Bermuda, Northern Ireland, the Republic of Ireland, South Africa, the United States and Viet Nam.

7
Reconciled Northern Ireland?

Building trust and confidence between and within communities and tackling sectarianism are key priorities for the Government. Northern Ireland remains a deeply divided society, with patterns of division that have become ingrained. There are many reasons for this including fear, mistrust and, in many cases, a weary acceptance of patterns of living that have developed over many years in response to conflict. The overall effect is that, all too often, the choices that people can make are limited – choices of where to live, where to work, or what services to use. (Des Browne, former Parliamentary Under Secretary of State at the Northern Ireland Office, 2003)

The road to peace

To all intents and purposes the Northern Ireland 'problem' has been 'solved' and political violence has significantly subsidised although not gone away. The killing of two soldiers and a policeman by dissident republican factions in March 2009 was a reminder that some paramilitary groups still pose a threat to political stability. The road to peace commenced as early as the 1980s when the British and Irish Governments co-operated more closely in a bid to reach a political settlement beginning with the *Anglo-Irish Agreement* in November 1985. This provided an opportunity for the Irish Government, much to the chagrin of unionists, to become involved in offering their views and proposals for the way forward in Northern Ireland. Both Governments agreed that any change in the status of Northern Ireland could only happen with the consent of the majority of its population and supported a policy of devolution, provided such arrangements could secure widespread community consent and endorsement. There followed (1991–92) a series of nugatory talks led by Northern Ireland Secretaries of State, Brooke and then Mayhew, in which the main constitutional parties (Ulster Unionist Party, Democratic Unionist Party, SDLP and Alliance) identified what they considered to be the key elements which would lead to an eventual political settlement. In December 1993 the then British Prime Minister, John Major and the Irish Taoiseach, Albert Reynolds, made a Joint Declaration which set out a charter for peace and reconciliation in Northern Ireland. It comprised the basic principles needed to achieve political consensus including safeguards for both communities. The British Government gave a statutory constitutional guarantee to uphold the democratic wish of the greater number of people in Northern Ireland. The Taoiseach, in turn, claimed it would be wrong to attempt to impose a united Ireland in the absence of the consent of the majority of people in Northern Ireland. The Declaration offered those linked to paramilitary violence a way of becoming involved in the political process through issuing a public statement to commit to exclusively peaceful methods and agreement to abide by the democratic process (Department of Foreign Affairs: Dublin).

In August 1994 the IRA announced a 'complete cessation of military operations' which was followed by the Combined Loyalist Military Command cease-fire in October 1994. As a consequence the two Governments began direct exploratory political talks with Sinn Féin and the two loyalist parties: the Progressive Unionist Party (PUP) and the Ulster Democratic Party (UDP). The basis of the exploration was to find ways in which these parties might become involved in the substantive talks process and to examine the practical consequences of ending violence. In February 1995 Prime Minister John Major and Taoiseach John Bruton launched *A New Framework for Agreement* which set out the British and Irish Governments' shared understanding of relationships within the island of Ireland and between the two governments. This was supplemented by a separate document *A Framework for Accountable Government* outlining the British Government's proposals for proposed new democratic institutions in Northern Ireland. Together these documents were offered as a possible way to secure broad support across the community in Northern Ireland for a peace settlement based on three sets of relationships – within Northern Ireland; between Northern Ireland and the Republic of Ireland; and between Britain and Ireland.

For unionists to take part in negotiations involving Sinn Féin required movement on decommissioning illegal paramilitary arms. Preliminary talks became bogged down when the Government did not judge that sufficient progress had been made on this issue to provide confidence for all-party negotiations. To kick-start the process the British and Irish Governments launched the *Twin Track Initiative* in 1995 to create the conditions necessary for all-party negotiations to begin. The 'twin tracks' comprised setting up an International Body to examine the decommissioning of illegal arms under the independent chairmanship of US Senator George Mitchell and, in parallel, to begin a phase of preparatory talks to examine the basis, participation, structure, format and agenda for all-party negotiations. Mitchell's report (January 1996) recommended six principles of democracy and non-violence, including the total and verifiable decommissioning of all paramilitary weapons. It also proposed a number of confidence building measures including an elective process to allow negotiations to take place. The Provisional IRA ended its cease-fire in February 1996 with the Canary Wharf bomb in London and resumed a campaign of violence. Both the British and Irish Governments resolved to push ahead with talks but without Sinn Féin until such times as the IRA restored its cease-fire. Multi-party talks, involving the two governments and the Northern Ireland political parties (excluding Sinn Féin), began on the three key relationships following elections in May 1996. All those elected became part of a deliberative forum aimed at promoting dialogue, understanding and consensus across the communities of Northern Ireland. They also committed to referendums to test the views of people on any proposed settlement. Negotiating teams were chosen by parties from amongst the delegates returned at the elections.

The talks, chaired by Senator Mitchell, spent most of the first year adopting rules of procedure but, once again, the arms decommissioning issue cast a shadow over progress in advance of the general election in May 1997. With Labour's landslide victory, the new British Prime Minister, Tony Blair, identified Northern Ireland as a high priority and injected momentum into the talks. Both governments committed to make progress on decommissioning through setting up an Independent International Commission on Decommissioning, alongside substantive political negotiations. The IRA announced a resumption of its cease-fire in July 1997 clearing the way for Sinn Féin's entry into the talks process and their endorsement of the Mitchell principles of democracy and non-violence. In response, the DUP and UKUP left the talks in protest at Sinn Féin's involvement. Substantive negotiations on the three strands of the debate did not commence until September 2007 and continued until April 2008.

On Friday 10 April 1998 the Belfast (Good Friday) Agreement was reached at a plenary session of the talks which set out a plan for devolved government in Northern Ireland that gave effect to the provisions of the multi-party negotiations (O'Leary, 2001; McGarry and O'Leary, 2004; McGarry and O'Leary, 2007). The Agreement provided for: the establishment of the Human Rights and Equality Commissions (Dickson and Osborne, 2007); the early release of terrorist prisoners; the decommissioning of paramilitary weapons, both within two years of the Agreement; and major reforms of criminal justice and policing in Northern Ireland. Importantly, the Good Friday Agreement underscored the constitutional position of Northern Ireland by recognising its legitimacy to continue to support the Union with Great Britain or a sovereign united Ireland, whichever the majority of people in Northern Ireland decided. It enshrines the principle of consent as follows:

> It is for the people of the island of Ireland alone, by agreement between the two parts respectively and without external impediment, to exercise their right of self-determination on the basis of consent, freely and concurrently given, North and South, to bring about a united Ireland, if that is their wish, accepting that this right must be achieved and exercised with and subject to the agreement and consent of the majority of the people of Northern Ireland. (Belfast/Good Friday Agreement, 1998: 1(ii) page 2)

In referendums held on 22 May 1998, the people of Ireland, both North and South, endorsed the Good Friday Agreement. In Northern Ireland 71.1 per cent of voters approved the Agreement. In the Republic of Ireland, 94.4 per cent voted in support. The combined approval in both parts of the island of Ireland was 85 per cent. The electorate in the Republic also approved amendments to the Irish Constitution which formed part of the Agreement. Elections took place to the new Northern Ireland Assembly in June 1998.

The Agreement established an interconnected group of institutions which made up the three strands of relationships. Strand 1 (Democratic Institutions in Northern Ireland) deals with relationships within Northern Ireland and created the Northern Ireland Assembly, its Executive and the consultative Civic Forum (Wilford, 2001b; Wilford, 2007). The 108 member Assembly is elected by proportional representation (single transferable vote) and ministers in the Northern Ireland Executive are appointed in proportion to party strengths in the Assembly. Key decisions are taken on a cross-community basis (parallel consent or a weighted majority). Strand 2 (Northern Ireland – Republic of Ireland relations) established the North–South Ministerial Council comprising members of the Northern Ireland Executive and the Irish Government bringing together those with executive responsibilities for the purposes of consultation, co-operation and action within the island of Ireland (Coakley, 2001). The North–South Ministerial Council also oversees the work of six cross-border implementation bodies. Strand 3 (East – West) deals with relationships within the British Isles. A British–Irish Inter-Governmental Conference was established to promote bilateral co-operation between the UK and Ireland. A new British–Irish Council was also created which includes members of all the devolved administrations within the UK and representatives of the Isle of Man and the Channel Islands alongside the British and Irish Governments.

Power was devolved to the Northern Ireland Assembly and its Executive Committee of Ministers on 2 December 1999 but disagreements between parties, largely over the decommissioning of paramilitary arms, led to a series of suspensions of the Assembly. The disruptions culminated in an indefinite suspension by the Secretary of State in October 2002 – the fourth time since its inception. While the devolved institutions operated for short spells only between 1999 and 2007, other aspects of implementing the Agreement continued. Significantly, police reforms recommended by the Northern Ireland Police Commission (chaired by Chris Patten) were given legal effect. The Royal Ulster Constabulary was replaced by the Police Service of Northern Ireland (November 2001). New associated accountability mechanisms included the Office of the Police Ombudsman (2000), Policing Board (2001) and District Policing Partnerships (2003). The Sinn Féin leader Gerry Adams argued (April 2005) that political alternatives to the armed struggle now existed which prompted a statement from the IRA (July 2005) that they would engage with the Independent International Commission on Decommissioning (IICD) to verifiably put their arms beyond use. The end of the IRA's armed campaign, confirmed by an IICD report that decommissioning had been completed, created the opportunity for greater political engagement. The Taoiseach, Bertie Ahern, and Prime Minister Blair set out a joint strategy to recall the Assembly and move to the restoration of power-sharing institutions (May 2006). This was followed by intensive talks (October 2006) between the two governments and political parties at St Andrews in Scotland where the former set out a road map aimed at reaching agreement on all outstanding issues. On the eve of the talks, then Secretary of State for Northern Ireland, Peter Hain wrote:

> Wherever I go people ask me, often in an incredulous tone: 'Do you really think Ian Paisley will agree to go into government with Sinn Féin?' When I reply in the affirmative, as I have been doing increasingly of late, the response often remains disbelieving. Historically, unionists have been wary of engaging with, let alone embracing, nationalism, while republicanism has been their implacable enemy. The suffering inflicted over 30 years of violence not only destroyed lives, but convinced unionists that their very identity was under threat and that they were being forced into becoming something they were not, and did not, want to be.
>
> Whatever reservations some unionists had about the Good Friday Agreement, it remains the only model for moving forward, precisely because it settled the constitutional issue. The Irish government removed their territorial claim, and the principle of consent was set with a united Ireland, only if the people of Northern Ireland vote for it. (Hain, 11 October 2006)

In pressing his case for progress Hain threatened 'devolution or dissolution' for the Assembly. The breakthrough came when Sinn Féin and the DUP, following elections to the Northern Ireland Assembly in March 2007, agreed to enter a power-sharing devolved government. The leaders of loyalism Ian Paisley and republicanism Gerry Adams, arch political enemies, had finally struck a deal. Adams stated at a hugely symbolic joint press conference (26 March 2007): 'I believe the agreement reached between Sinn Féin and the DUP, including the unequivocal commitment made by their party executive and reiterated today, to the restoration of political institutions on 8 May 2007, marks the beginning of a new era of politics on this island.' Ian Paisley commented: 'Our goal has been to see devolution returned in a context where it can make a real and meaningful improvement in the lives of all the people of this part of the United Kingdom. On 7 March 2007, the Unionist community gave us a mandate to deliver on this pledge.' The return of devolution and a power-sharing government which included the DUP and Sinn Féin as the major parties was greeted with euphoria by both the British Prime Minister and Northern Ireland Secretary of State, respectively:

> There are people who still think that compromises that were made along the way were unacceptable. But sometimes politics is about that in order to achieve a better end, and there are always two kinds of people in politics, those who stand aside and commentate and those who get their hands dirty and do (Tony Blair, *BBC News*, 8 May 2007).
>
> It's going to stick, I believe, because the DUP and Sinn Féin – Gerry Adams and Martin McGuinness on the one hand, Ian Paisley and Peter Robinson on the other – these are the two most polarised forces in Northern Ireland's politics, they have done the deal and that's why I believe it's here to stay for good. (Peter Hain, *BBC News*, 8 May 2007)

The politics of Northern Ireland had, at last, been 'resolved' but the legacy of some thirty-five years of violence has left in its wake a deeply divided society manifest in segregated communities, separate schooling, geographical areas bounded by 'peace' walls to protect their security, and single-identity social housing. It is to these issues that we now turn.

A divided society

After stop-start devolution from 1999 and the return of devolution and a power-sharing Executive in May 2007 to locally elected politicians, there were high expectations of the Northern Ireland Assembly whose primary role is to scrutinise and make decisions on the issues dealt with by government departments and to consider and make legislation. The Executive however has clashed on major policy issues such as: the end of academic selection in schools; granting legal status to the Irish language; the building of a 'conflict transformation centre' at the site of the former Maze prison (now rejected by the DUP Culture, Arts and Leisure minister); how to address the issue of victims of the conflict (four victims commissioners and the controversial

Eames-Bradley report); and devolution of policing and justice powers to the Assembly. These disagreements resulted in the Executive not meeting for a 5-month period from June 2008. The SDLP minister, in particular, and her party have felt isolated and politically vulnerable in an Executive which lacks consensus. The example in which the First Minister challenged whether the SDLP Social Development Minister had legal competence to provide emergency relief fuel poverty payments without Executive approval is a case in point. Overt co-operation between the two main parties in the Executive is difficult, mindful of their respective electoral bases. In short, the political process is still fragile, not least because of a challenge mounted by erstwhile DUP member and now rival Jim Allister (Traditional Unionist Voice) and the threat (and reality) of dissident republicans to mount violent attacks against the power-sharing arrangements.

Northern Ireland has moved incrementally to a form of political consensus as violence rapidly declined (see figure 7.1) but still remains a deeply divided society. From 1969–2009 (up to 31 May 2009) there were 3,377 deaths due to the security situation. For the same period, there were 4,741 paramilitary-style attacks (shootings and beatings). In the most recent figures (2008/09) there were 5 deaths and 40 paramilitary-style assaults but as the graph shows the trend is significantly downwards.

Segregation and division are best captured by a series of facts and statistics outlined in a consultation document (in 2003) aimed at putting in place a policy (under a direct rule minister) which would improve community relations in Northern Ireland. The stark evidence of division was outlined as follows:

- Violence at interfaces between communities continues to affect lives, property, businesses and public services.
- Whilst levels of tolerance and respect for diversity within the Protestant and Catholic communities have been improving, there is evidence that they have decreased recently.
- Housing has become segregated since the 1980s. More than 70 per cent of Housing Executive estates are over 90 per cent Protestant or more than 90 per cent Catholic.
- Around 95 per cent of children still attend separated schools. Despite evidence that more parents would prefer this option, there has only been a small increase in the number of children attending integrated schools.
- There are high levels of racial prejudice in Northern Ireland and the situation has recently become worse. The rate of racial incidents is estimated at 16.4 per 1,000 non-white population, compared to 12.65 per 1,000 in England and Wales.

RECONCILED NORTHERN IRELAND?

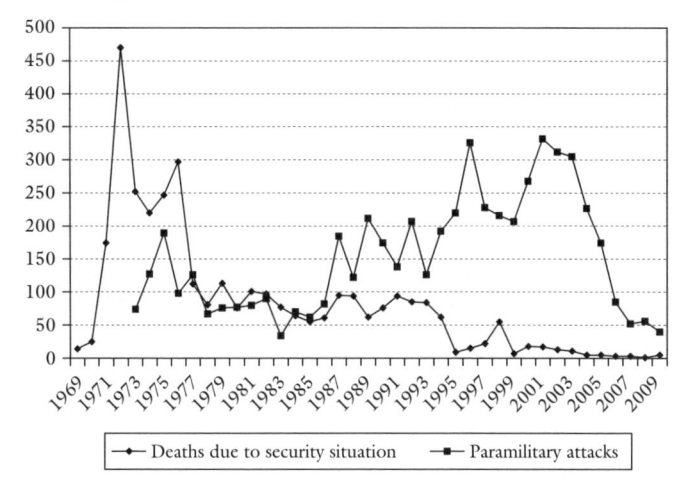

Figure 7.1 Declining violence in Northern Ireland

	1969	1970	1971	1972	1973	1974	1975	1976	1977	1978	1979
Deaths	14	25	174	470	252	220	247	297	112	81	113
Attacks					74	127	189	98	126	67	76

	1980	1981	1982	1983	1984	1985	1986	1987	1988	1989
Deaths	76	101	97	77	64	55	61	95	94	62
Attacks	77	80	90	34	70	62	82	184	122	212

	1990	1991	1992	1993	1994	1995	1996	1997	1998	1999
Deaths	76	94	85	84	62	9	15	22	55	7
Attacks	174	138	207	126	192	220	326	228	216	207

	2000	2001	2002	2003	2004	2005	2006	2007	2008	2009
Deaths	18	17	13	11	5	5	3	3	1	5
Attacks	268	332	312	305	227	174	85	52	56	40

- There is little change in the extent of inter-community friendship patterns.
- In some urban areas further divisions are emerging within local communities. This is linked to paramilitary influence, especially at interfaces.
- People's lives continue to be shaped by community division. Research suggests that, in some areas, community division plays a large part in the choices that people make about where they work, and how they use leisure facilities and public services.
- In summary, Northern Ireland remains a deeply segregated society with little indication of progress towards becoming more tolerant or inclusive (Office of the First and Deputy First Minister, 2003: 3).

What kind of society do people want?

In response to the deep-rooted segregation the government launched a process of consultation asking people what was their vision for Northern Ireland and eliciting suggestions for a more shared and pluralist society (Office of the First Minister and Deputy First Minister, 2003). The consultation document on improving relations engaged more than 10,000 people and generated 500 written responses. The removal of fear featured as a major theme in the consultation feedback and hence the need to strengthen security, law and order. To attain the goals of an integrated and shared society there was recognition that fear cements the *status quo*. This was expressed in the consultation responses as follows: 'fear keeps us frozen . . . fear of reprisal stops us intervening and so our sense of community is being destroyed by a few people who are capable of taking the law into their own hands and terrorising and intimidating their neighbours into a collusion of silence'. Hence, in moving to a shared and pluralist society, 'people's lives must change significantly if they are to feel the sense of safety and security necessary to enable them to engage with each other' (Darby and Knox, 2004: 17).

During the consultation concerns were expressed that developing integrated/shared communities where people wish to learn, live, work and play together was a middle-class concept predicated on citizens having the necessary finance and confidence to live in this way. The real challenge was to provide incentives for those in more disadvantaged communities to develop integrated living with safeguards to ensure their security. The key role here, it was argued by consultees, is for Government to take the lead by providing incentives to attract lower income families into affordable housing of mixed tenure and to tackle segregation. 'The responsibility is on Government to facilitate shared communities, since change cannot be easily brought about by people whose circumstances constrain their choices.' This point was made in a general sense by several contributors who argued that Government policy should privilege sharing over separation – this is not the case at present, they contended – Government is seen to facilitate separation by reinforcing the *status quo* (Darby and Knox, 2004: 22).

The issue of integrated education inevitably featured as part of the consultation feedback to government. A large number of respondents, including almost all the submissions from ethnic and racial minorities, advocated integrated education, sometimes as a proxy for improved relationships. A significant number of respondents wished to see integrated schools more proactively supported by mainstream government funding, under its statutory duty to encourage and facilitate integrated education, rather than parents having to prove the need existed in the first instance. Other consultees were less enthusiastic. A 'major concern about the document is that, even before consultation, integrated education seems already to be the preferred option, despite lack of a solid research base'. A substantial number of respondents defended Catholic schools, arguing the evidence that segregation caused division was anecdotal, and that Catholic schools also aimed 'to assist our society to move beyond its deeply ingrained divisions'. Some Catholic groups acknowledged that 'government has made a commitment to integrated education', but pointed out that the Department of Education 'also have a duty to support parental choice'. One comment which captured many responses on this theme was that 'it should never be implied that the existence of separated/Catholic schools is a cause of the deep divisions' in our society (Darby and Knox, 2004: 47). The British (direct rule) Government prioritised areas, following this widespread consultation exercise, which were deemed necessary to build a shared society such as: tackling the visible manifestations of sectarianism and racism; reclaiming shared space; reducing tensions at interface areas; supporting good relations through cultural diversity; and developing shared workspaces.

These provided the basis on which the (direct rule) government formulated a good relations policy document entitled *A Shared Future* (2005) in an attempt to address the divided society that is Northern Ireland. In the foreword and introduction to the document the (then) Secretary of State for Northern Ireland and Minister of State respectively, made the following comments:

> The essence of reconciliation is about moving away from relationships that are built on mistrust and defence to relationships rooted in mutual recognition and trust. Where relationships have been shaped by threat and fear over a long period we must make changes. We must make these changes through policy and law to address that threat and fear. (Murphy, 2005: 3)

> Good community relations policy, and its outworking, is the search for practical foundations of trust between all people in Northern Ireland who have been divided on the basis of perceived political, cultural, religious, class or ethnic background. (Spellar, 2005: 4)

The principles underpinning *A Shared Future* were also rooted in the political settlement. The Good Friday/Belfast Agreement (1998: 18) noted that 'an essential aspect of the reconciliation process is the promotion of a culture of tolerance at every level of society, including initiatives to facilitate and encourage integrated education and mixed housing'. In the St Andrews Agreement (2006) the British Government agreed to take forward a number of measures to build confidence in both communities and to pursue a shared future for Northern Ireland in which the culture, rights and aspirations of all are respected and valued, free from sectarianism, racism and intolerance. The

Shared Future policy document, drawing on the underpinning public consultation, argued that there was overwhelming support for a shared society with specific reference to: security, law and order, education and housing.

A shared future?

These compelling messages influenced the formulation of the *Shared Future* policy document (2005) and the type of society favoured by the people of Northern Ireland. The government was emphatic in its tone:

> Separate but equal is not an option. Parallel living and the provision of parallel services are unsustainable both morally and economically . . . No one is arguing for an artificially homogeneous Northern Ireland and no one will be asked to suppress or give up their chosen identity. However, the costs of a divided society, whilst recognising, of course, the very real fears of people around safety and security considerations, are abundantly clear: segregated housing and education, security costs, less than efficient public service provision, and deep rooted intolerance that have too often been used to justify violent sectarianism and racism. (*A Shared Future*, 2005: 15)

To illustrate the consequences of segregation, an empirical study was commissioned by the (direct rule) government to consider the financial cost of the Northern Ireland divide (Deloitte: 2007). The research concluded that an additional £1.5 billion per annum is spent on public services than a comparable region where such segregation did not exist. Set within the context of an £8.6b devolved budget (2009–10) this is a major drain on public resources. Not surprisingly the cost of 'normalising' policing and security (not yet a devolved matter) including the outworking of police reforms, compensation to victims of terrorist violence, public inquiries, prisons and policing civil disorder consume a large amount of public expenditure. In addition, however, government invests in: improving community relations and support for victims of the troubles; separate schooling systems for the two communities which duplicates provision; unquantified costs for the health sector associated with conflict related trauma; an inflated public housing budget because of the demand for single identity social housing; repairing damage to roads, railways and buses as a result of civil unrest; and duplication within the voluntary and community sector to support segregated communities. The report concluded:

> Looking to the future, research indicates that the likelihood is that Northern Ireland will remain a deeply segregated society in terms of where people live, work or are educated. However, the continued absence of violence coupled with an increased policy driven focus through *A Shared Future* may increase confidence, mobility and a willingness to access shared facilities. (Deloitte, 2007: 90)

The (then) Finance Minister, Peter Robinson, however, criticised the findings of the report as assuming large savings from a common education system in Northern Ireland, a highly unlikely prospect in the short term, in his view. He also pointed out the claimed savings accruing from security and policing services were outside the brief of the devolved administration. Other identified monies were for duplicate local government services such as public leisure facilities, of no direct monetary benefit to the Assembly.

Despite the direct rule administration's commitment to *A Shared Future* and evidence of the high costs of a divided society, the policy has been abandoned by the devolved Executive. Notwithstanding, the (then) First Minister (Ian Paisley) defended the role of his department, the Office of the First Minister and the Deputy First Minister (OFMDFM), arguing that it is totally committed to promoting equality and human rights. More generally Dr Paisley pointed to the fact the Executive recognised the importance of creating a shared society through ministers' affirmation in their pledge of office that they will promote the interests of the whole country which is represented in the Northern Ireland Assembly and work towards the goal of a shared future. Sinn Féin has argued against the whole basis of *A Shared Future* claiming that it defines the primary problem as a lack of tolerance between communities particularly in socially deprived areas, rather than tackling disadvantage on the basis of objective need and addressing structural inequalities. Sinn Féin cites examples where the principles of 'sharedness' are being used to limit building social housing in the name of creating neutral space.

In a bid to secure local ownership of the *Shared Future* agenda the Alliance Party which has championed this policy, called on the Northern Ireland Executive to make the creation of a shared society a top priority. The Northern Ireland Assembly in a debate on 4 June 2007 agreed that it would consider progress towards a shared future and bring forward detailed plans to promote the interests of the whole community towards that goal. Since then the Alliance Party accused the Executive of making little effort or progress in developing an alternative and equally comprehensive strategy: 'There is not a single reference to a *Shared Future*, or good relations, in the draft Programme for Government or in a single public service agreement, out of the 23 that are designed to promote them' (Assembly debate 26 November 2007). Naomi Long (Alliance) went on to argue:

> If people cannot live with the language of 'A Shared Future' - owing to its having the seal of approval of a direct rule Administration – by all means, change the name. It would be a huge mistake to simply throw the baby out with the bathwater.

With the restoration of devolved government in 2007, the expectation had been that local politicians would embrace the *Shared Future* policy agenda.

Interestingly, the word 'reconciliation' does not feature in the *Programme for Government 2008–2011*, instead it makes a rather oblique reference as follows:

> We must also continue our efforts to address the divisions within our society. Progress has been made, but at a time when our society is being transformed, sectarianism, racism and intolerance are still too evident. They mar our reputation, blight our economic prospects and have a corrosive effect on our society. For these reasons it is imperative that we all embrace the opportunity to create a shared and better future, based on tolerance and respect for cultural diversity. (*Programme for Government 2008–2011*: 12)

The devolved government has therefore jettisoned *A Shared Future* because of its direct rule antecedents and is currently developing a 'softer' policy document entitled *Cohesion, Sharing and Integration* due to be published sometime in the future after a very long gestation period. 'We will bring forward a programme of cohesion and integration for this shared and better future to address the divisions within our society and achieve measurable reductions in sectarianism, racism and hate crime' (Programme for Government 2008–2011: 12). Current disagreements between the DUP and Sinn Féin have delayed progress on a number of policies – this issue is part of the backlog of business. With no mention of *Shared Future* objectives in Public Service Agreements, the performance and accountability framework through which civil servants operate, the triennial action plan to deliver good relations on a cross-departmental basis has become redundant. The Office of the First Minister and Deputy First Minister now remains the sole guarantor of good relations in government.

Cohesion, sharing and integration

Early indications of what a new policy (on Cohesion, Sharing and Integration) will contain suggestions empowering local government in partnership with community organisations to develop relevant local responses to support cohesion, sharing and integration. Draft measures include:

- A significant increase in investment in the new policy from the current £21.7m to around £29m for the three-year period 2009/12.
- Enhanced support to local councils to build cohesive communities and to prevent and manage community tensions through the District Councils' Good Relations Programme.
- Independently produced good relations audits on which local action plans are based.

- A new interfaith group promoting dialogue between faiths and with government to develop enhanced understanding.
- Enhanced support to key local stakeholders in understanding and monitoring tension and conflict in local communities.
- Working with the private sector, including business and trades union representation on a Good Relations Panel (Source: Draft document, *A Shared and Better Future for All* – A Programme of Cohesion, Sharing and Integration (2008). Belfast: OFMDFM).

So what progress has been made towards a shared future? The Office of the First Minister and Deputy First Minister produced a baseline report and a comprehensive set of indicators which set out a methodology by which trends in good relations could be tracked (Office of the First Minister and Deputy First Minister, 2007). Therein the priority outcomes of *A Shared Future* and the *Racial Equality Strategy* are operationalised through quantifiable indicators. Although passé, now that *A Shared Future* has been jettisoned, we track two such indicators (amongst several) aimed at measuring whether 'Northern Ireland is a place where people of all backgrounds work, live and play together.' The data are gathered from yearly probability surveys (Northern Ireland Life and Times) of between 1,200 and 1,800 people randomly selected respondents throughout Northern Ireland.

(1) Percentage of young people (age 16) who think relations between Protestants and Catholics are better than they were 5 years ago (see figure 7.2).

Over the 5-year period (2003–2008), the proportion of young people who perceive relations between Protestants and Catholics as 'better' compared to 5 years previously has changed significantly (41 per cent in 2003 and 68 per cent in 2008, respectively). The data show a large increase in young people's perception of improving community relations between 2006 and 2007 with a continuing upward trend. This may well be linked, although no causal relationship can be inferred, to the restoration of devolution and a power-sharing Executive, – a much more positive political climate at the macro level.

(2) Percentage of adults who think relations between Protestants and Catholics are better than they were 5 years ago (see figure 7.3).

Over the 10-year period (1998–2008) the percentage of people who think that relations between Catholics and Protestants have got 'better' or compared

Figure 7.2 Improvement in community relations among young people

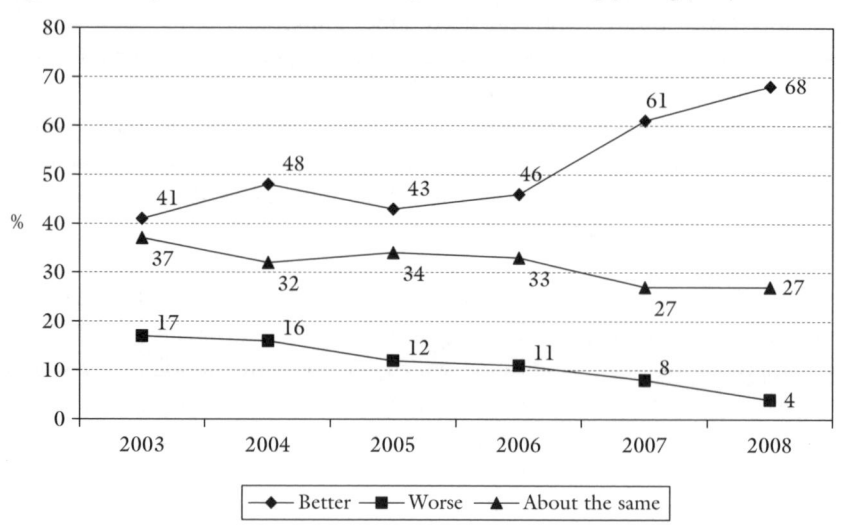

Figure 7.3 Improvement in community relations among adults

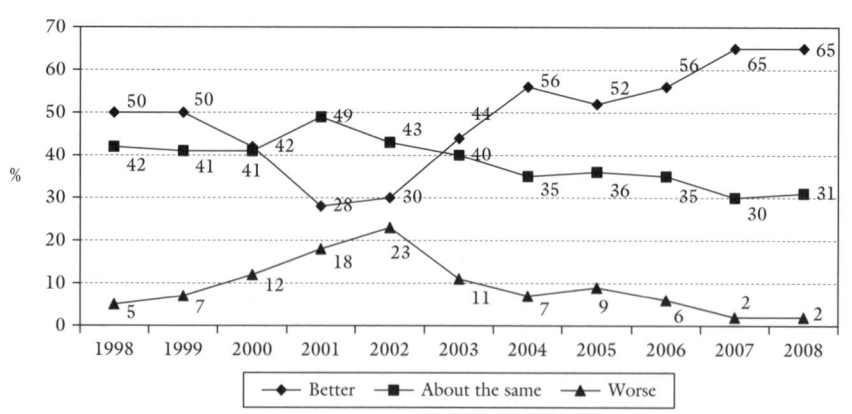

to five years previously has increased significantly from 50 per cent in 1998 to 65 per cent in 2008. The trend line is interesting over this period. Following devolution in 1999 the ensuing on/off status of the Assembly appears to have impacted negatively on perceptions of community relations. Perhaps surprisingly there seems to have been an acceptance that direct rule was a long-term prospect from October 2002 onwards. The restoration of devolved government in 2007 has not impacted on adults' perceptions of improved community relations, although no causal relationship can be inferred.

These trends in perceptions among young people and adults of improving community relations are encouraging for Northern Ireland as a post-conflict society but are likely to be little more than a welcome commentary on how its inhabitants read the macro-political signals – that the two main political protagonists are now prepared after years of hostility to share power. People view this as a hugely positive development for community relations. Yet systemic divisions remain in Northern Ireland society which must be addressed if we are to move beyond the poet Robert Frost's comment that 'high fences make good neighbours'. High physical fences in Northern Ireland are rather ironically referred to as 'peace' walls which are particularly prevalent at interface areas where Catholic and Protestant communities live cheek by jowl. In a study of segregation in Belfast, Shirlow and Murtagh (2006: 58) note that interfaces 'both divorce and regulate intercommunity relationships, and in so doing they compress space into sites that become notable places of violence and resistance'. They argue that interface areas vary in form and style – some are denoted by physical barriers, by flags, emblems and wall murals but all will most certainly be known and understood by those who live within segregated communities. Such is the pervasiveness of these barriers that it is difficult to estimate the numbers which exist. Jarman (2006; 2008) claims that the term interface barrier or 'peaceline' is generally used to refer to those barriers that have been authorised by the Northern Ireland Office in response to concerns for safety and security, but many other structures have been built in the course of regeneration projects to separate communities. In Belfast alone he estimates that there are over eighty barriers, half of which are Northern Ireland Office 'sanctioned' barriers. One would imagine that in a climate of improved community relations, as captured in the Northern Ireland Life and Times survey responses, the removal of 'peace' walls would be a tangible expression of this new found confidence. Yet in a study commissioned by US–Ireland Alliance in 2008, 60 per cent of a poll comprising over 1,000 residents in three interface areas in Belfast reported the walls should *not* come down at present but only when it was safe enough for them to do so. The three areas were: the Falls/Shankill, East Belfast (Short Strand and Templemore Avenue) and North Belfast (Antrim Road and Tigers Bay) where residents argued that walls made them feel safer by keeping the communities separated. Only 21 per cent of respondents wanted the walls to come down now (US–Ireland Alliance/Millward Brown, 2008).

In a review of the literature on factors which impacted on segregation and sectarianism in Northern Ireland, Hamilton, Hansson, Bell and Toucas (2008) found that in the main, place of residence, workplace and education were significant. They noted that, in general, high levels of residential segregation tend to be class based – mixed areas are more likely to be middle-class neighbourhoods and working-class areas segregated, although Protestant segregated areas are less deprived than their Catholic equivalents. This does not mean the absence of sectarian beliefs and attitudes within mixed, middle-class areas. The workplace offers the opportunity for cross-community contact but can also reinforce the segregated *status quo* particularly at times of increased sectarian tensions outside the work environment (e.g. marching season, terrorist atrocities). The education system is particularly divisive and the limited success of integrated education in terms of its relatively low uptake has been unable to challenge the controlled (Protestant) and maintained (Catholic) sectoral dominance of schools. The authors cite additional variables which have an impact on segregation and sectarianism: routines of daily living; parades and visual displays; gender; age; inter-generational transmission of attitudes and behaviour; mixed marriage/personal relationships; and the use of language in perpetuating sectarianism. The research offers some signs of optimism in the conclusions as follows:

> In some areas there are greater levels of mixing, sharing and integrating, while in others the legacy of the past, of hostility, fear and mistrust dominate the wider social environment. In most social environments the process of avoidance still appears to dominate interactions between members of the two main communities . . . The legacy of the troubles and recent experiences of violence remain factors in how people act as social beings, but people are not solely constrained by their past and there is some evidence of positive change, and greater levels of mixing in some aspects of social life in many areas across the North. (Hamilton *et al.*, 2008: 153)

In an attempt to capture the 'temperature' of Northern Ireland or the kind of society it has become, a recent Northern Ireland Life and Times Survey (2008) asked respondents their reactions to two key statements:

(a) Northern Ireland is a normal civic society in which all individuals are equal, where differences are resolved through dialogue and where all people are treated equally.

(b) The government is actively encouraging shared communities where people of all backgrounds can live, work, learn and play together.

In each case respondents were asked to score their answers on a scale ranging from 1–10 where:

1 = it has definitely *not* been achieved
10 = it definitely *has* been achieved

The results of these questions are displayed in figure 7.4.

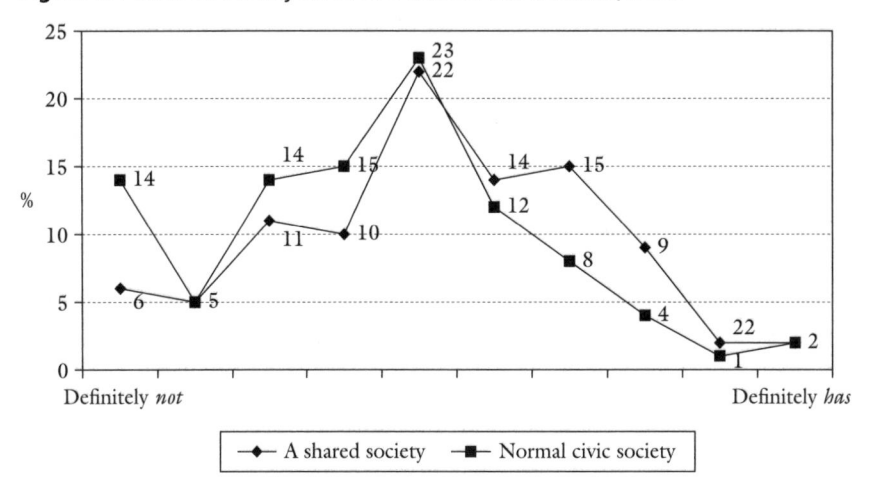

Figure 7.4 Kind of society Northern Ireland has become, 2008

Chart showing percentages across a spectrum from "Definitely not" to "Definitely has" for two categories: A shared society and Normal civic society.

A shared society: 6, 5, 11, 10, 22, 14, 15, 9, 1
Normal civic society: 14, 5, 14, 15, 23, 12, 8, 4, 2

The 2008 results show that a higher proportion of respondents feel that a 'normal civic society in which all individual are equal, where differences are resolved through dialogue and where all people are treated impartially' has definitely *not* been achieved, than has. Equally, a higher proportion of people disagree that 'government has actively encouraged shared communities where people of all backgrounds can live, work, learn and play together', than agree. Although views on these two issues broadly follow the same spectrum of opinion, a significantly higher percentage of respondents felt that 'a normal civic society' has not been achieved compared to attempts by government to encourage 'shared communities'.

Integrated education: a case study in reconciliation?

One frequency cited 'cause' and 'solution' to the conflict in Northern Ireland is the divisive education system. At its simplest, the argument is that children from Protestant and Catholic backgrounds are educated separately, making them both ignorant and suspicious of each other which merely compounds traditional ethno-national cleavages. It is not until they reach third-level education that they have the opportunity to mix and break down preconceived stereotypes, at which point attitudes have become entrenched and difficult to change. The integrated education movement promotes education that gives pupils the opportunity to understand, respect and celebrate all cultural and religious traditions. Integrated education brings together in one school, children, parents, teachers and governors from Catholic and Protestant traditions and those from other faiths or none. Parental involvement is a central value of integrated education, with a high level of parental representation on Boards of Governors (Northern Ireland Council for Integrated Education and the Integrated Education Fund, 2006).

The origins of the movement can be traced back to 1974 when a group of parents called *All Children Together* lobbied successfully for legislation which would allow existing schools to become integrated (Education (NI) Act 1977). The first planned integrated school (Lagan College) was established by parents in Belfast in 1981 followed by three others in 1985, initially as independent schools funded through charitable trusts. The sector emerged out of a sense of parental frustration that controlled schools served Protestant children almost exclusively, and the Catholic Church dominated the maintained sector – a chill factor for Protestants. As Donnelly and Osborne (2005: 152) argued 'the model of education continues to be academically selective and religiously segregated. Indeed the school system itself has been accused of not only reflecting sectarian division but of creating and reinforcing sectarianism'. Statistics for the current school year highlight how segregated the existing education system is. Less than 1 per cent of Protestants attend Catholic managed/maintained primary and secondary/grammar schools, and only 6.3 per cent of Catholics attend controlled schools. These contrast with integrated/transformed schools which have a 51:49 per cent Protestant/Catholic ratio. Overall though, only 6.3 per cent of the primary and secondary school population attend integrated schools (see tables 7.1 and 7.2).

Integrated education was given a major fillip through the Education Reform (NI) Order 1989 (article 64) which, for the first time, placed a statutory duty on the Department of Education to 'encourage and facilitate' the development of integrated education. The Order also gave the Department the power to fund a central, representative body to develop, support and promote integrated education in Northern Ireland – the Northern Ireland Council for Integrated Education (NICIE). There are two types of integrated schools: new build ('green field') schools known as grant maintained integrated (GMI), and controlled integrated (CI) where a majority of parents in existing Protestant or Catholic schools opt to transform to integrated status. When a grant maintained integrated school meets the Department of Education's enrolment criteria it will receive recurrent funding. It will however only access capital costs when the school can demonstrate a sustained viable enrolment (three consecutive intakes at the minimum level).

Transformation involves the change of an existing school to integrated status arising from a desire by parents to provide an integrated school in an area. The process is determined through consultation with the local community and a decision by parents expressed through a parental ballot.

Table 7.1 Religion of pupils by school type and management type 2008/09

Management type	Primary			Secondary[a]			Total[b]
	Protestant	Catholic	Others[c]	Protestant	Catholic	Others	
Controlled	53,903	3,605	14,497	52,142	3,578	11,977	139,702
Catholic managed/ maintained	746	72,268	1,102	476	67,793	636	143,021
Controlled integrated & grant maintained integrated	2,783	2,865	1782	5,049	4,597	1,818	18,894
Total	57,432	78,738	17,381	57,667	75,968	14,431	301,617

Source: Calculated from Department of Education NI, Annual Schools Census.

Notes: [a] Secondary schools include grammar and non-grammar schools here.
[b] Figures do not include nursery, preparatory schools or specialist schools.
[c] Others: other Christian, non-Christian, other and no religion recorded.

Table 7.2 Breakdown of religion by school management type, 2008/09 (%)[a]

Catholics enrolled in controlled schools	6.3
Protestants enrolled in catholic managed/maintained schools	0.9
Overall school population enrolled in integrated schools	6.3

Source: Calculated from Department of Education NI, Annual Schools Census.

Note: [a] Percentage calculations exclude 'others'.

Transformation is defined in the Education Orders as the acquisition of grant-maintained or controlled integrated status by an existing school (Department of Education, 2006). For schools to meet the conditions to transform to integrated status there must be at least 10 per cent of pupils from the minority religion and culture enrolled at the point of transformation with the expectation on the part of the Department of Education that this will increase to at least 70:30 within 10 years.

The two principal stakeholder bodies operating in support of the integrated sector are the Integrated Education Fund (IEF) and the Northern Ireland Council for Integrated Education (NICIE). The Integrated Education Fund was set up as a charitable trust in 1992 to provide a financial foundation for the development and growth of integrated education in Northern Ireland. A loan facility has been agreed between NICIE, the IEF and a consortium of the main local banks. This is available to fund capital development of schools which have been approved by the Department of Education. In addition, the Department provides recurrent grants to individual schools equivalent to the interest charges on the loan as 'rent' payable to NICIE for the accommodation (Department of Education, 2006). These measures accelerated the growth of the integrated sector but also created pressure on the capital budget of the Department because of the demand for grant maintained integrated schools. As a result, the Department reviewed its policy, raised the viability criteria for new schools and introduced measures to encourage schools to 'transform' to integrated schools. Viability criteria have reduced over time.

The Northern Ireland Council for Integrated Education was established in 1987 to co-ordinate efforts to develop the provision of integrated education in Northern Ireland and to assist parent groups in opening new integrated schools. NICIE is a registered charity in receipt of core funding from the Department of Education but also draws money from other donors. In 1991 NICIE, after consultation with all of the then existing integrated schools, agreed a 'Statement of Principles' which has underpinned the ethos and practice of integrated education ever since (NICIE). The 'Statement of Principles' provides for religious balance in pupil enrolments, teaching staff and governors. New schools agree to these principles as a pre-requisite of NICIE support and assistance. In the same year, the Department of Education, as part of its new statutory responsibility to encourage and facilitate integrated education, agreed to grant aid NICIE in its work.

The NICIE 'Statement of Principles' require that integrated schools seek to achieve a 40:40 balance in pupil admissions between Catholics and Protestants in order to ensure that no ethnic religious group can become dominant. As stated, the Department of Education accepts a balance of 70:30 (with 30 per cent coming from whichever is the smaller religious group in the area) as the minimum required for a new school to be recognised as integrated (Northern Ireland Council for Integrated Education, 2009). There are now 59 integrated schools in Northern Ireland which represents 4.6 per cent and 9 per cent of the number of schools in the primary and post-primary schools sector respectively (see table 7.3).

The impact of integrated education

In reviewing the development of integrated schools since the 1980s, Smith (2001: 570) noted:

> Despite the small number of integrated schools they have had a significant impact and posed implicit challenges to the existing system of separate schools. They have questioned whether it is appropriate for the churches to be directly involved in the management of schools in a divided society and provided models for the involvement of parents on a cross-community basis.

Table 7.3 Number of integrated schools, 2008/09

Type of school	Primary	Post-primary	Total
Number of grant-maintained integrated (GMI) schools	23	16	39
Number of controlled integrated (CI) schools	16	4	20
Total number of integrated schools	39	20	59
Total number of primary schools in NI	856		
Total number of post-primary schools in NI		223	
% of integrated schools in primary sector	4.6%		
% of integrated schools in post-primary sector		9%	

Source: Department of Education NI, Annual Schools Census.

Smith also suggested that transformed schools offered a model 'for a sort of co-owned institution that may be appropriate for a co-owned society' although felt it was too early (writing in 2001) to draw conclusions on their potential.

More recent research (McGlynn, 2007) posed the question as to whether integrated schools in Northern Ireland were really making a difference. The research design was based on a fairly small sample of 12 key stakeholders: 6 school principals (all from the integrated sector and, by design, supportive of the concept) and the remainder from NICIE, IEF, the Department of Education and the Office of the First and Deputy First Minister. This qualitative study did not directly answer the question which it posed but concluded that 'whilst the rights of religious communities to their own form of schooling are undeniable, such schools may not rebuild social cohesion as readily as integrated schools where contact between children is sustained' (McGlynn, 2007: 276). The study found no support for compulsory integrated education from the stakeholders, who argued that the benefits of integrated education need to be seen over a longer, more realistic, timeframe.

Research by Donnelly and Hughes (2006: 503) uncovered problems in transformed schools in what they describe as 'the imposition of integrated status on an existing segregated culture where most of the teachers are drawn from one community (Protestant) and where some are opposed to the transformation process'. They found a lack of consensus amongst staff and school governors on how to develop an integrated ethos and a culture of avoiding issues around cultural differences which might result in conflict. Beyond an official structural commitment (change in school's status) to integrated education, teachers, parents or governors had not therefore discussed or agreed its definition and outworkings in practice. The researchers concluded that an emphasis on obtaining good academic results in Northern Ireland schools 'coupled with a strong "avoidance ethos" left little room for participants to develop empathy with out-group members or to understand the uniqueness and differentiation among out-group members'. McGlynn (2007: 285) discounts the Donnelly and Hughes findings by arguing that 'constant reminders (about religion) might actually reify difference as social identification as "Catholic" and "Protestant" has been a defining feature of the Northern Irish conflict and intergroup boundaries are usually perceived as impermeable'.

The question as to whether integrated education works is also taken up by Hayes *et al.* (2007) who provide a review of the research literature as a preface to a quantitative study on whether or not experiencing a religiously integrated education has a significant effect on the political outlooks of Protestants and Catholics. In terms of the impact of integrated education they point out that:

> Previous empirical research on the relationship between integrated schools and relations between Protestants and Catholics in Northern Ireland is both limited and inconclusive. Although several studies stress the positive benefits of integrated schooling, particularly in promoting cross-community friendships, others are more ambiguous, suggesting that it has little or no impact in promoting shared cultural outlooks. Some commentators even suggest that integrated education may actually reinforce divisive ethnic and political views (Hayes *et al.*, 2007: 456).

Hayes *et al.* investigated the degree to which individuals from the two main religious communities who attended either a formally or informally integrated school differ in their political outlooks from those who attended a religiously segregated one. Their quantitative study used a pooled sample of the 1998 to 2003 Northern Ireland Life and Times Surveys and the 1998 and 2003 Northern Ireland Election Surveys – these amounted to about 11,500 people in the sample data analysis. The research provides a robust and comprehensive interrogation of the data and tests five key hypotheses as follows:

1. Whether individuals who had attended either a formally or informally integrated school are less sectarian in their views than those who did not.
2. Whether this reduction in sectarian attitudes is particularly the case among adults who attended a formally integrated school.
3. Whether this reduction in sectarian attitudes will result in an overarching in-group identity among the various individuals involved.
4. Whether this development of an overarching identity among those educated in a formally integrated setting is more common among Protestants than Catholics.
5. Whether, individuals who were in a clear minority position at schools

(Catholics in informally integrated schools) are more likely to abandon their traditionally established sectarian positions in favour of the dominant, or Protestant, view.

From the data analysis, researchers concluded the following:

> That attendance at a religiously integrated school – either one formally constituted as integrated or a religious school incorporating a proportion from the opposite religion – has positive long-term benefits in promoting a less sectarian stance on national identity and constitutional preferences . . . We conclude that as the numbers experiencing integrated schooling grow, these individuals have the potential to create a new common ground in Northern Ireland politics (Hayes *et al.*, 2007: 478).

Hayes *et al.* went on to probe the potential impact of integrated education on wider societal issues tolerance and reducing prejudice. They asked the following question: 'to what extent were parents and educators correct in their assumption that integrated schools would break down religious barriers and herald in a new era in community relations and politics in Northern Ireland?' The researchers concluded:

> While the results of our study cannot provide a definitive answer to this question, they do suggest that attendance at an integrated (both formal and informal) school has long-term benefits in weakening sectarian political outlooks and promoting a centre and common ground in Northern Ireland politics, and this is particularly the case within the Protestant community. (Hayes *et al.*, 2007: 480)

A recent study on interpersonal communication between Catholics and Protestants in Northern Ireland found similar support for integrated education. Hargie *et al.* (2008: 813) argued that by 'reversing the pattern of apartheid in schooling and bringing the two sides together at an early age, the resulting increased communication should help to foster greater disclosure, trust and attraction'. These findings were in line with a larger study by Stringer *et al.* (2009) which examined the effects of integrated and segregated schooling on Northern Irish children's self-reported contact and friendship with members of the other denominational group in school and community settings. The research sample involved over 1,700 pupils in 8 matched schools (integrated, Catholic maintained and Protestant controlled) across Northern Ireland and found that intergroup contact within and outside school was reported frequently in integrated schools but only occasionally in segregated schools. Cross-group contacts in school and outside school were both associated with less extreme political attitudes. The study provides support for educating Protestants and Catholics together as a means of moderating attitudes and creating cross-community friendships in a divided society.

This approach to reconciliation which advocates integrated education, however, is not without academic challenge. McGarry and O'Leary (1995a), for example, cite segregation as one of five key fallacies which constitute liberal explanations of the conflict in Northern Ireland. Drawing on Bruce's work (1994), they disparagingly describe attempts to break down segregation in this way as a 'mix and fix approach' espoused by the integrated education lobby, one which challenges stereotypes of the other religious group and addresses misconceptions and ignorance. In short, if segregation is the problem then mixing is the answer. McGarry and O'Leary dismiss this assertion outright. They argue that integrated education is impractical because residential segregation demands bussing children into hostile territory and mixed schools may simply exacerbate divisions on what separates groups rather than what they have in common. Whilst McGarry and O'Leary (1995a: 856) supported the idea that 'sufficient provision must be made for all those who wished to be schooled, live or work with members of the other community' they argued that 'many northern nationalists want equality and autonomy rather than integration'.

McEvoy *et al.* (2006: 86) argue that education has a key role to play in reconciliation and addressing the legacy of the past but are very critical of the community relations paradigm which informs this approach. They claim 'community relations was arguably always a softer and more palatable alternative (for progressive Unionists) to a rights discourse with its inevitable critique of the state'. The community relations paradigm was based on an erroneous analysis of the Northern Ireland problem as a war between two traditions, the 'solution' to which was to reconcile their differences by improving community relations, all of which conveniently absolved the role of the British state in the emergence and management of the conflict. They further suggest the education system, specifically integrated schools, which became a primary site for the outworking of reconciliation has yet to provide evidence of their success:

> Claims, reminiscent of those made by community relations activists during the late 1970s, have been made as to the accomplishments of these schools: their contribution to forgiveness and the reduction of intolerance, the development of social cohesion and more recently to the building of social capital. However, it is generally accepted that, to date, empirical evidence of their long-term success is at best inconclusive . . . the failure of increased contact in education, in its various guises, to make significant in-roads into producing genuine reconciliation equally points towards the fundamental flaws in the community relations paradigm. (McEvoy *et al.*, 2006: 96–97)

The researchers go further by suggesting that rather than reducing sectarianism, these schools are failing to create a climate in which pupils feel comfortable in expressing their *own* identity leading to the emergence of 'new *identikit* citizens who are, in the classroom at least, immune from the influences of the real world in which they live' (McEvoy *et al.*, 2006: 97). This community relations paradigm based on improving the quality of contact between the two dominant communities, they contend, fails to acknowledge the key role which ex-combatants played and continue to perform in promoting reconciliation. The researchers offer, with little detail, citizenship education as 'a more grounded understanding of the meaning of reconciliation to the next generation' (McEvoy *et al.*, 2006: 99).

In a similar vein McVeigh and Rolston (2007) argue that after the Good Friday Agreement, Northern Ireland has reworked rather than transcended sectarianism. One of the examples which they use to illustrate this point is integrated education which they described as an initiative that offered 'real possibilities' to challenge sectarianism but was 'only half-heartedly pursued' because of the 'good relations' paradigm adopted by government. They claim that the lack of public funding to build new integrated schools led to a policy shift in favour of transforming existing schools to integrated status. This resulted in two problems: 'first, given the opposition of the Catholic Church to integrated education, the only schools which have transformed, or are likely to in future, are in the state sector. Second, the threshold for integrated status in the transformed sector is lower than in the integrated sector' (McVeigh and Rolston, 2007: 17). This provides evidence of the feeble attempts by government to tackle an education system designed to institutionalise sectarianism.

The wider literature on conflict and peace building offers some insights into the segregated society of Northern Ireland. Oberschall (2007), for example, in a comparative study of the peace building processes in Bosnia, Israel–Palestine and Northern Ireland argues that peace settlements leave many loose ends on key issues in the conflict to be dealt with during the implementation process. He supports the need for social transformation or reconstruction policies that: encourage identities other than ethnicity, provide inducements for inter-ethnic co-operation where there are non-partisan public symbols, and shared institutions rather than segregation and avoidance – the converse of the principle 'good fences make good ethnics and good citizens'. He concludes:

> The reason that sharing is preferable to separation and avoidance is that recent history has repeatedly shown how 'live and let live' separatism rapidly descends into ethnic warfare in a crisis as in the Balkans. (Oberschall, 2007: 237)

When ethnic groups have different preferences, he argues, public policy should not support or subsidise these practices and institutions that make for separation, although at the same time it should not ban them as long as they are voluntary and benign. Taylor (2001; 2006; 2008; 2009) also advocates social transformation. In a critique of the consociational arrangements synonymous with the Belfast Agreement (McGarry and O'Leary, 2006) he suggests that political accommodation will regulate rather than transform the conflict. He argues for micro-level support to promote non-sectarian initiatives within civil society which advance democracy and justice such as integrated education and housing, and criticises consociational arrangements that 'work with and solidify intracommunal networks, rather than being concerned to promote intercommunal association' (Taylor 2001: 47).

Government's response

So why does the devolved administration appear to be dragging its heels on integrated education? The Minister and Department of Education find themselves in a dilemma over this issue. Their statutory duty to facilitate and encourage integrated education must be set within a context where other school management types are very protective of their schools and the retention of pupil numbers in a declining demographic scenario. If one overlays this with the all-consuming public controversy over the abolition of the 11-plus and post-primary academic selection, the need to rationalise the school estates, proposals to extend educational choice, and the Minister's personal conviction to increase Irish medium schools, then 'encouraging and facilitating' integration competes in a very crowded policy arena.

It is important to note, however, that the Department of Education has a statutory responsibility to 'encourage and facilitate' but *not* 'to promote' as that would be seen as favouring one form of education over another. As one departmental official put it:

> The difficulty is the Minister is trying to reconcile her statutory duty with the advice and evidence that she is presented with, and ultimately she is charged with the effective use of public resources. Balancing that against issues of need and parental choice is a difficult circle to square and development proposals for integrated schools will be disappointed and will continue to be disappointed. She has a very tight budget and has to live within her resources. (Interview with Department of Education official)

The role played by Government has been strongly criticised as failing to fulfil its statutory duty to encourage and facilitate integrated education. Critics ask how the Department of Education measures their discharge of this duty. The Department makes reference to how they grow schools in response to parental demand and directly fund NICIE to assess and respond to demand. NICIE, which is not a statutory body in turn argues that it cannot lobby for integrated education and its role is restricted to awareness-raising. Public funding for NICIE has therefore been a convenient relationship for the Department of Education. The IEF sees the integrated movement as having important challenge and championing functions to ensure the Government discharges its statutory responsibility to encourage and facilitate integrated education. The challenge function becomes even more important with excess capacity in the main education sectors as increasingly the Department can and do use the 'adverse impact on existing schools' criterion as a reason to reject development proposals coming forward for transformation and capping the numbers in existing integrated schools where there is evidence of demand for more places. NICIE claims that around 500 pupils per year are turned away from integrated schools because of over subscription. Not unsurprisingly, the Department rejects the criticism of not fulfilling its statutory role:

> The Minister takes her statutory duty to encourage and facilitate integrated education very seriously and takes it into active consideration when looking at development proposals for integrated schools. From the sector's point of view that is where 'the rubber hits the road' and they need ministerial attention. She often partners it with Irish medium education because there is a similar duty – she therefore takes it very seriously and has been active in visiting integrated schools. This stands in contrast to the Minister considering issues around community relations in schools – she would look at community relations funding proposals carefully and would not be immediately persuaded, but by comparison is very warm towards integrated education. (Interview with Department of Education official)

The integrated education movement needs to be convinced further, particularly in the face of rejections by the Minister following successful ballots of parents in support of existing school transformation to integrated status.

> The Department of Education will say it is a neutral player but we have seen time and time again that when it comes to decision-making, they will support the *status quo*. They will consider the impact of their decisions on the *status quo* rather than providing equality of opportunity for parents who want integrated education . . . In short, we need to see a change in attitude from the Department. (Interview with IEF official)

The Department remains, however, unconvinced about the ultimate goals of the integrated movement:

> There is a spectrum of opinion ranging from: 'the right way to deliver education in Northern Ireland is in this purist integrated way' through to the other end of the spectrum which says 'it is about integrat**ing** and *that* is the future'. The integrated movement should now be saying that we have a place in a bigger environment now and the rest of the world is catching up with us – so what do we have to offer the rest of the education community? That angle has the greatest legs for the future as it accepts that integrated education is continuing to evolve and must demonstrate relevance to the changing policy context. (Interview with Department of Education official)

The opportunity to promote 'integrating' as opposed to 'integrated' education has been financially supported by external organisations, the Atlantic Philanthropies and the International Fund for Ireland, through a programme entitled *Sharing Education*. Launched in September 2007 and managed by the Queen's University, Belfast the programme offers incentives to schools to support active collaboration through shared classes between schools from different sectors (Protestant and Catholic). In essence, the programme uses the delivery of the education curriculum as the mechanism for schools to share in the learning experience whilst at the same time building positive relationships between pupils from different backgrounds. So far, more than 60 schools and 4,600 pupils have been actively involved in the programme which is showing early signs of success and a new phase of the project commencing in 2010 will extend the number of schools (Queen's University Belfast, 2009). This approach to integrating education is seen as complementary to the longer established integrated education movement. One proponent of *Sharing Education* described it in this way:

> The Atlantic Philanthropies and the International Fund for Ireland can help break down the rigidities which exist in our segregated education system. The *Sharing Education Programme* is an excellent way of creating an 'integrated system' alongside the 'emerging sector of integrated schools'. In other words, take the zero-sum game out of it. Don't challenge existing patterns of school ownership/managing authorities but make the boundaries between them more porous and create a different dynamic for change. (Interview with Queen's University education specialist)

The fact that such initiatives have been taken by external organisations keen to support the consolidation of the political developments in Northern Ireland speaks volumes. The Department of Education has thus played a bystander role in which it questions the sustainability of sharing education, its value for money, and seeks evidence as to how it will improve education standards. What this case study has attempted to demonstrate is how lukewarm the key political partners in the devolved government are towards a public service that is central to the divided communities which characterise Northern Ireland, fearful that integration will challenge their *raison d'être*. The will, it seems, to move to a post-conflict or reconciled society is not yet present because it threatens the electoral base of the two key partners in a power-sharing devolved government

Shared housing

Even though the main parties in the Northern Ireland Executive (DUP and Sinn Féin) have eschewed the Shared Future agenda, the SDLP Minister for Social Development (Margaret Ritchie) sees it as central to her brief. In February 2008 she launched a new agenda for housing in Northern Ireland aimed at tackling the acute housing problem. The scale of the problem in stark statistical terms was set out as follows: over 38,000 people on the housing waiting list; over 20,000 people in housing stress; over 9,000 people officially homeless; and, average house prices over 10 times average incomes. The Minister announced plans to:

- Build more homes – at least 5,250 in the next 5 years.
- Make the existing co-ownership scheme more attractive for first-time buyers, including the abolition of house value limits.
- Bring forward proposals to establish a not-for-profit Mortgage Rescue Scheme.
- Allow existing social housing tenants the chance to buy a stake in their homes.
- Bring empty homes back into use through the development of an Empty Homes Strategy.
- Introduce a developers' contribution requiring future developments to include a proportion of homes for social and affordable housing.
- A new code for sustainable housing and a new procurement strategy that will increase the energy efficiency of new social houses whilst driving costs down.
(Ritchie, 2008a: 1)

Central, however, to the delivery of this plan was the Minister's commitment to a shared future. She noted that the *Programme for Government 2008–11* had been criticised for the absence of a specific commitment to *A Shared Future* but made it clear that its principles would inform her approach to the housing agenda.

> The drive to increase affordable housing and shared neighbourhoods is close to my heart. The Troubles have created a legacy of communities living separately. A shared future will not merely evolve — it must be built. Divisions must be bridged, and as part of the new housing agenda, we aim to deliver as many new-build social and affordable housing schemes as possible, in which the occupants are from mixed traditions and are signed up to a shared-future charter. The Shared Neighbourhood Programme will assist more communities in their desire to live together and involves communities and community organisations in 30 areas across Northern Ireland. (Ritchie, 2008b: 120)

The Minister's analysis was that although Northern Ireland had achieved a welcome level of political stability, it is a dysfunctional society which is deeply segregated on sectarian lines where people lived, were educated and socialised separately. She reasoned that to overcome this dysfunctionalism three things needed to happen: political stability, an improved economy and social development. Shared housing was a key element in social development which should be a catalyst for transforming society and dismantling the institutionalised divisions and segregation which characterised Northern Ireland. The Minister acknowledged that a shared ethos could not be forced. The Northern Ireland Housing Executive which is ultimately accountable to the Minister, for example, allocates houses on the basis of need and the personal choice of potential tenants. This allocation process is not driven by a value judgement on the part of the Northern Ireland Housing Executive between integrated or segregated housing but, rather, addresses need and accommodates people's choice of where to live.

To operationalise a shared future housing agenda the Minister has committed to deliver as many new build social and affordable housing schemes as possible, where occupants are from mixed traditions and are signed up to a 'Shared Future charter'. The prototype for this model was launched in Enniskillen (Carran Crescent), County Fermanagh where families signed up to a charter for their community and no more than 70 per cent of any one religion is allowed. She also plans to convert many existing social housing developments to shared future status. Alongside this agenda for change, the Minister committed to provided mixed tenure (private and social) housing as a way of achieving social and economic integration. In terms of existing homes (as opposed to new build) the Northern Ireland Housing Executive has developed a Shared Neighbourhood Programme (launched in August 2008 with financial support from the International Fund for Ireland) which works with communities who wish to develop shared neighbourhoods, celebrate diversity and bring people together from all backgrounds. The programme provides training and practical on-the-ground support through a dedicated team of cohesion advisors. In addition to grants to run official cultural awareness and community events, participating communities receive community relations training, community consultations and support to design their own Neighbourhood Charter and deliver their own good relations programme (Northern Ireland Housing Executive website). The aim is to work with 30 existing communities over a 3-year period – some 16 communities are already involved after 1 year of the programme's operation.

Is Northern Ireland a reconciled society? Although there are very positive indicators of improving community relations amongst both young people and adults, and a marked decline in levels of violence as measured by deaths and paramilitary-style attacks, there are insidious problems caused by a highly segregated society. The devolved government has been unable to face these problems head-on because they go to the heart of what separates the key partners in a power-sharing Executive. Integrated education is a case in point. Segregated schooling and the dominance of the churches in the education sector are difficult issues to tackle – better, from a political perspective, to skirt around these and make changes at the margins – the odd approval for a transformed school can be held up as 'encouraging and facilitating' integrated education. Despite criticisms of the discredited community relations paradigm upon which contact schemes are based, a preponderance of evidence is emerging to demonstrate that sharing as opposed to separation is a key ingredient in building a reconciled Northern Ireland whether that is in the workplace, education system or where people reside. Northern Ireland has some way to go on this.

8
Work-in-progress: community planning and central–local relations

Community planning

One of the most important new functions coming to local government in Northern Ireland is community planning. Community planning will be a key strategic responsibility for strong local government, working in close partnership with other key agencies within their area. It will allow councils to punch above their weight through influencing how the full range of services are planned and delivered in their area. The community planning process aims to draw together all service providers within the council boundary, thus allowing the council to address community needs in a more strategic, dynamic and flexible way. (Northern Ireland Local Government Taskforce Report June 2006)

Central–local relations

The key issue remains change in the central–local relationship with its implications for the working of central government. The problems that have to be overcome are:
- *The model of command and control leading to over-prescription, over-inspection and over-regulation.*
- *The lack of joined-up government leading to a failure to consider the full impact of the modernisation programme for departments of the inter-relationship between different initiatives.*
- *The absence of any adequate overview of developments in central–local relations, so that there has been little consideration of the overall impact of central government action upon local authorities.*
- *Attitudes in the culture of central government that prevent a recognition of the strengths of local government and of its councillors and officers.* (Stewart, 2003: 253–254)

The penultimate chapter in this book considers two key initiatives of central importance to the future governance of Northern Ireland: community planning and central–local government relations. At the time of writing (August 2009) these are very much work-in-progress and hence what follows is a cross-sectional account of the issues as they unfold. The author has been actively involved as an academic advisor in both areas, and material is included here which reflects that connection with the issues under consideration. In the case of community planning, the author (with colleagues) worked on the first pilot community planning process in Omagh District Council in Northern Ireland. In terms of central–local government relations, the author acted as an advisor to a taskforce set up by the Department of the Environment (NI) to examine how best to structure future relations in the changing governance environment which has emerged following the ongoing implementation of the Review of Public Administration. Writing about contemporary developments in Northern Ireland is a perilous affair as those trying to capture the on/off process of devolution in the Province will testify. This chapter therefore comes with a health warning to alert the reader that the material, whilst accurate at the time of writing, may well be subject to change as proposals for community planning and central–local relations move to full legislative approval in 2010/11.

Background: community planning

Community planning, according to Sinclair (2008), has various meanings. At a general level it refers to methods of public engagement and participation in local planning, particularly public involvement in local environment planning. More specifically, it refers to the development of joint strategies and partnership working between local agencies (Department of Communities and Local Government n.d. and Improvement and Development Agency, n.d. respectively, cited in Sinclair 2008: 373) – see table 8.1 which sets out the constituent elements of the community planning process. The Department of Environment (NI) Taskforce group set up to consider community planning defined it as 'any process through which a council comes together with other organisations to plan, provide for, or promote the well-being of the communities they serve' (Department of the Environment, 2006: 16). One of the key recommendations emerging from the outcomes of the Review of Public Administration (2006) was to provide local government in Northern Ireland with legislative powers in community planning and well-being. The (then) Secretary of State announced:

Table 8.1 The process of community planning

Objectives	Provide a guide to the process that sets out the principles, objectives and guidelines for working on the comprehensive strategy for well-being and sustainable development.
Partnership community involvement	Create a dialogue with people in the locality, community/voluntary organisations, private sector, other government agencies and departments; set out the strategic, thematic and sectoral partnerships
Vision	Set out a long-term vision that: • Promotes an outward focus on the needs of the community at large, its well-being and sustainable development • Promotes a holistic view of social, economic and environmental well-being and their interconnections • Focuses attention on tackling causes with preventive or anticipatory measures • Develops and monitors indicators of well-being together with 'general heath' and service specific performance indicators • Challenges or tests current services, policies and practice against their impact on current and future well-being
Action plan and Implementation	• Set out annual medium-term (3 or 5 years) and long-term aspirations (15–20 years and beyond) with clear targets and measures of success • Clarify the relationship to, and between, other statutory and non-statutory plans and processes including Best Value performance plans and seek to co-ordinate all consultation and involvement activities. • Encourage clear responsibilities amongst various agencies towards the overall wellbeing of the area, co-ordinate contributions of individuals and organisations and ensure effective use of public resources. • Link to regional and national, European and international strategies which support local well-being • Seek to link local moves towards well-being with their potential impact on the rest of the world. • Assess other plans and priorities against those set in the Community Strategy • Ensure that the council's 'in-house' activities respond to the aspirations of the community
Monitoring and Review	Provide a clear review and monitoring process (in partnership with stakeholders) with evaluation of outcomes and recommendations for improvement or change to the community plan.

Source: Local Government Taskforce, Community Planning Sub-group Report (2006).

Councils will have a new *power of well-being*. This will allow them to take any action, not already the responsibility of another agency, linked with the community plan, that will improve the well-being of the local community or the local area. Such a power allows great flexibility and, coupled with the additional functions transferring from other parts of the public service, will enable councils to respond creatively to local needs, ensuring accessible and citizen-focused services that make a real difference to people's lives.

Councils will be required to lead a *community planning process*. This will require the council to consult all its constituents about issues that affect their lives and allow people to have a say in the way in which their area is developed. All other statutory agencies will be required to work with councils in developing and delivering these plans. The community plan will be published allowing the whole community to take ownership of it, as well as assess how well the council and others are delivering against their commitments. (Review of Public Administration, 2006: 7)

Community planning, in particular, is acclaimed as a significant development for the new councils in Northern Ireland due to come into existence in 2011, following its introduction in other parts of the United Kingdom. What makes community planning particularly interesting in Northern Ireland however, is that the role of councils is much less prominent in the delivery of public services than Great Britain counterparts. The question is, in implementing the reforms proposed under the Review of Public Administration, whether community planning is merely a sop to the limited forum that is local government or if it will become a key mechanism in the governance of Northern Ireland in the future.

Community planning is now well established in the rest of the United Kingdom and the Republic of Ireland. Partnership working in the Republic of Ireland dates back to the late 1980s including the Irish model of 'social partnership' which was launched at national level. In 1991, area-based partnerships were established to address the problem of unemployment/disadvantage and social exclusion at local level (Walsh, 1998). These new local structures were largely independent of local government and operated outside formal local democratic mechanisms. In June 1998, an Interdepartmental Task Force was appointed to draw up a model for the integration of local government and local development systems. In its report the Task Force noted that what was missing from the process of developing the economic and social life of local areas in the Republic of Ireland was 'a coherent allocation of responsibilities among public agencies and a means for all local agencies and the community and voluntary sector to translate a shared vision into reality by working together at local level' (Interdepartmental Task Force, 1998: 33). The Task Force recommended setting up County/City Development Boards whose primary function was to draw up and work toward the implementation of a strategy (or shared vision) for economic, social and cultural development within the County/City. In 2000, 34 County/City Development Boards were given statutory recognition in Ireland under the Planning and Development Act 2000 and the Local Government Act 2001. The new strategies had a 10-year community planning parameter broken down into 3- to 5-year targets, and individual organisations retained responsibility for formulating and implementing more detailed operational plans. County/City Development Boards were required to explicitly 'proof' their strategies against wider regional/national policies and plans. Similarly, participating organisations are expected to 'proof' their operational plans against the County/City Development Board Strategy (Fenn, 2007).

The impetus for community planning in Great Britain stemmed largely from the Labour Party's search for democratic renewal during the 1990s (Rogers *et al.* 1999; Ilsley, 2001). That said, Williams *et al.* (2006) observed that the debate can be traced back at least as far as the 1969 Redcliffe Maud Report on local government reform and findings of the Bain Report 1972 which stated 'local government, in our view, is not limited to the narrow provision of a series of services to the community . . . It has within its purview the overall economic, cultural and physical well-being of the community.' In 1995 the term 'community planning' appeared for the first time in a consultative version of the Labour Party's policy statement for local government (*Renewing Democracy, Rebuilding Communities*) which suggested that local authorities should publish an annual community plan that would:

> Set out in clear terms the council's objectives and priorities for each service and establish the performance targets which would need to be met. Councils would publish the plan and be required to consult people generally and the users of specific services, spelling out the targets and cost implications for local people. (Cited in Williams *et al.*, 2006: 5)

The Local Government Act 2000 provided a legal framework for the development of local authorities' community leadership role in England and Wales including: a duty to develop a comprehensive strategy for promoting well-being – the community strategy; new powers to work in partnerships, in particular establishing local strategic partnerships; and, broad powers to promote the economic, social and environmental well-being of their communities. Additionally, local authorities were required to consult and seek participation in the preparation of the plan and to have regard to any guidance issued by the Secretary of State.

In Scotland, the Local Government in Scotland Act 2003 provides the statutory underpinning for community planning and linked to this, a duty to secure best value and the power of well-being. Statutory guidance issued by the Scottish Executive in 2004 to accompany the legislation identified two main aims for community planning:

- *Community engagement*: making sure people and communities are genuinely engaged in the decisions made on public services which affect them; allied to
- *Joint working*: a commitment from organisations to work together, not apart, in providing better public services.

These aims were supported by two further principles: rationalisation – an overarching partnership framework to co-ordinate other initiatives and partnerships which would rationalise and simplify the cluttered landscape; and connecting national and local priorities whereby community planning acts as a bridge to link national and local priorities better (Scottish Executive 2004). The Scottish model of community planning significantly influenced thinking in Northern Ireland as late-comers to the process.

Evidence of the community planning process in Great Britain is emerging which highlights some of the operational problems. Pemberton and Lloyd (2008) noted that the reality of partnership working was much more complex than anticipated and there were real difficulties in securing the integration of public services and activities. They cited Audit Scotland's conclusions (2006) that community planning had not helped in significantly rationalising the number or complexity of partnerships. Pemberton and Lloyd conclude:

> Even where obligations have been placed on partners to participate/collaborate within community planning structures, it appears that the evidence remains 'patchy' as to whether this has actually occurred in reality . . . Accordingly, the evaluations in England, Scotland and Wales have all generally identified that there potentially needs to be a much stronger - and broader - strategic framework for community planning to achieve the potential envisaged in the legislation. But the principal question is how to devise the most efficient and effective means of securing such integration in practice. (Pemberton and Lloyd, 2008: 449)

The researchers point out that the experience so far in Great Britain offers lessons for Northern Ireland in that even with placing a statutory duty on agencies to participate in the community planning process, this has not been easily achieved in practice. In seeking to address this problem of integration Lloyd (2008) suggests the idea of 'pooled sovereignty' (Morgan 2002) based on the use of contracts and agreements which he argues may be more appropriate for the complex and dynamic institutional relations and local circumstances involved in securing integration.

Sinclair's research (2008) on community planning in Scotland identified tensions in reconciling partnership working with local authority leadership:

between community planning as an additional or core duty of public agencies; between community engagement and the practical demands of policy-making; and between central government direction and local partnership autonomy. He concluded:

> Four years after the legislation introducing community planning in Scottish local government was passed, and 10 years since the formation of the Community Planning Working Group, a succession of analyses have concluded that it remains difficult to attribute any discernible impacts to community planning: it remains a process and method of working rather than a tangible set of outcomes. (Audit Scotland, 2006, cited in Sinclair, 2008: 385)

Similar findings emerged from a consultancy report which analysed case study examples of community planning across the United Kingdom and the Republic of Ireland which concluded that it was 'difficult to demonstrate hard outcomes (from community planning) in terms of both added value and impact'. Positive outcomes were described in terms of 'processes, such as closer partnership understanding and improved community engagement, rather than in harder outcomes such as efficiency savings through shared budgets' (Blake Stevenson and Stratagem, 2005: vii).

Sullivan and Williams' evaluation (2009: 177) of community strategies in Wales identified the complexity associated with designing and delivering community strategies and questioned 'the viability of the "joined-up" project as a whole, particularly in the context of multiple and often competing purposes'. They also had 'reservations about the potential to govern effectively in policy arenas that are over-populated with different actors and interests, operating within different spatial and temporal horizons' and concluded that 'operationalising community strategies presents significant challenges to government, practitioners and researchers'.

In Northern Ireland, the reorganisation of local government coming out of the Review of Public Administration led to the establishment of a Local Government Taskforce by the Department of the Environment and nine sub-groups to work on various aspects of reform, one of which was on community planning. Although Northern Ireland had no direct experience of community planning, its involvement in European Union funding initiatives in the early 1990s witnessed a growth in partnership working. The introduction of an EU *Special Support Programme for Peace and Reconciliation* (valued at £300m) to reinforce progress towards a peaceful and democratic society was delivered through 26 district partnerships drawing their membership from locally elected representatives, public bodies, the business sector, and community and voluntary organisations (Hughes *et al.* 1998). In a follow-up initiative (PEACE II), local strategy partnerships were given the task of developing an Integrated Local Strategy which was to provide a framework for the sustainable regeneration and development of their areas. In this sense the whole concept of partnership working was not new in Northern Ireland and provided useful context for proposals on community planning.

The NI Community Planning Sub-Group reported in June 2006, recommending a modified Scottish model which included best practice identified elsewhere but a process/strategy which was 'uniquely suited to the Northern Ireland situation. Such a model would include a duty to advance the process of community planning through partnership and the production of a community plan' (Department of the Environment, 2006: 15). The Sub-Group on Community Planning also recommended that it become a statutory duty for the following agencies to participate in the core community planning partnership: the Health and Social Care Board and Public Health Agency; Education and Skills Authority; Policing Board and Chief Constable, Fire and Rescue, Northern Ireland Housing Executive, Invest Northern Ireland and Translink. In addition, the sub-group recommended that a duty of co-operation and promotion should be placed on all government departments and public agencies. Naming public bodies in this way, one suspects, is borne out of past experience and frustration of local authorities in trying to provide an integrated response to the needs of people at local level. The sub-group also recommended that a number of community planning pilots be initiated across Northern Ireland to begin as soon as possible, although the Department of Environment provided no funding to kick-start this process. Omagh District Council decided to proceed to pilot community planning in its area – we consider this as a case study of the first community planning process in Northern Ireland (Carmichael *et al.*, 2007).

A pilot case study: Omagh District Council

Omagh District Council Omagh District covers an area of almost 113,000 hectares (440 square miles), making it the second largest district council area in Northern Ireland with a population of around 48,000. The market town of Omagh is at the centre of the region with the rest of the Omagh District primarily rural in character and its people living in scattered small towns and villages or in dispersed rural communities. Approximately 20,000 people live in Omagh town, the next largest centres are Fintona and Dromore. Omagh town (with the exception of Derry City) is now the largest in the west of Northern Ireland. Despite making international headlines following the Omagh bomb atrocity, in which 29 people were killed, the people of the area have pulled together under the leadership of the local authority and the area is recovering well.

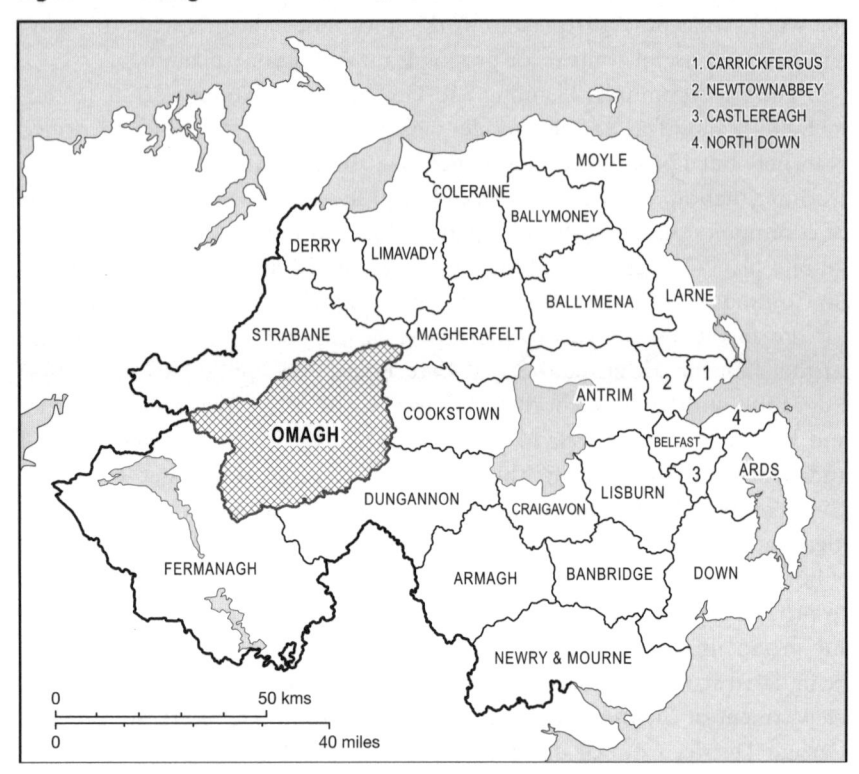

Figure 8.1 Omagh District Council, 2009

Some brief factual information on Omagh District Council (see figure 8.1) is as follows:

- On census day (2001) Omagh District Council had a resident population of 47,952.
- 25.9 per cent of the population was under 16 years old and 15.4 per cent was 60 and above.
- 69.1 per cent were from a Catholic background and 29.7 per cent from a Protestant and other Christian community background.
- The average age of the population in Omagh District Council was 34.1 years.

Looking specifically at multiple deprivation measures:

- 13 per cent of the Omagh population lives in the most deprived Super Output Areas (SOA) in Northern Ireland.
- Omagh ranks 7th out of 26 local government districts on the average

SOA measure (rank 1 = most deprived council: Strabane; rank 26 = least deprived council: North Down).
- Within Omagh District Council the most deprived SOA is Lisanelly 2 and the least deprived is Lisanelly 1.

In terms of the political composition of the local authority:

- Omagh District Council has 21 councillors: 10 Sinn Féin, 3 SDLP, 3 Ulster Unionist, 3 Democratic Unionist and 2 Independents.

Despite the absence of central government funding to pilot community planning, Omagh District Council took the decision to devise a community plan for the local authority area. It was acknowledged at the outset that such a proposal could only include the geography of the existing council area and not the reformed local government structure due in place by May 2011 in which Omagh District Council and Fermanagh District Council will amalgamate. Clearly this presented some limitations in the pilot but nonetheless allowed Omagh District Council the opportunity to 'road test' the community planning process for the first time in Northern Ireland. The Council also has an established history of partnership working in the area. It had been or is currently involved in several partnerships to include: Local Strategy Partnership as a mechanism for the implementation of EU funding; Community Safety Partnership; District Policing Partnership; and a taskforce on economic development.

The aims of the community planning process were:

- To produce a pilot community plan for Omagh District Council, within the confines of its existing boundaries, working with other statutory, private and voluntary/community sector providers in the area.
- To draw on Scottish exemplars of good practice in community planning to structure the process and production of Omagh's Community Plan.
- To establish collaborative arrangements (through a new Community Planning Partnership) with key service providers within the Omagh District Council area as a way of improving the quality of life of its residents.
- To initiate quarterly meetings of the Community Planning Partnership to oversee the monitoring and implementation of the community plan.

The process of developing the community plan began in 2006 and involved separate workshops with councillors, statutory organisations, and the private and voluntary/community sectors to agree a vision and priority themes for the area. When consensus emerged, Omagh District Council returned to statutory partners and sought agreement on a detailed action plan and associated targets. This stage of the process proved problematic. Statutory partners in key public services (health, education, roads, housing) had their own strategic plans with a wider geographical remit beyond the boundaries of Omagh District Council. How then did these plans align with the Council's proposed community plan – which was pre-eminent? Statutory partners needed to be convinced that the proposed community plan would not detract from or usurp their agreed work within the Omagh Council area: rather, it was intended to add value to existing public services through integrated planning. In other words, the whole (community plan) was greater than the sum of the parts (partner agencies service-specific plans).

The core elements of the community plan comprised:

1. An overall vision/mission statement for the Omagh District Council area.
2. A *small number* of *high-level cross-cutting themes* which required collaborative actions across community planning partners with an identified lead organisation.
3. An action plan linked to the cross-cutting themes with measurable targets and outputs. Each of the themes in the action plan was structured around three key questions: 'what will we do', 'how will we do it' and 'who will lead' on the actions identified.
4. A formal commitment to the community plan by partners through their own internal planning and decision-making processes.
5. Monitoring and evaluating progress in meeting the targets/outputs outlined in the community plan (through a proposed Community Planning Partnership).

The themes and actions were judiciously selected, few in number, high-level and cross-cutting to make the point that the community plan was **not** a composite of the internal and external plans of partner organisations (see figure 8.2).

Best practice evidence from community planners in Scotland (Scottish Executive, 2003) suggested that community planning partnerships needed to agree the following:

1. What the priorities are and how they will translate these into outcomes.
2. What actions need to be taken to deliver improvements?
3. What indicators will be used to measure progress on these outcomes?
4. What targets will be set for improvement?

Figure 8.2 Community planning process, Omagh District Council, 2009

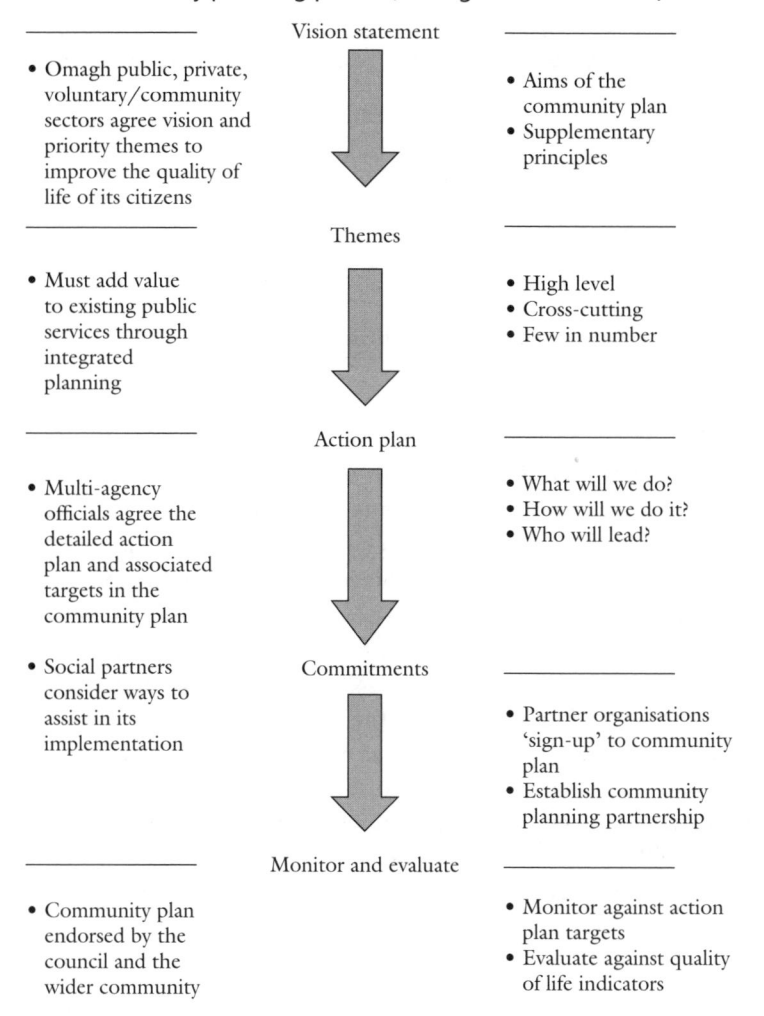

	Vision statement	
• Omagh public, private, voluntary/community sectors agree vision and priority themes to improve the quality of life of its citizens	⬇	• Aims of the community plan • Supplementary principles
	Themes	
• Must add value to existing public services through integrated planning	⬇	• High level • Cross-cutting • Few in number
	Action plan	
• Multi-agency officials agree the detailed action plan and associated targets in the community plan	⬇	• What will we do? • How will we do it? • Who will lead?
• Social partners consider ways to assist in its implementation	Commitments ⬇	• Partner organisations 'sign-up' to community plan • Establish community planning partnership
	Monitor and evaluate	
• Community plan endorsed by the council and the wider community		• Monitor against action plan targets • Evaluate against quality of life indicators

The community planning process therefore followed the steps set out in figure 8.2 above.

Vision statement

The agreed vision statement for the Community Plan was as follows:

> To make Omagh District an economically prosperous, healthy, sustainable and quality place in which to live and work, and to place the district at the heart of the administration of the Tyrone and Fermanagh region.

Themes

The six themes agreed by community planning partners to realise this vision were:

- Economic prosperity;
- Health and well-being;
- Education and lifelong learning;
- Infrastructure;
- Environment;
- Community safety and a shared future.

Action plan

The action plan followed from the agreed themes above. The format of the action plan broadly followed the headings: What will we do? How will we do it? What are our targets for action? Who are the lead partners? An example is included of *one* thematic area contained in the community plan (see table 8.2). The action plan was drawn up with the following criteria in mind:

- High level commitments to 'what we will do' – these had to add value to the existing work of planning partners.
- A relatively small *number* of actions which were truly collaborative, realistic and achievable – in other words, partners needed to co-operate to make them happen (cross-cutting, joined-up commitments).
- Measurable targets associated with 'how we will do it'.
- A community plan which was 'budget neutral' – making better use of existing resources.
- The ultimate test of community planning was whether its implementation improved the quality of people's lives in Omagh. There was a need to begin with baseline information in order to subsequently assess whether improvements had happened.

Commitments

The activities listed in the community plan required measurable targets for action identified under each of the themes. Ideally, each activity should have baseline information against which one would expect to see an improvement (or significant movement) over the period of the plan. Given the diversity of the activities gathered through the consultation process in developing the plan, some baseline measures did not yet exist.

Table 8.2 Omagh District council, Community Plan 2007–10 (extract)

What will we do?	How will we do it?	Lead partners

Health & Well-being: A Healthy Omagh
 	
We will promote and protect the physical and mental health of communities, provide high quality, accessible health services, and challenge health inequalities
	• Promote healthy lifestyles by:
	  – reducing obesity
	  – reducing number of smokers
	  – improving sexual health
	  – tackling drugs and alcohol abuse
	  – reducing suicides
	  – improving mental health
	  – reducing accidents in the home and workplace
	• Raise awareness of the above
	• Ensure the provision of, and access to, acute and related services locally that meet the needs of the Omagh area
	• Provide medical/clinical care of the highest standard
	• Improve emergency/crisis teams' response times
	• Address health inequalities – life expectancy
	• Promote the role of wider community partnerships e.g. promotion activities, preventative measures in health care
	• Promote work/life balance and leisure time
	• Promote 'happiness'
		Department of Health and Social Services
		Western Health and Social Care Trust
		Health and Social Care Board
		Public Health Agency
		NI Ambulance Service
		Omagh District Council
		Investing for Health Partnership
		Education and Skills Authority
		Community and Voluntary Sector

The approach taken to establish targets was therefore informed by a number of considerations as follows:

- What were the key indicators in the delivery of the community planning agenda in Omagh? By extension, was quantifiable information available which would allow progress to be tracked on these indicators over time?
- Following invitation, some participants in the consultation process (but not all) volunteered possible targets which could be used in progressing the community planning agenda.
- Where targets were not available, these were sourced through alternative means (Public Service Agreements – Northern Ireland Priorities and Budget, corporate and business plans of departments and agencies, adapted Quality of Life indicators drawing on the work of the Audit Commission (2005), statistical sources published by departments, and

database information gathered via the Northern Ireland Research and Statistics Agency disaggregated at local authority level).
- Some activities were not amenable to quantifiable measurement. These were listed in the plan and ways found to track the activities in a qualitative format.

An extract from Omagh District Council's Community Plan which shows targets under one theme *Health and Well-Being* is set out in box 8.1.

Box 8.1 Omagh District Council Community Plan 2007–10 (extract), commitments: targets for action health and well-being

A healthy Omagh

- To reduce the level of alcohol consumption from 7 per cent amongst adults (who drink either 'above sensible but below dangerous, or dangerous levels') in 2004/05 (Northern Ireland wide figure) to 5 per cent in the Omagh DC area. Sensible levels of alcohol consumption mean 21 units per week for men and 14 units for women.
- To improve ambulance response times in the wards of Dromore, Fairy Water, Fintona, Newtownsaville, Owenkillen, Termon and Trillick from an average of 33 minutes to 25 minutes.
- To reduce the number of individuals presenting for drug abuse in the Western Health and Social Care Trust area from 386 (2004/05) by 10 per cent.
- To reduce the number of admissions to hospital as a result of mood anxiety disorder from 38 in Western Health and Social Care Trust area (2004/05) by 10 per cent.
- To reduce infant mortality, the number of infant deaths (children aged 0 per 1,000 births) from 2.5 (in 1999–2003) to 2 in the Omagh DC area.
- To increase life expectancy in Omagh DC area from 76.6 (male) and 81.5 (female) in 2002–04 to 79 and 83 years respectively.
- To reduce the percentage of suicides per 100,000 persons (1999–2003) in Omagh DC area from 9.8 per cent to 8 per cent.
- To reduce the proportion of adult smokers in the Omagh DC area in line with the Northern Ireland target of 22 per cent or less.
- To equal the Northern Ireland average travel time of 12 minutes to reach the nearest hospital with an accident and emergency department including minor injury units.

Monitor and evaluate

To oversee the implementation of the plan a Community Planning Partnership was established comprising: 8 elected members, 10 nominees from statutory bodies, 2 nominees from the voluntary and community sector (urban and rural), and 2 private sector nominees. Statutory bodies on the partnership were targeted for selection on the basis of those most relevant to the delivery of the community plan's priorities. The planning partnership meets on a quarterly basis to monitor delivery against the action plan and review its activities accordingly. The partnership also reports progress on its achievements to the community it serves through Council bulletins.

Apart from reviewing progress against the action plan, Omagh District Council was interested in exploring, at a higher level, the impact of integrated service planning on the quality of life of its residents. If community planning is to be an effective process, then ultimately it must improve the quality of people's lives. In order to capture this, the community plan adapted the Audit Commission's quality of life (QoL) indicators for circumstances in Northern Ireland. Although designed for Great Britain with very different local government structures and functions, selective indicators were used to track progress on the themes agreed in the community plan. This represented a significant challenge in a number of ways:

- Adapting QoL indicators to the circumstances of Northern Ireland – not all of the data were available to operationalise Audit Commission indicators in the Northern Ireland context.
- Moving out of the 'comfort zone' of service-specific targets.
- Greater transparency and accountability for improving things that matter to the quality of citizens' lives.

Table 8.3 and figure 8.3 show the baseline information which were used by Omagh District Council as the basis of comparison with the indicators for Northern Ireland overall. The data were sourced from the Northern Ireland Neighbourhood Information Service (NINIS) area profile statistics (Northern Ireland Statistics and Research Agency: NISRA) and attempt to match the Audit Commission's local quality of life indicators.

Figure 8.3 shows that Omagh District Council is better than the Northern Ireland average on a number of the key indicators (owner occupied housing, school leavers going into further/higher education and higher earnings for those in work). Some obvious exceptions include crime (offences against the person) and economic and social well-being areas (higher levels of incapacity benefits, income support, and free school meals)

Table 8.3 Baseline information: quality of life indicators, Omagh District Council, community plan, 2007–10 (extract)

	Omagh	Northern Ireland	Better or worse
Crime/community safety			
% criminal damage of recorded crime (04/05)	25.3	26.6	+1.3
% burglary (04/05)	7.9	11.3	+3.4
% theft (04/05)	18.4	26.3	+7.9
% offences against the person (04/05)	34.9	24.8	−10.1
Housing			
% rented (census 2001)	28.0	30.4	+2.4
% owned outright (census 2001)	38.0	29.4	+8.6
% owner occupied (census 2001)	72.0	69.6	+2.4
Health and social well-being			
% teenage pregnancies by Board area (Western Board: 2004)	6.5	6.7	+0.2
Standardised mortality ratio for all ages (2000–04)	100	100	–
% people with long-term illness (census 2001)	20.4	20.4	–
Education and lifelong learning			
% degree level of higher qualifications (census 2001)	14.4	15.8	−1.4
% of school leavers into further and higher education (2002)	66.3	61.7	+4.6
% of school leavers with 5+ GCSEs at grade C and above (2002)	64.3	58.6	+5.7
Economic and social well-being			
% people (16–59/64) claiming incapacity benefits (2004)	12.7	10.7	−2.0
% people (18–59) claiming income support (2004)	11.5	10.8	−0.7
% school population entitled free school meals (2006)	19.3	18.9	−0.4
% unemployed (census 2001)	4.7	4.1	−0.6
Median gross weekly earnings all employees (2005)	£332.7	£320.5	+3.8
% economically active (census 2001)	61.2	62.3	−1.1

as well as a higher level of unemployment. Rather crudely, one interpretation could be a divide between the 'haves' and 'have-nots' best captured by the very high level of houses owned outright at one end of the quality of life spectrum, and at the other, the number of recipients on incapacity benefits.

WORK-IN-PROGRESS   251

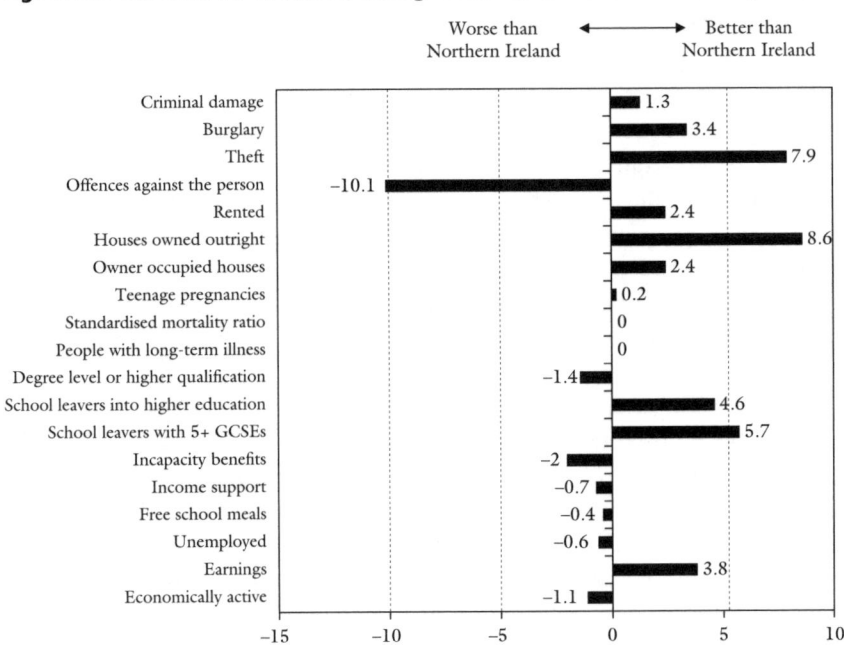

Figure 8.3 Baseline information, Omagh relative to Northern Ireland, 2008

Indicator	Value
Criminal damage	1.3
Burglary	3.4
Theft	7.9
Offences against the person	−10.1
Rented	2.4
Houses owned outright	8.6
Owner occupied houses	2.4
Teenage pregnancies	0.2
Standardised mortality ratio	0
People with long-term illness	0
Degree level or higher qualification	−1.4
School leavers into higher education	4.6
School leavers with 5+ GCSEs	5.7
Incapacity benefits	−2
Income support	−0.7
Free school meals	−0.4
Unemployed	−0.6
Earnings	3.8
Economically active	−1.1

Worse than Northern Ireland ← → Better than Northern Ireland

Learning from the pilot

What is clear from the pilot exercise is that much more work needs to be done to establish departmental 'buy-in' to the process of community planning in Northern Ireland. Part of the benefit of the pilot was educational and raising awareness. Government departments, agencies and non-departmental public bodies will, over time, become comfortable/confident working with local authorities, the private, and voluntary/community sectors. Statutory stakeholders will also know what is expected of them in the community planning process. One of the advantages of proposals emerging from the Review of Public Administration was co-terminosity under a 7-council model. Since this model was rejected and replaced with an 11-council 'solution', common boundaries for key public bodies have not happened (Knox, 2009). The pilot exercise demonstrated the limitations of stakeholders working across different geographical areas and its shortcomings for integrated service delivery. The status of a community plan will remain unclear in these circumstances. Indeed the burgeoning number of plans and strategies at the regionally, sub-regionally and local levels for spatial development, neighbourhood renewal and rural development, to name but a few, poses questions about the primacy of the community plan. Moreover, whether the local authority can, under whatever legislative arrangements emerge, act in a *primus inter pares* role within the community planning development and implementation process remains uncertain. Councils, despite the transfer of some powers under the reform of local government in 2011, remain marginal players in public service delivery. Their relative status could therefore limit their capacity to exercise leadership and influence at the community planning table.

To date the voluntary commitment of statutory bodies to the task is still tentative and uncertain. This can be explained, in part, by the fluidity of the current public sector environment in which they are working - the implementation of reforms under the Review of Public Administration and possible restructuring of government departments. More importantly however, central government bodies are unclear about how to address the intersecting lines of accountability posed by community planning. Can horizontal accountability through community plans sit easily alongside their own departmental vertical lines of accountability upwards to the Minister and the Assembly? This demands departmental 'buy-in' at the highest level from those participating in the community planning process. Indeed in the Omagh case study, those statutories whose baseline quality of life indicators were 'good' felt less obligated to take corporate responsibility to progress the community plan. The experience to date is that statutory organisations are good on process but tentative on target setting and a long lead-in time is required to secure commitment. Equally, the voluntary and community sector has argued that 'community' planning is a misnomer because of their limited numerical representation on the partnership – 2 nominees from a 22-membership community planning partnership. The Northern Ireland Council for Voluntary Action has lobbied for greater involvement of the sector in the community planning process. The response to this suggestion is that it is more important to have large statutory budget holders in the partnership who can deliver integrated services, and elected representatives can legitimately claim to represent the 'community' (McCullagh, 2009).

None of this is to devalue the contributions of willing and active participants in the pilot community planning process, but simply to acknowledge that it was a preliminary exercise and will demand formal commitment by statutories if the process is to take root and become a meaningful mechanism for 'joined-up' and responsive local service delivery. The scale of this task should not be underestimated. The Scottish experience is instructive here, where community planners argue:

> It is often relatively easy from community planning partners to reach agreement on the priorities for their area, but can be more difficult to agree the outcomes and what the targets should be for progress and how these can be measured, and who will take what actions to achieve those targets. (Scottish Executive, 2003: 12)

Legislative proposals in the form of the Local Government (Reorganisation) Bill will include provisions for the introduction of community planning and well-being. Subject to Northern Ireland Executive approval, it is anticipated that the Bill will be introduced to the Assembly by May 2010. Some concerns have been expressed that the powers of 'well-being' and 'sanction', key to the community planning process in other parts of the United Kingdom, have received little attention within the Northern Ireland debate. The pilot exercise in Omagh District Council has therefore exposed both strengths and weaknesses in community planning, all without the assistance of the government department whose remit it is to oversee local government reform – the Department of the Environment. Civil servants are experiencing some difficulties in the transition from Direct Rule to devolution, even if this only means collective engagement with other public service providers such as local authorities. We now move to consider the second key 'work-in-progress' agenda item, central–local relations.

Central–local relations

The outcomes of the Review of Public Administration were predicated on a two-tier model comprising a regional and local tier of governance in Northern Ireland. In essence, at the regional level the primary focus of Ministers and their departments is to formulate policy, strategically plan services, set and monitor the standards of service, and ensure Ministerial direction. At the local level, councils were intended to be at the centre of service delivery and civic life. According to the (then) Secretary of State, local authorities will 'be key to planning and delivery of services and to engagement with communities' (Hain, 2005: 2). With the return of devolution and a re-evaluation of the outcomes of the Review of Public Administration, the role of local government has remained marginal in terms of the functions over which they have direct responsibility. Separate health bodies (trusts, Health and Social Care Board, Public Health Agency), a new Education Skills Authority, and Library Authority have reduced the potential of local government to become a key stakeholder in the public sector. All of this is a far cry from Lord Rooker's assertion, as (then) direct rule Minister for the Environment, that 'local government would have a significant role in the overall governance of Northern Ireland' (Rooker, 2005: 5). Because of the significant which the Minister attached to the role of local government, it is not surprising that he called for a review of central–local relations. Given the minor role which local government had played since stripped of functional responsibilities in 1973, the issue of central–local government relations hardly featured. Councils felt that they were treated with contempt by civil servants who had a duty to consult them on centrally provided services in their areas such as planning, education and roads, but often ignored their input. Hence, Lord Rooker's statement of a new era in central–local relations heralded a welcome change based on co-operation rather than condescension when he announced:

> There will be a formal mechanism for central–local liaison. We will develop such arrangements in co-operation with local government. But it is vital that central and local government respect each other's role and work together for the good of Northern Ireland. (Rooker, 2005: 8)

Local government saw the opportunity to work as an equal partner with central government to ensure common purpose moderated through an effective mechanism of central–local relations. There is no power-dependent relationship between central and local government in Northern Ireland (Rhodes, 1986). The contrast with devolved government in Scotland and Wales is striking here (Laffin *et al.*, 2002; Bennett *et al.* 2002; McAteer and Bennett, 2005; McConnell, 2006). The Welsh Assembly Government sees local government as crucial in delivering effective public services. As Laffin (2004: 216 & 220) puts it 'for them (the Welsh Assembly Government) local government forms a vital implementation structure which absorbs about a third of the Assembly budget' and the Welsh Assembly Government is 'considerably more dependent on local government than central government is on English local government; and a similar argument can be advanced in Scotland'. Compare this to councils in Northern Ireland which deliver minor functions and, even under reform of local government due in 2011, will continue to be marginal players. In this sense Northern Ireland is more like England which is characterised by asymmetric central–local relations in favour of the centre. Devolved regional government in Northern Ireland has not resulted in regional centralism (where powers became more centralised at Stormont), rather it has simply reinforced the *status quo* of asymmetric relations with a strong centre and locally elected ministers reluctant to transfer functions to councils. Here again, the contrast with other parts of the United Kingdom is plain. Laffin (2007) argued that devolution does not inevitably lead to regional centralism particularly where a power balance or symmetry exists between regional and local governments, as in the case of Wales and Scotland. Yet in Northern Ireland regional centralism pre-dates devolution and is rooted in the abuse of power by local government which, in part, sparked the civil rights marches and 'troubles' in the late 1960s. With the emergence of devolution in 1999 and the lust for political power, largely denied for over twenty-five years, Members of the Northern Ireland Legislative Assembly did not feel inclined towards strengthening the role of local government.

To work as an equal partner, the Northern Ireland Local Government Association (NILGA) redefined the role which it envisaged councils playing in the reformed governance landscape. Councils, NILGA asserted, should have one key objective: 'to help create and sustain the social, environmental and economic conditions to enable our communities to thrive' (NILGA, 2006: 1). To achieve this objective, NILGA outlined three principal roles for local government in Northern Ireland: civic leadership, service delivery and local enablers:

1. *Civic leadership*. Civic leadership through local councils should provide the bridge between the citizen and the institutions of government. To facilitate this leadership role, councils would have defined and vibrant relationships with other public agencies, the voluntary/community sector, young people, the private sector and other social partners. Elected members play a vital role in this process. They act to balance the various sets of interest and the apportioning of scarce resources for the common good.
2. *Service delivery*. Councils should seek to deliver modern services which are democratically accountable, integrated, innovative and demonstrate value for money. They should be provided in a manner which increases accessibility of citizens to those council services. Services should be designed with the citizen in mind. Government at every level exists to serve the public, rather than the other way around. Therefore elected members must have effective mechanisms to hold regional and other agencies to account. Local government modernisation must involve changing cultures, not just structures.
3. *Enablers*. While councils, where possible, should be the principal service provider at local level, they also have a role in supporting and influencing the work of others to ensure local development is sustainable. Councils should act as the 'hub of the wheel' in a local community, helping to ensure that joined up solutions are provided to local problems. Both central government departments and other statutory bodies are often established and monitored in a fashion which encourages silo mentalities. Councils are likely to be the only body which can give an overview on any problem and perspectives to the issues facing that community. Councils must therefore be at the forefront of challenging existing practice and the development of new co-ordinated approaches (NILGA, 2006).

Local government therefore wanted to build a relationship with central government based on partnership for the common good, recognising the potential for mutual dependence and trust. Moran (2005) argues that there is no simple separation between the 'local' and 'central' and that the United Kingdom is best characterised as a multi-level system of governance within which there are numerous and often complex interactions between the levels:

> On occasion the relations are hierarchical: national government commands, or at least seeks to command. But more commonly, networks of governing institutions are joined in more subtle ways: they are obliged to co-operate with each other, to bargain with each other, and often to try and manipulate each other . . . Local governments are embedded in webs of relationships: with other local governments; with national institutions; and with regional bodies. (Moran, 2005: 249)

In the context of Northern Ireland, local government has relationships with other councils in tourism, economic development, and environmental health. Councils also interact with national and European institutions (e.g. UK departments - Department for Environment Food and Rural Affairs over BSE and bird flu; PEACE, Interreg EU initiatives) and with regional bodies (e.g. the Northern Ireland Housing Executive). On occasions the relations are hierarchical not least during periods of Direct Rule in Northern Ireland where ministers seek 'to command' (e.g. new rating system, water charges and education reform) but, as Moran suggests, networks are joined in more subtle ways. The complexity of central–local relations in Northern Ireland, despite the aspirations to reduce the number of public bodies and levels of bureaucracy, is unlikely to diminish with the outworkings of the Review of Public Administration. For example, the new powers of community planning given to local government, and discussed above, will require (by law) government agencies to work with councils in developing and delivering plans for the social, economic and environmental welfare of their areas. The production of community plans will typically involve representatives from health and social care, education, police, housing, voluntary and community sectors and the private sector. In short, central–local government relations are but one aspect of a more complex network in a multi-level system of governance in Northern Ireland.

Considering central–local relations in Great Britain, Stewart (2003) argued that Scotland and Wales offer more useful examples than England because of their necessary responses to devolution arrangements. He draws an important distinction in the relations between central government and the Local Government Association (LGA), and local authorities more generally. In fact, Stewart is critical of the top-down nature of central–local relations in England:

> The stress on command and control limits local choice and reduces the capacity for diversity through innovation and initiative that should be one of the strengths of effective local government. The failure to recognise the need for fundamental

> change in central–local relations remains a major weakness in the modernisation programme. (Stewart, 2003: 225)

The formation of the Scottish Parliament and the Welsh Assembly prompted renewed thinking about the relationship between the centre and locality and therefore provide better comparators for Northern Ireland. But the Northern Ireland governance system is different in that the Assembly's dependence on local authorities for service delivery is relatively limited. Core functions such as education, housing, health and social services still remain centrally controlled. The remit of the civil service and its agencies has been relatively untouched by the reform process. Hence the need or propensity for a partnership of equals is less obvious in the circumstances of Northern Ireland. In other words, as noted above, there is asymmetry in the power dependence relationship. It becomes all the more important in Northern Ireland, therefore, to establish good central–local relations as a counterbalance to a highly centralised system.

Accepting the distinctiveness of Northern Ireland, it is helpful to consider the experience of other devolved regions. The Scottish reforms came in the shape of the McIntosh Commission (Sir Neil McIntosh also sat as an expert on the Review of Public Administration team in Northern Ireland) which in its final report argued that 'relations between local government and the (Scottish) Parliament ought to be conducted on the basis of mutual respect and parity of esteem' (Scottish Office, 1999: para. 20). However, an evaluation of central–local relations in Scotland since the advent of a Scottish Parliament in 1999 concluded:

> Scottish local government has not experienced the type of shift in central–local relations that had been hoped for by those who campaigned for a more vital local democracy as part of a genuinely equal partnership between the Scottish Executive and local councils. Continuity is far more prominent than change . . . Fundamental patterns of political relationships essentially remain the same. Scottish local authorities still struggle to shift the balance of power towards the locality. (McConnell, 2006: 81–82)

The research found that the overall pattern of central–local relations was little changed from the pre-devolution period, which is partly explained by the self-interest of Scottish Executive Ministers to retain control over local government.

The Welsh reforms provide a more useful comparison when considering a review of central–local relations in Northern Ireland and hence these are outlined in greater detail than either the English or Scottish experience. Laffin *et al.* (2002) and Laffin (2004) described four formal mechanisms which regulate central local relations in Wales: The Partnership Council; The

Welsh Local Government Association; Professional Associations; and Policy Agreements. We consider the Partnership Council and Policy Agreements in more detail.

The Partnership Council for Wales

Section 113 of the Government of Wales Act 1998 required the National Assembly for Wales to adopt a scheme setting out how it proposed, in the exercise of its functions, to sustain and promote local government in Wales. Section 72 of the Government of Wales Act 2006, required Welsh Ministers to establish and maintain a body known as the Partnership Council for Wales. The Government of Wales Act 2006 effected formal separation between the Welsh Assembly Government and the National Assembly. The Local Government Partnership Scheme requires the Welsh Assembly Government to consider the interests of local government in all aspects of its work. In determining what should be included in the local government scheme, the Welsh Ministers must take into consideration any advice which has been given, and any representations which have been made to them by the Partnership Council for Wales.

The Partnership Council for Wales therefore represents the key formal mechanism to conduct relations between the Welsh Assembly Government and local government in Wales and is a statutory body set up to promote joint working and co-operation. The Partnership comprises members from: all parties in the Assembly, local government, national park, police, and fire and rescue authorities.

Its remit is to:

- give advice to the Welsh Ministers about matters affecting the exercise of any of their functions;
- make representations to the Welsh Ministers about any matters affecting, or of concern to, those involved in local government in Wales; and
- give advice to those involved in local government in Wales (Welsh Assembly Government, 2008a).

The Partnership Council works by consensus and produces joint papers representing the views of the Assembly Government and local government where this is possible. It is supported by a joint secretariat of officials from the Welsh Assembly Government and officers of the Welsh Local Government Association although it is not a decision-making body; rather, it has an advisory role. The Partnership Council provides a forum for collaboration between Welsh Ministers and local government in promoting major cross-cutting themes such as equality of opportunity and sustainable development.

Policy agreements

Policy agreements were orginally introduced to link local and national priorities. They contained specific measures of success to gauge progress in transparently improving the delivery of public services. Local authorities therefore agreed targets with the Assembly Government against a set of 16 measures intended to improve service outputs. Half of these measures were nationally prescribed and common to all authorities, the other half were devised locally by each authority with the aim of reflecting local priorities. Policy Agreements therefore set out the service improvements which councils' committed to deliver and, in turn, were rewarded for meeting output targets with a specific grant by the Assembly Government. Policy Agreements ended in March 2007 and were replaced with 'Improvement Agreements' which still retained the focus on local government service improvements incentivised by a central government grant (Welsh Assembly Government, 2009).

Local service boards and local delivery agreements

More recently, Local Service Boards (LSBs) have been introduced as a mechanism for bringing together key local service providers to agree joint action where it will result in better outcomes and services for others. They are described by the Welsh Assembly Government as follows:

(1) Fundamental to Local Service Boards is the need to integrate services across institutional boundaries, pooling resources if necessary, where it will enable more effective, responsive and often, more efficient, services. Local authorities have a key role in convening the Boards and driving the agenda.
(2) The Welsh Assembly Government will develop with each Board a Local Service Agreement (LSA) that identifies a limited and tangible number of national or local priorities to be delivered through the Local Service Boards. The Local Service Boards should lead the development and then delivery of the community strategy and help to ensure that it takes account of, and links appropriately to, other local strategies and is founded on a strong local commitment to delivery.
(3) Informed by six pilots, the aim is to have local delivery agreements in place across Wales by April 2010. Once developed, they will form part of the community strategy action plan. (Welsh Assembly Government, 2008b: 26)

The key purposes of the Local Delivery Agreement are:

- to provide a public service wide framework for aligning national and local priorities, and translating these into deliverable projects which are integrated across sectors and make best use of existing resources to improve outcomes for citizens;
- to define the outcomes which the Local Service Board commits to delivering,

with an agreed project plan specifying milestones and timescales, and benefits for citizens;
- to establish a framework for the Local Service Board to prioritise the actions it needs to take to improve partnership performance over the short, medium and long term;
- to encourage innovative approaches which transcend organisational perspectives.

The Local Delivery Agreement is not a new performance management system. It provides a framework for the Local Service Board to identify and develop innovative projects which add value to existing activity, and address strategic challenges beyond the reach of any individual organisation. It should be a rolling programme of work based on the community strategy action plan, comprising those projects which need leadership at the strategic level to move them forward – see box 8.2 as an example of local delivery agreement projects in Cardiff Council. (Welsh Assembly Government, 2008c: 41–42).

Box 8.2 Cardiff Council: example of local delivery agreement projects

1. Integrating Health and Social Care Project

Through a new joint LHB/local authority project team, develop joint commissioning of care provision and joined-up preventative and community-based services to support individuals through a comprehensive range of services, reducing reliance on institutional care.

Initial deliverables include:

- A reduction in delayed transfers of care
- An increased number of citizens with long-term care needs, are supported outside in-patient hospital settings.

2. Neighbourhood Transformation Programme

Designing and implementing a new approach to the local co-ordination and delivery of core community services across sectors within a neighbourhood to reduce the gap between neighbourhoods as measured by key economic, social and environmental indicators and citizen experiences.

Deliverables include:

- Multi-agency neighbourhood teams (and profiles) established in selected localities, phase one being led by the police and local

authority with participation from the fire & rescues service and voluntary sector. Early actions on youth services, youth employment, key street-scene issues, fly-tipping and arson, support procedures for community nurses etc. Phase two to involve the NHS and other partners.
- A multi-agency data hub/warehouse to enable better sharing of information and intelligence between LSB partners and enable effective and coordinated interventions through multi agency planning and service delivery.

3. **Governance and Performance Project**

Designing and implementing effective governance arrangements, including scrutiny, and a robust performance management mechanism through which the effectiveness of the LSB (and other partnerships) will be monitored and evaluated.

Deliverables include:

- A new public service scrutiny panel agreed with all local partners to scrutinise the work of the LSB and other local partnerships
- Evidence compiled to enable reduction of number of performance indicators, regulation and inspection regimes within the public services in Cardiff.

4. **Ask Cardiff Project**

Establishing a city-wide model of citizen engagement and consultation across the public sector and third sector that is recognised as best practice and informs actions to improve services.

Deliverables include:

- A co-ordinated approach to citizen engagement panels, the development of a Cardiff-wide consultation strategy and toolkit, information-sharing protocols, an annual Ask Cardiff services survey and expansion of the Council's *e-consult* to include public sector organisations.

Source: Welsh Assembly Government (2008c) *Local Service Boards in Wales: Realising the Potential: Route Map: Annex 4.* Cardiff: Welsh Assembly Government.

Modelling central–local relations in Northern Ireland

The Welsh model has attracted a good deal of attention in Northern Ireland as politicians and officials consider how best to structure future central–local relations. The core elements of that relationship currently under consideration would include: a Partnership Panel, Local Area Agreements, a lead Communities and Local Government Division for the local government sector, possibly within the Office of the First Minister and deputy First Minister and Minister, all bound by a set of partnership principles. The proposed framework therefore draws on the Welsh model of central–local relations suitably adapted for circumstances in Northern Ireland. The detail proposals include several specific elements which are set out here (Knox, 2006).

Advocacy

Both in symbolic and practical terms, there is a need for a core Communities and Local Government Division within the civil service, headed by a Minister for Communities and Local Government. The proposed Division for Communities and Local Government must be seen to be at the centre of government and hence in OFMDFM. This would offer several advantages. First, OFMDFM is at the hub of government in Northern Ireland and thus the status of local government, by association, would be enhanced. Second, a Division for Communities and Local Government within OFMDFM is better positioned to argue for a larger slice of the public sector cake in public expenditure negotiations. Third, given the emphasis within community planning on securing commitment from central government players, there is the potential for a Division for Communities and Local Government to influence 'joined-up' commitment. Fourth, the formation (in May 2006) of the Department of Communities and Local Government in Whitehall offers a useful comparator. Therein the department has a powerful new remit to promote community cohesion and equality, as well as responsibility for housing, urban regeneration, planning and local government. The conjunction of communities and local government in the Northern Ireland context symbolises a new era for councils which will have direct responsibility for *inter alia* urban and rural regeneration and community planning.

Political liaison

The composition of the Partnership Panel in a new era of local government in Northern Ireland needs to be a body with considerable clout and mutual respect between the sectors. Given the relatively small geographical scale, initial suggestions include a body comprising: local councillors representing the sector through each local authority (1 per new council) and the 5 largest political parties (1 from each party); the First Minister or deputy First Minister as chair of the Partnership Panel; the Minister for Communities and Local Government; and selected ministerial colleagues. The Partnership Panel will be supported by Council Chief Executives, Chief Executive of NILGA and Permanent Secretaries to the attending Ministers. These officials will be part of the discussions which take place in the Partnership Panel but without voting rights or decision-making powers. The day-to-day business of the Partnership Panel will be through a joint secretariat made up of NILGA officials and civil servants from the Division for Communities and Local Government. The Partnership Panel will:

1. Give advice to the Northern Ireland Assembly on matters affecting the exercise of any of the Assembly's functions.
2. Make representations to the Assembly about matters affecting those involved in local government in Northern Ireland.
3. Give advice to those involved in local government in Northern Ireland.
4. Negotiate the regional priorities of Local Area Agreements.

The central–local relationships conducted through the proposed Partnership Panel will be legally based (stipulating composition of the Panel, frequency of meetings, status of the decisions taken etc.).

Strategic and operational liaison

Pivotal to the process of a working relationship between central and local government is some form of policy agreement(s). Public Service Agreements (PSAs) (contained in the *Northern Ireland Programme for Government 2008–2011*) are the key mechanism for holding central government departments to account. In view of their widespread currency, a framework based on PSAs was considered as a way of accommodating the mutual needs of both central and local government sectors. PSAs, however, were seen as being too directive from the centre and more appropriate for government departments, accepting that whatever mechanism is applied it must meet the requirements of target setting and accountability against these targets. The potential for a PSA-based framework to be dominated by regional (Northern Ireland wide) priorities needs to be balanced with local policy objectives. The importance of community planning to articulate local priorities and feed these into some form of policy agreement offers an opportunity for 'a partnership of equals' approach.

Local Public Service Agreements (LPSAs) and Local Area Agreements (LAAs) were considered as alternative mechanisms for strategic and operational liaison from the experience of other parts of the UK. A Local Area Agreement is a three-year agreement, based on local sustainable community strategies, that sets out the priorities for a local area agreed between central government, a local area (represented by the lead local authority), and other key partners through Local Strategic Partnerships (LSPs). Local Public Service Agreements are a voluntary agreement negotiated between a local authority and the Government. The overall aim of LPSAs is to improve the delivery of local public services by focusing on targeted outcomes with support from Government.

At the heart of local PSAs is an agreement between a council, its partners and government about the priorities for improvement locally. The agreements provide a way of maximising the impact on local communities of locally responsive public services combined with government's commitment to national standards. The strong partnership focus provides a way of marshalling all the resources of the public sector locally, alongside the contribution of the community, voluntary and private sectors, to focus on what most needs improvement in the area. Success in delivering agreed outcomes attracts a reward grant from government and there is a contribution at the outset to 'pump prime' the improvements.

Considering the experience elsewhere, serious consideration is now being given to establishing Local Area Agreements in Northern Ireland based (from the top down) on the key priorities outlined in the *Northern Ireland Programme for Government 2008–2011* and (from the bottom-up) on locally determined priorities articulated via the community planning process. The Northern Ireland Executive and Assembly's priorities are:

- growing a dynamic, innovative economy;
- promoting tolerance, inclusion and health and well-being;
- protecting and enhancing the environment and natural resources;
- investing to build infrastructure;
- delivering modern high quality and efficient public services.

There must be an obvious alignment between local needs expressed through community planning and regional policy priorities, although local plans cannot be allowed to effectively veto ministers' policies. In short, the statutory duty for central government departments and agencies to work with local authorities through community planning should reinforce the engagement process voluntarily proposed in the Agreements. The resulting Local Area Agreements (for each of the councils) offer the opportunity for 'joined-up'

WORK-IN-PROGRESS   265

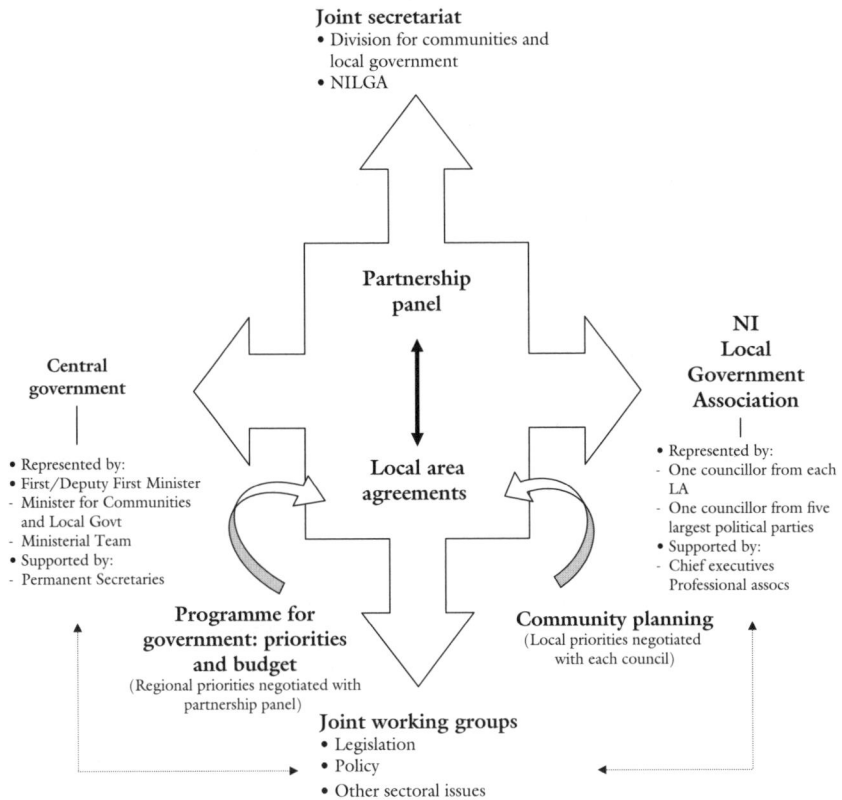

Figure 8.4 Proposals for central–local relations in Northern Ireland, 2009

Joint secretariat
- Division for communities and local government
- NILGA

Partnership panel

Central government
- Represented by:
- First/Deputy First Minister
  - Minister for Communities and Local Govt
  - Ministerial Team
- Supported by:
  - Permanent Secretaries

Local area agreements

NI Local Government Association
- Represented by:
  - One councillor from each LA
  - One councillor from five largest political parties
- Supported by:
  - Chief executives
    Professional assocs

Programme for government: priorities and budget
(Regional priorities negotiated with partnership panel)

Community planning
(Local priorities negotiated with each council)

Joint working groups
- Legislation
- Policy
- Other sectoral issues

government in which the key stakeholders (central and local government) are mutually accountable through the Partnership Panel – these proposals are depicted in figure 8.4.

Joined-up thinking also informs how councils conduct business at the local level. This is where local authorities interact with other sectors in the direct provision or oversight of public services within their boundaries. In this model, local government is at the hub of government departments and agencies operating in their areas – *primus inter pares*. Councils are the only democratically accountable body for people in the area and provide the link with local partners in the public, private, and voluntary and community sectors. By extension, local people can, through elections, exercise greater control over what is happening in their areas. This will drive public service delivery improvement. In the proposed model the critical issue is not what services local authorities deliver, but, rather, their capacity to provide effective leadership in their areas and to bring together the key players from the public, private and voluntary/community sectors to work in partnership. If the new local authorities in Northern Ireland can act as leaders and partnership builders, this will stimulate new models of service delivery, including cross-cutting approaches involving other public, private and voluntary/community agencies. The Local Government (Reorganisation) Bill is due to be introduced to the Assembly by May 2010 and will contain recommendations on the provisions for central/local government relations in Northern Ireland.

This chapter has set out two key initiatives, community planning and central–local government relations, both of which are under active consideration as part of the wider reform agenda in Northern Ireland. What is described here is tentative and subject to improvement and change as it moves to, and through, the legislative processes in the Assembly. As a general observation however, it is interesting to note that Northern Ireland should benefit from the experiences of other devolved regions in both these initiatives – from Scotland where it is closely following the model of community planning and from Wales in developing central–local relations. Learning from other devolved regions as opposed to Whitehall (or England) has significant political appeal for one of the main parties in the power-sharing Executive in Northern Ireland, Sinn Féin. The late arrival of Northern Ireland in terms of both embedding devolution and as a recent proponent of a public sector modernising/reform agenda may serve the region well if it is willing to learn the lessons of Scotland and Wales.

9
Conclusions

This book began by considering the most fundamental change since the introduction of direct rule from Westminster in 1972 – the move to devolved government in Northern Ireland in December 1999. We looked in some detail at the key structures of public administration under devolution: the Northern Ireland Civil Service and the modernising agenda therein; the history, evolution and reform of local government; reduction in the number of quangos under the Review of Public Administration; the changing role played by the third sector; whether Northern Ireland can become a shared society; and some work-in-progress in the areas of community planning and central–local government relations. It is perhaps timely at this point to reflect on where we are with devolution and what are the portents for its longer term direction and success?

Political context

Bradbury and Mitchell's (2002: 311) comment that 'devolution is a process rather than an event' is particularly apt as the starting point for some reflection on where we are. It has been a tortuous journey to reach some level of stability in the devolved institutions. It is clear (as discussed in chapter 1) that devolution suffered by association with the long-standing constitutional, security and human rights/equality issues with which Northern Ireland has grappled since the 1970s. The on/off nature of devolution between December 1999 and May 2007 created a politics of despair amongst the Northern Ireland electorate whose expectations had been lowered by years oscillating between impasse, political break-through and stagnation. The events of March 2007 changed all that. The enormity of Sinn Féin's Gerry Adams and (then) DUP leader Ian Paisley agreeing to share power in government was difficult to absorb – a kind of political manna. This was quickly followed by Sinn Féin taking its place on the Northern Ireland Policing Board for the first time – a major step of symbolism and substance. As the euphoria died down and the reality of power-sharing arrangements got underway, the electorate demanded public policy delivery from the Executive and Assembly. Several popular measures followed – the delayed introduction in water charges, free prescriptions, freezing the regional rate, and free public transport for older people, to name a few, but difficult issues have emerged which clearly illustrate the political fault lines. These include: how best do deal with the legacy of victims of the troubles; the replacement of academic selection between primary and secondary schools; and legislation to support the Irish language as an expression of nationalist/republican cultural identity. The ongoing row over academic selection which the DUP will not discuss as an item on the Executive's agenda resulted in unregulated admission tests for many of the grammar schools in Northern Ireland – teachers, primary school pupils, and their parents have been caught up in the ensuing education policy chaos. As one politician put it:

> There is a huge asymmetry between the political parties in the Executive with the DUP very much in control and Sinn Féin the junior partner. Both the SDLP and UUP see themselves are marginal in government. In theory, the DUP and Sinn Féin are co-equals with a mutual veto but, in practice, the former is the lead partner and republicans are frustrated that they have not been able to secure radical changes. This fed into the crisis at the end of 2008 when there were no meetings of the Executive and gridlock resulted . . . We avoid the hard issues because we don't want them to impact negatively on power-sharing arrangements. The threat in these circumstances is not as it was in the past to the overall stability of the institutions but massive under-performance or missing out on opportunities. (interview with Alliance Party MLA)

It should, of course, be noted that the stability of the institutions was tested to the full over the brutal killings of two soldiers at Massereene army base in March 2009 by the Real IRA, a splinter group born out of dissention about Sinn Féin's direction in the peace process, and the murder of a police officer by another dissident group, the Continuity IRA, in the same week. The First and deputy First Ministers moved quickly and their combined and unequivocal condemnation of these terrorist acts buttressed political stability at the centre of devolved government. The announcement by the INLA in October 2009 that its 'arms struggle is over' was seen as further progress towards normalisation of the political landscape.

The DUP remains deeply conscious of a group of its supporters who are, at best, equivocal about their partnership in government with Sinn Féin. The dissenters find a voice in former DUP member of the European Parliament, Jim Allister, and now leader of the Traditional Unionist Voice (TUV). The European elections in June 2009 were a real test of his support base and level of disaffection amongst DUP voters about power-sharing. Although Allister failed to be re-elected he nonetheless secured 13.7 per cent of the vote or just over 20,000 votes short of the DUP's candidate Diane Dodds moving her party from top of the polls to third position (in the election of 3 MEPs). There may also be a future challenge to the DUP in the 2010 Westminster elections in the North Antrim constituency, Ian Paisley's heartland and sitting MP. This has prompted caution amongst the DUP political hierarchy and served as a reminder that they cannot ignore a sizeable minority of their traditional voting base who simply refuse to accept what they would see as former (or unreformed) terrorists in government. The so called final act of the peace process, the devolution of policing and justice powers, is moving only at a pace dictated by the DUP's assessment of unionist confidence, however measured.

One observation of the ongoing power-sharing arrangements is offered by Dawn Purvis, East Belfast MLA and leader of the Progressive Unionist Party, who warned against what she described as 'the politics of fear'. She conveyed this message to the DUP and Sinn Féin:

> The impact a war of words at Stormont has on the ground in working class loyalist and republican areas should not be underestimated. Out-greening Eirigi (dissident republicans) or pandering to the dirty dozen to out-orange Jim Allister only serves to destabilise already vulnerable areas . . . You need to move away from the politics of fear. Instead you seek to maintain division through fear in order to serve your own interests. You offer no shared future for the people of Northern Ireland; you offer no policies to bring people together in order that we know each other; instead you offer the notion of 'separate but equal' – it didn't work in the USA and it is certainly not an option for us. Wake up to sectarianism! (Purvis, 2009: 1)

Working the institutions

Notwithstanding the fact that there are issues on which the two main parties in the power-sharing Executive cannot agree, First Minister, Peter Robinson, actively promotes the benefits of devolved government - 'despite our differences of working in a four-party enforced coalition, we have made real progress'. He argues that Northern Ireland is experiencing the longest period of continuous devolution and constitutional stability in almost forty years and, as a result, people's lives have improved through capital investments in schools, roads, and hospitals – almost £1.7 billion in 2008/09. In addition, he claims that the average household is £500 per year better off than under direct rule government because of the deferment of water charges and freezing the regional rate, and the poorest in society received an additional £150 to deal with fuel price increases.

> I am a convinced devolutionist; I have always been so, and part of my conviction that devolution is the best way forward for the people of Northern Ireland comes from my 30 years at Westminster, most of which were served during periods of direct rule. I will never agree with anybody who thinks that it is better for the people of Northern Ireland to be part of a system of government that allows people who have no roots in this community to take decisions on its behalf . . . We know the procedures, whereby Orders in Council were passed after an hour and a half of debate, sometimes at 3.00 am. Those matters were shoved on to the end of business because people did not want to keep English, Scottish and Welsh MPs from getting home to their bed. People may be a little bit unhappy about structural aspects, and there are many things that I want to see changed, but we must not start questioning devolution itself. (Robinson, 2009c: 210)

That said, the First Minister makes clear that the 'present arrangements are merely a staging post to a more normal form of devolution'. Although the St Andrews Agreement provides for a review of devolved institutions by 2015, Peter Robinson has proposed reforms to the operation of the Executive and Assembly and acknowledged the difficulties in working the present arrangements: 'let's be honest, Sinn Féin and the DUP in government was never going to be easy. Two ministers in a department with certain decisions requiring joint approval is not easy either' (Robinson, 2009c: 3). The First Minister made what he described as several 'modest suggestions for changes to the arrangements that could significantly improve and help to normalise politics in Northern Ireland'. The DUP proposals included the following:

- The abolition of community designation in the Assembly and, as a consequence, new voting arrangements in both the Assembly and Executive. Community designation was seen as entrenching division and, in practice, meant that the votes of all Assembly members were not equal.
- In place of community designation a weighted majority system was proposed. Where a cross-community vote is required by legislation or triggered through a petition of concern, a proposal would require 65 per cent of Assembly members present and voting to pass.
- The 65 per cent rule would mean that any proposal would need to command widespread support across the community but would not permit a small minority to frustrate the will of a cross-community majority. It would also mean that no single party would have the capacity to block proposals which had widespread support.
- The 65 per cent rule would also allow various combinations of parties to form a coalition to pass any proposal, thus increasing the relevance of all Assembly members and, at the same time, encouraging compromise between parties. Different coalitions could be formed around different issues to provide the required majority, with neither the DUP nor Sinn

Féin alone having a veto, but support needed from both sections of the community.
- An amendment was proposed to the ministerial code which would require the First Minister and deputy First Minister, within a reasonable period of time, to table and permit a vote at the Executive on any matter proposed by any Minister (Robinson, 2009c).

In summary, these proposals, according to the First Minister, would still ensure cross-community support without giving any single party the power of veto.

> This would be a first step to normalising politics here, and under this system compromise would be encouraged and deadlock could be avoided. I believe that such a voting system could re-energise politics and could potentially unlock many of the issues that are presently stalled. (Robinson, 2009e: 8)

Robinson espoused these proposals on the basis that devolution had reached an acceptable starting point and it was now time to improve the implementation arrangements.

The suggested changes were greeted with total opposition by Sinn Féin's deputy First Minister who accused Peter Robinson of 'going on something of a solo run in terms of promoting an end to checks and balances contained within the power-sharing framework in Stormont' (McGuinness, 2009: 30). The deputy First Minister viewed the DUP proposals as a fundamental change to the cross-community voting arrangements which were the foundation of the Belfast (Good Friday) and St Andrew's Agreements and motivated by 'looking over their shoulder' at the threat posed by the Traditional Unionist Voice and Ulster Unionists. McGuinness argued that checks and balances had been built into the decision-making process to ensure that the days of unionist majority rule never returned and the only way forward was to exercise political power on the basis of equality and partnership with nationalists and republicans. Any attempt by the British Government to intervene and support the abandonment of existing checks and balances would, according to the deputy First Minister result in the end of nationalist and republican participation in the institutions themselves. McGuinness concluded:

> The argument has been put that because of the nature of the current arrangements they are deadlocked and unable to deliver. I disagree. The reality is that the institutions can deliver and in many instances have delivered. But they only deliver when they are operated as they were intended – on the basis of partnership, inclusion, compromise and acceptance of all as equals. Not on the basis of a requirement by any one party that it gets its own way all of the time, nor on the basis that the rules are changed when it doesn't. This means that the Assembly cannot deliver solely on the agenda of any one party. That what's power-sharing means. That's what the DUP must come to understand. (McGuinness, 2009: 30)

The DUP has defended their proposals on the basis that of the 108 MLAs in the current Assembly, 55 (51 per cent) are designated as 'unionists', 44 (41 per cent) are designated as 'nationalists' and there are 9 'others' (8 per cent). Given this breakdown, no coalition of unionists, or unionists plus 'others', would be sufficient to carry a vote. The DUP argued that neither their party alone, with their representation of 36 (33 per cent) seats, nor Sinn Féin which holds 28 (26 per cent) seats could thwart the majority wishes of the Assembly. DUP Enterprise Minister, Arlene Foster concluded: 'there have indeed been real achievements under devolution but we would be foolish to pretend that more could not be achieved with arrangements which have good government as their main focus' (Foster, 2009: 35).

Public expenditure squeeze and public reforms

Devolved government in Northern Ireland also faces future challenges because of the significant cuts in UK public spending likely to take effect following the general election in 2010. The Northern Ireland Programme for Government 2008–11 highlighted the fact that UK public expenditure was planned to grow at its slowest rate since the comprehensive spending review (CSR) process was introduced at around 2 per cent in real terms per year. As a result, Northern Ireland developed an efficiency plan in order to deliver resource-releasing efficiencies during the 2008–11 budget period with a baseline target of 3 per cent per year across central and local government, net of implementation costs. Aside from efficiency savings the Northern Ireland Executive has cut the overall rate of under-spend by departments and significantly reduced the amount of money it returns to the Treasury from 3.5 per cent in 2006–07 to 0.2 per cent in 2008–09, equating to around £300 million pounds which is available for public services (Robinson, 2009f: 2). The First Minister argues that more is needed in the face of a squeeze on public expenditure in the form of a radical review of the size and shape of the public sector. He warns that unless reforms take place then service delivery standards will fall behind those in Great Britain. The DUP analysis is that the introduction of water charges and increase in the regional rate will not solve the problems of public expenditure, rather they contend that the public sector is too large compared to the private sector. First Minister Peter Robinson has therefore floated proposals such as reducing and reorganizing the number of civil service departments, MLAs, quangos and commissions in Northern Ireland. As an opening salvo in this campaign to cut expenditure, the DUP Finance Minister announced (September 2009) that he would not permit the payment of bonuses, and would cap pay uplifts, within the senior civil service and wider public sector.

The SDLP has however accused the DUP and Sinn Féin of being unwilling to review the budget priorities of the Executive despite what they estimate as a £2b shortfall in the capital budget as a result of receipts which did not materialize (public sector housing sales) and additional pressure on the public purse (civil service equal pay claims). The SDLP has called for a complete review of the budget to address the global economic downturn. The Ulster Unionist Party has been equally critical of the DUP's handling of the economy and identified what they describe as a black hole of some £400 million in the revenue budget.

The pips are beginning to squeak in the health service. Ulster Unionist Minister Michael McGimpsey has spoken of a 'bleak future' for the health service claiming that his department has 'given all it can give' in efficiency savings leading to financial stress in hospital trusts and major deficit budgets, an example of which is a proposal to cut 150 beds across the Royal and City Hospitals in Belfast (Gordon, 2009: 12). Faced with extra spending to deal with swine flu, the Finance Minister secured Executive agreement to cut almost £40m from other government departments to fund the outbreak, in addition to a £20m contribution from the Department of Health, Social Services and Public Safety. The Health Minister has, in turn, been criticized by his DUP opponents on the Assembly's health committee for cynically manipulating the need to make efficiency savings by targeting cuts in areas which attract media attention for political purposes.

Achievements?

In chapter 1 of this book we asked the question whether devolution had made a difference and concluded that as a legislative and executive forum the achievements of the devolved administration had been modest so far. Politicians, particularly those from the two largest power-sharing parties (DUP and Sinn Féin), are quick to stress what they see as the significant benefits. The First Minister has argued, for example:

> Devolution is good in theory but it has also been good in practice. However, I concede that one area where we have failed has been selling the benefits of devolution. Significantly, devolution provides the foundation for peace and prosperity, but it also allowed us to make a real difference to people's everyday lives. (Robinson, 2009e: 2)

In short, the political message is that devolution has been good for the people of Northern Ireland in terms of a more peaceful society and a better quality of life – it simply hasn't been sold. The Northern Ireland Life and Times (2008) survey results, which we drew on in chapter 1, revealed that a majority of

DUP supporters (some 78 per cent) felt the Assembly had achieved 'a little' or 'nothing'. This seems to be at odds with the First Minister's assessment that devolution has made a real difference to the quality of people's lives in Northern Ireland. Another useful way of making an assessment is to ask the electorate their views on key public services. The 2008 Northern Ireland Life and Times Survey asked respondents the following question:

Looking back over the last 10 years, do you think that Northern Ireland is better, worse or just the same in terms of the economy, health care provision and education provision?

The 10-year time cycle coincides approximately with the introduction of devolved government, although there were intermittent periods of suspension (one for over 4 years) during that decade. The results of these 3 separate questions are set out in figure 9.1.

Overall, the results show that:

- 58 per cent of respondents felt education provision had remained the same or got worse.
- 64 per cent of respondents felt health care provision had remained the same or got worse.
- 55 per cent of respondents felt the economy had remained the same or got worse.

While Northern Ireland has suffered from the effects of the global economic downturn and hence responses on the economy can be explained, it is clearly disappointing that such a high percentage of respondents see core public services such as education and health under a devolved government remaining

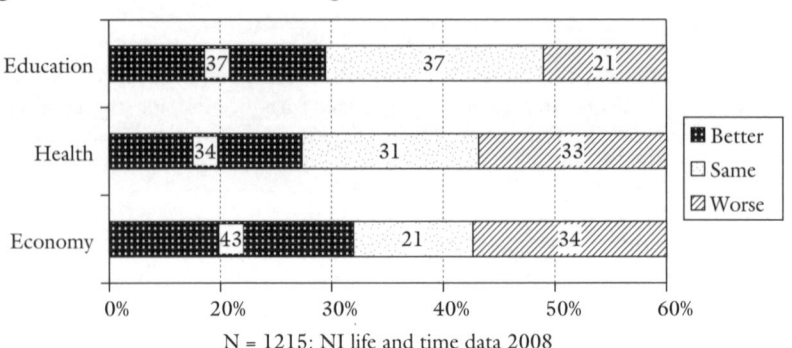

Figure 9.1 Has Northern Ireland got better?

	Better	Same	Worse
Education	37	37	21
Health	34	31	33
Economy	43	21	34

N = 1215: NI life and time data 2008

CONCLUSIONS 275

the same or getting worse. The economy in Northern Ireland has been less severely affected than other parts of the United Kingdom which is, in part, cushioned by the relatively large public sector and also because of the surge in cross-border shopping from the Republic of Ireland where the euro has been strong against the pound sterling.

The Office of the Minister and deputy First Minister compiled its first delivery report (1 April 2008 to 31 March 2009) on the Executive's *Building a Better Future: Programme for Government 2008–2011*. The report noted the more challenging context in which it now operates than when the *Programme for Government* was first developed and agreed by the Northern Ireland Assembly. The report set out progress against the goals, commitments and public service agreement (PSA) targets set up to 31 March 2009. It used the traffic light system of red/amber/green as a framework for assessment of progress in the following way:

- *Red*: where little or no progress has been observed.
- *Amber*: where the rate of progress has been less than planned.
- *Amber/green*: where progress has been good but may not be sustained towards targets OR there is confidence in getting close to targeted outcome.
- *Green*: where progress is on track or targets have been met.

The delivery report is highly mechanistic in its reporting of progress made by the devolved administration (see table 9.1). In broad terms it categorises the key goals, commitments and PSAs targets and provides an assessment of their status on the traffic lights system above. In summary, it reports that of the 66 key goals and commitments monitored, 5 (8 per cent) were reported as red, with a further 20 (30 per cent) reported as amber. In terms of the spread of goals and commitments reported as red or amber, the highest concentration can be found in priorities areas: *Protect and Enhance our Environment and Natural Resources* (priority 3 in PfG) and *Grow a Dynamic, Innovative Economy* (priority 1 in PfG), respectively. Of the 331 PSA targets monitored, 27 (8 per cent) were rated as red, with a further 62 (18 per cent) rated as

Table 9.1 Monitoring delivery: Programme for Government 2008–11

Priorities	Red	Amber	Amber/green	Green	Total
Key goals and commitments in PfG – 5 priorities	5	20	19	22	66
All PSA targets in PfG	27	62	82	160	331

Source: Delivery Report 2008/09, Programme for Government, OFMDFM.

amber – overall a creditable performance on delivering the *Programme for Government*.

The monitoring report concluded that a relatively high number of targets across the PSAs and PfG key goals and commitments were assessed as amber but these could be explained by two factors: the economic outlook rather than performance to date; and delays in the availability of robust data to gauge progress or justify a positive assessment of progress at this stage. Although logical in its presentation against the commitments outlined in the Executive's *Programme for Government*, the value of this report is fairly limited. Civil servants set the original PSA targets in their own departments and they now self-assess against their achievement, although the report indicates that the ratings 'were quality assured and agreed by a central team to ensure they constituted a robust, comparable and accurate reflection of progress' (OFMDFM, 2009: 4). Despite this assurance, the delivery report provides no evidence as to how judgements were made to arrive at the traffic light status of the priorities and targets outlined in the *Programme for Government*.

We consider just one example of potential anomalies. Public Service Agreement number 20 is:

- To improve the quality and cost effectiveness of public services to include delivery of the wider public sector reform programme and efficiency savings and outworkings of decisions on the Review of Public Administration.

The delivery report made a judgement on the 23 targets contained within this priority area and arrived at the conclusions listed in table 9.2.

There is no commentary or evidence on how the civil servants reached these judgements and the reader must take this on trust. In crude statistical terms we can conclude that just over one-quarter of the targets (n = 6 or 26 per cent) made no progress or less than planned; or conversely, that about three-quarters of the targets (n = 18 or 74 per cent) have been achieved or are on track. Yet, how does this conclusion accord with the fact that a high percentage of respondents in the probability survey, discussed above, see

Table 9.2 Monitoring delivery: PSA 20, improving public services

Priorities	Red	Amber	Amber/green	Green	Total
Improving public services	2	4	6	11	23

Source: Delivery Report 2008/09, Programme for Government, OFMDFM.

Note: n = 23 targets.

services such as education and health care provision remaining the same or getting worse over a 10 year period?

There are also important questions being asked about the implementation of the Review of Public Administration. As noted in chapter 3 the Minister, initially responsible for its implementation, claimed 'improving services to the public lies at the heart of any new model of public administration' (Pearson, 2004) and savings of £200m per year were estimated as a result. To date some politicians claim that the costs of the review have been spiraling out of control and it has yet to be fully implemented. One SDLP MLA and local councillor, Patsy McGlone, asked ministers in each of the 11 departments how much had been spent since the launch of the review in 2002. Although the figures were incomplete since only 8 departments could provide the information, there has been £90m spent thus far and this does not include the reorganization of local government due to take place in 2011. Mr McGlone stated:

> The costs of the Review of Public Administration are 'an elephant in the room'. There was supposed to be a cost–benefit analysis report due in September 2009 from PricewaterhouseCoopers (management consultants). That was pulled and according to reports I am hearing the findings weren't pretty beneficial. My concern is that we are sleepwalking into a situation where the costs are spiralling out of control. There needs to be much more discussion at Executive level, a big reality check to get to grips with the cost of this review. (McGlone, 2009)

The role played by one of Northern Ireland's leading quangos has also come under scrutiny in a recent report (Barnett, 2009). Invest Northern Ireland, an executive non-departmental public body, located in the Department of Enterprise, Trade and Investment, has an annual budget of £193m (2009/10) and its principal role is to help create wealth for the benefit of the whole community by strengthening the economy and helping it grow. It does this by supporting business development, helping to increase export levels, attracting high quality inward investment, and stimulating a culture of entrepreneurship and innovation. Invest NI has been the subject of an independent review of economic policy and while the report acknowledged that it had contributed significantly to Northern Ireland's economic performance in terms of employment growth, it was criticised on a number of fronts, including:

- The number and complexity of their programmes to businesses.
- The assistance offered to companies for enterprise, innovation, research and development, and trade promotion (the stated aims of Invest NI) amounted to only one-quarter of all offers of financial support.
- The projects assisted by Invest NI have been successful in job creation, however, their impact on productivity has been limited.
- The cost of additional jobs created is high.

One of the report's 58 recommendations was that as part of the review of Strand One institutions in the Northern Ireland Executive, the core economic functions (covering existing Department of Trade Enterprise & Investment and Department for Employment and Learning) should be brought together under a single Department of the Economy headed by a Minister for the Economy. Given the centrality of growing the economy to the Executive's *Programme for Government*, this report is hugely important in a number of ways. It must pose questions about the role of quangos, as discussed in chapter 5, particularly given the accountability and performance arrangements for a function so central to the work of the devolved government now and into the foreseeable future. It also raises wider issues around the structure of the civil service and the increase in the number of departments following devolution for reasons of political expediency. As the report on Invest NI shows, splitting functions which impact directly on the economy (employment and learning – trade and investment) makes no sense. Aside from the substantive and important business of economic development discussed in this report there are wider governance issues raised for the Northern Ireland Executive in the way it structures its business.

Retrospective and prospective summation

In the period since devolution was first introduced in Northern Ireland we have witnessed a remarkable chain of events. We began by arguing in chapter 1 that both the introduction and implementation of devolution in Northern Ireland were inextricably linked to key political events. The Belfast/Good Friday Agreement and the St Andrews Agreement were not only important political milestones but they led directly to devolved government in Northern Ireland and a power-sharing Executive and Assembly, respectively. Yet this direct association has had a major influence on the both the structures of governance and the ways in which the policy agenda are set and matters expedited. Hence the mechanisms established to protect the political process and embed power-sharing have, by association, made the policy-making process more anodyne and less ambitious. As one senior civil servant put it 'we will not fail with our public policies but we will not succeed spectacularly either'. Moreover, the electoral process has not matured sufficiently for politicians to feel accountable on public policy issues. Tribal voting will continue for the foreseeable future in Northern Ireland.

We should not of course underestimate the distance travelled since the inception of devolution and the truly momentous occasion in 2007 when Ian Paisley and Gerry Adams made a public declaration to share power. Combine this with an improving security situation (although far from perfect with dissidents still posing a threat) and Sinn Féin's endorsement of the PSNI and participation in the Northern Ireland Policing Board. These political gains are however a necessary but insufficient condition for good governance. The structures of governance which are in place have evolved to facilitate political stability rather than necessarily the expedition of public policy. One politician described it in this way:

> The further we move away from conflict the greater the expectation amongst the public will be of the benefits of devolution. They are asking questions like: is devolution making any difference to our lives; are we benefiting from the 'folks on the hill'; and, are our public services improving. What was good for power-sharing has not been good for public policy-making – power-sharing does not equal good governance in Northern Ireland. (Interview with senior politician)

The wider political scandal in Westminster over MPs expenses has resulted in greater probing and media commentary on claims of political parties and MLAs in the Northern Ireland Assembly. Political disagreements over high profile issues, in particular a failure on the part of politicians to tackle academic selection for children entering secondary level education, have caused public frustration. Populist public policies such as a delay in the introduction of rates, free travel for older people, and no charges for prescriptions have been 'pocketed' and there are greater expectations on the Executive and Assembly to deliver changes that will positively impact on the quality of people's lives. The push-pull factors are clear: a demand for more and better public services within the constraints of an ever tighter public expenditure budget. The developing row over health service cuts could be the thin end of a wedge which will see a radical review of public services provision. Can this be achieved by a more efficient public sector, as the First Minister suggests?

The Review of Public Administration, launched in 2002, has not yet been fully implemented and there are already further calls to reform the public sector by reducing the number of departments, commissions and quangos. Experience with the Review of Public Administration would suggest this is not as easy to implement. From the beginning of the RPA, civil servants captured the process and successfully fought against an independent review body. Instead the review was conducted by civil servants with an advisory panel of independent experts. It was politically expedient for officials that civil service departments were excluded from the process so as 'not to rock the devolved government boat' but the review was controlled by Permanent Secretaries keen to ensure minimum change to their functional responsibilities. Any future proposals for a radical overhaul of the public sector will face the same departmental resistance. Although the role of civil servants has undoubtedly changed, their capacity to actively resist changes which they perceive as adversely impacting on their departments should not be under-rated. Civil servants were powerful figures under direct rule (by default they will maintain) and the shift to devolution has not been easy. The level of public scrutiny and accountability to locally elected representatives brings a new dimension to their jobs. Infrequent appearances before the Public Accounts Committee in Westminster have been replaced by regular reporting to a statutory oversight committee in the Assembly, line responsibility to a locally elected minister, and daily interactions with specialist political advisors to manoeuvre the minefield of a mandatory coalition government. The modernisation agenda in the civil service which lagged behind other parts of the UK is now well underway and its impact remains to be seen – thus far there has been mixed success.

Local government in Northern Ireland, so long the locus of sectarian politics, has shed this image and worked constructively to rebuild its credibility as a responsive elected forum delivering local services, albeit with a limited functional role. That said, local government despite early ministerial claims in support of decentralized public services gained little from the Review of Public Administration. There is much optimism about future statutory powers in community planning and well-being which will be conferred on the new councils in 2011. These powers have been heralded as the mechanism to ensure local input and accountability for public services provided by a plethora of civil service departments and agencies at the central level. The pilot exercise in Omagh District Council demonstrates that there is a long way to go before the centre feels compelled to the local. The wider efforts to develop a model of central–local relations will again challenge the centripetal system of public administration in Northern Ireland.

Quangos have played a key role in the governance of Northern Ireland in the past and the reduction in their number, as envisaged under the Review of Public Administration, is proving much more difficult in practice. In fact, the new reorganized structures under the RPA, particularly in health and social care, education and libraries, have simply replaced one type of quango with larger super quangos (Birrell, 2009). Appointments to these bodies are much more strictly regulated through the Commissioner for Public Appointments although not without some pain for senior civil servants and politicians who have found 'ownership' of this process difficult to release. The quangocrats are alive and well in Northern Ireland and their future is guaranteed in the medium term unless their remit has a distinct political flavour (human rights, equality, and parades).

The voluntary and community sector has played, and will continue to play, a vital role in the governance of Northern Ireland although its role has undoubtedly changed under the devolved administration. Some politicians resented what they would have perceived as the sector's privileged access to senior officials during direct rule and, as a result, their significant influence within the decision-making process. Initial antipathy appears to have subsidized and the voluntary and community sector is attempting to forge a relationship with Government through a proposed White Paper that would strengthen participative democracy.

Has devolution resulted in Northern Ireland becoming a reconciled society? The outcomes of a long peace process are now clear to be seen. Northern Ireland is now a post-conflict society with a local power-sharing administration and minimum levels of political violence. There are however problems which impact on the daily lives of people due to the highly segregated society that characterises Northern Ireland. Are politicians ready to tackle this issue? Former Chief Constable, Sir Hugh Orde, on his departure from Northern Ireland (September 2009), warned the two main power-sharing parties, DUP and Sinn Féin, that unless they published the long awaited strategy on *Cohesion, Sharing and Integration* then it would 'create a vacuum for those wishing to perpetuate the divisions of the past'. In its absence 'sectarian and racial hatred was evermore apparent' (Orde, 2009: 12). Following this call, Sinn Féin unilaterally issued its own proposals which it claimed could become a blueprint for the way forward. In response, the DUP then released the previously unpublished and uncompleted *Cohesion, Sharing and Integration* document and claimed that internal discussions on the strategy had been blocked by Sinn Féin. Major recriminations followed and there are no immediate prospects for political agreement on the pledge outlined in the *Programme for Government* 'to build a shared and better future for all'.

Devolution got off to a rocky start in Northern Ireland and has now stabilised. The power-sharing institutions have become embedded and local politicians are actively participating in a broadly constructive way for the benefit of the people of Northern Ireland. Political stability and compromise must be weighed up against a process which had resulted in gridlock over key public policy decisions. It could be argued that this is a price worth paying. On the other hand, there is a level of frustration building up amongst the public, not helped by the wider political expenses scandal, that MLAs are self-serving and need to deliver more tangible quality of life benefits for local people. In a harsher public expenditure climate these will be more difficult to secure. In short, political agreement and power-sharing have happened and are hugely welcome, but it is now time to deliver local, responsive and high quality public services. The evidence to date is that the public is under-whelmed.

References

Acheson, N, and Williamson. A. (2007) 'Civil society in multi-level public policy: the case of Ireland's two jurisdictions', *Policy & Politics*, 35 (1): 25–44.
Alexander, A. (1979) 'Local government in Ireland', *Administration*, 27 (1): 3–29.
Alexander, A. (1982) *The Politics of Local Government in the United Kingdom*. London: Longman.
Attwood, A. (2009) 'Civic Forum', *Hansard*, Official Report, 3 February.
Audit Commission (2005) *Local Quality of Life Indicators – Supporting Local Communities to Become Sustainable: A Guide to Local Monitoring to Complement the Indicators in the UK Government Sustainable Development Strategy*. London: Audit Commission.
Audit Scotland (2006) *Community Planning: An Initial Review*. Edinburgh: Audit Scotland.
Barnett, R. (2009) *Independent Review of Economic Policy: DETI and Invest NI*. Belfast: DETI.
Beirne, M. (1993) 'Out of the bearpit', *Fortnight*, May: 6–8.
Belfast/Good Friday Agreement (1998), *Agreement Reached in Multi-party Negotiations*. Belfast: Northern Ireland Office.
Bell, P. N. (1987) 'Direct Rule in Northern Ireland', 189–226 in R. Rose (ed.) *Ministers and Ministries*. Oxford: Oxford University Press.
Bennett, M., Fairley, J. and McAteer, M. (2002) *Devolution in Scotland: The Impact on Local Government*. York: Joseph Rowntree Foundation, York Publishing Services
Bevir, M., Rhodes, R.A.W. and Weller, P. (2003) 'Traditions of governance: interpreting the changing role of the public sector', *Public Administration*, 81 (1): 1–17.
Birrell, D. (1978) 'The Northern Ireland Civil Service', *Public Administration*, 52 (2): 305–320.
Birrell, D. (2008a) 'Devolution and quangos in the United Kingdom: the implementation of principles and policies for rationalisation and democratization', *Policy Studies*, 29 (1): 35–49.
Birrell, D. (2008b) 'The final outcomes of the Review of Public Administration in Northern Ireland: tensions and compatibility with devolution, parity and modernisation', *Public Administration*, 86 (3): 779–783.
Birrell, D. (2009) *Direct Rule and the Governance of Northern Ireland*. Manchester: Manchester University Press

Birrell, D. and Hayes, A. (1999) *The Local Government System in Northern Ireland*. Dublin: Institute of Public Administration.

Birrell, D. and Murie, A. (1980) *Policy and Government in Northern Ireland: Lessons of Devolution*. Dublin: Gill and Macmillan.

Blair, T. (2003) 'Prime Minister confirms postponement of Assembly elections'. Belfast: Northern Ireland Office Press Release, 1 May.

Blake Stevenson and Stratagem (2005) *Case Study Analyses for the Review of Public Administration on Community Planning in Operation within the United Kingdom and Ireland*. Belfast: OFMDFM.

Bloomfield, K. (1998) 'Central Government', 142–151 in K. Bloomfield and C. Carter (eds) *People and Government: Questions for Northern Ireland*. York: Joseph Rowntree Foundation.

Bogdanor, V. (2001) *Devolution in the United Kingdom*. Oxford: Oxford University Press.

Bradbury, J. and Mitchell, J. (2001) 'Devolution: new politics for old?', *Parliamentary Affairs*, 54 (2): 257–275.

Bradbury, J. and Mitchell, J. (2002) 'Devolution and territorial politics: stability, uncertainty and crisis', *Parliamentary Affairs*, 55 (2): 299–316.

Bradley, C. (1994) 'Keeping a Secret', *Fortnight*, January (335): 25–26.

British–Irish Council (2009) available at: www3.british-irishcouncil.org, accessed 25 February.

Browne, D. (2003) *A Shared Future: A Consultation Paper on Improving Relations in Northern Ireland*. Belfast: Office of the First Minister and Deputy First Minister.

Bruce, S. (1994) *The Edge of the Union: The Ulster Loyalist Political Vision*. Oxford: Oxford University Press.

Buckland, P. (1981) *A History of Northern Ireland*. Dublin: Gill and Macmillan.

Budge, I. and O'Leary, C. (1973) *Belfast: Approach to Crisis*. London: Macmillan.

Business Development Service (2005) *Review of the Joint Government Voluntary and Community Sector Forum*. Belfast: BDS.

Byrne, S. (2001) 'Consociational and civic society approaches to peacebuilding in Northern Ireland', *Journal of Peace Research*, 38 (3): 327–352.

Cabinet Office (1999) *Modernising Government*, Cm 4310. London: The Stationery Office.

Cabinet Office (2006) *The UK Government's Approach to Public Service Reform: A Discussion Paper*. London: Prime Minister's Strategy Unit.

Cabinet Office (2007) *Building on Progress: Public Services*. London: Prime Minister's Strategy Unit.

Cabinet Office (2008a) *Excellence and Fairness: Achieving World Class Public Services*. London: Prime Minister's Strategy Unit.

Cabinet Office (2008b) *Public Bodies: Making Government Work Better*. London: Cabinet Office.

Cabinet Office (2009a) *Civil Service Reform: Working Paper*. London: Prime Minister's Strategy Unit.

Cabinet Office (2009b) *Working Together: Public Service on Your Side*. London: Prime Minister's Strategy Unit.

Cameron, D. (2009) 'People power: reforming quangos', speech by the Conservative Party Leader, 6 July, available at: www.conservatives.com/News/

Speeches/2009/07/David_Cameron_People_Power_-_Reforming_Quangos. aspx, accessed 31 July.
Carmichael, P. (2002) 'The Northern Ireland Civil Service: characteristics and trends since 1970', *Public Administration*, 80 (2): 23–49.
Carmichael, P. and Knox, C. (2005) 'The reform of public administration in Northern Ireland: from principles to practice', *Political Studies*, 53 (4): 772–792.
Carmichael, P. and Osborne, R. (2003) 'The Northern Ireland Civil Service under direct rule and devolution', *International Review of Administrative Sciences*, 69 (2): 205–218
Carmichael, P., Cleary, S. and Knox, C. (2007) *Omagh District Council: Community Plan 2007–2010*. Omagh: Omagh District Council.
Carmichael, P., Knox, C. and Osborne, R. (1996) *Mapping the Public Sector in Northern Ireland*. University of Ulster: Ulster Paper in Public Policy and Management No. 63.
Chartered Institute of Public Finance and Accountancy (CIPFA) and Local Government Training Group (1997) *Councillors' Guide to Local Government Finance in Northern Ireland*. Belfast: Local Government Staff Commission.
Coakley, J. (2001) 'The Belfast Agreement and the Republic of Ireland', 223–244 in R. Wilford (ed.) *Aspects of the Belfast Agreement*. Oxford: Oxford University Press.
Coakley, J. (2007) 'Wider horizons: cross-border and cross-channel relations', 261–277 in P. Carmichael, C. Knox and R. Osborne (eds) *Devolution and Constitutional Change in Northern Ireland*. Manchester: Manchester University Press
Cochrane, F. (2001) 'Unsung heros? The role of peace and conflict resolution organisations in the Northern Ireland conflict', 137–158 in J. McGarry (ed.) *Northern Ireland and the Divided World: The Northern Ireland conflict and the Good Friday Agreement in Comparative Perspective*. Oxford: Oxford University Press
Commission on the Future of the Voluntary Sector (1996) *Meeting the Challenge of Change: Voluntary Action into the 21st Century*. London: NCVO Publications.
Connolly, M. (1983) 'What happens when the government takes over?', *Local Government Policy-Making*, 10 (2): 7–21.
Connolly, M. (1996) 'Lessons from local government in Northern Ireland', *Local Government Studies*, 22 (2): 71–91.
Connolly, M. and Knox, C. (1988) 'Recent political difficulties of local government in Northern Ireland', *Policy and Politics*, 16 (2): 89–97.
Connolly, M. and Loughlin, S. (1990) 'Policy-making in Northern Ireland', 1–18 in M. Connolly and S. Loughlin (eds) *Public Policy in Northern Ireland: Adoption or Adaptation?* Belfast: Policy Research Institute.
Cooke, P. and Clifton, N. (2005) 'Visionary, precautionary and constrained "varieties of devolution" in the economic governance of the devolved UK territories', *Regional Studies* 39 (4): 437–451.
Craig, G., Taylor, M., Szanto, C. and Wilkinson, M. (1999) *Developing Local Compacts: Relationships between Local Public Sector Bodies and the Voluntary and Community Sectors*. York: Joseph Rowntree Foundation.
Darby, J. (1976) *Conflict in Northern Ireland: The Development of a Polarised Community*. Dublin: Gill and Macmillan.

REFERENCES

Darby, J. and Knox, C. (2004) *A Shared Future: Consultation Responses*. Report to Office of the First Minister and Deputy First Minister. Belfast: OFMDFM.

Deloitte (2006) *Exercise to Estimate the Costs and Efficiencies of the Review of Public Administration Proposals*. Belfast: OFMDFM.

Deloitte (2007) *Research into the Financial Cost of the Northern Ireland Divide*. Belfast: Deloitte.

Democratic Unionist Party (2009) *Driving Forward a Reform Agenda: DUP Policy Proposals*. Belfast: DUP.

Denton, M. and Flinders, M. (2006) 'Democracy, devolution and delegated governance in Scotland, *Regional and Federal Studies*, 16 (1): 63–82.

Department for Social Development (1993) *Strategy for the Support of the Voluntary Sector and for Community Development in Northern Ireland*. Belfast: Voluntary Services Unit.

Department for Social Development (1998) *Compact between Government and the Voluntary and Community Sector in Northern Ireland*. Belfast: DSD.

Department for Social Development (2001) *Partners for Change: Government's Strategy for Support of the Voluntary and Community Sector 2001–2004*. Belfast: DSD.

Department for Social Development (2003) 'New task force to shape the voluntary and community sector', 7 February. Belfast: DSD press release.

Department for Social Development (2004) *Investing Together: Report of the Task Force on Resourcing the Voluntary and Community Sector*. Belfast: Task Force Secretariat.

Department for Social Development (2005) *Positive Steps: The Government's Response to Investing Together: Report of the Task Force on Resourcing the Voluntary and Community Sector*. Belfast: DSD.

Department for Social Development (2006) *Partners for Change: Government's Strategy for Support of the Voluntary and Community Sector 2006–2008*. Belfast: DSD.

Department for Social Development (2007) *Evaluating Progress: Government's Report on the Implementation of Positive Steps*. Belfast: DSD.

Department for Social Development (2008) *Updating Progress: Government's Report on the Implementation of Positive Steps*. Belfast: DSD.

Department of Communities and Local Government (DCLG) (n.d.) *Department for Communities and Local Government Community Planning* available at: www.communityplanning.net/, accessed 27 March 2009.

Department of Education (2005) *Financial Management in Education and Library Boards*, Jack Report. Belfast: DENI.

Department of Education (2006) *Transformation: An Information Pack for Schools*. Bangor: DENI.

Department of Finance and Personnel (2007) *Public Bodies: A Guide for Northern Ireland Departments*. Belfast: DFP.

Department of Finance and Personnel (2008) *Northern Ireland Public Bodies 2008*. Belfast: Reform Delivery Unit.

Department of Finance and Personnel (2009) 'Termination of Workplace 2010 procurement', *News Release* 29 February. Belfast: DFP.

Department of Foreign Affairs *Political Background and Chronology of Peace Process* available at: http://foreignaffairs.gov.ie/home/index.aspx?id=2, accessed 16 July 2009.

Department of the Environment, Northern Ireland (2006) *Local Government Taskforce Community Planning Sub-Group: Recommendation Paper*. Belfast: DoE.

Department of Trade, Enterprise and Investment (2009) *Economic Overview of Northern Ireland*. Belfast: DETI.

Dickson, B. and Osborne, R. (2007) 'Equality and human rights since the Agreement', 152–166 in P. Carmichael, C. Knox and R. Osborne (eds) *Devolution and Constitutional Change in Northern Ireland*. Manchester: Manchester University Press.

Disturbances in Northern Ireland (1969) Report of the Commission, Cameron Report. Cmnd 532. Belfast: Her Majesty's Stationery Office.

Dixon, P. (1997) 'Consociationalism and the Northern Ireland Peace Process: the glass half full or half empty', *Nationalism and Ethnic Politics*, 3 (3): 20–36.

Dixon, P. (2005) 'Why the Good Friday Agreement in Northern Ireland is not consociational', *Political Quarterly*, 76 (3): 357–367.

Donnelly, C. and Hughes, J. (2006) 'Contact, culture and context: evidence from mixed faith schools in Northern Ireland and Israel', *Comparative Education*, 42 (4) 493–516.

Donnelly, C. and Osborne, R (2005) 'Devolution, Social Policy and Education; some observations from Northern Ireland', *Social Policy and Society*, 4 (2) 147–156,

Dowdall, J. (2004) *Hansard*, Official Report, Select Committee on Public Accounts, 23 February.

Dubs, A. (1997) 'District partnerships', *Northern Ireland Information Service*, 17 June, 1–2.

Economic Research Institute of Northern Ireland (2009) *Mitigating the Recession: Options for the Northern Ireland Executive*. Belfast: ERINI.

Electoral Office for Northern Ireland available at: www.eoni.org.uk/index.htm, accessed 20 February 2009.

European Commission (1995) 'Special Support Programme for Peace and Reconciliation in Northern Ireland and the Border Counties 1995–1999', *Eurolink Supplement*, No. 9. Belfast: European Commission Office.

Farrell, M. (1976) *Northern Ireland: The Orange State*. London: Pluto Press.

Farry, S. (2009) 'Consociationalism and the creation of a shared future', 165–179 in R. Taylor (ed.) *Consociational Theory: McGarry and O'Leary and the Northern Ireland Conflict*. London: Routledge.

Fearon, K. (2000) 'Life in civic society', *Fortnight*, September: 26–27.

Fenn, C. (2007) *A Comparative Research Study of Community Planning Practices across the United Kingdom and the Republic of Ireland: Lessons for Northern Ireland*. Jordanstown: University of Ulster.

Fitzgerald, M. (1978) 'Northern Ireland: where is local democracy?', *Local Government Chronicle*, No. 5817, 6 October, 1079–1082.

Foster, A. (2008) 'Ministerial statement: the Review of Public Administration', *Hansard*, Official Report, 31 March.

Foster, A. (2009) 'Why is Sinn Féin running scared of voting reform?', *Belfast Telegraph*, 2 October.

Frost, P. (2002) 'Selecting the appropriate structure', 89–92 in W. Cox (ed.) *Commonwealth Public Administration Reform 2003*. London: The Stationery Office.

Gaster, L. and Deakin, N. (1998) 'Local government and the voluntary sector: who needs whom – why and what for', *Local Governance*, 24 (3): 169–194.

Gay, O. and Pak, A. (2007) *The Northern Ireland (St Andrews Agreement) (No. 2) Bill*, Research Paper 07/32. Westminster: House of Commons Library.

Glentoran, Lord (2004) *Hansard*, Offical Report, Northern Ireland Orders Grand Committee 20 July.

Gordon, D. (2008) 'The civil service chief, the quango watchdog, and their frosty letters', *Belfast Telegraph*, 14 November: 1.

Gordon, D. (2009) 'Our finances are in an unhealthy state', *Belfast Telegraph*, 24 September.

Graham, E. (2002) 'More than just a talking shop', *Scope*, March: 20–21.

Greenwood, J., Pyper, R. and Wilson, D. (2002) *New Public Administration in Britain*, 3rd edn. London: Routledge.

Greer, A. (1999) 'Policy-making', 142–166 in P. Mitchell and R. Wilford (eds) *Politics in Northern Ireland*. Boulder: Westview Press.

Greer, J., Hughes, J., Knox, C. and Murray, M. (1999) 'Reshaping local governance in a divided society: district partnerships in Northern Ireland', 79–93 in G. Haughton (ed.) *Community Economic Development: Linking the Grassroots to Regional Economic Development*. London: The Stationery Office.

Greer, S.L. (2004) *Territorial Politics and Health Policy: UK Health Policy in Comparative Perspective*. Manchester: Manchester University Press.

Gribbin, V., Kelly, R. and Mitchell, C. (2005) *Loyalist Conflict Transformation Initiatives*. Belfast: OFMDFM.

Hadden, T. (1975) 'Local government: where are we heading for?', *Fortnight*, 7 (March): 10 and 15.

Hain, P. (2005) *Statement by the Secretary of State for Northern Ireland on the Outcome of the Review of Public Administration*, 22 November. Belfast: Northern Ireland Office.

Hain, P. (2006a) 'It is time for Northern Ireland to govern itself', *Independent*, 11 October.

Hain, P. (2006b) 'Review of Public Administration: quangos announcement', speech by Secretary of State on the outcomes of the review of non-departmental public bodies. Belfast: Northern Ireland Office.

Hall, M. (2007) *Building Bridges at the Grassroots: The Experience of Suffolk–Lenadoon Interface Group*. Newtownabbey: Island Publications.

Hamilton, J., Hansson, U., Bell, J. and Toucas, S. (2008) *Segregated Lives: Social Division, Sectarianism and Everyday Life in Northern Ireland*. Belfast: Institute for Conflict Research.

Hamilton, S. (2008) Private Members' Business, 'Voluntary sector', *Hansard*, Official Report, 25 November.

Hansard (2002) *The Review of Public Administration*, Official Report, Northern Ireland Assembly, 24 June.

Hansard (2009a) 'Reducing the number of government departments', Private Members' Business', Official Report, Northern Ireland Assembly, 19 January.

Hansard (2009b) 'Restructuring of the Executive and the Assembly', Private Members' Business, Official Report, Northern Ireland Assembly, 18 May.

Hargie, O., Dickson, D., Mallet, J. and Stringer, M. (2008) 'Communicating

social identity: a study of Catholics and Protestants in Northern Ireland', *Communication Research* 25 (6): 792–821.
Hayes, B., McAllister, I. and Dowds, L. (2007) 'Integrated education, intergroup relations and political identities in Northern Ireland', *Social Problems*, 54 (4): 454–482.
Hayes, M. (1967) 'Some aspects of local government in Northern Ireland', 23–36 in E. Rhodes (ed.) *Public Administration in Northern Ireland*. Londonderry: Magee University College.
Heald, D. (2009) 'Should Northern Ireland wish the abolition of the Barnett formula?', lecture by Professor David Heald at the University of Ulster, 2 April.
Hewitt, C. (1981) 'Catholic grievances, Catholic nationalism and violence in Northern Ireland during the civil rights period', *British Journal of Sociology*, 32 (3): 362–380.
HM Treasury (2002) *The Role of the Voluntary and Community Sector in Service Delivery: A Cross Cutting Review*. London: HM Treasury.
HM Treasury (2008) *Public Expenditure Statistical Analyses 2008*. London: HM Treasury.
Hodgett, S. and Johnston, D. (2001) 'Troubles, partnerships and possibilities: a study of Making Belfast Work development initiative in Northern Ireland', *Public Administration and Development*, 21 (4): 321–324
Holme, Lord of Cheltenham (2002) House of Lords, Constitution Committee: Minutes of Evidence, 10 June.
Home Office (2004) *Central Government funding of Voluntary and Community Organisations*. London: Home Office.
Hood, C. (1981) 'Axeperson spare that quango', 100–122 in C. Hood and M. Wright (eds) *Big Government in Hard Times*. Oxford: Martin Robertson.
Hood, C. (1991) 'A public management for all seasons?', *Public Administration*, 69 (1): 3–19.
Hood, C. (1998) *The Art of the State: Culture, Rhetoric and Public Management*. Oxford: Oxford University Press.
Hughes, J., Knox, C., Murray, M. and Greer, J. (1998) *Partnership Governance in Northern Ireland: The Path to Peace*. Dublin: Oak Tree Press.
Hunter, J. (2009) *Review of Local Government Staff Commission for Northern Ireland*. Belfast: Department of the Environment.
Huston, F. (2008) *Office of the Commissioner for Public Appointments for Northern Ireland Annual Report 2007–08*. Belfast: OCPA NI
Illsley, B. (2001) *Community Planning in Scotland: The Role of the Community*, available at: http://hippogfx.richardkenyon.co.uk/tcpss/papers/pdfs/2001CM04.htm, accessed 30 January 2009.
Improvement and Development Agency (IdeA) (n.d.) *It's All About . . . What Community Planning is All About* available at: www.idea.gov.uk/idk/aio/404115, accessed 22 April 2009.
Insight Consulting (2006) *Suffolk Community Plan*. Belfast: Suffolk Community Forum.
Interdepartmental Task Force (1998) *Report on the Integration of Local Government and Local Development Systems*. Dublin: Government Publications.
Irish Times (2009) 'The enemies of democracy', 11 March: 15

REFERENCES

Jarman, N. (2006) *Working at the Interface: Good Practice in Reducing Tension and Violence*. Belfast: Institute for Conflict Research.

Jarman, N. (2008) 'Security and segregation: interface barriers in Belfast', *Shared Space*, 6: 21–34.

Jenkins, S. (1993) 'A bomb for all bigots', *The Times*, 27 October: 16.

Keating, M. (2007) 'Devolution and public policy-making', 231–242, in P. Carmichael, C. Knox and R. Osborne (eds) *Devolution and Constitutional Change in Northern Ireland*. Manchester: Manchester University Press.

Keenan, D. (2008) 'Ex-prisoners "helped resolve conflict"', *Irish Times*, 1 March: 10.

Kilmurray, A. (1981) 'Assessing local government – Politely!', *Scope*, October: 13.

Kilmurray, A. (2007) *Core Funding for Politically Motivated Ex-prisoner Groups*. Belfast: Atlantic Philanthropies

Knox, C. (1996) 'The emergence of power sharing in Northern Ireland: lessons from local government', *Journal of Conflict Studies*, 16 (1): 7–29.

Knox, C. (1998) 'Local government in Northern Ireland: emerging from the bearpit of sectarianism?', *Local Government Studies*, 24 (3): 1–13.

Knox, C. (2003) 'Democratic renewal in fragmental communities: the Northern Ireland case', *Local Governance*, 29 (1): 14–36.

Knox, C. (2006) *Central–Local Relations Sub-group Paper to Local Government Taskforce*. Belfast: Department of the Environment.

Knox, C. (2008a) 'Policy-making in Northern Ireland: ignoring the evidence', *Policy and Politics*, 36 (3): 343–359.

Knox. C. (2008b) *The Northern Ireland Housing Council: Future Role*, submission to the Minister for Social Development. Jordanstown: University of Ulster.

Knox, C. (2009) 'The politics of local government reform in Northern Ireland', *Local Government Studies*, 35 (4): 435–456.

Knox, C. and Carmichael, P. (2005a) 'Improving public services: public administration reform in Northern Ireland', *Journal of Social Policy*, 35 (1): 97–120.

Knox, C. and Carmichael, P. (2005b) Devolution – the Northern Ireland way: an exercise in "creative ambiguity"', *Environment and Planning C: Government and Policy*, 23 (1): 63–83.

Knox, C. and Carmichael, P. (2006) 'Bureau shuffling? The Review of Public Administration in Northern Ireland', *Public Administration*, 84 (4): 941–965.

Knox, C. and McHugh, M. (1990) Management in government: the next steps in Northern Ireland, *Administration*, 38 (3) 251–270.

Laffin, M. (2004) 'Is regional centralism inevitable? The case of the Welsh Assembly', *Regional Studies*, 38 (2): 213–223.

Laffin, M. (2007) 'Comparative British central–local relations: regional centralism, governance and intergovernmental relations', *Public Policy and Administration*, 22 (1): 74–91.

Laffin, M., Taylor, G. and Thomas, A. (2002) *A New Partnership? The National Assembly for Wales and Local Government*. York: Joseph Rowntree Foundation.

Lenadoon Community Forum (2003) *The Development of Lenadoon Area and the Community Forum 1992–2002*. Belfast: Lenadoon Community Forum.

Lidington, D. (2004) 'Northern Ireland Grand Committee', *Hansard*, Official Report, 8 July.

Lijphart, A. (1968) *The Politics of Accommodation: Pluralism and Democracy in the Netherlands*. Berkeley: University of California Press.

Lijphart, A. (1975) 'The Northern Ireland problem: cases, theories and solutions', *British Journal of Political Science*, 5 (1): 83–106.

Livingstone, S. and Morison, J. (1995) *Reshaping Public Power: Northern Ireland and the British Constitutional Crisis*. London: Sweet and Maxwell.

Lloyd, G. (2008) 'Towards a "pooled sovereignty" in Community Planning in Scotland?', *Local Economy*, 23 (1): 58–68

Local Government (Northern Ireland) Taskforce (2006) *Community Planning Sub-group, Recommendation Paper*. Belfast: Department of Environment.

Local Government Staff Commission (2005) *Response to the RPA Second Consultation*. Belfast: LGSC.

Local Government Staff Commission (2008) *Annual Report and Accounts 2007–2008*. Belfast: LGSC.

Local Government Staff Commission (2009) *Corporate Plan 2009–2011 and Business Plan 2009/10*. Belfast: LGSC.

Loughran, G. (1965) 'The problem of local government in Northern Ireland', *Administration*, 13: 35–38.

Lyons, M. (2007) *Lyons Inquiry into Local Government – Place-shaping: A Shared Ambition for the Future of Local Government*. Belfast: The Stationery Office.

Mackintosh, J. (1971) 'The Report of the Review Body on Local Government in Northern Ireland: The Macrory Report', *Public Administration*, 49: 13–24.

Mandelson, P. (1999) Debate on Northern Ireland devolution of powers, *Hansard*, Official Report, 30th November.

Mandelson, P. (2000) House of Commons, *Hansard* Debates on Northern Ireland, 3 February.

Maskey, A. (2009a) 'Restructuring of the Executive and Assembly', Private Members' Business, *Hansard*, Official Report, 18 May.

Maskey, P. (2009b) '£3 billion reform agenda under scrutiny', Press Release PR/06/08/09, Public Accounts Committee, Northern Ireland Assembly, 15 January.

Massey, A. (1993) *Managing the Public Sector: A Comparative Analysis of the United Kingdom and the United States*. Cheltenham: Edward Elgar.

Massey, A. and Pyper, R. (2005) *Public Management and Modernisation in Britain*. Basingstoke: Palgrave Macmillan.

McAdam, N. (2009) 'Ritchie: no regrets over decision to axe funding', *Belfast Telegraph*, 1 May.

McAteer, M. and Bennett, M. (2005) 'Devolution and local government: evidence from Scotland', *Local Government Studies*, 31 (3): 285–306.

McCall, C. and Williamson, A. (2001) 'Governance and democracy in Northern Ireland: the role of the voluntary and community sector after the agreement', *Governance*, 14 (3): 363–383.

McConaghy, D. (1978) 'The collapse of a local government system', *Municipal Review*, 49 (585): 139–140.

McConnell, A. (2006) 'Central local relations in Scotland', *International Review of Administrative Sciences*, 72 (1): 73–84.

McCrea, I. (2009) 'Civic Forum', *Hansard*, Offical Report, 3 February.

McCullagh, A. (2009) 'The evolution of community planning process in Omagh

District Council', *Northern Ireland Best Practice Scheme*, 21 May. Belfast: Department of Finance and Personnel.

McEvoy, L., McEvoy, K. and McConnachie, K. (2006) 'Reconciliation as a dirty word: conflict, community relations and education in Northern Ireland', *Journal of International Affairs*, 60 (1): 81–106.

McGarry, J. and O'Leary, B. (1995a) 'Five fallacies: Northern Ireland and the liabilities of liberalism', *Ethnic and Racial Studies*, 18 (4): 837–861.

McGarry, J. and O'Leary, B. (1995b) *Explaining Northern Ireland: Broken Images*. Oxford: Blackwell Publishers.

McGarry, J. and O'Leary, B. (2004) *The Northern Ireland Conflict: Consociational Engagements*. Oxford: Oxford University Press.

McGarry, J. and O'Leary, B. (2006) 'Consociational Theory, Northern Ireland's conflict and its agreement', *Government and Opposition*, 41 (1): 43–63.

McGarry, J. and O'Leary, B. (2007) 'Stabilising the Northern Ireland Agreement', 62–82 in P. Carmichael, C. Knox and R. Osborne (eds) *Devolution and Constitutional Change in Northern Ireland*. Manchester: Manchester University Press.

McGarry, J. and O'Leary, B. (2009) 'Power shared after the deaths of thousands', 15–84 in R. Taylor (ed.) *Consociational Theory: McGarry and O'Leary and the Northern Ireland Conflict*. London: Routledge.

McGimpsey, M. (2007) 'Minister shelves plan for single health board', *Belfast Telegraph*, 7 July, p. 1.

McGimpsey, M. (2008) 'Historic day for Health Service as McGimpsey announces end to prescription charges', DHSSPS Press Release, 29 September.

McGlone, P (2009) 'Administration review costs £90m', *BBC News Report*, 13 October, available at: http://news.bbc.co.uk/1/hi/northern_ireland/8304442.stm, accessed 16 October 2009.

McGlynn, C. (2007) 'Rhetoric and reality: are integrated schools in Northern Ireland really making a difference?', *Irish Educational Studies*, 26 (3): 271–287.

McGuinness, M. (2009) 'Robinson plan of a return to majority rule is just fantasy', *Belfast Telegraph*, 18 September.

McVeigh, R. and Rolston, B. (2007) 'From Good Friday to good relations: sectarianism, racism and the Northern Ireland state', *Race and Class*, 48 (4): 1–23.

Meehan, E. (1997) 'Smaller public bodies', 167–181 in K. Bloomfield and C. Carter (eds) *People and Government: Questions for Northern Ireland*. York: Joseph Rowntree Foundation.

Moran, M. (2005) *Politics and Governance in the United Kingdom*. Basingstoke: Palgrave Macmillan.

Morgan, K. (2002) 'The new regeneration narrative: local development in the multi-level polity', *Local Economy*, 17 (3): 191–199.

Morison, J. (1996) 'Waiting for the big fix', in *Reconstituting Politics*. Democratic Dialogue Report No. 3.

Morison, J. (2000) 'The government–voluntary sector compacts: governance, governmentality, and civil society', *Journal of Law and Society*, 27 (1): 98–132.

Moutray, S. (2009) 'Civic forum', *Hansard*, Official Report, 3 February.

Murphy, C. (2002) 'Neutral working environment', *Hansard*, Official Report, 18 June.

Murphy, P. (2005) Foreword to: *A Shared Future: Policy and Strategic Framework for Good Relations in Northern Ireland*. Belfast: OFMDFM.

Nolan Committee (1995) *Committee on Standards in Public Life*, Vol. 1, Cm 2850–1. London: HMSO.

Nolan, P. (2000) 'The plump Cinderella or politics without politics', *Fortnight*, September: 29–30.

North–South Ministerial Council available at: www.northsouthministerialcouncil.org, accessed 17 June 2009.

Northern Ireland Act (1998) 'A summary guide', London: Northern Ireland Office.

Northern Ireland Assembly (2002) *The Executive Committee*, Government Series No.5. Stormont: Research and Library Services.

Northern Ireland Assembly (2007a) 'The outworking of the task force report on resourcing the voluntary and community sector', Briefing Note 58/09. NIA: Research and Library Services.

Northern Ireland Assembly (2007b) *Northern Ireland Assembly Election 2007*, Research Paper 01/07. Stormont: Research and Library Services.

Northern Ireland Assembly (2008a) 'Government and voluntary and community sector in Northern Ireland: timeline of key developments', Briefing Note: 113/08. NIA: Research and Library Services.

Northern Ireland Assembly (2008b) *The Legislative Process for Public Bills*. Belfast: Northern Ireland Assembly, Public Information Service

Northern Ireland Assembly (2009a) *Northern Ireland Assembly Standing Orders*. Belfast: NIA.

Northern Ireland Assembly (2009b) *The Barnett Formula*. Research Paper 49/09. Stormont: Northern Ireland Assembly – Research and Information Services.

Northern Ireland Assembly (2009c) available at: www.niassembly.gov.uk/io/5.htm, accessed 9 July 2009.

Northern Ireland Audit Office (2004) *Financial Audit and Reporting 2002–03: General Report by the Comptroller and Auditor General for Northern Ireland*. Belfast: NIAO.

Northern Ireland Audit Office (2008) *Shared Services for Efficiency: A Progress Report*, NIA 206/07–08. Belfast: NIAO.

Northern Ireland Audit Office (2009a) *Public Service Agreements: Measuring Performance*. Report by the Controller and Auditor General NIA 79/08–09. Belfast: NIAO.

Northern Ireland Audit Office (2009b) *Review of New Deal 25+*. Report by the Controller and Auditor General NIA 111/08–09. Belfast: NIAO.

Northern Ireland Audit Office (2009c) *The Management of Social Housing Rent Collection and Arrears*. Report by the Controller and Auditor General NIA 104/08–09. Belfast: NIAO.

Northern Ireland Civil Service (2002) *Review of the Northern Ireland Civil Service: Response to Devolution*. Belfast: NICS.

Northern Ireland Civil Service (2004) *Fit for Purpose: The Reform Agenda in the Northern Ireland Civil Service*. Belfast: NICS.

Northern Ireland Council for Integrated Education and the Integrated Education Fund (2006) *A Brighter Future through Learning Together: A Guide to Integrated Education*. Belfast: NICIE and IEF.

Northern Ireland Council for Integrated Education available at: www.nicie.org/, accessed 18 March 2009.

Northern Ireland Council for Voluntary Action (2008a) *Positive Steps: Final Monitoring Report.* Belfast: NICVA.
Northern Ireland Council for Voluntary Action (2008b) *The Potential for a White Paper on the Relationship between Government and the Voluntary and Community Sector in Northern Ireland*, Belfast: NICVA.
Northern Ireland Council for Voluntary Action (2009a) *State of the Sector V.* Belfast: NICVA.
Northern Ireland Council for Voluntary Action (2009b) *NICVA Strategic Plan 2009–2012.* Belfast: NICVA.
Northern Ireland Executive *Programme for Government* (2001). Belfast: Office of the First Minister and Deputy First Minister.
Northern Ireland Executive (2007) *Ministerial Code.* Belfast: NIA.
Northern Ireland Executive (2008a) *Budget 2008–11.* Belfast: Department of Finance and Personnel.
Northern Ireland Executive (2008b) *Programme for Government 2008–2011.* Belfast: Office of the First Minister and Deputy First Minister.
Northern Ireland Housing Executive available at: www.nihe.gov.uk/index/yn_home/community_cohesion/shared_future_housing.htm, accessed 25 August 2009.
Northern Ireland Local Government Association (2006) *NILGA's Commitments and a Vision for Local Government.* Belfast: NILGA.
Northern Ireland Local Government Association and Local Government Training Group (2006) *Local Councillor's Handbook.* Belfast: NILGA and LGT.
Northern Ireland Office (1998) *Building Real Partnership: Compact between Government and the Voluntary and Community Sector in Northern Ireland*, Cm 4167. Belfast: Stationery Office.
Northern Ireland Office (2006) *Better Government for Northern Ireland: Final Decisions of the Review of Public Administration.* Belfast: Northern Ireland Office.
Northern Ireland Prison Service available at: www.niprisonservice.gov.uk/index.cfm/area/information/page/earlyrelease, accessed 24 June 2009.
Northern Ireland (St Andrews Agreement) Bill (2006) EN: 54/2. London: The Stationery Office.
Nutley, S.M., Walter, I. and Davies, H.T.O. (2007) *Using Evidence: How Research Can Inform Public Services.* Bristol: The Policy Press.
O'Dowd, L., Rolston, B. and Tomlinson, M. (1980) *Northern Ireland: Between Civil Rights and Civil War.* London: CSE Books.
O'Halloran, C. and McIntyre, G. (1999) *Addressing Conflict in Two Interface Areas.* Belfast: Belfast Interface Project
O'Leary, B. (2001) 'The character of the 1998 Agreement: results and prospects', 49–83 in R.Wilford (ed.) *Aspects of the Belfast Agreement.* Oxford: Oxford University Press.
O'Neill, A. (2001) 'Quangos, accountability and devolution: the Northern Ireland Case', unpublished PhD. University of Ulster.
Oberschall, A. (2007) *Conflict and Peace Building in Divided Societies: Responses to Ethnic Violence.* Abingdon: Routledge
Office of Public Services Reform (2002) *Reforming Our Public Services: Principles into Practice.* London: The Stationery Office.

Office of the Commissioner for Public Appointments for Northern Ireland (2007) *Code of Practice for Ministerial Appointments to Public Bodies*. Belfast: OCPA NI.

Office of the Commissioner for Public Appointments for Northern Ireland (2008) *Annual Report 2007–08*. Belfast: OCPA NI.

Office of the Commissioner for Public Appointments for Northern Ireland available at: www.ocpani.gov.uk/index/our-role.htm, accessed 16 June 2009.

Office of the Deputy Prime Minister (2004) *The Future of Local Government: Developing a 10 Year Vision*. London: Office of the Deputy Prime Minister.

Office of the First Minister and Deputy First Minister (2002) *Programme for Government 2002–03*. Belfast: OFMDFM.

Office of the First Minister and Deputy First Minister (2003) *A Shared Future: A Consultation Paper on Improving Relations in Northern Ireland*. Belfast: OFMDFM.

Office of the First Minister and Deputy First Minister (2003) *The Review of Public Administration in Northern Ireland*. Belfast: RPA.

Office of the First Minister and Deputy First Minister (2004) *The Public Appointments Annual Report 2003–2004*. Belfast: OFMDFM.

Office of the First Minister and Deputy First Minister (2005a) *A Shared Future: Policy and Strategic Framework for Good Relations in Northern Ireland*. Belfast: OFMDFM.

Office of the First Minister and Deputy First Minister (2005b) *The Review of Public Administration in Northern Ireland: Further Consultation*. Belfast: RPA.

Office of the First Minister and Deputy First Minister (2007) *A Shared Future* and *Racial Equality Strategy: Good Relations Indicators Baseline Report*. Belfast: OFMDFM.

Office of the First Minister and Deputy First Minister (2008) *Public Appointments Annual Report, 2007/08*. Belfast: Central Appointments Unit.

Office of the First Minister and Deputy First Minister (2009) *Building a Better Future: The Northern Ireland Executive's Programme for Government – Delivery Report 1 April 2008–31 March 2009*. Belfast: OFMFM.

Office of the First Minister and Deputy First Minister (undated), *Make Your Mark: A Guide to Public Appointments in Northern Ireland*. Belfast: Central Appointments Unit.

Oliver, J. (1978) *Working at Stormont*. Dublin: Institute of Public Administration.

Orde, H. (2009) 'Stormont failure to agree sectarianism strategy "dangerous"', *Belfast Telegraph*, 17th September.

Osborne, R. (1992) 'Fair employment and employment equity policy learning in a comparative context', *Public Money and Management*, 12 (4): 11–19.

Osborne, R. (1998) 'Advising the committee', *Public Administration*, 76 (4): 793–803.

Osborne, R. (2002) 'Making a difference? The role of statutory committees in the Northern Ireland Assembly', *Public Administration*, 80 (2): 283–299.

Osborne, R, and Shuttleworth, I. (eds) (2004) *Fair Employment in Northern Ireland: A Generation On*. Belfast: Blackstaff Press.

Osborne, S. and McLaughlin, K. (2002) 'Trends and issues in the implementation of local "voluntary sector compacts" in England', *Public Money and Management*, 22 (1): 55–63.

Paisley, I. (1999) Debate on Northern Ireland devolution of powers, *Hansard*, Official Report, 30 November.
Paisley, I. (2007) DUP Statement on the return of devolution, 26 March.
Pearson, I. (2004) Speech delivered by Minister at BMF Conference, Belfast 29 June.
Pemberton, S. and Lloyd, G. (2008) 'Devolution, community planning and institutional decongestion?', *Local Government Studies*, 34 (4): 437–451.
Pliatzky Report (1980) *Report on Non-departmental Public Bodies*, Cmnd 7197. London: HMSO.
Pollitt, C and Bouckaert (2004) *Public Management Reform: A Comparative Analysis*, 2nd edn. Oxford: Oxford University Press.
Pollitt, C. and Summa, H. (1997) 'Trajectories of reform: public management change in four countries', *Public Money and Management*, 17 (1): 7–18.
Public Accounts Committee (2004a) *Housing the Homeless*, 21st Report, HC599, 20 May. London: The Stationery Office.
Public Accounts Committee (2004b) *Northern Ireland: The Management of Industrial Sickness*, 50th Report, HC561, 2 December. London: The Stationery Office.
Purdue, D. (2001) 'Neighbourhood governance: leadership, trust and social capital', *Urban Studies*, 38 (12): 2211–2224.
Purvis, D. (2009) Speech to Progressive Unionist Party Conference, 10 October.
Queen's University Belfast (2009) *Sharing Education Programme* available at: www.schoolsworkingtogether.co.uk, accessed 17 August.
Reid, J. (2001) Statement by Secretary of State for Northern Ireland to the House of Commons, *Hansard*, 24 October.
Reid, J. (2002) Statement by Secretary of State to the House of Commons, *Hansard*, 15 October.
Review Body on Local Government in Northern Ireland (1970) Macrory Report, Cmnd 546. Belfast: Her Majesty's Stationery Office.
Review of Public Administration (2006) *Better Government for Northern Ireland: Final Decisions of the Review of Public Administration*. Belfast: OFMDFM.
Review of Public Administration in Northern Ireland (2003). Belfast: Office of the First Minister and Deputy First Minister, RPA.
Rhodes, R. (1986) *The National World of Local Government*. London: Allen & Unwin
Rhodes, R. (1997) 'Reinventing Whitehall 1979–1995', 43–60 in W. Kickert (ed.) *Public Management and Administrative Reform in Western Europe*. Cheltenham: Edward Elgar.
Ritchie, M. (2008a) 'New housing agenda', *Hansard*, Official Report, 25 November.
Ritchie, M. (2008b) Private Member's Business, 'Voluntary Sector', *Hansard*, Official Report, 25th November.
Ritchie, M. (2008c) 'Ritchie unveils new housing agenda for Northern Ireland', Department for Social Development, Press Release, 26 February.
Ritchie, M. (2009) Minister for Social Development's speech to the Housing Council, 10 June.
Robinson, B. (2008) Extracts from a speech by the Head of the Northern Ireland Civil Service to the Londonderry Chamber of Commerce to the Londonderry Chamber of Commerce, 24 October. Belfast: NICS.

Robinson, P. (2008) quoted in *Irish Times*, 'Devolution beats critics' alternative', by G. Moriarty, 23 April.
Robinson, P. (2009a) 'DUP driving forward radical reform agenda', DUP Press Release, 12 May.
Robinson, P. (2009b) 'Robinson blasts Equality Commission', *News Letter*, 27 July.
Robinson, P. (2009c) Executive Committee Business, *Hansard*, Official Report, 22 September.
Robinson, P. (2009d) 'Proposed voting changes would build on success of the Assembly', *Belfast Telegraph*, 15 September.
Robinson, P. (2009e) 'Making devolution work', speech by Peter Robinson at Ulster Hall, Belfast, 8 September.
Robinson, P. (2009f) 'Government not designed to deal with delivering expeditiously', speech by Peter Robinson to Bankers Annual Dinner, 8 October.
Rogers, S., Smith, M., Sullivan, H. and Clarke, M. (1999) *Community Planning in Scotland: An Evaluation of the Pathfinder Projects*. Edinburgh: Convention of Scottish Local Authorities (COSLA).
Rooker. J. (2005) *Reform of Local Government: Outcome of Review of Public Administration*, 2005. Belfast: Northern Ireland Office, 22 November.
Rose, R. (1971) *Governing without Consensus: An Irish Perspective*. London: Faber.
Ross, K. and Osborne, S. (1999) 'Making a reality of community governance: structuring government–voluntary sector relationships at local level', *Public Policy and Administration*, 14 (2): 49–60.
Ruane, C. (2007a) 'Minister Ruane outlines education reforms', Department of Education Press Release, 4 December. Belfast: DENI
Ruane, C. (2007b) Minister of Education: letter to Department of Education staff, 19 July. Bangor: Department of Education.
Scottish Council for Voluntary Organisations available at: www.scvo.org.uk/scvo/Home/Home.aspx, accessed 9 July 2009.
Scottish Executive (2003) *Local Government in Scotland Act 2003: Community Planning Advice Note 9*. Edinburgh: Scottish Executive.
Scottish Executive (2004) *The Local Government in Scotland Act 2003: Guidance for Community Planning*. Edinburgh: Scottish Executive.
Scottish Office (1999) *Report of the Commission on Local, Government and the Scottish Parliament* (MacIntosh Commission). Edinburgh: Scottish Office.
Semple, S. (1982) Speech to the Association of Local Authorities in Northern Ireland Conference, 28 April, Newcastle, Co. Down.
Shirlow, P. (2008) *Politically Motivated Former Prisoners: Evaluation of the Core Funding Project 2006–08*. Belfast: Community Foundation for Northern Ireland.
Shirlow, P. and McEvoy, K. (2008) *Beyond the Wire: Former Prisoners and Conflict Transformation in Northern Ireland*. London: Pluto Press.
Shirlow, P and Murtagh, B. (2006) Belfast: *Segregation, Violence and the City*. London: Pluto Press.
Shirlow, P., Graham, B., McEvoy, K., O hAdhmaill, F. and Purvis, D. (2005) *Politically Motivated Former Prisoner Groups: Community Activism and Conflict Transformation*. Belfast: SEUPB Report.
Sinclair, S. (2008) 'Dilemmas of community planning: lessons from Scotland', *Public Policy and Administration*, 23 (4): 373–390.

Skills Sector Council for Central Government (2008) *Building Professional Skills for Government – A Strategy for Delivery: Action Plan for Northern Ireland*, Stage 5 Report. Belfast: Government Skills.
Smith, Lord, of Clifton (2004) Northern Ireland Orders Grand Committee, *Hansard*, Office Report, 20 July.
Smith, A. (2001) 'Religious segregation and the emergence of integrated schools in Northern Ireland', *Oxford Review of Education*, 27 (4): 559–575.
Smith, J. (1973) 'A city where abnormal is normal', *Municipal Review*, 44 (April): 104–107.
Social Democratic and Labour Party (SDLP) (2009) *Supporting the Economy. New Priorities in Difficult Times: A Discussion Paper on the Revision to the Northern Ireland Executive's Budget: 2008–11*. Belfast: SDLP Offices.
Spellar, J. (2005) Introduction to: *A Shared Future: Policy and Strategic Framework for Good Relations in Northern Ireland*. Belfast: OFMDFM.
Stewart, J. (2003) *Modernising British Local Government: An Assessment of Labour's Reform Programme*. Basingstoke: Palgrave Macmillan.
Stringer, M., Irwing, P., Giles, M., McClenahan, C., Wilson, R. and Hunter, J.A. (2009) 'Intergroup contact, friendship quality and political attitudes in integrated and segregated schools in Northern Ireland', *British Journal of Educational Psychology* 79 (2): 239–257.
Sullivan, H. and Williams, P. (2009) 'The limits of co-ordination: community strategies as multi-purpose vehicles in Wales', *Local Government Studies*, 35 (2): 161–180.
Sweeney, P. (1997) 'A view from the voluntary sector', 58–67 in K. Bloomfield and C. Carter (eds) *People and Government: Questions for Northern Ireland*. York: Joseph Rowntree Foundation.
Taylor, R. (2001) 'Northern Ireland: consociation or social transformation?', 37–52 in J. McGarry (ed.) *Northern Ireland and the Divided World: Post-Agreement Northern Ireland in Comparative Perspective*. Oxford: Oxford University Press.
Taylor, R. (2006) 'The Belfast Agreement and the politics of consociationalism: a critique', *Political Quarterly*, 77 (2): 217–226.
Taylor, R. (2008) *Global Change, Civil Society and the Northern Ireland Peace Process: Implementing the Political Settlement*. Basingstoke: Palgrave Macmillan.
Taylor, R. (ed.) (2009a) *Consociational Theory: McGarry and O'Leary and the Northern Ireland Conflict*. London: Routledge
Taylor, R. (2009b) 'The injustice of a consociational solution to the Northern Ireland problem', 309–329 in R. Taylor (ed.) *Consociational Theory: McGarry and O'Leary and the Northern Ireland conflict*. London: Routledge.
The Reshaping of Local Government: Statement of Aims (1967) Cmnd 517. Belfast: Her Majesty's Stationery Office.
The Reshaping of Local Government: Further Proposals (1969) Cmnd 530. Belfast: Her Majesty's Stationery Office.
The Review of Public Administration in Northern Ireland: Further Consultation (2005). Belfast: RPA.
Tomlinson, M. (1980) 'Relegating Local Government', 95–118 in L. O'Dowd, B. Rolston and M. Tomlinson *Northern Ireland: Between Civil Rights and Civil War*. London: CSE Books.

Tonge, J. (2008) 'From conflict to communal politics: the politics of peace', 49–72 in C. Coulter and M. Murray (eds) *Northern Ireland after the Troubles: A Society in Transition*. Manchester: Manchester University Press.

Toonen, T. (2003) 'Administrative reform: analytics', 467–477 in B.G. Peters and J. Pierre (eds) *Handbook of Public Administration*. London: Sage.

Trimble, D. (2002) 'Review of Public Administration', *Hansard*, Official Report, 25 February. Belfast: Northern Ireland Assembly.

US-Ireland Alliance/Millward Brown (2008) 'Belfast residents asked if peace lines should come down', available at: www.us-irelandalliance.org, accessed 14 September.

VolResource: information on voluntary and community organisations available at: www.volresource.org.uk/index.htm, accessed 18 August 2009.

Voluntary and Community Unit (2002) *Voluntary and Community Research in Northern Ireland*. Belfast: Department for Social Development.

Walker, G. (2001) 'The British–Irish Council', 129–141 in R. Wilford (ed.) *Aspects of the Belfast Agreement*. Oxford: Oxford University Press.

Walsh, J. (1998) 'Local development and local government in the Republic of Ireland: from fragmentation to integration', *Local Economy*, 12 (4), 329–341.

Weiss, C.H. (1999) 'The interface between evaluation and public policy', *Evaluation*, 5 (4): 468–86.

Welsh Assembly Government (2008a) *Local Government Partnership Scheme*. Cardiff: Welsh Assembly Government: Local Government Policy Division.

Welsh Assembly Government (2008b) *Local Vision Statutory Guidance from the Welsh Assembly Government on Developing and Delivering Community Strategies*. Cardiff: Welsh Assembly Government: Department for Social Justice and Local Government.

Welsh Assembly Government (2008c) *Local Service Boards in Wales: Realising the Potential: Route Map*. Cardiff: Welsh Assembly Government

Welsh Assembly Government (2009) *Local Government Partnership Scheme: Report 2007–2008*. Cardiff: Welsh Assembly Government: Local Government Policy Division.

Whyte, J. (1983) 'How much discrimination was there under the Unionist regime 1921–68?', 1–35 in T. Gallagher and J. O'Connell (eds) *Contemporary Irish Studies*. Manchester: Manchester University Press.

Widdis, H. and Moore, T. (2002) *Public Appointments and Public Bodies in Northern Ireland*. Paper 04/02. Belfast: Northern Ireland Assembly, Research and Library Services.

Wilford, R. (1999) 'Regional Assemblies and Parliament', 117–141 in P. Mitchell and R. Wilford (eds) *Politics in Northern Ireland*. Boulder: Westview Press.

Wilford, R. (2001a) 'The Assembly', 59–72 in R. Wilson (ed.) *Agreeing to Disagree? A Guide to the Northern Ireland Assembly*. Belfast: The Stationery Office

Wilford, R. (2001b) 'The Assembly and the Executive', 107–128 in R. Wilford (ed.) *Aspects of the Belfast Agreement*. Oxford: Oxford University Press.

Wilford, R. (2007) 'Inside Stormont: the Assembly and the Executive', 167–185 in P. Carmichael, C. Knox and R. Osborne (eds) *Devolution and Constitutional Change in Northern Ireland*. Manchester: Manchester University Press.

Wilford, R. (2009) 'Consociational government: inside the devolved Northern Ireland Executive', 180–195 in R. Taylor (ed.) *Consociational Theory: McGarry and O'Leary and the Northern Ireland Conflict*. London: Routledge.

Wilford, R. and Elliott, S. (1999) 'Small earthquake in Chile: the first Northern Ireland Affairs Select Committee', *Irish Political Studies*, 14 (1) 23–42

Wilford, R. and Wilson, R. (2003a) 'Northern Ireland valedictory', 79–118 in R. Hazell (ed.) *The State of the Nation 2003: The Third Year of Devolution in the United Kingdom.* Exeter: Imprint Academic Press.

Wilford, R. and Wilson, R (2003b) 'Public policies', in *Nations and Regions: The Dynamics of Devolution*: Report 16. ESRC and Leverhulme Trust, UCL Constitution Unit.

Wilford, R., MacGinty, R., Dowds, L. and Robinson, G. (2003) 'Northern Ireland's devolved institutions: a triumph of hope over experience?', *Regional and Federal Studies*, 13 (1): 31–54.

Williams, P., Rogers, S., Sullivan, H., Evans, L. and Crow, A. (2006). *People, Plans and Partnerships: A National Evaluation of Community Strategies in Wales.* Welsh Assembly Government: Cardiff.

Williamson, A.P., Scott, D. and Halfpenny, P. (2000) 'Rebuilding civil society in Northern Ireland: the community and voluntary sector's contribution to the European Union Peace and Reconciliation District Partnership Programme', *Policy & Politics*, 28 (1): 49–66.

Wilson, R. (2001) 'The Executive Committee', 73–79 in R. Wilson (ed.) *Agreeing to Disagree? A Guide to the Northern Ireland Assembly.* Belfast: The Stationery Office

Wilson, S. (2005) 'Quit now, education row chiefs are told', *Belfast Telegraph*, 6 April.

Wilson, S. (2009a) 'Is Sammy's rant on racism just a new red herring?', *Belfast Telegraph* 11 August.

Wilson, S. (2009b) 'Decisions on the future of the Local Government Staff Commission', *Ministerial Statement*, 30 June. Belfast: Department of the Environment Press Office.

Wright, V. (1994) 'Reshaping the state: the implications for public administration', *West European Politics*, 17 (3): 102–137.

Index

Note: page numbers in **bold** refer to figures, page numbers in *italic* refer to tables.

A Framework for Accountable Government 203
A New Framework for Agreement 203
A Shared and Better Future for All 215
A Shared Future 5, 211–12, 212–14, 230–1, 231
Account NI 103
accountability 3, 77–8, 84–5, *170*, 171, 179, 252, 265
achievements 273–8, **274**, *275*, *276*
Adams, Gerry 12, 206–7, 267
administrative reform 84–6, 87
Agriculture and Rural Development, Department of *18*, *58*
Ahern, Bertie 206
Alexander, A. 111, 121
All Children Together 219–30
Alliance Party of Northern Ireland 22, **23**, *23*, *24*, 213
Allister, Jim 208, 268–9
Anglo-Irish Agreement 1985 5, 125, 202
arms, decommissioning 9–11, 203–4, 206
Association of Local Authorities 124
Association of Public Service Excellence (APSE) 164
Atlantic Philanthropies 191, 201, 230
Audit Commission 249

Barnett formula, the 56–7
Belfast 217
Belfast City Council 116, 126–7
Belfast Corporation 122
Belfast/Good Friday Agreement 1998 2, 3, 8–9, 12, 24, 25, 28, 29, 30, 31, 85, 87, 90, 191–2, 204–7, 271, 278
Bell, P. N. 87, 97, 217–18
Better Government for Northern Ireland 92–3, 135
Bevir, M., *et al.* 86
Birrell, D. 47, 96, 120, 123, 159–60
Blair, Tony 8, 204, 206, 207
Bloomfield, Sir Kenneth 81

Bogdanor, V. 8
Bouckaert 86
Boundary Commission 120
Bradbury, J. 267
British–Irish Council 3, 8, 29–30, 205
British–Irish Intergovernmental Conference 3, 8, 30, 205
Brown, Des 183
Brown, Gordon 37
Bruce, S. 226
Bruton, John 203
Buckland, P. 115
Budge, I. 116
Building on Progress: Public Services 80–1
Building Real Partnership 178
Business Services Organisation 95

Callaghan, James 117, 117–18
Cameron, David 5, 160–1
Cameron Commission 118
Canary Wharf bomb, 1996 204
capital investments 269
Cardiff Council 260–1
Carmichael, P. 48–9
Castlereagh Police Station, break in 11
Central Community Relations Unit (CCRU) 129
central–local relations 6, 234–5, 253–8, 266
advocacy 262; Great Britain 256–7; Local Delivery Agreement 259–61; Local Service Boards (LSBs) 259; model 262–6, **265**; networks 256; Partnership Panel 262–3; policy agreements 259; political liaison 262–3; Scotland 254, 257; strategic and operational liaison 263–6; Wales 254, 257, 257–61
Centre for Applied Learning 103
Charities Act (NI) 2008 187
Charity Commission for Northern Ireland 186, 187
Child Support Agency 60, 64
Children's Commissioner legislation 76

INDEX

chronology, power-sharing and devolution 32–4
Citizens Online Programme 102–3
citizenship, active 179
citizen/user empowerment 82, **83**
Civic Forum 25–8, 46, 198, 199
civic leadership 255
civil rights movement 88, 116
Civil Service, UK 47, 82
Cohesion, Sharing and Integration 5, 214, 214–19, **216, 219**
Cohesion, Sharing and Integration Strategy 69–70, 281
Colombia 11
Combined Loyalist Military Command cease-fire 203
Commissioner for Public Appointments in Northern Ireland (OCPANI) 155–8, 280
Committee of Culture, Arts and Leisure 171
community: evaluation research 6; shared 210–12, 212–14
Community Investment Fund 187
community planning 6, 234–5, 235–41, 262, 266
  action plan 246, *247*; commitments 246–8; County/City Development Boards 237–8; lessons of pilot exercise 251–3; local strategy partnerships 240–1; monitoring 249–50; Omagh District Council 235, 241–51; process *236*, 243–4, **245**; statutory partners 243–4; themes 246; vision statement 245
Community Planning Sub-Group 241
community relations 129, 214–19, **216, 219**
Community Relations Council 191
compacts 178–80, 180–3, 184, 196, 197
comprehensive spending review (CSR) 272
Comptroller and Auditor General, the 62, 64, 88, 107–8
conflict transformation centre 207
conflict transformation initiatives 192–3, 194, 194–5
Connolly, M. 123–4
consociationalism 13–15, 30–1
contentious policy issues 73
co-terminosity 94
cross-border services 3
Culture, Arts and Leisure, Department of *18, 58*

Darby, John 116
Deakin Commission 178
Deloitte 212
demilitarisation 192–3
Democratic Unionist Party 12, 22, **23**, *23, 24*, 27, 38, 39, 41, 49, 66–7, 68, 69, 73, 125, 192, 206–7, 268–9, 270, 272, 281
Departments (Northern Ireland) Order 1999 47, 49–50
deputy First Minister *16*, 24, 26, 28, 36

devolution architecture 13–15, **14**
consociational arrangements 30–1
Direct Rule 1, 1–2, 9, 37, 48, 75, 81, 87, 88, 176, 211
  policy-making 68, *71–2*
district partnerships 128–9
District Policing Partnerships 131
Division for Communities and Local Government 262
Dodds, Diane 269
Dodds, Nigel 38
Donnelly, C. 220, 223–4
Driving Forward a Reform Agenda (Robinson) 27, 66–7
Dubs, Lord 128
Dungannon District Council 125–6, 129

Economic Research Institute of Northern Ireland (ERINI), 38–9
economy 274–5, **274**
education 274, **274**
  academic results 223–4; academic selection 268; government response to integration 228–30; impact of integration 222–8; integrated 210–11, 219–30; and interpersonal communication 225; public service agreements (PSAs) 60, *61*; pupil numbers, by religion 220, *221*; reforms 39–40; Review of Public Administration final decisions 96; schools, by management type 220, *221*; schools, number of integrated 222, *223*; segregation 208, 218, 225; transformation 219–22; Travellers 29
Education, Department of *16, 58*, 211, 223, 228–30
Education (NI) Act 1977 220
Education and Skills Authority 39, 94, 96
Education Reform (NI) Order 1989 220
elections: 1998 22; 2003 11–12, 22, 23; 2007 22, 23
  European 268–9; local government 111–12, 121–2, *121, 122*, 125, 126, 139
electoral system 14, 112, 205
  single transferable vote (STV) proportional representation 22
Emerging Findings Paper 166–7
Empey, Sir Reg *18*
employment, public sector 51–3, *51*, **52**, *53*
Employment and Learning, Department for *18, 58*, 65
Enniskillen 232
  bombing, 1987 126
Enterprise, Trade and Investment, Department of *17, 58*, 277
Environment, Department of the *18, 58*, 235, 253
equality and diversity 163, 179
Equality Commission, the 27–8, 204
European Union 30, 57, 198
  partnership arrangements 127–9

Excellence and Fairness: Achieving World Class Public Services (Cabinet Office) 82–3, **83**
Executive Committee of Ministers 2, 8, 24–5, 36, 38–9, 69–70
  composition 12, 24–5; Devolved Functions *16–18*; role 25
ex-prisoner groups 191–6
  developing capacity groups 194–6; Policy Development Group 194; re-integration groups 193–4

Fair Employment Act 1976 68
Farry, Dr Stephen 30–1, 50–1
Faulkner, Brian 118
Fearon, K. 177
Finance and Personnel, Department of *16, 58*, 104, *107*, 108, 149
Financial Assistance Act (Northern Ireland) 2009 36
First Minister *16*, 24, 26, 28, 36
Fit for Purpose: The Reform Agenda in the Northern Ireland Civil Service (Northern Ireland Civil Service) 98–9, 101
Fitzgerald, M. 123
Foster, Arlene *17*, 94, 135–8, 164–5
Freedom of Information 99
Frost, P. 96–7
fuel poverty payments 208

Gardiner, Barry 152
general exchequer grant 133–4
Gildernew, Michelle *18*
Glentoran, Lord 89
Good Relations Challenge Programme 129, 211
government agencies, creation of 82
Government of Wales Act 1998 258
Government of Wales Act 2006 258–61
Government's Approach to Public Service Reform, The 80
Great Britain: central–local relations 256–7
  community planning 238–40; modernisation, government 79–84; Northern Ireland's peripheral status 81–2

Hadden, T. 122–3
Hain, Peter 92, 135, 146, 206, 207
Hamilton, Nigel 157–8
Hamilton, Simon 195–6, 217–18
Hanson, David 166
Hansson, U. 217–18
Hayes, B., *et al.* 224–5
Hayes, Maurice 114, 115
Heald, D. 57
health 274, **274**
  budget cuts 273; community planning *247*, 248; Patient and Client Council 95; Review of Public Administration final decisions 95

Health, Social Services and Public Safety, Department of *17, 58*, 62, *63*, 273
Health and Social Care Board 95
Health and Social Services Authority 94
Health Services Board 149
Hewitt, C. 115
Holme, Lord 31
homelessness 64
Hood, C. 161, 171
housing 149–50, *200*
  discrimination 115–16, 117, 118, 208; prices 231; removed from local government control 117–18; shared 230–3; social 65–6; waiting list 231
Housing (Northern Ireland) Order 1981 167
Housing Associations 65–6
Housing Executive Act 1971 124
HR Connect 103, 107
Hughes, J. 223–4
human rights 77–8
Human Rights Commission 204
Hunter, John 165–6
Huston, Felicity 155

ICT Shared Services 103
Independent International Commission on Decommissioning (IICD) 9, 10, 204, 206
Integrated Education Fund (IEF) 221, 223, 229
Integrated Local Strategy 240–1
integration 210–12, 212–14
  see also education
interface areas 217
International Fund for Ireland 190, 230
interpersonal communication 225
Invest NI 277–8
Investing Together 5, 183–4
IRA: cessation of military operations 203
  decommissioning 9–11, 203–4, 206; dissident groups 268
Ireland, Republic of 28, 202–3

Jarman, N. 217
Jenkins, S. 122
Johns Hopkins Comparative Non-Profit-Making Sector Project 174
joined-up thinking 265
Joint Declaration, Major and Reynolds, 1993 203
Joint Government/Voluntary and Community Sector Forum 179–80, 181, 182, 199

Keating, M. 69
Kelly, Gerry *16*
Kilmurray, A. 123, 193

Laffin, M. 254, 257
Laffin, M., *et al.* 257
Land & Property Services Agency 132
language 29

INDEX

legislative process 20–2, 36
Lenadoon Community Forum 189
Lenadoon Estate, Belfast 187–91
Library Authority 96
Livingstone, S. 153
Lloyd, G. 239
Local Area Agreements (LAAs) 264–5
Local Authorities Association 114
Local Delivery Agreement, the 259–61
local government 4, 83, 139–42, 280
  budget 89; centralisation 124; civic leadership 255; community relations 129; council budgets 130–1; councils 94, 95, 110, **111**, 113–14, 119–22, **119**, 123, 136, **136**, *137*; councils by political party **111**; elections 111–12, 121–2, *121*, *122*, 125, 126, 139; enablers 255; expenditure 110, 113, 131, *131*, 133; finance *131*, 132–5; functions 130–2, *130*, 136–7, 140; history 110–14; housing responsibilities removed 117–18; implementation structures 138–9, **138**; income sources 133–4, **134**; innovation 126–7; Macrory review 118–20; networks 256; partnership arrangements 127–9; policy development panels 139; political composition 121, *121*, *122*; politicisation 122–6; reform 88, 116–17, 163; reorganisation 135–8, **136**; responsibility sharing 125–6; review 94–5; Review of Public Administration final decisions 95; and sectarianism 114–17; service delivery 255; statutory committees 113; Strategic Leadership Board 138–9, **138**; Unionist hegemony 115–16; and voluntary and community sector 183; *see also* central–local relations
Local Government Act 2001 238
Local Government Act (Northern Ireland) 1972 88, 124, 162
Local Government Association (LGA) 256
Local Government in Scotland Act 2003 238–9
Local Government (Ireland) Act 1898 111
Local Government (Miscellaneous Provisions) (NI) Order 1992 162
Local Government (Northern Ireland) Act 1922 112
Local Government (Reorganisation) Bill 253, 266
Local Government Staff Commission 5, 162–6
Local Government Taskforce 240
Local Government Temporary Provisions Northern Ireland Order 1986 125
Local Government Training Group 165
Local Public Service Agreements (LPSAs) 264
Local Service Boards (LSBs) 259
Local Strategic Partnerships (LSPs) 264

Londonderry, County Borough of 118
Loughran, G. 113
Lyons Inquiry 140–1

McCausland, Nelson *18*
McConaghy, D. 124
McConnell, A. 257
McEvoy, L., *et al.* 226–7
McGarry, J. 31, 180, 226
McGimpsey, Michael *17*, 38, 93–4, 273
McGlone, Patsy 277
McGlynn, C. 224
McGuinness, Martin *16*, 39, 40, 271–2
McIntosh Commission 257
Mackintosh, J. 120
McLaughlin, K. 183
Macrory, Patrick 118–20
Macrory gap, the 121
Macrory Report (Review Body) 88
McVeigh, R. 227
Major, John 203
Mandelson, Peter 8
Maskey, A. 148–9
Massereene army base killings 268
Massey, A. 80, 85
Meehan, E. 151
Members of the Legislative Assembly (MLAs) 68–9, 72, 74, 87, 254, 281
ministerial code 25
Mitchell, George 203–4
Mitchell, J. 267
modernisation, government *see also* Review of Public Administration
  Great Britain 79–84; Northern Ireland 87–90; Northern Ireland Civil Service 80; public administration 87–9; public sector reform 84–6; public service reform 97–109, **98**, **102**, *105–6*, *107*; reform programmes and projects 101–9
Modernising Government (Cabinet Office) 4, 68, 80, 97
Moran, M. 255–6
Morison, J. 151, 153, 178
Murphy, Conor *17*, 37, 211
Murtagh, B. 217

Network NI 103, 108
New Deal 25+ Programme 64–5
Newton, Robin *16*
Nolan, P. 177
Nolan Committee on Standards in Public Life 154–5, 156
Nolan principles, the 158, 159
non-contentious policy issues 73–4
non-departmental public bodies 4–5, 143–9, 161–2
  accountability 152–3, 153–4; appointments 151, 154–8, *156*; expenditure *150*; funding *150*; guidance notes 146; impartiality 144–5; numbers 149, *149*; review 146, *147–8*, 148–9; staffing *150*; types 144, *145*; *see also* quangos

303

Northern Ireland Act 1998 2, 8, 12, 20, 26, 47–8, 77
Northern Ireland Act 2006 12
Northern Ireland Affairs Select Committee 152
Northern Ireland Assembly 2, 3, 6, 8, 15–24, 38–9, 87, 197, 205, 205–6, 213, 264
  achievements 40–1, **45**, *45*, 46, 274; acts 41, *42–4*; Civil Service reform proposals 67; composition 22–3, **23**, *23*, 270–1, 272; constitution 15; decision making process 15, 19; departmental expenditure *58*; Devolved Functions *16–8*; Education Committee 40; elections 22, 23, *24*; ethnic self-designation 19; legislative process 20–2, 36; ministers 12; powers 15; Public Accounts Committee 108, 109; reform proposals 270–2; statutory committees 19–20, 73–4; suspensions 9–12; veto 270–1
Northern Ireland Audit Office 3, 60, 62, 106–8, 109
Northern Ireland Best Practice Scheme 99–100
Northern Ireland Charities Commission 184
Northern Ireland Civil Rights Association (NICRA) 116
Northern Ireland Civil Service 3, 47–8, 157–8
  access 102–3; best practice case study 100–1; budget allocations 57; capability building 99; committees 49; core values 53, 54; departmental expenditure 57, **58**, *58*; departmental structure 48, 49–51, *50*, 67; functions 48–51; funding 56–7; modernisation 80; new working methods 103; performance 64–7; performance culture 104; policy-making 68–71, *71–2*, 72–8; Professional Skills for Government initiative 53–6; reform and restructuring 66–7, 97–109, *107*; responsibilities 52; and the Review of Public Administration 90; staff 51–3, *51*, **52**, *53*; structure 47–8; technological foundation 103–4; working environment 104
Northern Ireland Constitution Act 1973 120–1
Northern Ireland Council for Integrated Education (NICIE) 220, 221–2, 223, 228–9
Northern Ireland Council for Voluntary Action (NICVA) 154, 173, 175–6, 185–6, 196–8, 252
Northern Ireland Direct 100–1, 102–3, 106
Northern Ireland Election Surveys 224–5
Northern Ireland Executive *16*, 28, 35, 40, 47, 49, 52, 56, 66, 67, 94, 135, 198, 199, 205, 207–8, 230–1, 253, 264, 270, 278
  see also Programme for Government

Northern Ireland Executive Budget 2008–11 195
Northern Ireland Hospitals Authority 113, 149
Northern Ireland Housing Council 5, 166–70
Northern Ireland Housing Executive 64, 65–6, 82, 117, 151–2, 166, 168, 169–70, *170*, 208, 232
Northern Ireland Housing Trust 113, 149
Northern Ireland Joint Council for Local Government Services (NIJC) 163
Northern Ireland Life and Times Surveys 217, 218–19, 224–5, 273–5, **274**
Northern Ireland Local Government Association (NILGA) 130, 255
Northern Ireland Neighbourhood Information Service (NINIS) 249
Northern Ireland Office 37, 178, 217
Northern Ireland Police Commission 206
Northern Ireland (St Andrews Agreement) Act 2006 12, 25
North–South implementation bodies 8, 67
North–South Ministerial Council 3, 8, 28–9, 205

Oberschall, A. 227
Office of the First Minister and deputy First Minister *16*, 26, *58*, 73, 90, 213, 214, 215, 223, 262, 275
O'Leary, B. 31, 180, 226
O'Leary, C. 116
Oliver, John 117–18
Omagh District Council 6, 235, 241–51, **242**, 280
  baseline information 249, *250*, *251*; Community Plan 246, *247*; community planning commitments 246–8; community planning lessons 251–3; community planning monitoring 249–50; community planning process 243–4, **245**; community planning vision statement 245; deprivation 242–3; political composition 243; population 241–2; themes 246
O'Neill, Terence 117
Opening Up Quangos 158–9
Orde, Sir Hugh 40–1, 281
Osborne, R. 220
Osborne, S. 183
Outer West Belfast Neighbourhood Renewal area 189

Paisley, Dr Ian 8, 12, 31, 206–7, 213, 267, 269
Parades Commission 67
parallel consent 19
participative democracy 196–200
Partners for Change (DfSD) 5, 181–2, 184–5, 199
Partnership Council for Wales, the 258

Partnership Panel 262–3
peace, road to 202–7
peace building 187–91, 193, 194
PEACE II 240
peace walls 217
Pearson, Ian 92
Pemberton, S. 239
petition of concern 19
Planning and Development Act 2000 238
pluralist society 210–2, 212–14
police and policing 40–1, 206, 267–8, 279
Policy Development Panel 165
policy-making 67–71, *71–2*
  accessibility 72; accountability 77–8; civil servants role 75; contentious issues 73; cross-border issues 73–4; Direct Rule 68, *71–2*; evidence and 76–7; factors shaping 70; new thinking 74–5; NGO group's lack of coordination 75–6; non-contentious issues 73–4; Scotland 69
political settlement 202–7
Pollitt, C. 85–6
Poots, Edwin *18*
Positive Steps 5, 184–7, 197, 198–9
power-sharing 1, 6, 12, 31, 34–5, 207–8, 267–9, 278, 281
  achievements 40–1; chronology 32–4; policy-making 69–70
Preparation for Employment Programme 65
prescription charges 37–8, 39
prisoners, early release 191–3, 195–6
Private Security Industry (NI) Order 2009 20
Professional Skills for Government initiative 53–6
Programme for Government 3, 25, 26, 48, 59–63, **59**, *61*, *63*, 74–5, 77–8, 84–5, 101, 104, *105–6*, 180–1, 195, 199, 214, 231, 263, 272, 278, 281
  delivery report 275–7, *275*, *276*
Progressive Unionist Party (PUP) 203
Public Accounts Committee (PAC) 1, 3, 64, 151–2, 157–8, 280
public administration 2, 87–9, **89**
  two-tier model 92, **93**, 94–5; *see also* Review of Public Administration
public appointments 154–8, *156*; Code of Practice 156–7, 157, 159
Public Authorities (Reform) Bill Northern Ireland Assembly Bill 19/07 21–2
public expenditure 2, 56–7, 272–3
Public Health Agency 95
public sector 79
  borrowing 56; budget 89; employment 51–3, *51*, **52**, *53*; mapping 91; reform 84–6; reform trajectories 85–6
Public Sector People Managers' Association (PPMA) 164
Public Service Agreement Framework 59
public service agreements (PSAs) 3, 60, 104, *105–6*, 106, 199, **200**, 214, 263–4, 276–7, *276*

Public Service Improvement Unit 100
public services 101–9, 280
  access 102–3; best practice case study 100–1; dissemination of good practice 99–100; external scrutiny 64–7; funding 3; joined-up service delivery 99; modernisation 4; new working methods 102–3; reform 80–4, 97–101, **98**, **102**, *105–6*, *107*
Purvis, Dawn 269

quality of life (QoL) indicators 249, *250*, 273–5, **274**
quangos 4–5, 88–9, 143–4, 149–54, 277, 280
  accountability 152–3, 171; culling 158–61, 162–71
Queen's University Belfast 230

Race Relations Order (Northern Ireland) 1997 129
Racial Equality Strategy 215
racial prejudice 208, 211
rates: domestic 39, 56, *131*, 198
  regional and district 132–5
reconciliation 5–6, 225–6
Records NI 103, 108
referendums, 1998 205
Regional Development, Department for *17*, *58*, 64
Reid, John 10
Reinvestment and Reform Initiative (RRI) 56
religious discrimination. *see* sectarianism
Renewing Democracy, Rebuilding Communities 238
Report on Non Departmental Public Bodies (Cabinet Office) 143
Reshaping of Local Government, The (Cmnd 517) 114
Reshaping of Local Government: Further Proposals, The (Cmnd 530) 114
responsibility sharing 125–6
Review of Public Administration 2, 4, 6, 87–8, 90–7, 109, 131, 135, 140, 140–2, 146, 148–9, 151, 161–2, 164, 166–7, 235, 237, 240, 251–2, 253, 256, 279–80
  achievements 277–8; final decisions 95–7; savings from 93
Review of the Northern Ireland Civil Service: Response to Devolution 97–8
Reynolds, Albert 203
Rhodes, R. 85
Ritchie, Margaret *17*, 35–6, 167, 170, 186–7, 192–3, 231–2
Roads Service 64
Robinson, Bruce 104, 106
Robinson, Peter *16*, 27, 40, 66–7, 135, 193, 213, 269–71, 272, 273
Rooker, Lord 253–4
Ruane, Caitríona *16*, 39–40, 94

St Andrews Agreement (2006) 5, 12, 24, 30, 31, 37, 49, 206, 211, 270, 271–2, 278
Scotland 35, 48, 159
  central–local relations 254, 257; community evaluation research 6; community planning 238–40, 244, 252; policy-making 69; prescription charges 38
Scottish Council for Voluntary Organisations (SCVO) 173
SDLP 22, **23**, *23*, *24*, 27, 41, 66, 273
sectarianism 68, 70, 114–17, 180, 187, 187–91, 211, 217–18, 220, 227, 280, 281
segregation 5, 14, 187–91, 208–9, 217–18; cost 212–13; education 208, 218, 224
Shared Future charter 232
Shared Neighbourhood Programme 232
Shared Services for Efficiency: A Progress Report 106–8
Sharing Education Programme 230
Shirlow, P. 194, 217
Sinclair, S. 235, 239–40
Sinn Féin 9, 11, 22, **23**, *23*, *24*, 38, 41, 49, 68, 69, 73, 73–4, 124–5, 192, 199, 203, 204, 206–7, 213, 267–8, 279, 281
Smith, A. 222–3
Social Development, Department for *17*, 35–6, 64, 66, 170, 184–7
  Voluntary and Community Unit 181–2
social justice 179
social partnership 237–8
Social Security Agency 64
Society of Local Authority Chief Executives (SOLACE NI) 164
Special Support Programme for Peace and Reconciliation 127–8, 240
Spellar, John 36–7, 186, 211
Statutory Transition Committees 165
Steps to Work Programme 65
Stewart, J. 256–7
strand 1 institutions 3, 13, 205
  see also individual institutions
strand 2 institutions 3, 13, 28–9, 205
  see also individual institutions
strand 3 institutions 3, 13, 29–31, 205
  see also individual institutions
Strategy for the Support of the Voluntary Sector and for Community Development in Northern Ireland 177
Stringer, M., *et al.* 225
Suffolk and Lenadoon Interface Group (SLIG) 5, 189–91
Suffolk Community Forum 189
Sullivan, H. 240
Summa, H. 85–6

Taoiseach, the 28
taxation 56
Taylor, R. 180, 227–8
Tomlinson, M. 112, 113, 116, 121

Toonen, T. 85
Toucas, S. 217–18
Travellers 29
Treasury, the (UK) 37
Trimble, David 9, 10
Twin Track Initiative 203–4

Ulster Democratic Party (UDP) 203
Ulster Unionist Party 9, 10–11, 12, 22, **23**, *23*, *24*, 41, 273
unemployment 64–5
US–Ireland Alliance 217

Valuation and Lands Agency 133
violence: decline in 208–9, **209**, 281; republican 40–1
voluntary and community sector 5, 89, 280–1
  accountability 179; beneficiaries 176, *176*; call for White Paper 196–200; and community planning 252; compact 178–80, 180–3, 184, 196, 197; definition 172–5; engagement 180–7; ex-prisoner groups 191–6; funding 185–6; and local government 183; and participative democracy 196–200; partnership arrangements 177; peace building 187–91, 193, 194; purpose 175–6, *175*; role 176–80, 196–200; size 175, 182; Task Force 183–4; threats to 183; Working Together 181

Wales 35, 48, 159
  Assembly 254, 258; Cardiff Council 260–1; central–local relations 6, 254, 257, 257–61; community evaluation research 6; community planning 240; Local Delivery Agreement 259–61; Local Service Boards (LSBs) 259; the Partnership Council for Wales 258; policy agreements 259; prescription charges 38
Water and Sewerage Services (NI) Order 2006 37
water charges 36–7, 39, 66
Water Service Agency 36, 64
Weiss, C.H. 70
Westminster, expenses scandal 279
Whyte, J. 116
Wilford, R. 24–5, 34–5, 69–70, 151, 152
Williams, P. 240; *et al.* 238
Wilson, R. 34–5, 48, 84
Wilson, Sammy *16*, 161, 166
winter fuel payments 35–6
Women in Local Councils initiative 163
Women's Coalition Party 26
Work and Pensions, Secretary of State for (UK) 36
Working Together: Public Service on Your Side (Cabinet Office) 4, 83–4
Workplace 2010 104